S0-BRT-679

973.91
Sal

157646

Salter.
The American politician.

Learning Resources Center
Nazareth College of Rochester, N. Y.

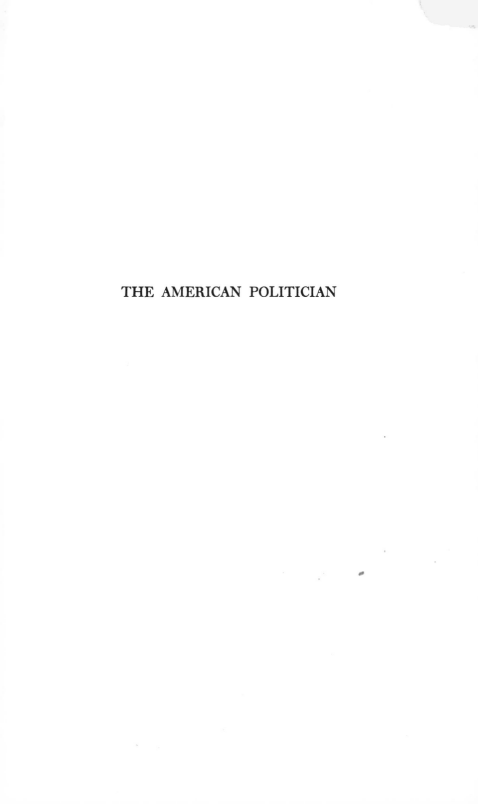

THE AMERICAN POLITICIAN

★ ★

The

American Politician

Edited by

J. T. SALTER

DISCARDED
LEARNING RESOURCES CENTER
NAZARETH COLLEGE

GREENWOOD PRESS, PUBLISHERS
WESTPORT, CONNECTICUT

★ ★

Library of Congress Cataloging in Publication Data

Salter, John Thomas, 1898-   ed.
    The American politician.

    Reprint of the ed. published by the University of
North Carolina Press, Chapel Hill.
    Includes bibliographical references and index.
    1. Statesmen--United States--Biography.
2. United States--Politics and government--1901-
1953--Addresses, essays, lectures. I. Title.
E747.S29 1975   973.91'092'2 [B]   75-17541
ISBN 0-8371-8239-5

Copyright, 1938, by The University of North Carolina Press

Originally published in 1938 by the University of North
Carolina Press, Chapel Hill

Reprinted with the permission of The University of North
Carolina Press

Reprinted in 1975 by Greenwood Press,
a division of Williamhouse-Regency Inc.

Library of Congress Catalog Card Number 75-17541

ISBN 0-8371-8239-5

Printed in the United States of America

157646

13.91
Sal

*

*

To

FRED EDINGER,
JOHN PALMER GAVIT,
ROGER HINDS, JOE ROTHSCHILD,
FRANCIS BLOODGOOD,
JOHN ALLEY,
FRANCIS FISHER KANE,
WILLIAM T. BISSELL,
WILLIAM ALLEN WHITE,
RICHARD WELLING, R. L. DUFFUS,
WALTER R. AGARD,
MAX KADUSHIN,

and some millions of other citizens unknown to me, this book is dedicated by its editor, because they have risen above the political indolence of the many and have always maintained an interest in political happenings and community problems that has fitted them to identify and to support those candidates who serve the common good, and because from time to time they take a stand that helps their fellow citizens choose between truth and error in our Great Society.

*

*

"To bring home the newness of democracy let us imagine the period of the existence of mankind from the date of the Pekin man to be represented by the life of a man aged fifty years. He would have been aged forty-nine years and nine months before the idea of justice had dawned upon him. His first experience of democracy in Greece was six weeks ago; after an age of darkness lasting a few weeks he has, during the last seven days, been experimenting in England in developing our present form of democracy. In fact, democracy is in its swaddling clothes. There is nothing so encouraging in the history of man as its astounding and rapid growth in the last few thousand years. It is not surprising that there should be setbacks."—E. D. Simon, "Education for Democracy," *The Political Quarterly*, V (No. 3, July–September, 1934), 310

INTRODUCTION

THE MOST IMPORTANT TASK CONFRONTING THE PEOPLE IN A democracy is that of picking the right politicians. Some of these politicians are leaders and others are just symbols of the status quo. They are the men elected to the 800,000 or so elective offices in the United States, and the authentic politicians among them are elected not once, but many times. They—and in some cases their sponsors, who send them rather than hold office themselves—are the government—national, state, and local. They chart the public policies which, in this day of the positive-service state here and of the threat to our democratic processes by the ideologies of fascism and communism, may literally determine the life and death of a people—policies which, in any event, will largely set the conditions under which life is to be carried on in this country.

Nearly everyone believes that the politician who is interested in his constituents only at campaign and election time is not worth much. I, for one, believe this to be true; and I just as strongly believe that the voter who cannot quite pay attention to what his politicians are doing save when a pre-election campaign is on, is equally disappointing in a democracy.

I once knew a boy who worked in a grocery store. He was filling an order for bananas, and one of the older clerks happened to see that some of the bananas that he had put into the sack were past their prime. The older clerk said, "For goodness' sakes, Johnnie, don't send those bananas to Mrs. Abbott! She is very particular about what she gets, and if the stuff isn't right, she'll send it back! Now bananas like that are all right for Mrs. Brown—but never send rotten bananas to Mrs. Abbott!"

The politician, like the grocer, is forever trying to find out what the people want. He is often pictured with his ear to the ground, and the person he is most certain to hear is someone like Mrs.

Abbott—and she is the one whose wishes he is most likely to heed. And this lady may be Mrs. Abbott herself, or she may be any one of a number of pressure groups—a crusading newspaper, a labor organization, a chamber of commerce, an American Legion chapter, a business group, a Father Coughlin, a Liberty League, the bar association, the party organization. In short, the ever-recurring problem in a democracy is the contest that goes on between the articulate and organized minority and the often silent and unorganized majority.

Every politician is subject to a great fear. This fear conditions the basic processes of democracy. Sometimes the politician does not do what he wants to do, but does what he must do, or thinks he must do, in order to keep power. The member of Congress, for example, nine times out of ten, does not vote or speak without weighing possible repercussions and recriminations. If he does not or cannot judge correctly the probable reaction of his constituents, he will not survive as their alter ego. Theoretically, a member of Congress is free to vote as his own mind and conscience dictate. Actually, however, and on any number of important measures, his mind and conscience cannot dictate until some individual organization, newspaper, or pressure group dictates to them. On other measures, the legislator may have a very definite opinion as to how he wants to vote, and (1) he votes that way, or (2) he does not vote at all, or (3) he votes contrary to his personal preference in the matter. First, he votes according to his own preference when there is no particular reason why he shouldn't—that is, when any powerful force that he is amenable to, such as the President, or a newspaper, or some organization has either not advised him on the matter, or has expressed an opinion that coincides with his own. In the second case, we may think of the legislator at bay; he may look out on his constituency and hear such a jarring discord of voices, one group urging him to vote for the measure, another fraction promising punishment if he does, that he cannot vote either way without feeling that he will alienate support. And, in the third place, he may vote against his own conviction when he finds that to do otherwise would cost him support. A congressman recently told me that he certainly wanted to vote for the reorganization bill that has just been defeated. I asked him why he hadn't favored it then, instead

of voting against it. He said, "Because of Bill Johnson's big stick!"
(Johnson is the editor of a very powerful newspaper in the congressman's constituency.) Another congressman that I know voted
for the reorganization bill. He said to me, "I could not have voted
any other way without being ridiculous in my own eyes." He
added, however, that he had received ten times as many letters
against the reorganization plan as he had for it. Yet he felt so
strongly on this matter himself that he had no choice. He happens,
however, to be one of the two or three strongest and most forthright men in Congress. Unfortunately, he is not so strong in his
own constituency, and whether or not he is returned this November will depend on the personal campaigning that he does between
now and then, as well as on the nature of his opposition at that
time.

As I have said, this congressman is an exception. The average
legislator and politician is more amenable to public pressure. It
must be obvious that if Mr. Frank Gannett and his nineteen newspapers, William Randolph Hearst and his nineteen million readers, Father Coughlin and his two million and more listeners, Dr.
Ed A. Rumley and his wealthy supporters, the American Legion,
the C.I.O., the National Grange, the American Federation of
Labor, the American Farm Bureau Federation, the National Association of Manufacturers, the National Committee to Uphold Constitutional Government, and other individuals and pressure groups
oppose some measure whether in the public interest or not, the
measure is most likely to fail. This will be particularly true if, on
the other hand, the larger public that has no private interest involved, has no adequate spokesman and does not, itself, tell its
congressman how to vote.

Democracy's goal is the development, the well-being, and the
supremacy of the individual. Under our plan of government, the
individual is the measure of whether or not a governmental arrangement is good or bad. And just as the individual's possible rewards in a democracy are greater than in other systems, so are his
obligations. For democracy is the governmental system that is most
difficult to keep running true to form, and it is therefore the most
exacting.

People who live under dictators are asked to give only one thing

—obedience. Totalitarian states think with their blood; democracies require minds. And in a democracy, no single man is big enough to be its leader alone. He needs the help of millions of others—as many others as there are individual voters. The individual must be able to judge general results of governmental policies; he must know what he can know, and what he cannot know. He must keep his eyes open; he must know and evaluate a politician's record; and he must express an opinion according to the evidence. The entire system depends on the ability of the individual to support those public officials who are working for the public good and to oppose those who are not. One must agree with Pericles that the citizen in a democracy who is too busy to pay attention to public affairs is not merely without ambition, but he is useless. The lone voter is important. A million times zero is still zero, but a million times one is a number of very great size.

The contributors to this book believe that one can learn more about the realities of American politics by studying the lowly or the noble politician than by reading conventional histories, textbooks, and the Constitution. Politics is life, and politicians and voters are the warp and woof of this life. They are to be found in society at large and not between the covers of a book. Next to observing the politician on the hoof, the best thing is to read an honest biography of one, written by an experienced Boswell who has stood close enough to his subject actually to see him, hear him talk, and learn how he functions in the democratic process. And one politician is, in large measure, descriptive of all politicians.[1] *They are all vote-getters, and they are all men who know the ropes.* However, getting votes in New York City presents problems not confronting those who campaign in a rural state. The man who knows the ropes that enable him to win through to office in Wisconsin might find that still other techniques are needed to bring a plurality behind his banner in Ohio. But basically, and whether or not the politicians live in an urban or rural environment, in the prairie country or in the mountains, and are candidates for national,

---

[1] For a definition of the politician and his characteristics, see J. T. Salter, "The Politician and The Voter," in *The American Political Scene*, edited by E. B. Logan, New York, 1936. For a picture of the ward politician in his daily work and of a powerful party organization in an urban environment, see *idem, Boss Rule: Portraits in City Politics*, New York, 1935.

state, or local offices, they are all in the same business—politics. Yet the differences as well as the inner core of sameness among the politicians presented in this volume (and, I believe, existing among all politicians), will be seen here. For example, Norman Thomas, one of the two men in this book who have not been elected to public office, differs from the others in kind as well as degree. He is not the prototype of the people as are the "regulars" in politics who are elected again and again. He is an expression of the intellectual and ecclesiastical rather than the usual self-made, grammar-school American tradition. John L. Lewis, the other person in this book who has not been elected to public office, is here to represent a new voice of labor in our politics—a labor that is becoming so well organized and articulate that labor and not the employer may receive the first attention of the politician.

The other subjects in this book of biographies are representative American politicians. Most of them hold public office today, and nearly all of them have been elected to public office many times, and many will continue to be elected until they die. ("Politics gets into your blood. You say you will quit, but you never do.") The sketches that follow indicate this, and many other things, about the *zoon politikon.*

Farley likes people, has unusual energy and a remarkable memory for names and faces, and is typical of the species. All politicians have something of Farley in them, or want someone like Farley to work for them. He means organization; and either in political or military battle, victories go to the side that is most thoroughly organized. Organization means economy of effort; it enables the few to defeat the many; it is indispensable in football, church affairs, politics, or wherever a number of people must act in unison. Farley represents the epitome of the power to build such organization.

Norris, La Follette, La·Guardia, Vandenberg, McNutt, Wagner, Tydings, Maverick are national politicians of varying significance. All represent viewpoints in American politics, and all except one are most likely to be increasingly important in the days ahead. Dan Hoan is a politician who has been socialist mayor in a non-socialist city for twenty years. He is the administrator and politician par excellence. Governor Chandler of Kentucky is a personality that wins in a state where school teachers are sometimes, and in some parts, warned to keep away from the polls on election day lest they get shot. S. Davis Wilson is a personality that is particularly identified with these present times. In the recent past he has shifted, with surprising ease, from the Republican party to the Democratic, and back again to the Republican; and while fighting strenuously under that banner was elected mayor of Philadelphia; and then in 1938 he became a Democrat again in order to campaign for the United States Senate in that party's primaries. Sol Levitan is a Jewish personality of such appeal that he repeatedly wins in the German-Scandinavian state of Wisconsin. His history best illustrates the value of publicity to the man in politics. Joseph Sickler and Anna Brancato are local politicians who are as authentic a part of politics as are certain governors or presidents. Robert Heuck is an exception; his life is more or less of a peg on which the Honorable Murray Seasongood has hung a sermon. It is included because Mr. Seasongood was mayor of Cincinnati at a most exceptional time, and his voice in American politics is worth hearing here. Honest Tom McIntyre is real although his name is not. He is the one subject in this book that stands under a pseudonym. He is important because of his place and function in American politics, because he is a system or an institution rather than an individual, and because there are vastly more Honest Toms in Politics than there are Norrises, La Guardias, or La Follettes. He reminds one, furthermore, of the idea that no amount of "oughtness" can ever equal a tiny bit of "is-ness."

I regret that I do not have sketches of other Republicans in national politics, of a typical politician from the deep South, and of a politician prominently identified with organized crime. A sketch here of a district attorney controlled by the owners of slot machines and by men who run the number game and other rackets would be of value in pointing out an important phase of present-day politics. (I have a sketch of Nicholas Fishbourne, a gangster politician, in *Boss Rule: Portraits in City Politics,* and I will have another in my next book of sketches of contemporary politicians, but I was not able to get the desired sketch for the present volume.)

Abraham Lincoln once said that a man's legs should be long enough to reach to the ground. I think that a biographical sketch should be long enough to say what the biographer has to say. I have not tried to keep these sketches the same length. Neither do I believe that the best known politician necessarily deserves the most space. Furthermore, I believe that there may often be more political truth to be found in a concrete detail than in a general statement or abstract principle. This partly explains the length of the sketches of Sol Levitan and Honest Tom McIntyre. I have stood near these men long enough to become aware of an atmosphere, and I have tried to put this on paper. I hope, therefore, that the reviewers will not be too unkind because I have given Honest Tom more space than Mr. McNutt's biographer has given to his subject.

I was urged by several important people in the field of political biography to edit this volume on the American politician. Because I believe the subject most important to the American voter, I willingly undertook the very interesting task. I invited the foremost literary and scholarly men in this particular field to write the biographies. The writers I approached invariably welcomed the idea, but in several cases, earlier commitments prevented them from accepting the assignment offered.

I am most grateful to the contributors who have joined with me in this undertaking. Each, in his own way and according to the nature of his subject, has done a portrait. I have sought individuality rather than sameness. For example, Farley is presented in terms of his organizing ability, Norris is revealed through his record of solid achievement, and Chandler appears as one who owes most to personality. Although I believe each sketch to be an honest and intelligent one written by a contributor who had no purpose other than to present a lifelike portrait, yet I find that all save one are favorable rather than unfavorable. That is, they present their politicians more largely in terms of the voters who support them; and I think that this is fortunate, if one is interested in giving a portrait of a politician which explains how he wins through to public office. One cannot put fifty years in five or ten thousand words. Moreover, the art of biography involves the selection and evaluation of data. In the case of my sketch of Sol Levitan, for example, I think I have given a pertinent, vivid, and realistic portrait; I know, however, that I could have merely described him as a candidate who gets votes by this simple formula: "First, he demands votes; second, he asks for votes; third, he begs for them; and fourth, he weeps for them." This brief formula calls attention to one aspect of this particular politician's campaign technique, but it does not describe the man or his strength. These sketches present the politicians as they are, but they do not, nor do I here, produce a yardstick by which to measure a man in order to determine his fitness for public office. Some professor may know or have a slide rule that will enable him to measure a politician's fitness for a given office to which he has been repeatedly elected by the people. My colleagues and I, however, have used our time and energy to present facts, and more facts. The reader, here, like the voter at the polls, must do the judging.

My gratitude is due the editors of the *Public Opinion Quarterly*, the *Dalhousie Review*, and the *National Municipal Review* for permission to reprint materials that appeared in part in their journals. To my part-time secretary, Miss Emily Blenis, I express my hearty thanks for her unfailing help in preparing this work for publication. To my contributors I express my fullest appreciation. They are the book. And if this book, or any portrait of it, leads some voter to follow more closely the politicians in his own community or in Washington, we shall have accomplished our purpose.

J. T. SALTER

Greenport, Long Island
June, 1938.

CONTENTS

THE AMERICAN POLITICIAN

FIORELLO H. LA GUARDIA*

By Paul J. Kern

CONGRESSMAN FIORELLO H. LA GUARDIA WAS COMING HOME from Washington one torrid day in late July, 1932. With him, in a rattletrap eight-year-old car piled high with household bric-a-brac, was a young man, his secretary. They mounted the main span of the George Washington Bridge, and over the Hudson in the blazing afternoon sun the mighty panorama of Manhattan came into view.

"It is a great city," said the secretary. "It is good to be home."

"I love it," said La Guardia. "I am going to be its next mayor."

Strange words, these, for a man who had but recently been disastrously defeated for that very office by the flamboyant and corrupt Jimmy Walker, and who was soon to taste defeat in his own bailiwick for Congress. But they were not words of idle conceit or futile self-assurance. For this statement typified the most significant La Guardia trait—a profound and penetrating intuition for public reaction.

Despite the brazen cheers for "Jimmy" and the boos and catcalls for the venerable Judge Samuel Seabury at the open hearings, La Guardia knew that the devastating exposures of the Seabury investigation had shaken Tammany to its back teeth and shocked the decent citizens of New York. Despite the bland self-assurance of Tammany Hall in the face of abject poverty and economic collapse, La Guardia knew that the "great minds" of Tammany stood as children before the simplest economic phenomena, and that the old formula of the "Christmas basket and the ton of coal" was no longer working in 1932.

It was the turning point of the La Guardia career. Before him,

* All rights reserved by Paul J. Kern.

to be resolved within the next year, lay political triumph or oblivion.

The preparation for triumph had been painstaking. Over a public career of two decades in a metropolis ravaged by corruption and political betrayal, the impeccable La Guardia character had remained untarnished. While the "night club Mayor" was touring the hot spots and lavishing gifts upon a movie actress, La Guardia was at home, reading and thinking and calling attention on the floor of Congress to the fact that it was a false prosperity and couldn't last. The struggle through these years was a struggle to be heard.

Fiorello was born, without benefit of silver spoon, on New York's Varick Street, December 11, 1882. A career of Army bandmaster took the elder Achille La Guardia to northern New York State, Fort Sully, South Dakota, and Prescott, Arizona, where Fiorello and his brother, now dead, and his sister, now married and living in Hungary, grew up in the culture of the pioneer West.

Equivocation about a career as cornetist, jockey, baseball player, or newspaper reporter was ended by the outbreak of the Spanish American War. Achille La Guardia was sent to Tampa and soon thereafter died, a victim of putrefied army beef. Fiorello had followed as an unsalaried, but expense-paid correspondent of the *St. Louis Dispatch*. At the age of eighteen, just as another American boy of the same age, destined for contemporary political distinction, was entering Harvard, Fiorello was cast loose in a strange world to fend for himself and assist in the support of his mother. John Hay, secretary of state, appointed him to a minor position in the consulate at Budapest. Later he was made consular agent at Fiume, where he was paid $300 a year at the start.

La Guardia's diplomatic career was so highly successful that he soon became the subject of official protest. The Immigration Racket was then in full swing. He alarmed the steamship companies by insisting upon medical inspection of emigrants before sailing; and most serious of his offenses was *l'affaire* of the Archduchess Maria Josefa. The Archduchess, a pompous and pouter-pigeonish member of the royal family, descended on Fiume for a royal visitation. Emigrants interested the Archduchess and she was determined to see an embarkation even though the day was Monday and the ship was not to sail until Saturday.

La Guardia was not so much concerned with the dilettante preoccupations of royalty as with the suffering of the emigrants for five days without ventilation in steerage. So he refused clearance. Contrary to popular belief, the consul at Fiume was not removed as a result of this incident, but voluntarily resigned a year later.

To New York City returned La Guardia at the age of twenty-three. It was his birthplace, but it was not a home-coming. For La Guardia was a westerner, in whom the misery and suffering of the slums engendered a bitter and smoldering resentment quite unlike the callousness and apathy of those who, by daily contact, have grown to accept them as an indispensable part of urban culture. He has never lost this resentment, nor has he lost his yearning to provide the million New York children with space and air and a place to play away from the wheels of trucks. As Jay Franklin says of him in a recent biography: "The man is still the Western boy, who lived and loved the 'old' army, who drank in the national tradition of America which the East and the South had long since lost and which the West is now losing. . . . His background is the background of Henry Clay, Abe Lincoln, the elder La Follette, George Norris and other men who saw America steadily and saw it whole. The man is sensitive, eager to promote the Anglo-Saxon concept of the common good, to foster self-reliance and to contribute, without thought of personal advantage, to the welfare of his fellows. As he talks, the man looks out through the mask and the mask itself melts away."

For four years, 1906 to 1910, La Guardia worked as a stenographer, as an interpreter at Ellis Island, and as a law student. In 1910 New York University gave him the degree LL.B. and he was admitted to the bar. But his restless soul was not content with law alone. Into the labor movement and politics plunged young Attorney La Guardia.

For many years, by vested right, the liquor interests of New York City had a congressman. Because the Constitution, by sheer oversight, had made no provision for an alcoholic congressional district, Tammany had obligingly set one aside for this proper purpose, the Fourteenth District, in Greenwich Village. The Republican party acquiesced in this lofty plan and quietly gave the biennial nomination to some prominent nonentity who would have no chance of upsetting such a high-minded compact. So in the late summer of 1914, as the secretary of the Republican Club was making up the nominations for the ballot, he came to the candidate for Congress. He had never heard of the candidate and could not spell his name. It was late at night and the legal dead-line was upon him. In desperation he shouted out into the clubroom: "Who wants to run for Congress?" La Guardia was sitting there, hopefully looking for a client or two. "I will," said he, without the slightest hesitation. "What's *your* name?" said the secretary. "F. H. L-a-G-u-a-r-d-i-a," said the late-stayer. For a generation the voters of New York were to see that name often.

Political baptism was a bit painful to the newcomer. He found that he would not be allowed to speak at meetings; that there was to be no campaign. So he bought an old open Ford, waited until meetings were over, and addressed the crowds on the street as they left, from a platform built on the back seat. "Virtue," of course, triumphed, and the liquor congressman beat him badly. But so well known had he become that two years later the Republicans had to give him the nomination again.

The same sort of campaign ensued. But on election night the returns showed La Guardia a winner. Very much excited, the thirty-four-year-old congressman proceeded at once to his Republican Club to thank the boys and receive congratulations. The Club was deserted and the lights all out but one. In the back room the boss was on the phone. He was talking to the Tammany leader of the District.

"I don't know how it happened," he said. "I was never so surprised in my life."

"No, we didn't give him a bit of help."

"Yes, I know I'm a goddam fool for letting him run."

"I know. . . . I know. . . . I know. . . . Yes, it's too late now. . . ." He looked up. "Hullo, what'r you doing here? Y'gotta leave now. I'm closing up. G'night." The boss reached for his hat, lit a cigar, snapped out the light.

Scarcely had the gavel called Congressman La Guardia to order for the first time when sounded the call to arms. To make the world "safe for democracy" the young congressman voted for war, marched to the well of the House and resigned to join the air force. A brief course of training at Mineola by Joseph Bellanca, later famed airplane designer, and then the Italian front with the American army. Distinction and decorations and the rank of major. Valiant service as propagandist behind the Italian lines. Re-election to Congress while at war. Home and marriage and the tragic end of that marriage in the death of wife and infant child.

The election of Al Smith as governor left a vacancy for president of the Board of Aldermen. Casting about for a candidate, the Republicans struck upon War Hero La Guardia. After a rollicking campaign, and by a paper-thin margin, "The Major" was elected— went to the City's second-high elective office to serve with the ineffable Mayor Hylan in the strange interlude between the reform of Mayor Mitchel and the buccaneering days of the tin-box brigade.

Life was interesting as usual for the Aldermanic President. When Tammany raised the salaries of all aldermen and failed to raise his, he retaliated by wearing a khaki shirt to a Board of Estimate meeting. This horrified no end the Tammany stuffed shirts, who recalled with nostalgia the days, a decade previous, when Mayor Gaynor used to wear a silk hat from his office on the first floor of City Hall to the Board of Estimate chamber on the second. An unprincipled personal feud developed between the Mayor and Comptroller Craig, whereupon La Guardia seized the opportunity to foment the worst possible relationship between these two high Tammany officials. His slight comforts to the plodding Hylan brought cries of pain from Craig, who shouted, "Hit the little wop over the head with the gavel" and generally referred to him as "Blackguardia."

Significant of this period was a gradual impregnation with City affairs. Fourteen years before he was to face the crisis of municipal bankruptcy, he warned, "The financial condition of the City requires care in the spending of money and the utilization of property." [1] And, "The only way to meet the situation is spend less

[1] Opening address to the Board of Aldermen, 1920.

money and to run the City of New York within the limits of our resources. Unless you do this, gentlemen, you will have a difficult problem confronting you by the end of this year and the taxpayers of 1922 and the years thereafter will have to pay the price of our present lack of prudence or our unwillingness to economize at the proper time. I am indeed concerned with the future financial condition of this City. . . ." [2]

He recommended centralized purchasing, harbor development, administration of public relief "without embarrassment or humiliation," and a myriad other reforms. But his gay and carefree colleagues from Tammany conscientiously disregarded all his advice and suggestions, set their course firmly toward the rocks, and pulled down the throttle for full steam ahead.

Significant of all these years was the forthright intellectual honesty which later made him great, but which at this point merely made him singular. There was no effort during these years to deceive either the public or himself. What he said was the truth; the fact that few believed him was due to a public cynicism that recognized the New York City political cesspool for what it was and disbelieved all public officials.

Back to Congress, but not from his old district. From Greenwich Village he moved uptown to the heavily populated Jewish and Italian section of East Harlem, the Twentieth. Five times he was elected from this district and served continuously until March 4, 1933, in the United States Congress. In 1924 he ran with La Follette on the Third Party ticket, and won by the largest majority of his career. When Tammany once nominated a prominent Jew against him and spread the story that he was anti-Semitic, he promptly posted the entire district with huge posters challenging his opponent to a debate in the largest hall in the area. Only *one* condition (a fair one), said La Guardia, the debate must be in *Yiddish*. On the night of the debate, five thousand howling constituents packed the hall. La Guardia spoke in Yiddish, a talent from his Ellis Island days. His opponent (who could not speak a word of Yiddish) was "ill." His opponent was more genuinely ill after the returns were in.

[2] Opening address to the Board of Aldermen, 1921.

WIDE WORLD PHOTOS

FIORELLO H. LA GUARDIA

"I say that the most inefficient, wasteful self-government is worth more than the most efficient dictatorship."—La Guardia, April 15, 1932.

These campaigns abounded with the political ingenuity of La Guardia. As he became more prominent in Congress, it became more and more important to certain well-financed interests to defeat him, and large sums of money were spent by his opponents. He met their unimaginative campaign literature with billboards screaming the names of his detractors and their financial and political antecedents. To dramatize his fight against the high cost of living, he pulled lamb chops from his pocket to show the slight nourishment available to his underprivileged constituents for thirty cents. To show the evils of prohibition and the ease of evasion, he experimentally made beer on a street corner.

His district was not affected by the pious endorsements of the Citizens Union or the City Club. Campaigns had to be won on the street corners, and as he became more and more of a menace to the things that Tammany stood for, that organization resorted to violence and open terrorism. Guerrillas and thugs, supported by the organized crime which Tammany assiduously protected (the district was a Dutch Schultz fiefdom) hurled brickbats and drove heavy trucks into La Guardia street meetings. Ultra demagogic use was made of the facts that La Guardia, though of Italian extraction, was anti-fascist and that he was a Protestant and a Mason, contrary to usual Italian custom. The City's main Italian newspaper, *Il Progresso*, whose owner received huge sand and gravel contracts from Tammany Hall, was, "strangely enough," anti-La Guardia. A huge fraudulent vote in the district added to his difficulties.

Despite these obstacles, however, "The Major" was successful each time until the obstacle of running on the same ticket with Herbert Hoover in 1932 proved too much for him. Added to this handicap of 1932, was the fact that the Jewish population of the district, always progressive and difficult for Tammany to organize and own, had moved uptown, and in its place had come Puerto Ricans with less sophistication in New York City politics and, in 1932, less responsible leadership.

Seven terms in Congress were full of activity and rich with achievement. Highlights of that career show a record of consistent liberalism. It was a record that paralleled the elder La Follette and George Norris in the Senate across the way. And, in full justice, it should be pointed out that the widespread popularity of liberalism, both pseudo and real, is very recent. Now everyone is a "liberal," or claims to be. In the decade of Coolidge and Hoover, however, liberalism was heresy and anyone who disagreed with Andrew Mellon on taxation was a menace to constitutional government. Through this dank period of American history moved La Guardia with a sure-footed rebelliousness and considerable success.

He fought for the Child Labor amendment and saw it pass Congress. He fought for Woman Suffrage and saw it pass. He fought for the Lame Duck amendment, which later passed.

Andrew Mellon gravely proposed that the way to dispose of a treasury surplus was to reduce the tax on large incomes. La Guardia urged the application of the treasury surplus to the reduction of the public debt.[3] No one paid any attention to this ridiculous idea, of course, but with a small group of willful irreconcilables he did contrive to beat the Mellon tax bill.

He was lethal to pork-barrel appropriations and crooked federal judges. The House of Representatives had a unanimous consent calendar, where local district pap was speeded through without the embarrassment of debate or a recorded vote. It was considered very gauche for a congressman actually to study this calendar and file objections. But La Guardia did. "Mr. Speaker, reserving the right to object, I call the attention of the House to these bridge bills that are coming up. . . . This bill is typical of the type of bill that should be objected to." [4] So dozens of times. He fought for the sale of public property at public auction rather than at private sale. He blocked a bridge franchise to a man who had previously retailed a similar franchise. He blocked a plan to lease for no consideration other than "upkeep of the premises" a $12,-700, 000 naval base.

In his spare time he conducted raids on corrupt federal judges. Most congressmen, even those on the Judiciary Committee, avoid this burdensome duty because of the heavy investment of time and energy involved. But La Guardia had the energy and found the time. Judges English and Winslow left the bench under his assault. Judge Louderback escaped by a hair. Judge Anderson was

[3] December 8, 1926.
[4] December 17, 1928.

harried for months, and so on. He exposed the expense account padding of federal judges and secured the passage of an amendment to prevent them from giving their secretarial allowances to their wives, daughters, etc. These efforts availed him nothing politically, for they were of no interest to his own congressional district. But they satisfied his inveterate yearning to improve the character and honesty of the public service, and many incidents in his career are due only to such scruples.

He never yielded to postwar jingoism. He passed an amendment to speed demobilization at the war's end. He fought to reduce postwar military expenditures; opposed increase in army personnel; defeated efforts to buy more Liberty motors after the war ended with hundreds of them already on hand.

He demanded that the wartime espionage laws be repealed; that the wartime taxes be ended. He spoke out against the expulsion of socialist members of the New York State legislature, and was branded a radical while others who spoke out similarly (Charles Evans Hughes, Alfred E. Smith) lost no standing at the Union League Club.

Foe of extravagance, he none the less fought for the welfare of public employees. In April, 1920, when salaries of high City officials were raised twenty-five to a hundred per cent, he asked for a minimum wage of $1,200 for City employees. On February 3, 1925, he said: "Let us get action on this postal salary increase . . . the wives of our postal employees cannot pay rent and the butcher and grocer on promises." In January, 1926, he fought for the merit system for Civil Service employment and adequate budget support for the staff of the Civil Service Commission. He attempted to extend the competitive employment of public servants in the federal courts. He asked for the forty-four-hour week in the postal service in 1930, and introduced a bill in 1932 to provide a five-day week for those employed on government works.

Throughout, he fought for the repeal of national prohibition. His was a district where he witnessed at close range the rise and spread of gangsterism and racketeering financed and supported by the illegal traffic in liquor.

He struggled for government operation of Muscle Shoals and against proposed private leasing, long before the TVA. Always busy as a bee, he steadily grew in prestige and influence among his colleagues, until the climactic events of the seventy-second Congress (1931–1933). An iconoclast about great financial power and a skeptic concerning the "wizards" of industry and finance, he had attacked American Bond and Mortgage and the Harriman Bank as early as 1928. "It takes more than a pair of spats and a love-nest on Park Avenue to make a banker," he acidly commented. When bond and mortgage companies commenced to collapse and Harriman was indicted and a general cataclysm ensued, his words took on a prophetic cast and his more sober colleagues began to view him with an awesome respect.

He attacked Samuel Insull on the floor of the House as early as January, 1931, and received at the time only a shower of brickbats. When Insull protested that La Guardia hid behind his congressional immunity to make libelous charges, La Guardia repeated the speech from the steps of the House office building. Insull, told of the speech, "laughed."

When his own alma mater, New York University, presented Richard Whitney, president of the New York Stock Exchange, with an honorary degree, he wrote New York University a letter asking them why they didn't give a degree to Scarface Al Capone. This may or may not have accounted for the fact that he received no honorary degree himself until 1938, after Richard Whitney had been sent to Sing Sing as a further recognition of his financial genius. This was a source of peculiar satisfaction to the Mayor, for it was Richard Whitney who had taken special pains to turn his back squarely on La Guardia when testifying before a congressional committee in 1932.

These matters were not lucky coincidences but the result of a keen understanding of the forces at work in the profession which he scornfully called "banketeering." Many thousands of thoughtful people knew and understood what was going on, but few public officials had the courage to tell the truth, and thereby risk the enmity of the rich and powerful. And few of them saw steadily and saw whole the economic picture, as did La Guardia. From the first he saw the Stock Market collapse of 1929 not as an isolated and transitory phenomenon, but as a symptom of an epochal economic event, marking the end of an era. He was reaping, for the first time, the reward of thoughtful study and attention to basic economic issues. While the wiseacres, including President Hoover, were predicting prompt and rapid recovery "just around the corner," La Guardia was saying: "Let us act with our eyes open. We are going to have a deficit next fiscal year and the year after that." [5]

He saw accurately that the development of labor-saving machinery and the elimination of the frontier paralyzed those forces which had previously lifted us out of depressions automatically. And as the government remained inert in the face of disaster, waiting for the "inevitable" and automatic economic cycle, which never arrived, La Guardia was stating the case for the brave new world on the floor of the House: "We must have modern conditions to meet modern machinery. As labor-saving devices are installed and used for production we must necessarily shorten the number of hours per day, and we are now at that stage where we will necessarily have to come to a five day week because, gentlemen, you cannot have prosperity unless you have employment. . . . This is 1930, not 1898. We have not only arrived at a 44-hour week but in this machine age we are arriving at the time when all workers will soon be given a 40-hour week," [6] "We must give the benefit of machinery and improved methods of production to all of the people, and not to a few who happen to own the machines." [7]

These were happy days; days of vindication and achievement. For a full month in the spring of 1932 he and his "allied progressives" routed the leadership of the House, massacred the sales tax, which had the blessing of William Randolph Hearst, Bernard Baruch, and the conservative leadership of both parties, and rewrote the tax bill. His anti-injunction bill, jointly sponsored with Senator Norris to strip the federal courts of power to break strikes by injunction, finally passed. He brought a trunk-load of documents to the Senate Banking and Currency Committee and triumphantly proved that crooked newspapermen had conspired with crooked brokers and speculators to rig stock prices on a large scale for the shearing of innocent investing lambs. Successfully

[5] December 5, 1929.   [6] May 3, 1930; July 1, 1930.   [7] December 21, 1932.

stifled by the Republican controlled committee, these exposures came to life a year later, were whipped into a flame by Ferdinand Pecora, special Senate counsel, and resulted in the SEC. La Guardia was floor leader for organized labor. Life was good.

Most of all he saw the hope of passage for social legislation of basic importance. He renewed his crusade for social insurance, old-age pensions, and unemployment relief. "Immediate relief for the unemployed this winter is necessary," he said on December 21, 1932. "I would suggest now, and I don't care what you call it, immediate, substantial appropriations by the federal government to supplement state and local appropriations to carry us through this winter. In the meantime we must adopt a real building program that will put hundreds of thousands of men to work immediately." Unknown to him he was sounding the tocsin for a New Deal and a new economic and political philosophy that was to sweep the country like a prairie fire within a year. But on November 8, 1932, the day that the New Deal triumphed, La Guardia was defeated for Congress.

The bitterness of this defeat was not softened by the fact that his friends told him it was wholly undeserved. Nor was it much consolation that after the writer introduced him to A. A. Berle, Jr., trusted Roosevelt adviser, the New Deal thought so well of him that he was chosen to pilot some vital emergency measures through the House in the lame duck session of December, 1932, including the now famous 77B of the Bankruptcy Law.

Back came La Guardia to the City scene with a bounce. He had loved the cosmic power of the United States government to make basic economic and social adjustments in our body politic, but he swiftly became oriented again to the realities of the local City picture. Events were swiftly moving in his direction, and ere a month had passed he was gravitating again to the vortex of the local political whirlpool. This was not sheer luck. The way had been carefully prepared three years previous, and he was about to reap the first fruits of his lifelong and betimes single-handed crusade against Tammany Hall.

The way had been prepared in 1929, in his violent campaign

for mayor against Jimmy Walker, with its bitter ending of overwhelming defeat. But he had told the truth in that campaign, and three years had made a great difference in the popular reception of that truth.

In 1929, for instance, he had charged that the lower criminal courts were nests of corruption and that magistrates bought their appointments.

"Reckless and irresponsible statements," retorted Walker.

"Reckless and irresponsible statements," echoed the hostile press.

Came the Seabury Investigation of the Magistrates' Courts. Removed and resigned in 1930, 1931: Magistrates Silbermann, Jean Norris, McQuade, Goodman, G. W. Simpson, Leo Healy, Vause, Vitale, and Ewald.

In 1929 he charged larceny in paying of excessive prices for school sites controlled by politicians.

"Reckless and irresponsible statements," echoed Walker and his press.

Followed the Wallstein report: Tammany politician F. T. McEneny had made $67,000 profit on $900 investment; Boss McCooey of Brooklyn made $69,656 on the notorious gas house school site bought by the City at five times its assessed value; Officers A. C. Kerwin, W. P. Jewett, of the Tammany Board of Education, were dismissed and suspended on bribe charges; Tammany state senators, borough presidents, aldermanic president, district leaders implicated.

La Guardia charged graft in bus franchises.

"Reckless and irresponsible," came the echo.

Seabury said of Equitable Bus: ". . . the conditions which motivated the Mayor in granting this franchise were improper . . . the scheme was a conspiracy . . . the Mayor exerted himself, in violation of his duty, in the furtherance of that conspiracy." [8]

In 1929 La Guardia charged sewer building scandals.

"Reckless and irresponsible."

On May 7, 1930, the grafters were convicted.

In 1929 La Guardia charged zoning law graft in the Board of Standards and Appeals and declared that zoning laws did not apply to persons "on the inside."

[8] Seabury's Second Intermediate Report, p. 76.

"Reckless and irresponsible."

Seabury reported: Dr. Doyle, operating at the Board, deposited more than $1,000,000 in a few years, and split his fees. Large Real Estate firms had to retain Tammany lawyers to get fair treatment. W. J. Flynn, Bronx Public Works Commissioner, had blocked a permit for a competing garage across the street from one for which he himself obtained permission.

La Guardia accused Tammany of grafting on a huge scale; called it a "cash register administration"; said graft was as large a burden on business as taxes; charged that no Tammany politician could afford to have his bank accounts examined.

"Reckless and irresponsible."

Seabury found: Tammany politician McQuade banked $520,000 in six years on $50,000 total salary; Perry, $135,000 in four years on $30,000 total salary; "Tin Box" Farley, $96,000 in seven years on $90,000 salary; Kavanaugh, $250,000 in twelve years; Flaherty, $21,000 in four months; Cruise, $80,000 in excess of salary; Mac-Cormick, $200,000 in excess of salary; Dennis Wright, a policeman, $99,000 in eleven years on $2,500 salary ("loans from a seafaring man," said he); Mullerkey, police inspector, $27,800 in thirteen months on a $5,900 salary. And so on. The mayor had large brokerage accounts concealed through one Sherwood; received large sums in bonds from taxicab interests before passing the Taxi Control Bill. Everything from newsstand license and dumping permit to bus franchise called for a "price" to the politicians and was ridden with graft. "The graft and corruption established by the evidence is part of a system controlled by Tammany Hall and permeating the City," summarized the understating Seabury.[9]

Now it was La Guardia's turn. He had come back. The overwhelming defeat of 1929 was three years past and his charges had resulted in the Seabury Investigation and the Seabury Investigation had ripped off the lid. Jimmy Walker had fled to Europe. The filthy trail of corruption and graft ran from the meanest district clubhouse to the steps of City Hall. Graft in markets, pushcarts, busses, ash removal, assessments, sewers, docks, zoning, condemnation, the milk racket ("baby poisoning" La Guardia

[9] Intermediate Report, p. 67.

called it), the open alliance between organized crime and the Tammany organization, the Central Park Casino, the murder of the Tammany gambler, Rothstein, all led the same miserable, odious trail back to Tammany Hall.

Meaner and more spectacular were the exposures of Lowell Limpus, ace muckraker of the *Daily News,* and his stool pigeon, Chile Acuna. They showed how crooked policemen and crooked judges framed innocent girls on prostitution charges to "shake down" their decent families. (An innocent girl, from a decent family, Tammany found, would pay almost any price to escape from a framed-up charge of prostitution.) Large contracts paying millions; petty graft, paying pennies (one Tammany Alderman was nicknamed "Two-bit" because nothing was too small for him to take), were all part of the tribute to the loathsome system of Tammany. Rotten to the core, reeking in its own stench, Seabury laid it bare. It was just as La Guardia had said it was—*in 1929.*

"RECKLESS AND IRRESPONSIBLE!" He flung it back in their teeth! It was no longer 1929. It was the spring of 1933!

But, even so, the nomination of La Guardia for mayor in 1933 by Reform was not foreordained. The "respectable" reformers looked with some trepidation on this "radical" who had been identified so closely with labor and liberal causes. An abortive attempt was made by former Governor Whitman and some other conservatives to nominate a "respectable" candidate, General O'Ryan. La Guardia called the nominal leader of the "Fusion" groups into his office the next morning, strode up and down the room, shouted, gesticulated, pounded the desk, threatened to demand a Grand Jury investigation. He profanely pointed out that it was a typical sell-out to Tammany Hall, whereby the reform vote would be split between himself, who had already announced his candidacy, and a conservative. The Fusion leader left, much impressed.

"You just have to put on an act sometimes," said La Guardia calmly.

But the dominant, self-made leadership of La Guardia in New York City reform could not be denied. Roy Howard, with his powerful, reforming *World-Telegram,* brought up his heavy guns for La Guardia. C. C. Burlingham, venerable ex-president of the City Bar Association and leading citizen of New York City for half a century, brought Republicans, reformers, Fusionists, and all into one joint committee of fourteen. Even the arch conservatives were gradually becoming resigned to the one immutable truth—that there was only one person who could beat Tammany and that person was La Guardia.

The Committee of Fourteen met one August night. La Guardia sat at home with about ten of his most intimate friends awaiting the outcome. That night the fate of New York City, and who knows what greater ultimate issue, hung in a very delicate balance. The ordinarily gregarious friends of the Major, Corsi, Marcantonio, and others who have seen him through many tough campaigns, were unnaturally tense and silent. The third highest elective office in the United States dangled in the balance for five hours. Then, shortly after midnight the telephone rang. It was Judge Seabury. The Committee of Fourteen had nominated—La Guardia.

"I promise you faithfully you will never regret this," said La Guardia to Judge Seabury. "I hope I shall be able to make you proud of me."

In the history of New York City the fall of 1933 will stand as one of its very critical periods. Tammany Hall, sterile intellectually in the face of economic disaster and bankrupt morally, clung like an octopus to the great power of the City government. Tammany was indeed in low repute publicly. Not only had the organization sunk deep in the mire of scandal and corruption, but its reactionary leaders had opposed Roosevelt at Chicago in 1932 and part of them had opposed Lehman for governor. The victory of both at once did not help the "Hall." But Tammany had the great prestige of consecutive power over a century. It nourished for itself the idea of invincibility. It possessed, indeed, an army of thugs and guerrillas for the poorer districts and an army of doorbell ringers on the city payroll for the middle class.

It protected Dutch Schultz and his slot machine and policy racket, and his hundreds of professional and well-paid criminals would be out working at election time. They had a real stake. It was Tammany's police commissioner who would discipline any headstrong detective who might lay a hand on "the Dutchman." It was Tammany's district attorney who would return the bloody evidence to a faithful henchman charged with murder and accept a plea of guilty to disorderly conduct for any heinous offense. So with the trucking racket, the live poultry racket, the artichoke and vegetable rackets, the building racket, the loading racket, commercialized prostitution, dope, gambling—everything. They were all protected by the "Hall," and on election day and before, they would supply their army for the intimidation, coercion, and murder if necessary of decent voters and for the fraudulent registration and voting of thousands of illegal Tammany floaters.

On top of these was the army of jobholders. Tammany had smuggled in the back door of Civil Service nearly twenty thousand favorites without examination, who had the main job of canvassing their friends, families, and neighbors for weeks before election day. They pleaded, cajoled, and, as a last resort, told the voter how their wives and children would surely starve if Tammany should lose. Always effective before, how could Tammany suspect that this tactic would one time fail?

In the old days, under Boss Charley Murphy, the great man of the "Hall," it had been felt that, no matter how rotten the motives, the "front men" should be respectable and have a popular appeal. Murphy brought out such popular heroes as Al Smith, Bob Wagner, and, in his day, Jimmy Walker. But when Murphy died, "the brains of Tammany were laid away in the cemetery," [10] and the small men who succeeded him decided that this business of popular appeal was all the bunk and that a political organization with plenty of doorbell ringers and plenty of money was invincible. Sad was their awakening.

On this theory Tammany nominated and elected in 1932 for the short term to succeed Walker and again in 1933, a lovable, God-fearing, and personally honest ex-Surrogate, whose unblemished personal life glittered like diamonds in comparison with his exiled predecessor—his name was John P. O'Brien. For all that, he was as a candidate, the most ingenuous slob who had run for mayor of New York City in a long time.

While the effervescent La Guardia was touring the highways

[10] Jimmy Walker, 1937.

and byways, his rapier thrusts dealing out death to the dragon Tammany, and his lightning-like mind striking about a week ahead of his opponent, the stodgy O'Brien was orating: "Mr. President, and may I say brothers? when I get in a room with chairs I get the fraternal spirit." [11] And, "I've come up here to be received and lifted on a higher plane." [12] And, "During the week I have momentous matters to attend to. I meet great people and I must go here and there to make up the addenda that goes with being Mayor of the City. Therefore, when I come here to this great forum and see before me flowers and buds, ladies, girls and widows, emotion is running just riot with me." [13] It was reported that, in speaking at a school graduation, he told the children that he had always loved the classics ever since he translated Horace from the original Greek.

By the middle of September, even Tammany commenced to get worried. Always a vigorous and devastating campaigner, who thought nothing of four to ten meetings a night and who pulled no punches, La Guardia was drawing huge crowds, winning straw polls, and receiving mighty newspaper support. The La Guardia campaign headquarters in the Paramount Building, classic as usual for their disorganization, were humming with activity and were filled with important and respected citizens, able and determined. William Chadbourne, an old Bull Mooser and prominent Republican, was campaign chairman. Even La Guardia's fatal campaign weakness, to return large contributions on the theory that their source was immoral, did not deter this campaign.

La Guardia on the stump was telling the truth again, and people were listening. And as the tide rolled in and confidence increased, La Guardia put forward a program for municipal rejuvenation, and the people were interested. And underlying his whole campaign was the strident cry for social justice, a cry that had risen from the halls of Congress for almost sixteen years without any great effect. Now it had effect.

As things looked blacker and blacker, Tammany became more and more desperate and, with ignorance characteristic of profes-

[11] Speech at the Samuel Tichnor Society, January, 1933.
[12] Speech at the Riverdale-on-Hudson Club, April, 1933.
[13] Speech before the Ladies of the Theatre Assembly, Hotel Astor, April, 1933.

sional politicians in such crises, became more and more inane. Inanity reached a peak with a pamphlet entitled "No Red, No Clown, Shall Rule This Town," which attempted to make high fun of La Guardia's congressional disclosures about the Stock Exchange. In a city where thousands had been ruined by crooked stock manipulation, and while many of the perpetrators were still awaiting trial, this technique was hardly over-astute, and certainly abysmal in its failure to appraise the temper of the times.

From the start, the campaign of Tammany fooled no intelligent citizens, and finally it even ceased to fool Tammany Hall. Puffing and panting, from Washington rode Jim Farley, to add a climactic debacle to the already badly "debacled" mire of the machine. Tammany had opposed Roosevelt. Farley would lick Tammany and at the same time gain control of the third highest office and second largest budget in the country. So out of a hat, from the friendly Bronx Democratic organization of Ed Flynn, Farley pulled Joseph V. McKee. And at the last legal moment, the race became three-cornered.

"Holy Joe" McKee had been president of the Board of Aldermen under Walker and had frequently praised that regime. As such he had succeeded Walker for a brief spell as acting mayor in the fall of 1932. During that brief spell he had looked like a reformer and gained the appellation "Holy Joe," which overlooked the fact that in his office had transpired some of the smelliest real estate deals of all in the good old days. His campaign started like a Kansas cyclone, and ended like one, with "Holy Joe" lucky to save his pants and vest. The reason was that he insisted upon bringing up some old magazine articles he had written casting very unflattering aspersions upon the Jewish citizens of America.

La Guardia had known about these articles from the start, but refused to use them or allow his supporters to use them. Then, by inadvertence, Judge Seabury made a speech attacking Governor Lehman for something. Whereupon "Holy Joe" sent La Guardia a telegram demanding that he repudiate this attack by his main supporter upon "a great representative of a great race." The telegram arrived while the Major was attending a rodeo at Madison Square Garden with some neighbor children on a Saturday afternoon. Quick as a flash came the reply: "Are you trying to draw a red herring across the trail . . . of your scurrilous attacks . . ." etc. Thunder and lightning struck down McKee. Samuel Untermyer, Jewish leader, attacked him in screaming headlines. By Monday morning the *New York Times* was printing the whole text of the McKee articles. There are two million Jews in New York. La Guardia had previously won their respect by leading an anti-Hitler parade to the battery, before he was a candidate. Farley retreated in disorder.

At one minute after midnight on the morning of January 1, 1934, at the home of Samuel Seabury, Fiorello H. La Guardia was sworn in as the ninety-ninth mayor of the City of New York.

No "basket party on the lawn" awaited La Guardia at City Hall. As Tammany breathed its last, it commenced to reap the whirlwind it had sown by its wild orgy of waste and graft. Even as the election approached, the all-important relief funds were exhausted and Tammany had to go begging to the bankers again and again for aid. The grim spectre of payless payday for City employees loomed larger and larger. In desperation to raise funds, Tammany entered the iniquitous "Banker's Agreement," which placed the City revenues in hock and put the City in a financial strait jacket as the price of a $70,000,000 loan at election time. Even so, the bankers did not save Tammany or improve the financial condition of the City, and on January 1, 1934, the City of New York was hair-hung and wind-blown over the yawning abyss of bankruptcy.

Otherwise Tammany's closings days were orthodox. It faced the great darkness unrepentent and unpurged by its experience. In the last week the lights were lit all night at the Mayor's office and a roaring grate fire consumed the damning personal files of four Tammany mayors. A few twenty-five-year bus franchises were handed out to some specially loyal henchmen; and an army of the faithful found a sweet and comforting repose upon the City pension rolls, as a fitting reward for their long and faithless service. This even included some who had resigned in confusion and disgrace under fire but who now managed to return for a few weeks and qualify for fat pensions (such as ex-Magistrate McQuade).

All the idyllic hopes of the new mayor were, at the outset, circumscribed by the brutal fact of bankruptcy. All of his grand schemes and beatific dreams for the "City of the Future," with its parks, housing, health stations, express highways, and whatnot, awaited the one inevitable condition—funds. La Guardia had never appeared in the light of a hard-headed business man. In Congress he had always come somewhat in the role of the starry-eyed idealist. Even his friends were a little surprised at the vigor and realism with which he commenced to solve the fiscal problems of his $650,000,000-a-year business.

Immediately he demanded from the state legislature power to economize. The Tammany legislature called him a "would-be dictator" and all the usual names, but after a brief and sanguinary struggle he got substantially what he wanted. He had to cut salaries of City employees. Tammany laughed and knew that this would be fatal—would kill him politically. They cleverly called him "Furloughello" on the floor of a meeting of the Board of Aldermen when he furloughed City workers, and rejoiced in his misfortune. But again they had failed to appraise accurately the temper of the times, and the response of the City employees as a whole was cool but realistic—they knew what he was up against and they faced the facts.

The Tammany budget had never been balanced. Such minor items as coal and food for the City hospitals were omitted to a large extent because they knew that no one could seriously complain about a forced loan in the middle of the year to fill out these vital appropriations. La Guardia set to work to balance their budget. And he did. That year, and the year after, and the year after that, until the present.

The relief load was rapidly reaching a peak, with nearly a million of his fellow townsmen unable to support themselves. There was no way out except to impose new taxes. Again Tammany laughed. This would surely be fatal. Swiftly there came into being an inheritance tax, income tax, general business and sales tax, utility tax, and minor personal property tax. The income and inheritance taxes were withdrawn when the Tammany-supported governor, a millionaire banker, Herbert Lehman, threatened to withdraw the City's taxing power entirely. But upwards of $70,000,000 a year poured into the coffers of the City through the remaining taxes, and New York City became the only large municipality in the

United States paying for relief entirely out of the current revenues.

All this was not easy for La Guardia. He had been in Congress long enough to learn the time-worn rule for re-election: "Vote for every appropriation and against every tax bill." But he set his face firmly toward the absolute exigencies of the case. He never weakened publicly even in the face of criticism by his old liberal friends about the sales tax. They called it regressive taxation and reminded him that he had fought and beaten it single-handed on the floor of Congress in 1932.

"It has every defect you say," he replied. "In fact the sales tax is wholly wrong except for one thing—it raises the money we need."

But after he held the public hearing required by law on the tax bills and retired to his own office, alone with his law secretary, he picked up his pen and said, "I still think it's lousy," as he signed it in a big, bold hand. The statement was very significant. La Guardia was gradually making the difficult adjustment to the limitations of executive office that had looked impossible to some of his best friends. He was no longer able to clamor for cosmic change from the floor of a sovereign legislative body; he was an executive of a great corporation, bound by technical and legal limitations of all sorts and bound to do the best possible job within the established framework even though the best be only mediocre and sometimes quite disagreeable.

The budget was balanced; relief was financed, and City bonds leaped back to par from a wobbly 82, in the hands of this "radical" mayor. When short-term financing was necessary, to anticipate taxes in the first year, and the bankers downtown expected to do as they had done with Tammany—fix their own interest rate (as high as six per cent), he called the biggest banker of them all on the telephone and called him a cheap, contemptible, chiseling pawnbroker (in effect) for keeping up interest rates in the face of sound credit. The interest rates came down. On July 16, 1935, the City sold bonds at the lowest interest rate in thirty years. New York City avoided default and probably by so doing avoided a national cataclysm in municipal credit.

Once financed, the relief administration was also rehabilitated internally. Instead of a politician, the Mayor appointed a highly

experienced welfare administrator, William Hodson, recommended
by the president of the Welfare Council. Instead of cards from
political clubs qualifying applicants for public aid, an army of in-
vestigators, later made Civil Service, checked the validity of their
claims. Tammany bitterly resented all this, and through their
control of the Board of Aldermen commenced an "investigation."
La Guardia swiftly maneuvered them into the position of enemies
of the unemployed, and when the investigation coined the word
"boondoggling" to describe Federal Works Projects, the relief
workers became very restive and apprehensive and the whole en-
terprise blew up in Tammany's face.

Of all the difficulties at the outset, however, the worst was over-
turning the long established political mores of the metropolis. The
inertia of Tammany's cultural system was tremendous. When La
Guardia announced during the campaign that he believed in "non-
partisan, non-political city government," and when he said at his
inauguration that "to the victor belongs the responsibility for good
government," the calloused citizenry put it down as just another
shrewd political stunt. He said that there was "no republican, no
democratic, no socialist way to clean a street or build a sewer but
merely a right way and a wrong way," and after election he stated
that he was "out of politics for four years."

The reception of these statements was symptomized by an incident which befell the writer. After election a meeting was called
at Mecca Temple for the purpose of having the Mayor-elect thank
the Republican leaders for their support. There they were (the
leaders) full of bubbling good fellowship. La Guardia spoke. He
thanked them sincerely for their support; said that he thought
they had done their City a service and hoped he would justify their
confidence. "But," he said, in effect, "I want to repeat again that
this administration will be non-partisan and non-political. We did
not defeat Tammany Hall of the Democratic party merely to bring
back the same system through the instrument of the Republican
party." The writer was in the third row, next to a district leader,
from lower Manhattan. "Ain't he cute?" said the leader, leaning
over. It took four years to convince that leader, who opposed La
Guardia in 1937.

One Republican district leader merely wanted a concession from the Police Department for a little gambling joint on Sixth Avenue. "A clean little place," he suggested. Another was indignant because a gas station permit in a restricted area was denied him. All wanted jobs and jobs. All were disappointed. The Mayor appointed career men who had come up through the Civil Service ranks to head four departments, Police, Fire, Docks, and Water Supply. In the Police Department this was particularly gratifying because he was able to appoint as Commissioner, Lewis J. Valentine, who had been demoted and transferred to the hinterland by Tammany for raiding politically protected gambling in the old days.

Other commissionerships were filled by competent men without political affiliations, some of them experts from outside the City, such as Austin MacCormick of the Department of Correction, who came from the Federal Prison Service, and Dr. John Rice of the Department of Health, who was commissioner of health in New Haven. Others were outstanding experts, like Robert Moses, Parks; Dr. S. S. Goldwater, Hospitals; Paul Blanshard, Investigation; Professor Russell Forbes, Purchase, etc. Where an occasional political figure gained high office it was because the Mayor thought well of his qualifications, and the political organization gained slight solace. What started as a crusade against Tammany ended as a devastating blow to the whole theory and philosophy of district leader, machine-controlled, city government.

Not only were the jobs important, but the prestige of the leaders was emasculated. For the power of the leader and his standing in the community depend on his ability to do favors and his ability to do favors depends on his intimacy with the officials of government. This was lost, irretrievably.

Just as the professional politicians were coming to earth with a dull thud, the general public rubbed its eyes again at the unfolding of a new standard of official civic virtue. After the crass and open stealing of Tammany, the most that the public expected was decent restriction on official graft in keeping with hard times. They reckoned without the almost fanatical morality of the new Mayor. He loudly announced that anyone in his administration who accepted a nickel cigar would be fired forthwith, and just as the warning grew cold, he drove it home by dismissing, with paralyzing dispatch, a respected deputy commissioner who had given a load of City gravel to a Boy Scout camp.

From top to bottom every department felt and knew the meaning of this new crusade. Eleven City marshals, under direct discipline of the Mayor's office, were swiftly fired for such formerly common misdeeds as holding public auctions in a back room. Dozens of petty grafters, holding over in minor positions, went the hard way. Deputy commissioners in the Sanitation Department descended on the street cleaners and fired several dozen who took tips for loading trade waste on City trucks. But the Sanitation Department found it could not break the long established graft in the City dumps whereby private truckmen used the City dumps by slipping the City men a trifling "honorarium." So La Guardia legalized the whole thing, raised the fee to a half dollar, printed tickets for sale, and collected thousands of dollars a year for the City treasury out of money formerly spent for private graft.

One of the Mayor's best friends, a pompous and elegant Colonel, was arrested for speeding. After bawling out the cop, the Colonel took the ticket, sent it to the Mayor, and demanded immediate discipline for the offensive policeman who had given him, a friend of the Mayor, a ticket. The Mayor sent out for a box of cigars and sent it to the cop with a note of congratulation.

With inside graft on the run, he proceeded against outside excrescences. Typical was the artichoke racket. Terranova, the Artichoke King, had lived in a swank suburb in royal splendor on the "take" from this racket for years. Strong-arm men forced merchants to buy artichokes only from "the boss." So Terranova's company, grandiloquently styled the "Union Pacific Produce Company," handled all artichokes shipped into New York City. It performed no services; did not load, unload, deliver, or even keep accurate books. It occupied a hole in the wall with a telephone number for the headquarters of the "mob." For these services, Terranova added about a hundred per cent to the price of the commodity, and took about a million dollars a year net profit.

Detectives were sent with pushcarts to the markets to sell artichokes bought through outsiders. Sure enough, the Terranova thugs came in and ordered them out. The wheels started to move.

Terranova was arrested on general principles each time he crossed the City line. The Mayor went to the Bronx Terminal Market himself, with fanfare and bugles, at six o'clock one cold winter morning to read a proclamation against the racketeers. The hostile *New York Sun* made fun of this circus byplay, but missed the fact that while the Mayor was telling the pushcart peddlers he would protect them, by use of trumpets, his own law secretary was in Washington, before the Department of Agriculture, quietly securing the cancellation of Terranova's license to sell artichokes under the Perishable Agricultural Commodities Act. Soon the sympathetic wheels of the federal government were grinding Terranova and his racket into pulp as the Mayor had planned. The artichoke empire was wrecked beyond repair; and the twilight of the "Artichoke King" and the "Green Pepper King" and Socks Lanza of the fish market, and all other racketeering "kings" was fast drawing near.

La Guardia knew that these crusades would crack Tammany Hall; and eventually they did. Finally a "runaway" Grand Jury, headed by an eminent real estate man and prominent citizen, Lee Thompson Smith, sickened of the efforts of the Tammany district attorney to suppress damaging evidence against Tammany men, and demanded that the Governor appoint a special prosecutor. The Governor did. Came Thomas E. Dewey as such. La Guardia gave Dewey his ace detectives; Dewey recruited an ace legal staff. And the havoc and destruction caused thereby to organized crime with political protection is still being written by Dewey with flaming headlines into the history of the City of New York.

Other urgencies impeded the development of the great constructive civic program that seethed within La Guardia. Strikes and labor disputes were acute in 1934, 1935, and 1936. From the taxi strike to the building service strike, these disputes were frequent and serious. Many times La Guardia spent the entire night at City Hall, with the employers in one room and the strikers in another, bringing them closer and closer by attrition as he wore them thinner and thinner, and generally settling in the end. Throughout, he kept his police force neutral, using force only when force was used by one party or the other, and allowing unions and employers both an opportunity for self-discipline. On occasion the police were sent in force to the scene of a strike, without night sticks. Some excesses occurred, but while Chicago had its Memorial Day Massacre and riots and violence abounded throughout the country, New York was free of a single fatal disturbance. The proof of the pudding was the eating thereof.

Gradually the swirling, madcap days of the early months tapered off into a less jaded time of constructive effort. As the critical period of City finance ended, Dewey took over crime, state and federal labor boards took over labor disputes, and the vast machinery of City government was geared more and more to the great social welfare program La Guardia had planned.

For years he had ridden about the City indignant at the social myopia of its rulers. "What a beautiful park this could be," he used to exclaim, riding up through shabby Central Park at night from his office to his home before he was mayor; and no indignation matched his contempt for the failure of Tammany to attack slums, disease, mass recreational facilities, and the like. Now it was his turn.

For park commissioner he appointed the hard-hitting, fire-eating, overbearing, and incomparably efficient Robert Moses. In the first two years 253 new playgrounds were built in congested areas, most of them on undeveloped and unused land already owned by governmental agencies. Ten swimming pools, eleven large parks, ten golf courses, two great new beaches, a tremendous park and athletic field at wasted Randall's Island, all blossomed overnight. Nor were these the ordinary Tammany jobs, with a few cinders scattered over a rubbish heap and an enclosure of chicken-wire. Parks by La Guardia's Commissioner Moses were a new experience for the citizens of New York City. Carefully landscaped, carefully built, each wading pool chlorinated, each small playground hard surfaced for easy cleaning, sanitary field houses, shade trees, adequate apparatus, were the new technique. Almost all of the few previously constructed playground were rebuilt and rehabilitated. Political concessionaires were thrown out. Political appointees were ousted and Civil Service staffs replaced them. Moses was "hellbent" and La Guardia swelled with deeper satisfaction at every new dedication.

To supplement the internal park system, a great parkway network was constructed for the auto-traveling, suburban recreationists. The Tri-Boro Bridge, the Henry Hudson Bridge and Parkway, the great Grand Central Parkway in Queens, and the Riverside Parkway in Manhattan, literally cut hours from the sweaty, interminable traffic jams of the old days for the beach-bound and country-bound week-enders.

All this was associated with a new philosophy of public administration. At Orchard Beach a squatters' colony had grown up under Tammany, with politically favored individuals actually building bungalows on the City-owned beach. Overnight these were swept away and a great new public beach, à la Moses, rose like a Phoenix from the debris. The Flushing Dumps became Flushing Meadow Park and the site of the World's Fair (as Moses said, "from dump to glory"). The teeming throngs at Coney Island had swum for years in the mouth of the Coney Island Creek, where Tammany carefully dumped raw sewage from a large portion of the City. When holdover doctors of the Department of Health advised the Mayor that the water was pure despite the sewage, he sent them down to swim in it themselves. They had their pictures taken on the beach in swimming suits but did not go near the water.

A sewage disposal plant cleared the creek. Moses took over the park.

In Central Park a main attraction was an expensive night club, charging eighty cents a cup for coffee (operated under lease by a Tammany politician, friend of Jimmy Walker, who also made large "loans" to politicians). The Mayor and Moses tossed out the lessee, ripped down the building, and made the site into another children's playground. On Riverside Drive hundreds of acres of potential park were left as an ash-dump by Tammany Hall, between the Hudson River and the railroad. A colony of tar-paper houses grew in this desolate strip of land and a favored yacht club occupied a piece of the water front. The Mayor and Moses swept away the yacht club and the tar-paper shacks at once, covered the tracks, and built a great waterfront drive and park, a model for the world.

The methods of Moses were sometimes high-handed, but always effective. When four city blocks of waste space were left over after the construction of a new bridge approach in the teeming lower

East Side, Tammany wanted to use the land for more teeming apartments so that the Tammany merchants of the area would have more business. The Mayor and Moses decided to make it a park. For months the contest raged in the Board of Estimate, but it was all academic, because Moses had the streets closed, playgrounds built, and shrubbery planted all the while. Sometimes Moses' precipitate haste even exceeded the Mayor's, as when he decided to build a park at a ferry slip and ordered a pile driver to tear down the ferry terminal (86th Street) while the ferry was still running. The Mayor had to send the police.

Symbolic of every department was the progress of the Department of Parks. Eight new health stations and twelve new baby health stations were built for the Department of Health; vigorous attacks were made on venereal disease and tuberculosis and the City made a new low record on infant mortality. The City markets were rehabilitated; new water and rail facilities were installed; and unsanitary open markets in the streets were in some cases enclosed (as on upper Park Avenue) or eliminated (as Harlem Market). A consumer's service was established which gave marketing advice to the housewives on the radio each morning. The Bronx Terminal Market, a $17,000,000 white elephant under Tammany, was completed and showed an operating profit of $192,000 in its first seven months.

The City prisons, where politically favored inmates occupied private apartments, had their own iceboxes, pets, and servants, and sometimes controlled an illicit traffic in narcotics, were cleaned out and the wardens became for the first time as important as the most politically powerful inmate. Centralized purchasing under one of the nation's leading experts, Commissioner Russell Forbes, saved millions of dollars. Fifty thousand dollars was saved on one fuel oil contract; $27,000 on a single printing contract alone in the first year, for example. The law department was rehabilitated and more than $3,000,000 was recovered from litigating a single crooked condemnation award contrived by Tammany (Lucmay's "Larceny Park") while $60,000 was recovered from a single crooked bus operator who had felt such confidence in his Tammany connections that he neglected to pay the City any compensation for the use of the streets. Ninety-six thousand dollars was recovered from the Third Avenue Railroad on claims upwards of twenty years old. A special corps of utility engineers and lawyers, headed by Oscar Cox and Paul Moses, fought a double bookkeeping system whereby large utilities claimed one low value against the City for taxation purposes and another high value against the State and City for rate purposes, and Cox and Moses added $205,000,-000 to the utility valuations for taxation.

Obsolete street railway systems, millions of dollars in default under old franchises, were litigated off the streets. The Queens bus problem, mélange of two dozen wildcat operators, had proved insoluble to Tammany because of its effort to award the phony Equitable Bus franchise on a grafting basis. It was solved in a few months by a special Bus Committee which gave short term franchises on a scientific zone basis to responsible operators, which paid the highest compensation to the City that any franchises had ever paid (10 per cent of the gross). In addition these franchises established a nickel fare, free transfers, and half fare for school children, and they assured the payment of the highest wage scale to employees ever paid in Queens. No better evidence was ever given of the amount the public had previously paid for the "cash and carry" policy of Tammany Hall.

Defaulting street railway companies that had known Tammany well enough to stay on the streets while in the courts for eighteen years, were suddenly jarred into sensibility and street car eyesores on main boulevards (Northern Boulevard, Queens Boulevard, etc.), were summarily replaced with busses and the tracks torn up.

Rampant rehabilitation proceeded apace, and La Guardia established a new concept of civic morality and a new philosophy of public service for his entire government. Reform at City Hall had a galvanic effect, which ran from the farthest section station and fire house right through the Commissioners' offices.

But La Guardia never became too entangled in administrative routine to press for basic reform. When federal funds became available for housing, he took the next airplane to Washington and begged and borrowed a hatful. In record time he condemned the huge Williamsburg site in Brooklyn for the largest public housing project ever built in America, and near by slum-ridden Harlem rose Harlem houses for five hundred Negro families.

Hard-driven bargains with private owners enabled the construction of "First Houses" on land bought with Housing Authority bonds, without cash consideration; and the commencement of his second term found him under way with all sails set with a public housing program the like of which the country has never seen. Filthy, disease-ridden firetraps, some without toilets, were locked and boarded and hundreds of them were demolished.

Allotment of federal funds for public power projects again found La Guardia on the job. He had a careful study made by City Engineers, concluded that a $50,000,000 public yardstick power plant would bring down rates, forced the Board of Aldermen to vote it to referendum, but the Court of Appeals intervened and, on a legal technicality, prevented the proposal from going to the people. Every dollar of federal relief funds available for construction was applied to some substantial and useful public project such as parks, health stations, college buildings, and the like.

Never in this triumphal march has La Guardia neglected the long-term aspects of reform. Close to his heart is his Civil Service Commission, and heavy-handed has been its strangulation of political patronage.

Six thousand jobs on the City-owned subway, formerly appointive, have become competitive: the entire staff of the housing authority to man and operate the huge public housing projects; the entire staff of the relief administration, more than twelve thousand persons, have been placed within the competitive class of the Civil Service. Successful assaults have been made on notorious nests of Tammany patronage, the municipal courts, the City clerk's office and the like. On a fair and even basis 107,000 jobs of the City government are filled by examination, and by 1937 his Commission was able to report to the Mayor that: "exempt (political) jobs have been reduced to the lowest point in the history of the City. Indeed so low is this percentage that it marks the maximum advance of the merit system in the United States. . . . It is an all-time, all-American record for the elimination of patronage. This . . . augurs well for the ultimate success of the vast social welfare program which you have undertaken on behalf of the City. Housing, transportation, health stations, parks, and relief are no longer hazardous undertakings for your government, for you have placed these facilities beyond the sordid control of patronage mongering political spoilsmen."

Under the New York State Constitution, these jobs, once made competitive, can never become political. These are permanent gains.

So with education. New York City, with one million children in school and the largest college and university plant in the world,[14] had placed the administration of these great institutions in the hands of politically appointed boards of little or no educational competence. Though the turnover of administration is slow (board members have terms for years), the dazzling accomplishments of the Board of Higher Education under such men as Ordway Tead, Lewis Mumford, John T. Flynn, Prof. Harry J. Carman, Joseph Schlossberg, Chauncey L. Waddell, Lawton Mackall, etc., bid fair to outrival in permanent stature even the more spectacular physical accomplishments of the present.

Just as important, finally, as this colossal physical rehabilitation of the City was its counterpart of personal rehabilitation. Contrasted with the clubhouse politicians who headed City departments under prior administrations, the Mayor appointed men of high competence to nearly every one of the vital posts in his "cabinet." The importance of these positions, paying in some instances more than the cabinet offices of the United States government and involving the responsibility for as many as twenty thousand employees or hundreds of millions of dollars in property, can scarcely be overstated. In the presidential campaign of 1936, for instance, a great point was made that one candidate, as governor of his state, had balanced his budget. The total budget of that state was well under the budget of the New York City Fire Department.

Just as the selection of Moses for park commissioner represented a selection based solely on competence, so also the selection of other officers of the government represented a search for quality never before experienced by the City of New York. As these men took hold with a firm and even hand, the wheels of government commenced to spin with a smoothness and efficiency that greatly

[14] The four city colleges, City, Hunter, Brooklyn, and Queens, have an enrollment of more than 40,000 degree-seeking students.

reduced the Mayor's sleepless nights and established a real high-water mark of public administration.

As his first term as mayor drew to a close, it became increasingly clear that there was no one in the City who could defeat him for re-election. Every important newspaper, with the exception of Hearst and the Conservative *New York Sun* (whose owner still resents the fact, apparently, that La Guardia once called him a "rum-smuggler"), supported him. In August, the American Labor Party set the tone of his campaign by calling him "The Greatest Mayor the City has ever had," and on this point there was amazing agreement. Ultra-conservative Republicans opposed him in the primary with Senator Royal S. Copeland, anti-New Deal Tammany-man, but La Guardia beat him badly. After some floundering, Tammany nominated Jeremiah T. Mahoney, in an attempt to secure a respectable candidate, but a campaign which must start with "My opponent is honest and capable, but . . ." is foredoomed.

Tammany stood on its record of unrelieved intellectual sterility and in the closing days of the campaign made a desperate attempt to drag in the red scare, which failed. The Mayor and his whole ticket were overwhelmingly returned. Dewey was officially elected as district attorney. The Tammany borough president of Manhattan was blotted out by La Guardia's running mate, Stanley Isaacs, and the presidency of the council and comptrollership, two offices lost to reform in the previous administration by the untimely deaths of the valiant Bernard S. Deutsch and W. Arthur Cunningham, were returned to La Guardia's support by the election of Newbold Morris and Joseph D. McGoldrick. And with them returned control of the all-important budget-making Board of Estimate.

Well under way in a second four-year term, full of high hopes, unquenchable idealism, and opportunity for bright new achievement, is Fiorello H. La Guardia today.

Contemporary appraisal of a man or the significance of his career or his place in history is always dangerous. This is especially true when the appraiser, as in this case, cannot be wholly objective. What immediately stands out about La Guardia, however, is that his career is the career of a new type of American politician and has no more in common with that of the orthodox old-time ward heeler, than does the career of Bishop McConnell with that of Aimée Semple McPherson.

This aspect translated into ordinary terms merely means that La Guardia made good government good politics. Reform in an American city is nothing new. But even his mightiest mayoral predecessor, the great Tom Johnson of Cleveland, lived on indignation more than on positive political strength, and La Guardia's New York City reform predecessors, Seth Low and John Purroy Mitchel, were stiff-necked and aloof, lasted a term and were gone.

"Tammany is the sea and reform is only a wave," and "No reform Mayor ever served two terms," were the political summaries of this condition. Reform never identified itself with the masses of the people, and the rich never had any basic interest in reform anyway, for while each ward heeler was taking his, they were able, under Tammany, to make the really big grabs on subways, busses, and the like. So temporary reform was confined to purity as a fetish, and it neglected government as the instrument of mass social improvement. Not so La Guardia. His dynamic fury about graft is dramatic and explosive; but the solid foundation of his political strength is his humanitarian, day-by-day output of things the people need and feel. Good government under La Guardia has not stopped with honesty and efficiency; it has transmuted these ideals into real and substantial tangible benefits to the people as a whole.

When John Purroy Mitchel ran for a second term as reform mayor in 1917, he was blasted by huge cartoons, showing him in a Park Avenue drawing room, saying: "Mr. Vanderbilt, call me Jack." When La Guardia ran for mayor a second time the great trade unions jammed Madison Square Garden for a sight of him, filled the Hippodrome for foreign language meetings, and mobbed him in the far corners of the Bronx and Brooklyn. This was no happenstance. The orthodox politician depends on an army of doorbell ringers, petty favors wrung by special privilege from the government, "influence" for his constituents, and over all the "hail fellow well met" conviviality. La Guardia had none of these to rely on. His reform Civil Service administration had eliminated the jobs necessary to support the doorbell ringers. His devastating morality eliminated special privilege all the way from a traffic ticket to a bus franchise. His hard work and long hours made conviviality impossible. He had to depend, therefore, on results, which the people could see and feel. He had to dramatize efficiency and social-mindedness in government. He couldn't dramatize the savings of money by the Department of Purchase, the efficiency of Civil Service personnel, but he could dramatize the tangible results of this efficiency when he dedicated housing developments, parks, playgrounds, health stations, schools and whatnot. And he did.

A city cannot live half slave and half free, and the political system could not survive side by side with free democracy. The menace to La Guardia's reform was the lingering middleman of politics, the merchant of special privilege, the district leader. The citizen could not go straight to government in the old days because he could not get consideration without the intervention of the "boss." The "boss" thereby performed service, put the citizen in debt, and wangled graft. La Guardia's government did more than sprinkle rosewater over the surface of this loathsome system. It went to the roots, and it did not replace one boss with another; it replaced all bosses with good government. Clamorous criticism, even by his friends, said this system would never work; that the voter required the "personal touch" of the district leader. La Guardia himself admitted it was an experiment, but he lashed out against the bosses of both parties and deliberately attempted to go straight over their heads to the people themselves. It worked by more than half a million majority in 1937.

In fairness, it must be admitted that this was no new idea with La Guardia; it was just an idea that had never been tried in New York City. Shrewd politicians had seen the possibility of such pure democracy for a long time, especially with the advance of public education, the dwindling of immigration with its large supply of less sophisticated voters, and the growing power of the press, radio, and motion picture. In fact, one night in 1920, at a public banquet, La Guardia, as president of the Board of Aldermen, was seated next to the great Boss Murphy of Tammany Hall. The Boss chided La Guardia for his Sunday-school ideals, but when the conversation ended, shot a parting remark something like this: "Keep it up, boy! You are on the right track and your day will come."

On top of this, La Guardia is not the chill and colorless reformer of popular renown. Quick-witted and often biting is his sarcastic humor. In the summer of 1933, when all of his friends were trying to convince the high-brow reformers that La Guardia was not a dangerous anarchist with bombs in both hands, Professor Berle arranged a speaking date for him at the ultra-rich, ultra-fashionable, ultra-ultra Fifteenth Assembly District Republican Club. The district is Park Avenue to the hilt, home of Ogden Mills and Ruth Pratt, and social prestige in the district is limited to newcomers whose ancestors came on the *Mayflower* and does not include those whose ancestors came with Columbus.

Into the palatial clubhouse of the "silk stocking" Fifteenth walked the Harlem Congressman. Back from the rostrum, row on row, stretched hundreds of icy stares, mostly insulated by pincenez. He was introduced to a polite kid-glove patter, looked around, shifted from foot to foot, and said: "Well, I don't know, either I have been made socially tonight or the Fifteenth Assembly District has gone slumming." From that point on, the audience was his.

When John McCooey, venal Tammany boss of Brooklyn, passed away, La Guardia dryly remarked that "He was a good husband and father," which had an added point when those present recalled that McCooey had made his son, a little-known lawyer, a Supreme Court justice and had the city pay roll full of relatives.

With the office full of commissioners whom he had just bawled out in his usual venomous manner for their many (according to him) shortcomings, a secretary, Clendenin Ryan, Jr., walked into the room, made a blunder. "If you were any dumber," said the Mayor, "I would have to make you a commissioner."

When a pious colleague in Congress in 1932 was felicitating the bipartisan collaboration which marked the sales tax proposal, La Guardia was on his feet in a minute: "I will grant that this demand for a sales tax is by no means bipartisan. There is no partisanship in anything that goes beyond a million dollars. That is a conclusion from my observation." When another colleague proposed the spending of large sums of money for education to combat communist propaganda, La Guardia dryly remarked: "It is empty stomachs, not empty heads that make communists."

When Tammany spent millions of dollars for a park at Jamaica Bay which turned out to be four feet under water, La Guardia went to visit it in a motorboat, named it "Larceny Park," and the name stuck. When a Tammany gambler built a whole suburb of cardboard houses in Juniper Swamp near Maspeth, to be condemned for the City at twenty-one times their evaluation by Tammany's Mayor Walker, La Guardia named it "Phantom Village," and the deal fell through.

A gifted raconteur, the drama and humor of thirty years of public service have not been lost on the Mayor, and his intimates avidly attend occasional sessions of La Guardia yarns. Typical is that regarding a poor old ex-Mayor, who in 1933, as a judge, was again feeling the urge to run for mayor. He talked to La Guardia about it; urged him to join his ticket as candidate for president of the Board of Aldermen. "I'm not interested," said La Guardia. "I've had the job once, and, what's more, I'm interested principally in the social aspects of government which go only with the mayoralty."

"Oh, that's all right," said the ex-Mayor. "I'm getting old anyway, and I would be glad to have you attend all the social functions for me."

Basically, however, a most important difference between La Guardia and the American Politician, Old Style, is La Guardia's very substantial understanding of basic economic and social issues. Imagine any previous mayor of New York City, for instance, speaking to the American Federation of Labor, as did La Guardia on Labor Day, 1934, and saying: "Old supply and demand may have been all right in their day—supply and demand where the supply was entirely created by hand and primitive machines; where there was no speculative credit upsetting the balance, no possibility of monopolies controlling and cornering supplies; and where demand really represented human requirements and production balanced that demand. . . . Today there is no limit to production. There is an artificial limit, however, placed upon demand. Demand today does not represent human requirements, but only ability to buy. They are very different things."

Kenneth Simpson, Republican county chairman of New York County, stated publicly in the summer of 1937 that "Mayor La Guardia, both in public utterance and in private conversations, has made it clear that he is an avowed radical." This was not and is not correct. La Guardia is a liberal and no more. He is not opposed to accumulations of wealth but to accumulation of poverty. There is a wide difference. The sight of a bloated millionaire does not arouse, by itself, his indignation, one whit, but the idea of an unemployed father with undernourished children brings indignation steaming from every pore. To his mind great wealth and widespread poverty are not necessary counterparts. He sees clearly the inequitable operation of the economic system and has spent his life fighting to correct it, but his has been a fight to help the underprivileged and not to eliminate the tycoons. His only forays against capitalists as such have been on moral, not economic grounds (such as Insull, Mitchell, Whitney, Harriman [in 1928] and others).

And as a liberal he believes most of all in democratic methods. In New York City he is the number one enemy of Adolf Hitler, and because of the popularity of this position it is generally overlooked that he is an anti-fascist of long standing. Even his most recent biographer, Jay Franklin, remarks that he never attacked Mussolini. Nothing could be less accurate. La Guardia has been an ardent, unrelenting believer in democracy and an enemy of fascism all his life. Before Hitler became a great local issue in New York City, La Guardia was stating on the floor of Congress: "Of course under our form of government it is natural that there should be waste and lost motion, but I say that the most inefficient, wasteful, self-government is worth more than the most efficient dictatorship." [15]

It was no new philosophy, but only more incisive diction, that led him to refer to Hitler in the spring of 1937, as a "brownshirted fanatic who menaces the peace of the world." And when he proposed a chamber of horrors at the World's Fair for dictators, the whole affair became a diplomatic incident which was only settled when our own State Department supinely apologized as is its practice.

[15] April 15, 1932.

But his liberalism and his belief in democracy are based upon a firm understanding of underlying economic forces. He sees fascism not only as a political system, but in its true light as an economic system as well. He clearly sees American capitalism strangled by its inability to distribute, and appreciates full well the temporary character of palliatives such as government spending. Yet he sees no need to alter the system basically, but would seek merely to control its operation more equitably, to bring about a more widespread utilization and enjoyment of the vast resources of the country. These ideas look like radicalism to Republican county chairmen. To economists they are no more than the advanced brand of American progressivism advocated for years by Norris and the La Follettes.

Of all the anomalies of this specimen of American politician, however, none is more distinctive than his personality, both official and home. He is generally reputed as a volatile and explosive firebrand, but the reputation is overdrawn. An ordinary politician, with plenty of guilt on his conscience, generally adopts a defensive "live and let live" philosophy toward derelictions of others. Not so La Guardia. His own impeccable morality supports a firm, subconscious feeling of inner righteousness, and in this light his enemies, if not incredibly stupid, often appear incredibly corrupt. He has no ulterior designs or motives. His motive is the public good alone, and he has a firm idea of how to achieve it. Those who would obstruct, therefore, are not to be treated chivalrously as honorable antagonists, but deserve the unmitigated contempt and bitter invective reserved for the antichrist.

The frequency with which this instinct has been correct in his public career has strengthened the reaction, and much that passes for volatility is really firmly premised thus.

Neither is his classic impatience with his subordinates wholly mysterious. He has a quick and active mind and a lightning-like perception. To him a normal secretarial reaction seems intolerably slow and stodgy, and his frequent abusiveness to his own staff is compensation for this reaction. This impatience extends to all who would routinize and organize his office and his work. As an administrator he has little use for formalism, and only recently has a time budget been arranged to allow regular weekly appointments for each department head. In the old days in Washington, he ran his office as a "grand artist" of high temperament might run an opera troupe. His desk was always piled knee-deep with unanswered mail, and his staff was always half mad with haste and overwork.

Despite these jaded days, his staff, or that part of it which survived, loved him and did not take their many "dismissals" too seriously. Generally the "Major's" explosions terrorized no one who knew him well, and the fact that his wife, Marie Fischer, a charming and gracious woman, served for fifteen years as his secretary before marrying him, is good evidence that life in his office bred, in some cases at least, mutual esteem and affection.

Notwithstanding the great pressure, haste, and excitement under which his office always worked, he required extreme care. Instances have already been given of how his 1929 charges against Tammany were completely validated. These instances could be multiplied many times over. On one occasion, for instance, a group of wags at Cornell University got together and sent a telegram to a number of politicians telling of a prospective testimonial dinner for that "great American and Republican, Hugo N. Fry," and asking for a few words of congratulations for the occasion. Vice President Curtis, a prominent congresswoman, and others promptly sent the usual slushy telegrams praising the long service of Mr. Fry. But La Guardia, never having heard of Hugo, sent his research man to the Congressional Library for information to support a telegram. A whole day passed. No data on Fry. A night, and still no data. La Guardia fumed and spluttered; fired the research man again; and paced the floor, profanely venting his opinion of members of Phi Beta Kappa (of which the man was one). Just as the second day passed and the incident promised to prove fatal, the whole hoax was exposed, the nonexistence of "you go'n fry" was confirmed, and the precarious tenure of the research man took a respite.

This caution and circumspection extended to more serious things. When the soldier's bonus, for instance, was before the House, in 1932, La Guardia had his researchers gather material. He made a study and came to the conclusion that such a large expenditure of government funds upon veterans at that time was an unscientific method of relieving distress. He appeared before a House Committee and stated his convictions; and he voted his convictions on the floor, realizing full well that a piece of demagoguery for the other side in this instance might well mean re-election. But the facts were conclusive to him at the time. Possessing the facts, he did not hesitate to act on them, even though the action jeopardized, as it did later, his re-election to the House.

Gradually this reputation for care and preparation permeated even lofty and conservative circles, and may have had more than anything else to do with the fact that Judge Samuel Seabury, who neglected to call La Guardia as witness in his investigation of Tammany even though he offered his services, came finally to regard him as the one real hope of reform in 1933. And probably Professor Adolf A. Berle, Jr., after meeting La Guardia in 1932, did more than any other one person to circulate the accurate picture of La Guardia in important circles where he had previously been regarded as wholly impulsive.

The fact that La Guardia takes great care on main issues, however, does not prejudice his generally tempestuous treatment of his subordinates. Especially during the chaotic first years of his mayoralty was life for those around him difficult. "Do so and so, at once, or I will find myself a commissioner who will," was a characteristic memorandum to a department head who seemed slow in effecting reform.

The inordinate pressure of overwhelming public business, caused by a really great crisis in the affairs of the City, induced an exhaustion and a mental fatigue even beyond the endurance of his hardy constitution. Hundreds of persons, many important, insisted on seeing him immediately. Board meetings consumed hours. Heavy demands were made for public appearances even though he cut them to a minimum. Relief and labor disputes added an extracurricular burden. Racketeering and political crime were still rife in Tammany offices. His own commissioners were in many cases new and inexperienced. Under these circumstances the secretary who went into his office at seven o'clock at night with a stack of papers to be considered and signed, ran the risk of immediate decapitation, no matter how important the papers or how mild his entry. Much of this difficulty was aggravated by the fact that in the early months La Guardia persisted in handling an overwhelming mass of detail, later successfully transferred to subordinates. When the *Nor-*

mandie arrived on its maiden voyage, for instance, the Mayor's time was taken in discussing the menu for the official dinner. Experience soon eliminated this type of thing.

Gradually, however, the pressure subsided and La Guardia's adjustment from legislative to executive technique became more complete. He was always, and probably always will be, a temperamental and ruthless taskmaster. He customarily makes excessive demands on those who work under him. While still in Congress, he used to wire on Thursday morning: "Look up law and prepare memorandum for me on question of establishing residence for purpose of transferring trial of action particularly law in Federal Courts stop need memorandum by Saturday morning," and, more classic: "Draft railroad reorganization bill make every effort to get this to me by Monday morning," which telegram arrived Saturday noon. He has had intense loyalty and generally high intelligence about him, principally because his own character justifies it. But he is quite without sentiment in important appointments, having permitted appointment of outright political enemies to high office, while devoted followers of years standing and some ability, occasionally gained no consideration.[16] It remains to be proved that the accomplishment of these former enemies, who saw the light at the eleventh hour, only after the election was over, will measure up to that of the hard-bitten, old-line reformers.

After the first two years at City Hall, however, as the work lightened, the impatience and irritableness of extreme fatigue subsided, and it turned out that the Mayor had concocted an amazingly efficient government. The department heads who stood up under his incessant pressure came out with colors flying and departments humming.

The administrative technique of constant pressure was not

---

[16] An instance of this was the appointment of William C. Chanler as assistant corporation counsel and then corporation counsel. In the *New York Times*, Nov. 1, 1933, Chanler wrote: ". . . I was equally amazed to find them supporting Major LaGuardia, who in August had been denounced by nearly all of his present supporters except Judge Seabury as unfit for the nomination, and who, as it had seemed to me at the time, forced his own nomination by a threat to run in the Republican Primaries and thus sabotage the Fusion movement itself." And, ". . . As to the relative ability, integrity, etc., of the two men, I think Mr. LaGuardia's latest outburst leaves no doubt that he is what everyone thought he was before he became the Fusion candidate—a man who will resort to any tactics to win votes."

wholly in the manner of Simon Legree. As time permitted and general competence of his appointees increased by experience, it became good-humored even more often than not. He donated a large bone, which he ceremoniously gave to the commissioner who had committed the most egregious blunder of the season. The growing satisfaction of good work, the increasingly happy home life in the arrival of two lovely children in the spring of 1934, and the expert ministrations of his personal physician, Dr. George Baehr, especially in the manner of limiting horrendous diets, all combined to bring increasing good humor and lightheartedness. Increasing experience by his staff and himself and an additional sense of real achievement day by day made the job of mayor less onerous and made the Mayor more himself—an immensely brilliant, humorous, and delightful person to be around.

Privately the life of La Guardia today is just as it was before his exaltation. He has made a rule that he has no social contacts, except official ones, with persons he did not know before 1933. He has guests to dinner often, but never official dinners. "My Commissioners bore me," is his excuse for this. He occupies the same apartment on upper Fifth Avenue, on the fringe of Harlem, that he did before he was mayor. His wife is exactly the same gracious and unassuming person she was five years ago.

Not interested in society, the La Guardias' home life is simple and devoted largely to Jeanne, eleven, and Eric, seven. The two children needed space and there was thought of moving. But when Mrs. La Guardia went out apartment hunting, a real estate man offered her free rent, and they decided to have nothing to do with the idea. They persuaded their own landlord to cut additional rooms into their present five-room apartment. They never partook of Washington society in the past. The types of guests they entertain, without pomp or drawing-room prattle, are newspapermen, writers, musicians, artists, college professors, and the like. Fourteen hours a day at work leaves little time for the merry-go-round of official society.

La Guardia has always been intensely fond of children. In Washington, for instance, he never went to the circus without buying extra tickets to distribute to the urchins standing longingly outside the gate. In the spring of 1933, when it looked as if he might have to earn a living practicing law, a brief in a case of utmost importance, imminently due, had to be written on a Saturday afternoon. On his way from his home to the Columbia Law Library, where the work was to take place, he disappeared. Two hours later his harassed colleagues found him quietly listening to a rehearsal of the boy choir in the Cathedral at 110th Street. Children and music had proved irresistible.

Aside from his children, who have become a major factor in his life, he has few personal distractions. He and Mrs. La Guardia are lovers of music and frequently attend concerts and operas. Occasionally they go to the theatre. He does not engage in sports or exercise—not even golf; he takes no formal vacations. He used to cook one night a week as high diversion, but rigors of the mayoralty have mostly ended that. All in all, the personal life of America's number one mayor, in sharp contrast to his official life, is just about as conventional as a personal life could be.

So stands the Mayor of the City of New York today—full of substantial accomplishment, replete with the laurels of conquest, and firm in the hearts of his fellow citizens. Certainly on the background of La Guardia is written one of the most absorbing political careers of our times. Where that career may still lead only the presumptuous would speculate. La Guardia himself professes no higher ambition than the private one to have the new North Beach airport named after him when he is dead. But he is in the prime of life; of rugged vitality. His record of achievement stamps him as an outstanding American mayor of all time. He is American Politician, New Style; a Liberal with Integrity. Today he stands astride the Metropolis, still growing in stature and prestige. His future is written in the stars.

2

ARTHUR H. VANDENBERG

By Paul M. Cuncannon

ONE SUMMER AFTERNOON SOME YEARS AGO THE GENTLEMEN of the fourth estate, as they whiled away the time in the press gallery, rated the senators much as the seniors at Yale or Princeton might grade their classmates. In that estimate of the solons debating beneath them, Carter Glass of Virginia was rated the most brilliant man on the Democratic side. Of the Republicans, David A. Reed of Pennsylvania was figured as the ablest and Arthur H. Vandenberg of Michigan the most ambitious and most likely to be president. It was like the New Haven rating of "most likely to succeed." Several years have passed, and much water has flowed under the bridge since then, but events have seemed to bear out that prophecy.

The *Philadelphia Record* draws this picture of Vandenberg in the Senate—"Tall, sparse-haired, Vandenberg swapped tortoise shell glasses for rimless ones to 'look less bookish.' Likes to match pennies, bowl, play bridge, billiards. He carries a pedometer, stops his regular morning walk when it shows four miles. Finger pointer and desk pounder in the Senate, he smokes heavily, likes dark suits, always double breasted, watches that his 180 pounds don't go up. Inflation fears constantly assail him; he carries German marks printed with 100,000,000 signs to give colleagues visual warning of its danger." [1]

Vandenberg, at fifty-four, and ten years a senator, is the actual leader of the Republican minority in the Senate of the United States. A member of the two best Senate committees—Finance and Foreign Affairs, twice the nominee of the Republican caucus for president pro tem of the Senate and recognized as his party's ablest campaigner on the hustings, the man looms up.

[1] June 23, 1937.

He is a big man, slightly over one hundred and eighty pounds, and stands six feet and a half-inch tall. He is very much the athletic type of individual. His dress is the somewhat unconventional dress of the middle westerner. In conversation he is aggressive and self-concerned. His voice is deep and resonant and quite pleasing. It is the voice of the orator. Vandenberg has much of the self-consciousness of the actor. He is aware that he made a good speech yesterday, and expects to make another one tomorrow. The sense of the oratorical is never or rarely absent from him.

Arthur Vandenberg was the fair-haired boy of Senator William Alden Smith of Michigan. Smith was the owner of the *Grand Rapids Herald* and for a quarter of a century (1894–1919) represented the Wolverine State in the national Congress, dividing that service almost equally between the lower and the upper houses at Washington. William Alden Smith was considerable of a figure in Michigan and to some extent in the America of his day. He gave Vandenberg, then a youth in his teens, a job on the *Herald*. Vandenberg stayed with the *Herald* for twenty-seven years, leaving it in 1928 to enter the United States Senate. Senator Smith taught this journalistic neophyte high politics. This was a great period in American politics. Theodore Roosevelt was president of the United States, John Hay was secretary of State, Elihu Root was secretary of war, William Howard Taft was governor general of the Philippines, Joseph H. Choate was our ambassador at London. Beveridge and Dolliver and Aldrich were in the Senate. It was a time to stir men's imaginations. Senator Smith, always remarkable on the personal side of politics, interested this young man of somewhat limited background in the national scene at Washington. And it has been in the Washington scene that Vandenberg has been interested from that day to this. He never cared for Michigan politics and never interested himself in them save as they might serve as a springboard to Washington. Senator Smith used Arthur Vandenberg as a kind of good-will ambassador for the *Grand Rapids Herald*. There is no indication anywhere that he intended to push Vandenberg into practical politics and actual office-holding. Smith taught him national politics and used his remarkable forensic abilities to increase the circulation of the *Herald* and add to its prestige.

WIDE WORLD PHOTOS

ARTHUR H. VANDENBERG

" 'One good term deserves another.' "

No person except Mrs. Vandenberg seems to have had as much influence over the Senator. The distinguishing feature of Senator Vandenberg's Washington office today is a large oil painting showing William Alden in all his pompous glory. In 1919 Smith, for some unknown reason and after considerable vacillation, retired from the Senate. A number of men were mentioned to succeed him —Henry Ford, Mayor James Couzens of Detroit, Commander Newberry, Governor Osborn, and Editor Vandenberg. Vandenberg apparently was willing, but he could get the office only with the very active support of Senator Smith, and the old man fooled so long making up his mind not to run that he was not a serious factor in the choice of his successor. Ten years later Vandenberg reached the Senate via the appointment route.

During the 1924 campaign a writer said that each of the three candidates was typical of the town from which he hailed—John W. Davis represented the urbanity and emphasis on classical statesmanship of Clarksburg, West Virginia; Calvin Coolidge exemplified the frugality and sturdy new England virtues of Northampton, and La Follette typified the interest in modern social problems for which Madison has long served as a laboratory. Now Vandenberg, save for his Dutch blood and his aggressiveness, is not particularly typical of Grand Rapids. There he was born fifty-four years ago, within two blocks of where he now lives. He is rather proud of this fact in a Congress where not one per cent of the members represent their birthplace. He is Dutch on his father's side and English on his mother's side. His people came from small towns in New York State. His grandfather, Dr. Aaron I. Hendrick, from whom he gets his middle name, was the long-time president of the village of Clyde. He was one of the rabid abolitionists of ante-bellum days and was a delegate from New York to the convention which nominated Abraham Lincoln for president. During the Civil War Dr. Hendrick ran an underground railroad to help the slaves northward to Canada. Vandenberg has lived in his present house in Grand Rapids for a quarter of a century. His father was a harness maker in Grand Rapids, and the family was poor. Vandenberg went to the University of Michigan Law School for one year. Sir Paul Vinogradoff, Regius Professor of Jurisprudence at Oxford, watching the students work at Ann Arbor, remarked that "there were

mean jobs but no mean men." The genuinely democratic atmosphere of an American state university in the Middle West permits
students to work their way. Arthur Vandenberg was one of these
students in the law class of 1904 at Ann Arbor. However, the
strain of earning every penny of his expenses proved too much for
his health, and at the end of his first year he had to retire from the
University. Senator Vandenberg says very frankly that the best
thing college gave him was a wife.

For more than a quarter of a century he lived the life of a middle-western newspaper editor and publisher with one brief interlude with *Collier's Weekly* in New York. He wrote three books on
Alexander Hamilton, none of which adds very much to our knowledge of the first secretary of the Treasury. He joined the Masons,
Elks, and other lodges and attended the Congregational Church.
There is an old saying that the prizes of politics go not to the men
who are really in politics, but to those who play around the fringes.
Vandenberg is a good illustration of this truth. He was really not a
part of Michigan politics. He spoke, he wrote, he traveled for the
Republican State Committee, but he was not a real part of the process. The drudgery of practical politics did not appeal to him. He
never visited the legislature or busied himself with party organization. He was not a mixer with the county chairmen and with the
boys who brought in the vote in the wards. He was with but not of.
To this day he is not particularly popular with the typical party
politician in Michigan save in those periods when they think he
may be president, with honors and jobs to hand out. Vandenberg
was a gifted man, respected, but he was an outsider.

Vandenberg's opportunity came with the candidacy of Fred W.
Green of Ionia for the Republican nomination for governor. Ionia
is about twenty miles from Grand Rapids. Green dared to challenge the movement to renominate the sitting Governor Alexander
Groesbeck. The latter had already been governor two terms. He
was a Detroit lawyer, a millionaire, and, with the exception of
Chase Osborn, the most brilliant governor Michigan has had this
century. A shrewd politician, Groesbeck had used the patronage of
the governor's office to build up a powerful state-wide machine. He
was no easy man to lick.

Fred W. Green was a unique figure. In the gallery of a century

of Michigan's governors at Lansing, his painting stands out among
the frock-coated notables. He was painted in a red hunting coat of
brilliant hue, standing in the great outdoors beneath that marvel-
ous sky of the Upper Peninsula, with a gun in his hand and with
two of his favorite hunting dogs at his feet. A poor boy obtaining a
hurried education at Ypsilanti and Ann Arbor, he faced the world
on his own. He made himself a millionaire through his reed furni-
ture factory at Ionia. He journeyed to the Straits Settlement at Sing-
apore to get the wood for that factory, and the labor he took from
the convicts in the state prison at Ionia. Fred Green became wealthy
and developed into the local tycoon. In the city and county of
Ionia he bossed the politics, became the leading banker, and more
or less ran the community. In fact, he did everything in the community, including the riding of the elephant in the annual Ionia
County Fair. Shrewd, bold, unconventional, generous, gregarious
—the friend of prize fighters and movie actors, he seemed to some
a strange person to aspire to gubernatorial honors. Green was short
of stature and not impressive looking, and those who had seen him
reviewing troops realized that ceremonial was not his forte. However, he was keen, energetic, and at that time well supplied with
funds. He challenged Groesbeck. Vandenberg was among the first
to declare for Green. With voice and pen he advocated the nomination in the September primaries of the Mayor of Ionia. The support was more than welcome. Fred Green, who, by various means,
had built up a powerful organization in the counties, easily defeated Groesbeck. The Vandenberg support gave a tone and a certain early vigor to his candidacy.

Michigan at this time was represented in the United States Senate by James Couzens and Woodbridge N. Ferris, a former Democratic governor. The term of Ferris was drawing to a close. Vandenberg began openly to covet the seat of Ferris in the Senate.
When Ferris suddenly died, Vandenberg became a candidate for
appointment by the Governor. There was considerable support in
the state for Vandenberg, and it was expected that Governor Green
would appoint him in return for the help Vandenberg had given
him in the gubernatorial campaign. Two things held up the appointment. The first was a movement to have Vandenberg wait for
the primary and run with full party support and in the meantime

157646

give the temporary appointment to Joseph Fordney of Saginaw, for many years chairman of the Ways and Means Committee in the House. This program would have permitted "Uncle Joe" Fordney to round out his congressional career with a brief tenure in the Senate. Vandenberg did not cotton to this at all. The second obstacle to Vandenberg's appointment was the demand of Green that if he appointed Vandenberg to the Senate, the federal patronage be dispensed by the Governor. This Vandenberg flatly refused. However, Green, after some slight hesitation, appointed him, and thus Vandenberg in the year 1928 came to Washington.

At Washington it has been a march of triumph for Vandenberg. In Browning's phrase, it has been "roses, roses all the way." The psychologist tells us that we know what we are today by remembering what we were yesterday. Yesterday Vandenberg was an obscure editor in a small city of the American Middle West. Today he is first on the list as a possible nominee of the Republican party for the presidency. Arriving in Washington ten years ago, Vandenberg found a lifelong friend, Borah of Idaho, one of the leaders of the United States Senate. The friendship of Borah in the Senate has helped him very much. He managed to get on good committees. The attitude of the members of the Senate toward Vandenberg has been a friendly one. In the atmosphere "of the greatest chamber of free debate in the world" the man has grown and developed. The Senate has been for him in very truth what Woodrow Wilson used to say a classroom in Politics should be—namely, a seminary of statesmanship.

Vandenberg ranks number three on the Finance Committee and number five on the Foreign Relations Committee on the Republican side. He works hard in the Committee hearings, and both there and in personal conferences his affability is a great asset. His mail is enormous. He writes to all kinds of people all over Michigan concerning all kinds of things. His office never closes with a letter unanswered. He makes it a solemn rule never to leave Washington while Congress is in session. He has no business connections of any sort on the outside.

In campaigns his chief asset is his oratorical ability. He is not a political organizer. His habit is to go into the principal cities of Michigan, hire the largest hall, and orate. And he does a good job.

Many a governor remembers his oration on "The Spirit of Mackinac" at the Governors' Conference at Mackinac Island, when Fred Green played host to the chief executives of the states. Another factor in his campaigns for the Senate is the general feeling throughout Michigan that he is an asset to the state at Washington. In a state which has produced very few national leaders, this is a real thing. In his successful campaign against Frank Picard in 1934, he put enormous billboard signs around Detroit stating that "one good term deserves another."

In Michigan politics Vandenberg is a lone wolf and glories in the fact. Unlike the late Senator Couzens, he does attend Republican state conventions and observe the formal party amenities, but he is not a part of the political scene. He has no close advisers among the politicians and more or less goes it alone. He mixes with the politicians a little better than he used to, but he has little in common with them, and to this day he is much more at home in a meeting of the state newspaper editors.

Michigan state politics are very odd. There is no regular organization. There are no real county leaders like the old Penrose leaders in Pennsylvania. Detroit is probably the only large city in America without a political machine. Scattered through the state there are numerous individuals long active in politics, and here and there a local chieftain of real power. Detroit has certain racial solidarities like the Negroes and the Poles and an occasional individual aspiring to power. Michigan politics are in reality a group of divergent influences rather than any definitely organized efforts. The result is that the sitting governor runs the politics of the state. The last seven governors have each in turn, been temporary state bosses. This suits Vandenberg. He had little enough interest in Michigan politics when he lived in Grand Rapids; he has less at Washington. His prestige is sufficient to re-elect him.

Speaking at Indianapolis in the 1936 presidential campaign, President Roosevelt said that he and Vandenberg were such good friends that if the Republicans had nominated the Michigan Senator for president, the two candidates could have stumped the country from the same platform. Vandenberg goes often to the White House and thoroughly enjoys his times there. He and Mr. Roosevelt are very, very different, and yet they get along.

LEARNING RESOURCES CENTER
NAZARETH COLLEGE

Vandenberg is a born newspaperman. He loves the smell of printer's ink. In fact, he frankly says that he would probably be happier managing one of the great eastern daily newspapers than as senator or president. He has the born newspaperman's flair for publicity. Only Borah, among the senators, excels him in this. He is very well treated by the press because, after all, he is one of the craft and belongs to the guild. Newspapermen take a certain pride in him as one of themselves. Being a newspaperman himself, he knows how to handle the press. He knows what is news. It is noteworthy that he has received very little criticism from the papers during his public career.

Vandenberg in the present Senate is the "leader of His Majesty's opposition." In this position he has had notable success and considerable advertising. His tactics and strategy are to praise the administration when he thinks it is right, and object only when objection is proper. He does not particularly like his job, on the grounds that it is not a constructive job. He feels that he has helped the administration in some of the things he has blocked and in this sense has been constructive. Borah, who has been over thirty years in the Senate, says he expects to be remembered for the things he has prevented. The same might well be said of Vandenberg as minority leader. He blocked the Passamaquoddy project and the Florida Ship Canal. He is leading the fight on the $47,000,000,000 reserve fund created by the Social Security Act. He has helped create a commission to study it and wants to rewrite the law to get it out. He thinks he will succeed. He forced disclosure of big payments to corporation farmers under the AAA. He is the author of the Amendment to the Banking Act of 1933, which created insurance for bank deposits. He led the fight for the Reapportionment Bill, and was responsible for forcing the passage of the 1931 Reapportionment Act, which took care of existing inequalities and created a formula for automatic reapportionment after each census. Vandenberg has introduced a substitute for the Child Labor Amendment which has been reported favorably to the Senate by a unanimous vote of the Judiciary Committee. This substitute forbids the employment "for hire" of children under sixteen. It avoids many of the controversial features of the Amendment, which has so long hung fire and has so far failed of ratification by the states.

Vandenberg has ability to gauge public sentiment. He is a genius at offering to the Senate workable compromises. He has plenty of self-confidence and the ability of the journalist to write clearly and well. In his activities in the Senate he offers to that body very definite propositions. These are usually worked out in proper legal form. There is nothing vague or inchoate about his suggestions.

Vandenberg has proposed three amendments to the Wagner Act. His amendments: (1) Would authorize the employer to appeal to the National Labor Relations Board for an election to determine the representatives of his employees. Under the present law only the employees can demand an election. (2) Require that agreements "resulting voluntarily from collective bargaining" be set down in writing and permit strikes only when called by a majority vote of all employees. If any group of employees broke a contract and refused to correct it upon order of the Labor Board, the Board would be empowered to suspend its right of representation. (3) Establish a "fair practice code" for labor which would prohibit compulsory political assessments on union members and require that all union officers, agents, and representatives be United States citizens. The Senator said, "I believe that labor is entitled to a constantly broadening share in the fruits of its own production, but it will do labor no good to achieve these benefits if a profitable economy and an orderly society in which to enjoy them is jeopardized or destroyed."

Elihu Root once defined himself as an "animated conservative." Vandenberg is conservative but he marches with the times. He has traveled far since he learned his politics at the feet of William Alden Smith. He is a man given to reasonable compromises and has a wonderful sense of the possible and the practical. On things he firmly believes in he will fight to the last ditch. He is a great believer in the American system of checks and balances, in which his faith amounts almost to a religion. He was strongly opposed to both the President's Court scheme and his plan of executive reorganization, as striking hard at this system of checks and balances.

In the Senate he loves dialectics and is skilled and practiced in debate. He is extremely resourceful. He has shown great ability to find the flaws in the Democratic armor and to thump them vigorously. With it all he is courteous, fair, no violent partisan; in all his leadership of the opposition, he has been able to keep the good will of the Democratic majority and of its leaders.

Walter Lippmann in his *Preface to Politics* said of Woodrow Wilson that he could state a principle better than the expert from whom he borrowed it. The same was true of Theodore Roosevelt. Vandenberg, with his flair for writing, has this gift of phrase making. It makes him effective in the rough-and-tumble debates of the Senate and out on the hustings. It permits him to focus attention on certain issues. In his Lincoln Day address at the Waldorf-Astoria in 1937, Vandenberg displayed real skill in stating the case against the New Deal. This power of trenchant phrase making, carried over from his journalistic days into the political arena, helps him to be a leader.

Vandenberg's growth has been steady, from the old type of spellbinding politician into a speaker who has mastered the facts and proceeds to state his case. He used to be a good deal of a hot-air artist. He was very much the view-with-alarm and point-with-pride type. Now he proceeds to get the facts. The years and experience have toned him down. He still has the oratorical manner, but there is a substructure of facts. There is some bombast to him, but no senator is wholly free from that.

Vandenberg is not strong on foreign affairs and is somewhat restricted in his grasp of international realities. In Grand Rapids he followed Lodge and in Washington Borah, and both have led him in the wrong direction. He still believes America entered the World War because Wall Street wanted to save its money. The testimony of men like Newton Baker, who were Wilson's daily companions in the crisis at a time when Vandenberg was writing editorials for the *Grand Rapids Herald* in the hinterland, he blithely ignores. Franklin K. Lane, speaking of the Cabinet meetings within six weeks of the declaration of war, said, "We couldn't get the idea out of his [Wilson's] head that we were bent on pushing the country into war. . . . The President believes, I think, that the munitions makers are back of the Republican plan." [2] Thus Wilson held out to the last. On Armistice Day, nineteen years after, the *New York Times* said, "The dream of a world of free men and free governments was the dream for which we fought." But Vandenberg firmly believes that we went to war to save our money, showing no understanding whatever of the Wilson psychology or the moods of our people. He proves this by quotations from that self-confessed liar, the German Ambassador Count von Bernstorff, and by statements of Mr. Page in London, who was so pro-British that he would say anything to get us into the war, whether it was straight or not.

Vandenberg has also been one of the leaders in Congress in the so-called neutrality movement. The senators who have pushed this plan to put the President in a strait jacket in the conduct of foreign relations have really made for war. Nothing is so calculated to involve us in hostilities as these laws which tie the President's hands in the conduct of foreign affairs. We may get into war if he has a free hand; we will certainly get into war if his actions are restricted.

Vandenberg has today political sagacity of high degree—not inherent but a product of his later years. He is accused by the senators of being a headline hunter. There is a certain personal vanity about him which you are apt to find in musicians or actors. He lacks the smooth manners and gracious urbanity of the late Warren G. Harding. He is friendly and cordial enough, but in a sense remote. Withal, one's impression is that of fundamental decency and absolute honesty.

A large factor in Vandenberg's success is his wife. He married Miss Hazel Whitaker of Fort Wayne, Indiana. She and the Senator were classmates at Ann Arbor. She taught school in Saginaw, wrote editorials for the *Chicago Tribune*, and worked on the advertising staff of the J. L. Hudson Company in Detroit. She is a graduate of the University of Michigan and a Delta Gamma. She is possessed of high character, is very able, and altogether charming. Henry Adams used to say that Mrs. Lodge would have made a better senator than Cabot. One can certainly say of the Vanden-

[2] *The Letters of Franklin K. Lane* (Cambridge, Mass., 1922), p. 240.

bergs that he is a much better senator because of his wife. Her influence on the Senator has been all to the good.

Vandenberg is the sort of man who if he had been a lawyer would have become a judge. He has a well-balanced mind. It used to be said that when he wrote editorials for the *Grand Rapids Herald,* he had the Sir Roger de Coverley attitude that there was much to be said on both sides. Picard, his Democratic opponent for the Senate, used to ridicule Vandenberg's attitude on the stump of now on the one hand and then again on the other. This quality is deep in his mind. He sees both sides of a question. He is no extremist and can weigh evidence. It is one reason why it irks him to lead the Republican opposition in the Senate and to be cast in the role of chief critic of the administration. Even today he sees much good in the New Deal, and he likes and admires the President. He is no fanatic. In a *Saturday Evening Post* article lambasting the administration's civil service record, he had many good things to say of Mr. Farley.

Vandenberg, as he looks ahead to 1940, sees the need of a great spiritual crusade to redeem the country from the dangers which beset it. He believes that this campaign should be realistic—that the Republican party cannot carry water on both shoulders. He fervently believes that the American system of government, with its checks and balances at Washington, this "indestructible union of indestructible states," is a priceless thing. He believes it is a thing apart, which stands in danger of being worked over in the world mould. He would like to be a part of this great spiritual crusade to save the nation.

"Jim" Reed of Kansas City used to say that Mr. Hoover landed in the Cabinet running for president. The same might be said of Vandenberg in the Senate. When Woodrow Wilson took his first trip to the Pacific Coast in 1911, he explained to the crowds at the various stations en route that he was not interested in the presidency. Finally Mrs. Wilson sent him a telegram from Princeton, telling him not to say that as everybody knew it wasn't true. Vandenberg doth protest too much that he is not a candidate. Would he make a good president? No and Yes. In the first place, he is without administrative experience, and that is important today. Stanley Baldwin says, "Administration is the essence of government, and its quality is a

prime condition of civic comfort." In the latest reorganization
scheme Mr. Roosevelt asks six highly paid administrative assistants
to aid him in the White House. And apparently not without some
basis. The other day in New York John L. Lewis said what this
administration needed in the White House was less balancing of
personalities against each other and more application of the seat of
the pants to the seat of the chair. It will be increasingly so at
Washington. Vandenberg has never been mayor of a city, governor of a state, chief of a diplomatic mission, manager of a political
campaign, or head of an industrial corporation. His only managing experience has been to run a newspaper in a small city of the
Middle West. Now writing editorials for the *Grand Rapids Herald* and making speeches in the United States Senate is one thing,
and running the United States government is another. Woodrow
Wilson wrote a brilliant essay on administration when he taught
at Bryn Mawr, but he was a poor administrator at both Trenton
and Washington.

In the next place Vandenberg is not particularly effective in dealing with individuals. Queen Victoria said Gladstone addressed her
as though she were a public meeting. Vandenberg likes to speak to
public meetings. He has amazingly little sense of the importance
of the individual and how to deal with him. Old William Alden
Smith, from whom he learned his politics, was a past master at
this, but Vandenberg did not absorb it from him. Vandenberg has
none of the devoted following throughout Michigan which Smith
had. People admire Vandenberg, but they wouldn't fight, bleed,
and die for him.

There are word men and thing men. Vandenberg is a word
man. He is a thumber of the dictionary. His life has been spent in
writing editorials and making speeches, rather than in managing
affairs. He lacks a broad education. He has had no liberal education beyond high school, and his law course was interrupted near
its beginning. In such a man's equipment there are broad inter-
stices which no amount of private reading can make up or fill in.
He lacks a knowledge of technique and insight into the significance
of things.

When Calvin Coolidge was in the old State House above the
Common in Boston, Barrett Wendell predicted he would be presi-

dent of the United States. He said, "He is a kind of Yankee Lincoln—a local lawyer capable of directing great affairs." That prophecy was fulfilled. The qualities of high leadership were there, and so they may be with this Dutch editor from Grand Rapids. Two men as diverse as Herbert Hoover and William E. Borah picked him as the best man to lead the Republicans in 1936, and they both knew him well. If the Republicans hadn't nominated Landon, they would undoubtedly have named Vandenberg; as it was, they kept pressure on him for fifty-six hours to accept the nomination for vice-president. He was smart enough to avoid the debacle of 1936. His position of leadership in the Senate, his ability to force the fighting out on the hustings with his oratory, his resourcefulness, his amazing sense of the workable and the practical, combined with the good will manifested towards him by Republicans of different types, all make him stand out. Men who know him think the nation would be safe in his hands. He would be progressive without being radical and would keep his feet on the ground. His pouncing ability for the issues of the moment and his dynamic drive would help him.

One compares him with senators of the past. He lacks the graceful periods of Albert Jeremiah Beveridge. Mr. Dooley said you could waltz to Beveridge's speeches. You couldn't do that to Vandenberg's. He lacks the broad culture of the late Henry Cabot Lodge. He has no Harvard Ph. D. or thirty summers in Europe. He lacks the practical prescience of Nelson P. Aldrich. He could never draw a complete banking act. He lacks the almost religious fanaticism of the late Robert M. La Follette. Vandenberg is no tilter at windmills. He lacks the political organizing ability of a Penrose or the grasp of legal principles and wide diplomacy of a Knox. But Vandenberg has enough of what each of these men had to make him a successful senator. He can talk, he reads, he has a wonderful sense of the possible and the necessary. He fights with fervor for what he believes, and he has amazing ability to land on his feet politically and to avoid trouble. In the four years since he licked Frank Picard by the narrow margin of 43,000 (piled up in Detroit) to return to the Senate, he has grown in wisdom and in senatorial stature, and he has become increasingly a thorn in the side of the administration. He has increasingly seen less and less good in the New Deal and has displayed amazing resource in fighting it.

He looks toward 1940. Why any man should, I don't know. The twenty-year cycle has rolled round again. No man who has taken his seat in that cycle since Harrison in 1840 has lived his administration out. In his heart Vandenberg thinks he will make it. A traveled man—he knows Europe, South America, and the Far East. While not rich, he is, as he likes to say, a man of reasonable means. A bookish man—he makes up for his early lack of advantages by constant reading. He is a likable man and above all an honest man. Like Garfield and Harding, he is willing to pass from the upper chamber to the White House. He awaits his country's call.

3

PAUL V. McNUTT

By Harold Zink

MORE THAN PASSINGLY BRILLIANT IN PERSONAL QUALITIES, A graduate with distinction of two well-known universities, the sometime dean of a reputable law faculty, member of the French Legion of Honor, and commander of the Polonia Restituta, Paul Vories McNutt might seem to a casual observer the very incarnation of the ancient philosopher-king ideal. But more careful study indicates that marks of greatness, not too often associated with political figures in the United States, stand alongside of practices made notorious by political bosses. All in all, one would go far to find a more complex admixture of political liberalism and machine orthodoxy.

From the standpoint of appearance, there are few more striking figures in American politics of the fourth decade of the twentieth century than Paul McNutt. His fine head of silver-gray hair alone would mark him. When one adds to that a rare combination of flashing eyes, well-proportioned forehead and chin, and slightly bronzed skin, it is scant wonder that McNutt has become a feminine idol. Furthermore, McNutt possesses the size, height, and bearing that constitute male elegance.

Nor does McNutt fall far behind his physical appearance in other personal qualities. His poise attains Hollywood proportions. Despite a lack of tact—recently exhibited in the toast episode in the Philippines—and an inclination toward impatience and arrogance, McNutt possesses not a little personal magnetism, although he does not always choose to use it. To those who criticize or disagree or seem unimportant he can present an aloofness and indifference of alienating chilliness.

Speaking both on public occasions and in the small talk of private dinner tables with an ease and fluency rarely encountered, McNutt possesses a mellifluent voice which charms listeners. He has the ability to present issues in such a fashion that coverage, even to intelligent persons, seems quite complete, and yet at the same time he glides over dangerous points with almost feline grace. Such is his persuasiveness that somewhat critical listeners emerge from a public utterance convinced that McNutt has handled almost every public problem to the point of perfection. To a student of psychology McNutt displays definite symptoms of exhibitionism when he makes a public appearance. Newspaper men remark on the good time he is having. No one can doubt that he loves the limelight.

In almost every respect McNutt is the product of Indiana. Born in Franklin, a small urban community in the central part of the state, July 19, 1891, he received his education in the public schools of that place and in Martinsville, another small county-seat town southwest of Indianapolis. Being an only child he received the doting attention of his middle-class parents and developed something of a reputation as a prodigy. According to his father, the boy developed presidential aspirations as early as his eighth year.

After being graduated from high school Paul moved a few miles from home to attend the state university. According to contemporaries he did not stand at the very front as a leader on the campus, but he did complete his liberal arts course with Phi Beta Kappa honors. Then he left Indiana for the longest period of his life—at least prior to the Philippine venture—and became a student at the law school of Harvard University. Considering his devotion to the Hoosier State and his feeling of Hoosier self-sufficiency, one wonders whether McNutt does not sometimes regret his Harvard lapse. At any rate he achieved second-group honors in law school and consequently was chosen president of the legal aid bureau.

Like some other law school professors and deans, McNutt has never essayed to do much in the way of practicing law. He assisted his lawyer-father for a few months in 1916. Then, in 1917, he accepted an assistant professorship in the law school of Indiana University. The same year he joined the army field artillery as a captain in the reserves and later, in 1918, he became an active major. A reserve lieutenant colonelcy, in 1919, and a reserve colonelcy, in 1923, followed the war. McNutt did not get overseas during the fighting.

After the conclusion of the war he returned to Indiana and, in 1919, became a full professor in the law school of Indiana University. After a time, in 1925, he received the post of dean and incidentally the distinction of being one of the youngest law deans in the United States. Altogether he made a good reputation in this capacity, raising the standards for admission, strengthening the faculty, and in general adding to the prestige of the school. But it may be questioned whether he ever found great satisfaction in his academic duties. Teaching a few young men something about the law could scarcely be called exciting. The administrative duties of a school with a small faculty and student body were not such as to bring great acclaim. Consequently McNutt looked about for fields which offered more in the way of what he wanted from life.

The American Legion for some time seemed the most likely field for cultivation. Hence, Dean McNutt spent more and more of his time in Legion affairs, assiduously attending Legion conventions both in Indiana and without. Eventually the efforts devoted to this brought reward in the form of election as head of his local post, then as commander of the department of Indiana, after a time as a member of the national executive committee, and in 1928 as national Legion commander. Perhaps no period of McNutt's life has proved more pleasurable than these years of commanding the Legion. He had almost unlimited opportunities of exhibiting his prowess as a public speaker. His speeches on Americanism and other patriotic subjects are still remembered in many communities and rank among the most eloquent, if not always the most rational, utterances of that type.[1] The office also gave numerous opportunities for otherwise appearing in the public eye. At conventions McNutt either presided or was a distinguished guest. In the Legion periodical, messages from the national commander always found a place. Finally there were the glorious parades with Commander McNutt, resplendent in uniform, occupying a prominent position.

Most politicians in the United States get their start as precinct committeemen. Commander McNutt used the American Legion for that purpose. As dean of the law school of Indiana University he had some scope for political maneuvering among lawyers and

---

[1] See Charles A. Beard, *The Navy: Defense or Portent* (New York, 1932), pp. 119-21, for background of an address delivered at the Mayflower Hotel in Washington.

teachers of law. But he was not particularly interested in lawyers. Besides, too many of them had their own political axes to grind. The Legion gave a much greater opportunity to emblazon himself as a coming public figure.

Indiana had been Republican for sixteen years when McNutt finally, in 1932, ran for the office of governor. Much of that period must rank with the darkest and most corrupt in Hoosier political annals. One governor served a term in the federal prison at Atlanta. Another saved himself from state penitentiary only by pleading the statute of limitation. Several years in the middle of the period had seen the state in the grip of the Ku Klux Klan and its notorious Grand Dragon, D. C. Stephenson, who serves a life term on a murder charge in the Indiana state prison.

At the time McNutt laid his plans for the governorship, the Republicans had retrieved some of their damaged reputation, but the progress had not been impressive. An easy-going governor allowed many of the politicians who had fattened off the state during Klan days to hold influential positions in the state government. What little popularity the Republicans could boast suffered severely at the hands of the depression.

With the Republicans in bad odor, a depression in full swing, and the Democratic party somewhat disorganized, McNutt quite easily won the governorship. He had his Legion contacts in virtually every community. He had spoken widely throughout Indiana, and the people remembered him. As the word spread that McNutt was interested in the gubernatorial nomination, widespread sentiment almost spontaneously developed in his favor. McNutt-for-Governor clubs sprang up everywhere. He himself visited several parts of the state, delivered more eloquent speeches, and allowed the citizens to admire him. In the state Democratic convention, despite some bitter opposition, his nomination came on the first ballot. With many voters holding the Republicans responsible for the depression, he won the election easily and decisively.

When McNutt took oath as governor of Indiana, in January, 1933, he found some difficult problems confronting the state. The peak of the depression made the relief situation particularly demanding. The question of adequate state revenues loomed high. Shortly after he took office came the closing of the banks. After the repeal of the Eighteenth Amendment the regulation of liquor needed attention.

How would the new governor proceed? There was much difference of opinion. Some who knew McNutt's love for the limelight believed that he would be satisfied with the semblance of power—the pomp of public office. Possibly the largest group of citizens actually expected little in the way of action. For a dozen years pressing problems had received inadequate attention in the state. Sometimes a governor recommended changes, but the legislature usually adjourned at the end of its constitutional term with little accomplished. Why expect the new governor to do more, especially since he was a schoolmaster rather than a man of affairs?

There are those who insist that little credit for the changes achieved during the four years of McNutt's term should be given to McNutt himself. They argue that the years 1933–1937 were years of progress everywhere, that the depression gave impetus, President Roosevelt furnished leadership, and all states found themselves forced to vigorous action. That it was easier to bring about reforms in this period, few can doubt. That public opinion demanded certain changes can scarcely be denied. But allowing for all of this, considerable credit still seems to belong to Governor McNutt. For one thing, he had his program well under way before Franklin D. Roosevelt took office. It is true that McNutt did not originate a great deal of significant legislation himself, but he could be persuaded to support important measures, whereas all too many governors remain diffident. Largely because of his backing, some exceptionally important laws found their way onto the statute books.

As one reviews the administration of McNutt, one cannot escape the fact that the Governor definitely believed in strong executive leadership throughout the state government. He wanted a legislature that would follow his dictates and administrative officials who would look to him for guidance. Hence, he lost no time in laying the foundations necessary for the establishment of such leadership.

Governor McNutt probably reasoned somewhat after this fashion: "The expert in government has usually failed because he has not been able to put through his program. The organization has controlled, in the last analysis. The first thing for me to do is to build a powerful machine of my own. Only in that way will it be possible to avoid the experience of my predecessors with a chaotic legislature and ambitious administrative officials."

It seemed to McNutt that the best way, perhaps the only way, to construct a powerful political machine in Indiana centered around the disposal of patronage. Very shortly after he assumed office, therefore, he fired virtually all state employees. Even the staff of the state library, which for many years had supposed itself above wholesale change, found itself involved. Of course the numerous places thus vacated went to deserving followers of McNutt and his associates. It may be added that McNutt openly admitted a belief in party reward, but he also maintained that those who received the jobs should render efficient service or get out.

The Governor allowed Pleas Greenlee, one of his political managers, to handle most of the patronage in jobs. Greenlee did the job with a vengeance. To get on the state payroll Democrats had to show what they had contributed to McNutt's election. Furthermore, they had to prove that they carried with them a number of votes other than their own. Having cleared out the Republicans, Greenlee did not rest. His eagle eye constantly surveyed the ranks of state employees. Democrats who proved themselves of doubtful political worth were replaced by more deserving members of the party.

Then there was the matter of beer and liquor franchises. Indiana had decided to legalize the sale of liquor after the repeal of federal prohibition. Why not limit such business to deserving Democrats? That ought to strengthen the organization. The Governor appointed a faithful follower to select one wholesaler of beer and one of liquors in each county. To start out, the number of retail licenses was limited. State distributors and importers also received commissions. In almost every case these lucrative appointments went to Democrats of the McNutt persuasion.

But an efficient machine needs more than jobs and liquor franchises: it requires money, and in large sums. The Indiana Democracy does not include within its ranks many men of great wealth. The Governor himself had no independent fortune. Why not expect the holders of state jobs and the recipients of liquor franchises to contribute toward a campaign chest? Let a club be created whose main purpose it would be to collect two per cent of the salaries of state employees as well as suitable contributions, according to report one month's profits each year, from the liquor dealers. The "Two Per Cent Club" became an integral part of the organization and provided generous sums for financing political programs.

With several thousand jobs, lucrative beer and liquor franchises, and the substantial treasury of the Two Per Cent Club at his disposal it is not strange that McNutt and his associates built one of the strongest political machines ever known in Indiana. Very few Democrats either within or without the government could withstand it. The members of the legislature literally signed over their votes in order to secure appointments and liquor franchises for themselves and their followers. Despite a constitutional prohibition, McNutt and Greenlee named approximately thirty members of the legislature to important state positions.

When after a time the recalcitrant branch of the Democratic party in Indiana attempted to dictate the nomination of a United States senator, the McNutt organization had an opportunity of demonstrating its effectiveness. The opposition found itself unable to make any headway. Governor McNutt nominated and elected his friend, Sherman Minton, to the office.

However brilliant the achievement of constructing a powerful political machine may have been, Governor McNutt discovered that a price had been paid. Some of his more idealistic friends had found themselves unable to go along with the Two Per Cent Club, the liquor franchise distribution, and the disposal of state jobs on a patronage basis. More serious was the break in the tone of the press. To begin with, the Governor had, with certain notable exceptions, received quite favorable attention from the press not only in Indiana but, perhaps even more, elsewhere in the United States. Periodicals, such as *Collier's* and *The Literary Digest*, ran articles and printed photographs.[2] Many writers pointed to McNutt as the most promising man in the Democratic party after President Roosevelt and predicted that he would succeed Roosevelt in the White House. After the machine had been built and the methods used had been brought to light, much of the press changed its atti-

[2] See *Collier's Magazine*, XCII (November 18, 1933), 10–11; *Literary Digest*, CXV (March 4, 1933), 12; *ibid*, CXVI (July 15, 1933), 9.

tude and became definitely critical. No longer did McNutt stand forth as the well-trained, brilliant expert in politics with a great political future. Instead he was held up as a huckster of public jobs and a racketeer in liquor franchises. Such criticism gave the Governor sorrow and caused him to slow up. The liquor system underwent modification. Some non-political appointments were made.

With the overwhelmingly Democratic legislature safely in his grasp, Governor McNutt began to put through a legislative program of ambitious proportions. Numerous bills "sold" by various groups to the Governor found their way into the legislative chambers. Lest undesired changes be made, a system was devised under which legislative proposals emanating from the executive department received "steam-roller" passage. In most cases rules of the houses were suspended and the bills bearing the McNutt "must" sign went through without opportunity for offering amendments and with little or no debate. Obviously such a method engendered restiveness among the members of the legislature as well as criticism in the press. Nevertheless, the Governor's control of the huge Democratic majority in the legislature reached such absolute proportions that the dissatisfaction had no practical repercussions. Whether in keeping with the traditions of American government or not, it must be admitted that such a system proved exceedingly efficient. Despite the inadequate period allowed by the Indiana constitution for a legislative session, McNutt found it possible to write upon the statute books a great deal of important legislation.

One of the first items which the Governor gave attention to involved a reorganization of the administrative departments of Indiana. A start in this direction had been made in 1919, but a department had been added here and a commission there through the years until Indiana had something like one hundred distinct divisions in its administrative setup. Some of these departments duplicated the work of other departments. Some of them looked to the governor for orders, and others had very slight relation to the governor. The popularly elected secretary of state, state treasurer, and superintendent of public instruction all had fairly large powers of appointment and were not closely subject to gubernatorial control. McNutt wanted real command over state administration. Nevertheless, he apparently feared the political consequences of a reorganization and only after considerable pressure from advisers did he finally commit himself.

Instead of calling in experts to plan an administrative reorganization which would be submitted either as an amendment to the state constitution or to the legislature for passage as a law, or even drafting his own bill, McNutt decided to support legislation sponsored by a member of the Senate. This bill provided blanket authority under which the governor could make such rearrangement as he wished by executive order. Of course the administrative agencies did not regard this plan with favor. But McNutt's machine functioned so efficiently that permission was wrung from the legislature.

Despite the somewhat questionable method chosen by the Governor to accomplish the much-needed administration reorganization, expert advice could still have been employed. However, McNutt feared that there would be a slip if anyone in addition to himself and his most intimate advisers had anything to do with the reorganization. Hence, although the opportunity for scientific grouping was a very good one, which may not soon come again, little or no expert assistance was used, with the result that the reorganization finds itself with a very unenviable reputation. All of the agencies were brought together into a small number of big departments, but many discovered that they had landed in strange company. Functions entailing a close relationship not infrequently had been widely separated. However, except for the state officers, such as the secretary of state, provided for in the state constitution, and their personal deputies, the reorganization did give McNutt complete control over state employees. No longer could the popularly elected state officers hire and fire the workers in their departments. The Governor did that and hence indirectly managed the affairs of those departments.

Possibly to offset the criticism growing out of his failure to use experts in the administrative reorganization, McNutt proceeded to appoint commissions, made up to some extent of specialists, to study such matters as poor relief and governmental economy. These commissions made some valuable reports. But the Governor, although expressing general agreement, failed to include their recommendations in his "must" list, and hence they did not become law.

Demand for tax relief had reached such intensity that a special session of the legislature shortly before McNutt became governor attempted to limit the general property tax rate in Indiana. On the ground that the state had restricted its share in such a rate to fifteen cents McNutt proceeded to put through a gross income tax as well as an intangibles tax to provide additional state income. At a time when many states found inadequate revenues a very serious problem, Indiana not only had money for the entire program of the Governor, but could point with pride to a balance in the treasury variously estimated at from twelve to seventeen million dollars when McNutt left office.

Toward the salary of every teacher in accredited schools McNutt-supported legislation provided that the state treasury should pay five hundred dollars per year. Such generosity toward education continued right up through the state universities. When the legislatures of all the surrounding states cut university budgets unmercifully, McNutt insisted that the appropriations of Indiana University and Purdue should remain generally untouched. Such thoughtfulness has enabled both institutions to make greater relative progress during recent years than perhaps any other state schools, at least in the Midwest.

It has already been noted that one of the very important problems confronting the state after McNutt took office involved the regulation of state banks. A commission appointed by McNutt's predecessor had drafted important legislation after considerable deliberation. McNutt agreed to support this proposed legislation. His backing and the bank holiday put it upon the statute books. At first sight it would seem that the new banking law merely extended the governor's power over banking. Actually McNutt regarded the regulation of banks as somewhat different from other state affairs. He brought in from Indiana University's department of economics an able young man to have charge of the new banking administration and gave him free rein. Instead of using the jobs in this department for partisan purposes the Governor allowed Mr. Wells to set up a system of examinations to test the general educational background and special qualifications of all prospective employees. Appointments went to the highest names on the list, subject to a provision that not more than half be from one political party. The banking department built up an enviable reputation.

Toward the close of his administration as governor, McNutt seemed to become increasingly interested in the application of the merit system to state appointments. Positions in the new department of public welfare were placed by law under the merit system. The Public Administration Service of Chicago received a commission to set up a modern personnel system for this department, the state employment service, and the unemployment compensation division. McNutt followed this with interest and, shortly before he left office, by executive order placed all of the state institutions under a merit system.

In retrospect McNutt's four years as governor impress an observer as a complicated combination of contradictions and inconsistencies. His liberal attitude toward education and banking, as well as his apparent interest in the merit principle, stand forth in contrast to the liquor legislation and the Two Per Cent Club. In a general way he wanted to be known as progressive. Those who sought his backing testify that half of the battle consisted in convincing him that such a scheme would place Indiana in the foreground as a sort of pioneer. As executive officer of the National Conference of Governors, he generally exhibited this side of his character. Yet it must be admitted that he distrusted anything smacking of radicalism. And his definition of radicalism was a broad one. Some of the most sensational episodes in his career as governor involved strikes and labor disputes. McNutt frequently called for martial law and sent in the state troops. Sometimes, as in Terre Haute, martial law remained in force for many weeks after normal conditions seemed to have been restored. Of course the labor forces resented such treatment and accused McNutt of being a "fascist," despite the fact that he claimed that more legislation favorable to labor had been enacted during his administration than in any other.

Although McNutt absented himself from Indiana quite frequently, he worked hard at his job as governor. His remarkable capacity for intensive work, his unfailing memory, and a general political fearlessness impress the student of politics. At times he

HOOSIER SENTINEL, INDIANAPOLIS

PAUL V. McNUTT

*"One would go far to find a more complex mixture
of political liberalism and machine orthodoxy."*

suffered not a little rather than do what was politically expedient. In connection with consumer-credit legislation, for example, he encountered bitter opposition and threats of reprisal in the national arena from a nation-wide lobby opposing such a scheme. When advisers counseled caution, he replied, "We make decisions based upon fairness and justice rather than political expediency."

As a Hoosier party leader McNutt's record displays confusion. He could deliver campaign speeches and handle crowds with unusual effectiveness. Not many have engineered a more powerful political machine. But individual political relations did not always fare very well. In his desire to be surrounded by those whom he regarded as loyal and sympathetic he made unfortunate choices which doubtless enhanced the excesses of his regime. He left the Democratic party divided—whether more so than when he appeared on the scene it is difficult to say. Shortly after his departure for the Philippines many prominent Democrats did not hesitate to speak in thinly veiled or even open hostility. Some of this is doubtless the result of reaction against strong leadership. Probably some must be attributed to McNutt's lack of tact. More is due to the long-standing division in the party.

Under the Indiana constitution a governor cannot succeed himself in office. Therefore, McNutt began during the last years of his term to look to the future both as to his own career and as to his successor in office. At one time there seemed some possibility that Vice-President Garner might retire and that McNutt might become the running mate of President Roosevelt in 1936. At other times a Cabinet position in the national government, especially that of secretary of war, appeared in the offing. But McNutt had not enjoyed the warmest support from the Roosevelt administration, although he actively favored the New Deal program. The Indiana delegation under McNutt's leadership had not been on the original Roosevelt bandwagon in 1932. As a result Indiana Democrats received but few pieces of important federal patronage. After some hesitation McNutt refused to back Pleas Greenlee as his successor and named Lieutenant Governor Townsend, who was duly nominated and elected.

When Governor McNutt's term finally came to an end, no other suitable position in public life had presented itself. It seemed that he might take the presidency of Indiana University, which had been held open for him. But before any decision had been made, President Roosevelt offered McNutt the high commissionership to the Philippine Commonwealth. After some hesitation he accepted, at the same time intimating to Indiana University that he might return within a year to take over its presidency.

McNutt's career in the Philippines did not begin auspiciously. He almost at once made himself unpopular by notifying foreign consulates that they must negotiate with the Philippine Commonwealth through his office and issuing a ruling that he must be toasted before the president of the Commonwealth. Some attempt was made to throw the responsibility for these actions on Washington, but the Manila newspapers blamed McNutt and violently castigated him in their editorials. With characteristic charm he largely saved his face by extending an unexpected courtesy to President Quezon. Under Filipino etiquette an inferior must light the cigarette of a superior. Commissioner McNutt took occasion to light the President's cigarette and then in turn received a light from him, indicating his recognition of equality.

Approximately a year after assuming the high commissionership McNutt decided to pay a visit to the United States to confer with President Roosevelt and to bring him personal knowledge not only of the Philippines but of the Far Eastern situation in general. Delayed by weather conditions, McNutt reached California with his executive secretary on a Pan American clipper too late to make by train an engagement to address the Indiana Democratic Editorial Association. Hence, he requested an army plane for transportation. Almost immediately after the flight the officer piloting the machine received orders transferring him from a good post in California to the Siberia of air fields, a run-down field in Illinois. Report had it that President Roosevelt was indicating his displeasure at the plans which had been made in Washington to launch a McNutt-for-President boom.

After being received with at least superficial warmth by Hoosier Democrats, McNutt went to Washington, where Senator Minton accorded him a big reception at the Mayflower Hotel, which was sensationally reported in the newspapers. Most of the political bigwigs of Washington received invitations, and while President

Roosevelt and Secretary Farley found it necessary to be out of the city, well over a thousand guests appeared. Incidentally they consumed twenty-five hundred dollars worth of elaborate refreshments. Although McNutt replied to queries from reporters that he intended to stay in the Philippines as long as the President wanted his services, there was little doubt in the minds of most observers that he had succeeded in launching one of the most daring and colorful presidential booms in recent years. The press throughout the country gave generous amounts of space and displayed cuts which indicated McNutt's unusual physical handsomeness. After the reception President Roosevelt conversed with McNutt on several occasions relative to Philippine and other matters.

Before returning to his post McNutt informed Indiana University that he was not a candidate for its presidency—which was interpreted as an indication of his confidence in his President-of-the-United States boom. Furthermore, McNutt delivered an address in which he urged the people of the United States not to free the Philippines despite the commitment already made. He maintained that the Philippines could not keep their independence if the United States gave them up and argued that the United States has a duty to remain in the Far East. What part such a question will play in the campaign of 1940, time alone will tell. One can scarcely doubt that McNutt will do everything within his power to capture the Democratic presidential nomination if Mr. Roosevelt does not run himself. In general his chances seem to be better than they were earlier when some political observers claimed that he was committing political suicide by going halfway around the world to the Philippines. His public record should make him fairly acceptable to the conservative group in the Democratic party.

During the summer of 1938 McNutt proved his continuing ability to control the Democratic organization in Indiana, even when personally far removed from the scene. Despite a formal notice served on Senator Frederick Van Nuys by Governor Townsend reading the former out of the party for his part in fighting the proposal of President Roosevelt to enlarge the Supreme Court, Commissioner McNutt and his manager, National Committeeman McHale, persuaded the Democratic state convention to renominate Van Nuys by acclamation as a gesture of party harmony. Moreover, McNutt greeted the delegates by radio message from the Philippines and in return received from them a formal endorsement for the presidency in 1940.

To conclude, there seems little question as to McNutt's native ability along political lines. He has the striking appearance, the verbal eloquence, and the magnetic personality which go far in attracting popular support in the United States. Furthermore, he is daring, persistent, and adaptable. Although he makes bad mistakes, he knows usually when to shift, and he has a considerable gift of making capital out of what might in many cases be political suicide. At the same time, and perhaps because of these very qualities, he is essentially an opportunist and an organization man. To gain personal success he will give public jobs to party workers, use public employees for party service on time paid for by public funds, levy assessments on the salaries of government employees for the filling of a campaign chest, and set up a system of liquor-political partnership. Nevertheless, McNutt has redeeming features, and these qualities would seem to place him somewhat above the average of political partisans. On occasion he gives his confidence to those who see in the public service more than mere personal profit, even to backing them in the face of strong opposition. At times he becomes interested in some public problem and without attention to political expediency throws himself into its solution, despite the fact that by and large he is definitely a conservative in his reactions.

4

GEORGE WILLIAM NORRIS

By Claudius O. Johnson

TRAITOR, PRO-GERMAN, COPPERHEAD, PACIFIST, SOCIALIST, BOL-shevik, predatory politician, demagogue, agitator, meddler, reformer, idealist, major prophet, monopoly hater, Wall Street baiter, friend of the common man, statesman unafraid, a living, perambulating Declaration of Independence—these are only a few of the terms which have been used in characterizing Senator George William Norris. Independent of party, he has held office for fifty years in a country which perfected the party system. Scorning almost every device which practical politicians have considered indispensable, he has remained in public life as others have fallen, often the stupid victims of their own orthodox practices. In a country and a period which definitely prefer young men, he won his most signal victory at the polls when seventy-five; and in a country which expects quick performance, he had passed three score and ten before he started winning major victories for his principles. Here is a man who placed his principles above himself and whom the people placed above his principles, even above their own principles. "He that loseth his life shall find it." The solution of the riddle of George Norris is relatively simple. Honesty, courage, and independence are the key words.

Norris's earliest years fit into any American success story. He was born in Sandusky County, Ohio, July 11, 1861. His father, Chauncey Norris, had come to Ohio from Connecticut, and his mother, Mary Mook Norris, was from Maryland. The parents were poor in everything but offspring, for George (who was called William at home), was one of twelve children, the youngest. He was but an infant when his only brother was killed in the Battle of Gettysburg and just four years of age when his father died of pneumonia. George grew up to help support his mother and sisters. As a boy he worked for farmers in the summer and attended school in the winter. With a meager public school training he taught for a few years in order to earn money to continue his education. He attended Baldwin-Wallace College in Ohio and Valparaiso University, receiving the degree of bachelor of science from the latter. Again he taught, but he wanted to become a lawyer, having developed a great interest in that profession through his experience as a college debater.

With a little cash in his pocket, he completed his legal studies at Valparaiso University, and he passed his bar examination in 1883. Once more he taught school, this time for the purpose of securing means to purchase a law library. He did this teaching in far-away Washington Territory, near Walla Walla. After seven months, he did a very unusual thing for an ambitious young man with a pioneering temperament who was making his own way. He left the Territory and went back to the Middle West, to Beaver City, Nebraska, a little town in the south central part of the state. There he hung out his shingle in 1885. Some years later, he moved to McCook, a few miles farther west. It might be a matter of some interest to record here that about the time Norris was leaving the Far West for Nebraska, two other future senators were leaving the Middle West for the Far West. Wesley Jones journeyed from Illinois to Washington State, and Borah pulled up his stakes in Illinois and put them down temporarily in Kansas before he went West to make his name synonymous with Idaho.

It is said that even as a young college student Jones had a burning ambition to go to Congress. Borah thought nothing of a political career until he became well established as a lawyer, although he did make an unsuccessful race for city attorney shortly after he arrived in Boise. Norris's plans seem to have been about the same as Borah's, but his law practice grew slowly and he was glad to make the race for prosecuting attorney of his county. He won the election (1889), and he has been holding elective office ever since. After six years as prosecutor, he came out in 1895 for the position of judge of the Fourteenth Judicial District. The Populists were strong in that territory and Norris won for the Republicans by a very narrow margin. The young judge did all he could to protect farm debtors and he gave general satisfaction except to mortgagees.

He was easily re-elected in 1899. Early in 1902, the Judge was suggested as a candidate for Congress. The idea appealed to him, and with characteristic candor he announced his desire to represent the Fifth District. The movement for Norris grew rapidly, and when the convention nominated him it "only voiced the sentiment of the people residing within the district." [1]

The Fifth District had been represented by fusion men (Populists-Democrats) for some years. In 1902, the incumbent, a fusionist, A. C. Shallenberger, was pitted against Norris. Judge Norris asked Shallenberger to meet him in joint debate on the issues. At first Shallenberger refused, but later, feeling that he had made a tactical error, he debated Norris on four occasions. Although Norris proved himself to be an excellent campaigner, it is probable that the Oxford *Standard* indicated the chief reason for his success in the election in its statement that "old General Prosperity and a big crop have this year emblazoned a way to Republican success." [2] Capitalizing on President Theodore Roosevelt's popularity, Republicans of the district made some use of the slogan, "A vote for Norris is a vote for Roosevelt."

The man who went to Washington in 1903 to represent the Fifth Nebraska District was not particularly striking in appearance. He looked solid and respectable like the average successful small-town lawyer of the Middle West. His fine black hair was reasonably well kept, his black eyebrows were not unusually prominent, and his drooping, almost "weeping walrus," mustache was not then absolutely out of style. The black hair is now gray, almost white. The eyebrows are still black, giving a certain melancholy appearance to the countenance of the man who often listens in sympathy and thinks in terms of human suffering. In time, the mustache was trimmed to bristles, which, unlike the eyebrows, in due course turned gray and finally disappeared. The nose is well proportioned, the chin protrudes but slightly, and the jaws are not particularly firm. The mouth is small, and from it flow, except when he is thoroughly aroused, gentle, pleading words. The few wrinkles in his face belie his seventy-seven years. His somewhat sombre countenance, expressive of sympathy, sometimes suggestive

[1] Beaver City *Times-Tribune*, June 20, 1902.
[2] Quoted in the Beaver City *Times-Tribune*, July 4, 1902, from the Oxford *Standard*.

of disillusionment, sometimes lighted with a quizzical smile, his soft-spoken words—in fact, practically every visible feature belies the fighting man that he is. He has always dressed for comfort rather than for style, carelessly but not with ostentatious carelessness. He has always been as independent of the commands of sartorial dictators as he has been of party organizations.

As a young attorney, George Norris married Pluma Lashley in 1890. This marriage was an entirely congenial and happy one. Mrs. Norris died in 1901, leaving the future senator with three daughters. Two years later, he married Ella Leonard, who had been principal of one of the public schools at McCook. Since 1903, they have lived quietly in Washington during the sessions of Congress. They shun Washington society; the Senator occasionally ridicules it. During recesses they enjoy their home and friends at McCook. In the summer they often motor to Wisconsin, where they live in a little forest cabin of which the Senator is the architect and builder. The Norrises enjoy motoring in their inexpensive car, and on the road they give every appearance of being just one of many hundred thousands of plain couples on limited incomes who are out for a little recreation and pleasure. The Senator enjoys doing the odd jobs about his yard, such as trimming trees and mowing grass. This work and simple living doubtless go a long way to explain why he has enjoyed such good health.

The Norris library is well stocked. Leisure time means to the Senator time to read and study. Indeed, this has been his education, for the formal instruction he received years ago was only the faintest introduction to the store of knowledge he now possesses. He loves stirring poetry, which he often reads aloud, and, as would be expected of a man so modest, he associates the triumphal lines with the deeds of his friends rather than with his own accomplishments. The greater part of his reading is on economic and social problems. It includes not only books and magazine articles but dry-as-dust reports. All of these he carefully analyzes, and on occasion he comes into the Senate with neat diagrams and charts, which he inserts in the record for the benefit of the few who will trouble themselves to look at them. Norris is a student. He is not the type of student the professor is supposed to be, the student who investigates with complete objectivity, for the Senator has very definite views which he has held for a generation and he is sometimes particularly interested in finding material which lends strength to his position. His very friendly biographers describe him as roaming "the continent, seeking proof for his claim that the blessings of electricity could be brought within the reach of the whole citizenry." [3]

In the earlier days of his public career, Norris was a leading member of the Independent Order of Odd Fellows. The Beaver Valley *Tribune* (September 23, 1898) describes him as an enthusiastic Odd Fellow who had been chosen to the highest office of the Grand Lodge, Grand Master of the State. In the same year he was elected delegate to the Sovereign Grand Lodge and attended the meeting in Boston. It seems that he never had any interest in other organizations of this character, and his interest in this one waned a bit as he grew older and became interested in promoting the welfare of men through legislation. In any case, he has never been a "joiner," a rider in the "Great American Bandwagon."

He has never been affiliated with any church, nor has he ever professed any kind of religion. He does not play to the religious groups by occasional church attendance and scriptural references in his speeches. On occasion he has been known to jest on the floor of the Senate that overly-optimistic senators are using too much Christian Science.[4] He says he is "one of the followers of the religion proclaimed by Abou ben Adhem . . . who loved his fellow men." [5] Kindliness, unselfishness, and humanity are the principal elements in the religion of George W. Norris.

The Senator reserves his supreme contempt and scorn for men who parade as Christian gentlemen and at the same time stoop to practices which contravene the fundamental principles of the religion the Senator profoundly respects. One of the men who took a leading part in the disgraceful "Grocer George" plot to defeat Norris for the Senate in 1930 was the national president of the Boy Scouts of America and a teacher of a very large Sunday school class. He admitted under oath that he had furnished four or five thousand dollars for the campaign. "Nobody suspected that this great Sunday school man, this great Boy Scout Christian, was en-

[3] R. L. Neuberger and S. B. Kahn, *Integrity: The Life of George W. Norris* (New York, 1937), p. 214. This volume is well written, interesting, and full of information.
[4] *Congressional Record*, 68th Congress, 2nd Session, p. 4402.
[5] R. L. Neuberger, "A Politician Unafraid," *Harper's Magazine*, October, 1936, p. 548.

gaged in the disreputable business," was Norris's vitriolic comment.[6]

A prominent minister in Nebraska wrote Norris that the "good" people of the State were ashamed of him, particularly for his support of Smith in 1928. "You do not represent us at all," added the minister. Norris wired for advice on how he should vote on a naval armaments bill then before the Senate. The minister was for it. Norris replied: "It may be that the way to save the heathen people is to do it by backing up our prayers with a big navy and with armed marines and flying machines dropping bombs upon the homes of innocent people. You, being an educated teacher of religion, perhaps know more about this than I do, but I hope you will pardon me, if, in my sinful way, I cannot see your viewpoint." [7]

Not a backslapper, not a hail-fellow-well-met, the Senator nevertheless has always had his friends. In the days when he was considered regular in politics and sound in economics, he may have had a greater number of the garden variety of friends than he has had since he entered the United States Senate, but if his heterodox ideas have limited the number of his friends, they have strengthened the remaining friendships. Perhaps the strongest friendships he has ever had were those he enjoyed with Senators Robert M. La Follette, Sr., of Wisconsin and Harry Lane of Oregon. In La Follette he found a man whose views on railroads, banks, and other business concerns he frequently shared and a man whose broader and longer experience in public life made him something of a teacher. There is no doubt that La Follette greatly influenced the Senator from Nebraska.

Lane and Norris entered the Senate as freshmen the same year (1913). They became constant companions, very dear friends. They fought with La Follette and a few others to keep the United States out of the World War. During the period immediately preceding the declaration of war, Lane became seriously ill. His doctors ordered him to avoid all excitement if he wanted to live. He told a member of his family that he would rather die at once than "back down on George and Bob." [8] Night after night Norris sat at

[6] Neuberger and Kahn, *op. cit.*, p. 238.

[7] *Ibid.*, p. 180.

[8] *Ibid.*, p. 94.

the bedside of his friend. Lane attended sessions when he had the strength to do so and was present to cast his vote against war on that memorable April 4. Six weeks later he died. Norris said that his colleague gave his life for peace, and that sacrifice of his friend became one of the great inspirations of the Nebraskan's later career.

Ask any newspaperman in Washington, even the most cynical, who is the most honest man in the Capital, and he will say Senator Norris. At a time when everyone else is acting, posing, saying one thing and thinking another, Norris goes right on doing exactly what he wants to do in a natural manner and saying exactly what he thinks without regard for consequences. His honesty is much more than just plain integrity; it is freedom from all forms of sham and pretense. Generally a warm supporter of President Franklin D. Roosevelt, often his adviser, he does not hesitate to say that the President is guilty of the sin of ingratitude when he thinks he is. And the President "takes it" from his "Uncle George." So do the Senator's associates. An unspotted record for integrity over two generations has given him the right, tacitly conceded by all, to pronounce harsh judgments.

Modesty is a quality which great men often lack. This is unfortunate, for few other qualities are more appreciated by the intelligent public. Modesty attached itself to young George Norris and it has remained with him, increasing with his years and achievements. Ordinarily he is mild, soft-spoken, unobtrusive. In his office he receives all who have any good reason to demand his time. Smoking a cigar or pipe (seemingly his only "bad" habit or extravagance) he just converses, exploring a question or problem. Often he lets the visitor do the greater part of the talking. He never pounds his desk, makes a grand declaration, or gives an oracular utterance. On February 12, 1936, some newspapermen had the not very bright idea of asking a number of public men what policies the Great Emancipator would advocate were he here to celebrate his one hundred and twenty-seventh birthday. Every statesman but one proceeded to put words into Lincoln's mouth praising or condemning the New Deal. Said Norris, "Lincoln would be just like me. He wouldn't know what the hell to do!" [9]

[9] *Ibid.*, p. 359.

In the day when Huey Long's histrionics were the chief attraction in the Senate Chamber, the many visitors who came to see him perform did not have to ask, "Which one is he?" for the Senator entering or leaving the Chamber, or getting up or sitting down, signaling or crossing over was of course the Senator from Louisiana. With the passing of this admittedly brilliant Senator, Norris is the one about whom visitors are most curious. Often they must have him pointed out to them, for the Senator from Nebraska sits quietly near the rear of the "picked chicken" [10] side of the Chamber, the only factor about his appearance which might cause one to look at him twice being his alertness to what is going on. Modest in debate, the Senator speaks in hardly more than conversational tones. Sometimes he is heard with difficulty. His speeches contain many such expressions as "I believe," "I think," "in my opinion," "maybe I am wrong," and "I hope I am wrong." His weapons are facts and figures and a sardonic humor. He is not eloquent and his voice is not particularly pleasing. His modesty does not prevent him from making a speech whenever he has something to say, which is fairly often, nor does it always cause him to bring to an end a speech which a number of his colleagues may think has been in progress long enough.

On the stump, having finally decided to be candidate, George Norris is not too modest to tell the voters that he wants them to do their duty by him. Unlike Borah, who almost never mentions his candidacy, Norris does not hesitate to say that he deserves re-election. Borah has never been so irregular that he could not expect some party support at a pinch. Norris has been so irregular that his party would use every pinch to accomplish his defeat. In the campaign, Norris goes it alone, except for the aid he might get from independents. He exposes the plots of the enemies of the plain people. He denounces reactionary newspapers. He reviews his stubborn fights against entrenched greed and outlines his program for a better country. He puts it up to the voter to sustain him and liberal government.

One of the little group of senators whom Wilson castigated as "willful men" in March, 1917, the Senator from Nebraska

[10] Norris's own words in characterization of the Republican side of the Chamber after the election of 1932.

UNDERWOOD AND UNDERWOOD

GEORGE WILLIAM NORRIS

"Intelligent voters have indicated their appreciation, although many of them do not agree with Norris that party-mindedness is a form of feeble-mindedness."

has been a most persistent follower of the War President's policy of "watchful waiting." He prepares himself and waits for his opportunities. Often the opportunity has been nothing more than the chance to enter, from the floor of the Senate, a protest against a proposition or to outline a plan of action. Defeats he can count by the score; victories, until 1932, he could count on the fingers of one hand. Yet he has never given up a fight. At times, discouraged at the prospects for ever putting through any liberal legislation, he has almost given up, but something has happened to prevent it. He reached the slough of despond in 1924, and only by a clever bit of strategy was he prevented from withdrawing from the senatorial campaign in that year. Ready to end his political career at sixty-three, Norris has never treated an issue so lightly. It was precisely his interest in the issues and the apparent hopelessness of settling them to the advantage of the great body of American people that caused him to want to quit the Senate during the Coolidge era. But having been re-elected in 1924, he declared, "We [Progressives] may lose, but we will keep on fighting to the very last." [11]

Norris does not refuse to compromise if compromise will advance his program. On the question of government operation of Muscle Shoals he refused to budge one inch because he felt that to compromise that issue was to lose the fight. But on the question of "reforming" the Supreme Court, he was willing to support President Franklin D. Roosevelt's plan to increase the number of judges if he (Norris) saw no possibility of putting through a plan which would limit the terms of judges and require a 7-2 majority of the Court to set aside an act of Congress. In 1928, Senator Norris, still advocating Prohibition, supported wet Governor Smith for the presidency because he was pleased with Smith's stand on other and more important social and economic questions. In like manner he supported Roosevelt in 1932 and again in 1936, although he has been a severe critic of some of his policies. In other words, Norris is willing to compromise, to take what he can get at the moment, provided that compromise does not block the road to the ultimate objective.

Senator Norris, being the independent radical that he is, very

[11] *New York Times*, November 8, 1924.

heartily dislikes the typical conservative party newspaper. The dislike is reciprocal, even such a well-mannered paper as the *New York Times* having on occasion spoken severely of the McCook statesman. It was during the days preceding America's entry into the World War that Norris made his most vigorous denunciations of the newspapers. They did not print the news impartially, he said, but were trying to stampede the United States into a declaration of war. In his famous speech at Lincoln, in which he defended his opposition to the Armed Merchant Ship Bill, he stated that he was telling the whole truth, some of which his hearers had not read in the newspapers. Nebraska newspapers countered with the statement that Norris had not co-operated with them in giving the people the news, that he had been asked for advance copies of his Lincoln speech, which he did not furnish, and that it was well understood by the Senator that newspapers were seldom able to give a full report of a speech without such co-operation.[12] As Norris's economic heresies increased and intensified after 1920, the dislike between him and the newspapers grew proportionally. On one occasion he met Mr. Hearst head-on. Printed in that publisher's newspapers was the absurd rumor that the Mexican government was planning to bribe certain senators, including Norris. In an open letter to Mr. Hearst, Senator Norris characterized him as "a man entirely without honor," the publisher of a chain of newspapers that constitute the "sewer system of American journalism." [13]

If the Senator's relations with newspaper publishers have not been altogether cordial, there has been compensation in his association with the newspaper correspondents. Sick of senatorial bombast, pomposity, and insincerity, these men love to talk to Norris, for whom they have profound respect and admiration. Norris tells them what he thinks, and he gives them the status of any question before the Senate unless a rule of that body binds him to secrecy. He may object to such rules, but he feels honor bound to abide by them. It is an old story that writers often have views totally at variance with those of their employers, and many are the Washington reporters who more nearly share the views of

[12] *State Journal*, March 28, 1917.
[13] *New York Times*, December 20, 1927.

George Norris than those set forth in the editorials of the papers they represent. Consequently, news articles favorable to Norris have often found their way into journals which have never supported him editorially.

The very serious, sad-eyed Senator from Nebraska does not lack humor. Sardonic, caustic humor is one of his weapons in debate. When the preparedness movement was gathering momentum in 1916, he ridiculed its proponents' fears that the widows and cripples left in Germany after the war were going to rig up a raft and come over and attack us. He denounced propagandists who shook the portrait of the Kaiser before the people in the East and frightened the children in from the streets after dark in San Francisco by crying, "The Japs are coming." [14]

Norris kept the senators and the galleries laughing as he spoke in opposition to the seating of Truman H. Newberry, who had paid some $200,000 for the toga. "They had a public sale up in Michigan," he declared. "The property that was placed on the auction block was a seat in the Senate of the United States. . . . The only question before the Senate is, shall that sale of a seat in this Chamber be confirmed? . . .

"It is said by some of those who are opposing the confirmation that this would establish a precedent by which the poor man would be eliminated from the Senate Chamber. Suppose it does? What business has a poor man here, anyway?" Mockingly he called upon senators to vote for the seating of Newberry, pointing out that if they were defeated at the polls at the next election for so doing they would be given better jobs by the Harding administration than they now held as senators.[15] It is a fact that the seating of Newberry did cause some senators to be unseated by the electorate, as Norris had intimated, and it is also a fact that these senators were given places by the administration even as the Senator from Nebraska had prophesied.

Never scrupulous to avoid personalities, on occasion the Nebraska humorist tickled his colleagues with the aristocratic plumage of the Senator from Massachusetts, Mr. Lodge. Once when he was ridiculing the fears of the State Department concerning Soviet

[14] *Congressional Record*, 64th Congress, 1st Session, p. 11188.
[15] *Congressional Record*, 67th Congress, 2nd Session, p. 1052.

propaganda in the United States, he ironically announced that an order had been given to seize every man with whiskers, and he warned Senator Lodge of the grave consequences likely to ensue if that Senator and Secretary of State Hughes should be seen together on Pennsylvania Avenue.[16]

Mr. Norris's humor sometimes takes the form of parody. When Vice-President Dawes rushed from the Willard Hotel to the Senate Chamber and failed to arrive in time to cast his vote for the confirmation of Charles B. Warren as attorney general, the Nebraskan was one of several who thought that that taxi ride deserved a place with Sheridan's famous horseback race. His parody concludes:

> And when his statue is placed on high,
> Under the dome of the Capitol sky,
> The great senatorial temple of fame,
> There with the glorious General's name
> Be it said, in letters both bold and bright,
> "Oh, Hell an' Maria, he has lost us the fight." [17]

When Secretary of State Kellogg tried to persuade the American people that they were in peril from a Bolshevik plot in Mexico, Norris ridiculed him by doctoring a few lines from James Whitcomb Riley:

> Onc't they was a Bolshevik,
> Who wouldn't say his prayers,
> So Kellogg sent him off to bed,
> Away upstairs,
> An' Kellogg heerd him holler an'
> Coolidge heerd him bawl,
> But when they turn't the kivvers
> Down, he wasn't there at all!
> They seeked him down in Mexico,
> They cussed him in the press;
> They seeked him 'round the Capitol,
> An' ever'wheres, I guess;

[16] *Congressional Record*, 68th Congress, 1st Session, p. 447.
[17] *Ibid.*, 69th Congress, Special Session, p. 150.

But all they ever found of him was
Whiskers, hair, and clout—
An' the Bolsheviks 'll git you
Ef you
Don't
Watch
Out! [18]

Even grim human tragedies find Norris ready with a relieving bit of humor. A state judge in Pennsylvania had enjoined striking coal miners from singing hymns on a lot owned by them because he thought the singing might intimidate "scab" miners who had to pass within fifteen hundred feet of the lot on their way to work. Denouncing this injunction, the Senator said, "I suppose when the miners ran up against United States marshals and the coal and iron police armed with clubs and guns, that 'Nearer My God to Thee' was a very appropriate hymn." [19]

Like many another caustic humorist, the Senator does not always enjoy a joke on himself. In 1922, at the time Henry Ford's offer for Muscle Shoals was before Congress, Senator Norris and other members of the joint committee of Congress studying the problem visited the Shoals country. At a barbecue tendered the Committee at Decatur, Alabama, a matron remarked to the Senator that she hoped he would change his mind and favor the acceptance of Ford's offer. The Senator replied that he might vote for the Ford bid if he could kiss one of the pretty girls at the barbecue. A young girl promptly kissed the Senator. A few months later the matron from Decatur related this incident before the Senate Committee on Agriculture, a Committee of which Norris was chairman. The Senator was indignant. In a voice that could be heard some distance down the corridor, he asked the reason for this testimony. "Was this fixed up in advance to browbeat me? Is this a put-up job? . . . The story you have told is a falsehood. I know a blackmail plot when I see it. If you were not a woman, this would not be the end of this, I tell you. I did not kiss that girl. She kissed me. Intimations were given to me that

[18] *Ibid.*, 69th Congress, 2nd Session, p. 1691.
[19] *Ibid.*, 71st Congress, 2nd Session, p. 8185.

if I did not favor Henry Ford's bid for the Muscle Shoals, some sort of thing would be hung over my head. I guess this is it." [20]

The incident just related not only indicates a certain lack of humor on the part of the Senator but also serves as an illustration of his inclination to be suspicious of the most innocent and worthy acts of those whom he deems to be enemies of the people. Back in 1925, this tendency caused him to make a few declarations which he later regretted. President Coolidge had nominated Attorney General Harlan F. Stone, an old friend, for the position of associate justice of the Supreme Court, and the question of confirmation was before the Senate. Norris attacked several appointments and pending appointments of President Coolidge—Charles B. Warren for the post of attorney general (to succeed Stone), W. E. Humphreys to the Federal Trade Commission, and T. F. Woodlock to the Interstate Commerce Commission. He said that the people had shown their preference for the Vermont farmer for president over John W. Davis, the Morgan attorney, and the "farmer" was now proposing to place a Morgan attorney (Stone) in the Supreme Court. "With Morgan and Company's attorney on the Supreme Bench," he cried, "with the Sugar Trust running the Attorney General's office, with the railroads themselves operating the Interstate Commerce Commission, with the greatest reactionary of the country sitting on the Federal Trade Commission, tell me, O God—tell me!—where the toiling millions of the honest, common people of this country are going to be protected in their rights as against big business." [21]

The Lone Lion of Idaho (Borah), himself interested in the "plain people" and usually duly suspicious of "Wall Street," stated to his friend from McCook that Stone was one of the most liberal-minded men who had ever been in the attorney general's office and added that his only regret in seeing him advanced to the Supreme Court was that the country would lose an extraordinarily able and conscientious attorney general. Mr. Justice Stone's career on the bench has confirmed the faith of Borah rather than the fears of Norris, and as the Idahoan long since came to regret his opposition to the confirmation of Justice Brandeis, the

---

[20] *New York Times,* May 25, 1923.
[21] *Congressional Record,* 68th Congress, 2nd Session, p. 3053.

Nebraskan is now sorry he opposed the appointment of Justice Stone.

The occasional unreasonable suspicions and unjust judgments of the Nebraska senator arise not from a suspicious and severe character but rather from his great dominant interest in the plain people, the relatively inarticulate masses. By nature he is not suspicious, or harsh, or bitter, but trusting, charitable, and kindly. Having devoted his life to farmers and wage-earners and having so often found their representatives break faith with them, as he sees it, he is eternally vigilant to protect the masses from laws which may hamper them and from men who may discriminate against them. Yet, aside from remarks in the heat of a debate, there is nothing personal in the Senator's criticisms of men who represent corporations rather than the people. Indeed, even in debate he often makes this clear. In voicing his opposition to the Coolidge nominees just named, he was careful to state that they were all honorable men, but men who saw "through the glasses of corporations." But once, while speaking, he is reported to have said of Coolidge, "He thinks he is a little Jesus Christ," a remark which a tactful clerk inserted in the *Congressional Record* as "He thinks he is the embodiment of perfection." [22]

Political independence is one of the outstanding qualities in the mature statesmanship of Senator George W. Norris. Republican politicians, with whom he was so long technically associated, could not conceal their irritation and disgust over this man who, in defiance of all the conventions of politics, time and again demonstrated the success of his method. Democratic politicians marveled. Intelligent voters have indicated their appreciation, although many of them may not agree with Norris that party-mindedness is a form of feeble-mindedness. As the orthodox view it, the Senator has tried many times to commit political suicide, but he misses, or the bullet penetrates a non-vulnerable spot, or strikes such a tough spot that it bounces off. Or to put it in other terms, the other politicians' poison is his political medicine. This is Norris since about 1910.

It was not the Norris of the days of Populism, for then, despite his Middle West and Far West background, despite the strength

22 Neuberger and Kahn, *op. cit.*, p. 162.

of Populism in Nebraska, he remained one of the few Republicans in his county. As we look back, we can now discover a few indications of a growing independence in Congressman Norris during Theodore Roosevelt's administration, but on the whole he was a good enough party man to praise the protective tariff and use such expressions as the "magic wand of Republican encouragement and enthusiasm," and mean them. Within three months after he took his seat in the House he committed a little offense against party rule. On Washington's Birthday, a Democratic member had moved that the House adjourn in tribute to the Father of the Country. Freshman Congressman Norris thought that this was a perfectly proper proposal, and he voted for it, the only Republican who did so. Leaders indulgently but gravely explained to him the impropriety of a Republican's supporting even such a patriotic resolution when introduced by a Democrat. Norris still could not understand why he should not vote for measures which he approved. A few months later he made a speech against his party's bill increasing the pay of an officer of the House, thus beginning a long and unbroken record against the spoils system. Despite such lapses in party regularity, Norris meant to be a good Republican, and he naïvely thought that voting and speaking his convictions was perfectly sound Republicanism. He did not change his course upon learning that the masters of the party disagreed with him most positively.

His irregularity was not marked in these years of Roosevelt and Taft, but it came to the attention of the leaders clearly enough for them to become lukewarm on Norris as a member of Congress. They gave him no patronage, which according to their political axioms would end his career. The innocent member from Nebraska had never thought of patronage as essential to a public career. In any event, he did not ask for or receive the privilege of naming even one man for an appointive position during the ten years he served in the House. The Senator thinks this is a record, and in all probability he is right.

Without patronage and without any other help from the party organization, Norris had to fight his own campaigns for re-election, and he fought them with vigor. During this decade of service in the Lower House of Congress, the man who put Nebraska on the political map, William Jennings Bryan, and not the man who has kept it on the map, Norris, was the state's most famous man. Incidentally, the Great Commoner was quite unlike Congressman Norris in his attitude on patronage, not being above doing what he could for "deserving Democrats" when he became secretary of state. Bryan was a strong party man and he came into Norris's district in every campaign, advocating with silver-tongued eloquence the election of Norris's Democratic opponent. After the third such campaign, one in which Bryan had been particularly active and which Norris had won by twenty-two votes, the Commoner told the Congressman that he had really preferred him to the Democrat whom he had supported for reasons of political expediency.[23]

Before 1910, Norris had been politically careless, some might say reckless, but he did not until that date attempt political suicide. Speaker Joseph Cannon ruled the House and had reigned as a tsar for some years. Few believed that his power could be broken. Some congressmen hoped that a well-timed attack might prove successful. The leader of this group was George W. Norris. This seemingly non-offensive but agile and sharp-toothed prairie wolf had already scratched Cannon's ankles several times in parliamentary encounters. He was eager to have a good big bite. He and several other insurgents prepared a resolution. Norris put it in his pocket, and, with that infinite patience which has always characterized his political tactics, he sat quietly in the House for months and months waiting for his opportunity. A resolution not on the calendar required a two-thirds vote for consideration unless the matter was made "privileged by the Constitution." On a rather dull day in the House, the Speaker had ruled that a motion relating to the census was "privileged by the Constitution" since the Constitution made the census mandatory. The Great Moment had arrived. Norris drew from his pocket the well-worn piece of paper on which was written his resolution (H. Res. 502) to deprive the Speaker of his authority to appoint the Rules Committee, and to confer that authority upon members of the House.[24] He stated that his resolution was privileged by

[23] Neuberger and Kahn, *op. cit.*, p. 33.
[24] *Congressional Record*, 61st Congress, 2nd Session, p. 3292.

the Constitution since that instrument required each House of Congress to make its own rules just as it required the Congress to provide for the census. The bitter struggle got under way. Norris and his coalition of Democrats and insurgent Republicans spread terror in the ranks of "Cannonism." The opposition tried to force a recess, but the coalition succeeded in beating this motion by three votes. The session went on through the night and well into the afternoon of the next day, during which time Norris had no rest or sleep. On the next day Speaker Cannon ruled Norris's resolution out of order. The Gentleman from Nebraska appealed to the House, and it overruled the Speaker's ruling. A dynasty had fallen, and the name of George W. Norris appeared for the first time in newspapers and magazines throughout the country.

Regular Republicans wanted Norris to run for governor of his state in 1912, but Norris supported Theodore Roosevelt and ran for the Senate. He has been in the Senate ever since, always against the wishes and best efforts of the Republican party and sometimes even against his own wishes. In 1924, he was discouraged and disillusioned. Seeing the hopelessness of La Follette's campaign for president and knowing no way to secure the enactment of a progressive program in this prosperous Coolidge era, he declared that he would not be a candidate for re-election. However, a newspaperman suppressed his telegram declining the nomination and he was re-elected by a comfortable majority. Six years later, the Republican regulars decided to retire Norris. Their patience was utterly exhausted as a result of his constant attacks on Coolidge and Mellon policies, his campaign against Vare in Pennsylvania in 1926, his support of Smith in 1928, and his failure to follow President Hoover. In 1930, the National Republican organization had the support of some of the good people of Nebraska who could not forgive Norris for advocating the election of Smith two years earlier. Even Mrs. Norris had publicly disagreed with her husband on the Smith candidacy. The Republicans found the now notorious grocerman, George W. Norris, and groomed him for the 1930 senatorial race. The Nebraska Supreme Court ruled "Grocer George" off the ballot on a technicality. Having failed to shelve Norris in the primaries, conservative Republicans supported the Democratic nominee, former

Senator Gilbert M. Hitchcock, in the November election. The vote stood Norris, 247,118; Hitchcock, 172,795.

Norris wanted to retire in 1936. This was the best news the regular Republicans of Nebraska had heard for years, and in view of the Senator's age (seventy-five) they had good reason to believe both he and they would be accommodated. They nominated a tried and true one hundred per cent Republican, Robert G. Simmons, to succeed Norris. The Democrats were unfortunate in their primary, which resulted in the nomination of a political accident, demagogic Terry Carpenter. Forty thousand Nebraskans nominated Norris by petition. The Democrats urged Carpenter to withdraw, but he refused. President Roosevelt, with Norris on the platform with him at Omaha, declared: "George Norris's candidacy transcends state and party lines. In our national history we have few elder statesmen who, like him, have preserved the aspirations of youth as they accumulated the wisdom of years. He is one of the major prophets of America. Help this great American to continue a historic career of service." Democrats, even anti-Roosevelt Democrats, anti-Landon Republicans, and independents heeded the President's call.

Why has Norris, considering his attitude toward the old parties and their discipline, not aided in the formation of a new party? The answer is that he has no more faith in new parties than he has in the old parties. Unless a new party's leaders were Christlike men, he says, "—in which case they would not be political leaders—its candidates would be dictated by a few bosses conferring in private, just as in the old parties." [25] He does not regard parties as necessarily positive evils, but he believes that dictation by the party organizations is a denial of the basic principle of democratic government, a grave danger to free political institutions.

Why will Nebraskans continue in public life a man who has such scant regard for party and who votes on the unpopular side of issue after issue? In 1931, one of their editors, Charles S. Ryckman of Fremont, won the Pulitzer Prize with an editorial in which he maintained that the people of his state returned Norris to the Senate time after time because through him they

[25] Neuberger and Kahn, *op. cit.*, p. 155.

could express their contempt for the East. Now it may be that a few voters have some such motive in mind, and it is a fact that the editor's theory sounds well. But it is said that Nebraskans generally deny being influenced by any such consideration. They vote for Norris because he is honest, unselfish, devoted to the people's interest, absolutely fearless, and the personification of independence. Only the old party hacks and stodgy party newspapers object to Norris's freedom from political restraint. Before each election their mutterings sound ominous indeed. But it ought to be an old story by now that the seeming unpopularity and certain defeat of a particular candidate is an illusion as easily created by political organizations and their newspaper allies as it is smashed by the majority of plain men and women who have a way of becoming very articulate on election day.

Not only does the Senator scorn the restraints of party, he scorns every other type of restraint which men may attempt to impose upon his judgment and conscience. In 1917, as the country was entering the World War, one of Nebraska's senators, Mr. Hitchcock, led in the movement while Norris, politically speaking, tied himself to the mouth of a cannon in opposing American participation in that war. In March, 1917, as Congress approached adjournment, he and his close friends, La Follette and Lane, and eight other senators, prevented from coming to a vote the bill which was to have authorized the arming of American ships against German submarines. This was the "little group of willful men, representing no opinion but their own," who rendered "the great Government of the United States helpless and contemptible." These men denied that they were conducting a filibuster since they confined their remarks to the subject at hand and made no use of quorum calls. They pointed out further that those favoring the measure did much of the talking during the so-called filibuster. Yet they did prevent the measure from coming to a vote and thus from becoming a law, and President Wilson's characterization of them as quoted above was heartily applauded by the country, particularly the East. The obstructionist senators were excoriated by all "patriots." Articulate elements in Nebraska denounced Norris as few men have ever been denounced. Norris offered to resign his seat in the Senate if the voters of Nebraska in a special election expressed that desire. He made this offer against the advice of La Follette who said that he would not have a chance against the war hysteria then raging. But the Governor of Nebraska refused to agree to Norris's proposal, thus saving Norris from possible repudiation by the people.

A few weeks after the memorable contest in the Senate, Norris went to Lincoln to explain his action. He arrived at Lincoln Sunday morning, and his speech was scheduled for Monday night. That Sunday was the darkest, most lonely day of the Senator's life. Few people came to see him, and nearly all of them advised him to leave town in order to escape violence. The only person who encouraged him was a reporter from the Nebraska *State Journal* who slipped in after dark, got Norris's version of the "filibuster," and assured the Senator that the story would appear in the paper as he had given it, since the *Journal* authorities had all gone home and would not be back at the office until the issue was off the press. The reporter told Norris that he approved of his position and admired his independence and courage. Norris was grateful for this to the point of tears, but he still did not know that he had another friend in the city. Grim and determined, he stepped out on the platform that Monday night, a lonely figure, and faced a very large and ominously silent audience. Serving as both chairman and speaker, he began, "I have come home to tell you the truth." Almost at once the realization that George Norris never told anything but what he firmly believed to be the truth seemed to spread over the audience. They listened attentively as he outlined the developments which were leading us to war. Presently they applauded and shouted, and they stood up and yelled when he denounced the newspapers for not giving the full story. His triumph was complete. He declared he "would be willing to go through it all again for such a vindication." His other speeches in Nebraska met with equally favorable receptions.[26]

His faith in the plain people restored, the Senator returned to Washington, and on April 4, with five other senators, voted against war with Germany. We are declaring war, he said, "all because we want to preserve the commercial right of American

[26] Neuberger and Kahn, *op. cit.*, pp. 99 ff.

citizens to deliver munitions of war to belligerent nations." "I feel that we are committing a sin against humanity and against our countrymen. I would like to say to this war god, You shall not coin into gold the lifeblood of my brethren . . . I feel that we are about to put the dollar sign upon the American flag." [27] This last sentence, deliberately spoken, brought upon the Senator a round of denunciation and condemnation seldom visited upon public men. In the Senate and in the pulpit and in the press the man who seemed to be throwing away his political career by courageously following his conscience was held up as the worst possible type of citizen. He had forfeited his place among God-fearing and patriotic men! Senator James A. Reed (Missouri), referring to the "dollar sign on the flag" sentence, said: "If that be not treason, it takes on a character and guise that is so near to treason that the enemies of America will gain from it much consolation." [28]

In a running debate with Reed, Norris said that he meant what he had said, no more, no less. "I have not, I know, intended to cast any reflections upon any living being . . . Reflections, however, have been cast here today upon me which are ten million times greater than anything I have said. I am not going to take them seriously, because I believe, as I have said, that there is at this time a feeling controlling not only the country, but Members of this body, by which men are not in full possession of all their reasoning faculties. The Senator from Missouri has said something that at some time he will regret, I believe." [29] Nine years later, standing in his place in the Senate of the United States, the Senator from Missouri manfully declared that the six senators who had voted against the war performed "the most superb act of courage this century has witnessed." [30] Of all the votes the Senator from Nebraska has cast in the Senate, the vote against the war gave him the most trouble and the greatest satisfaction.

Since the World War, Norris has become increasingly famous as a persistent battler for political reform, social legislation, and government ownership of public utilities. For years he advocated

[27] *Congressional Record,* 65th Congress, Special Session, p. 214.
[28] *Ibid.,* p. 215.
[29] *Ibid.,* p. 216.
[30] *Ibid.,* 69th Congress, 1st Session, p. 11651.

the abolishment of the "lame duck" session of Congress, the old Congress which held its session from December until March, although a new Congress had been elected the previous November. This historical curiosity (it dated from an act of the Confederation Congress and an act of the First Congress under the Constitution) was to Norris a political enormity. The least that could be said against it was that it was downright silly for a group of adults to continue in office for four months after their successors had been duly chosen. It was undemocratic for the people to be required to wait for thirteen months for their newly elected Congress to begin its work, and it was a gross violation of the representative principle for the old Congress, scores of whose members had been repudiated, to hold another session after the election. And this was not all. This "lame duck" session had to adjourn on March 4, and it was so rushed to get its work done that there was always a jam at the end of the session. Furthermore, the short session and the fixed date for adjournment gave filibusters excellent opportunities to ply their trade. Then, too, and this was very bad in Norris's opinion, representatives of the president's party who had been defeated (lame ducks) the previous November were subservient to the president during this session, having every reason to expect payment from the president in the form of administrative appointments.

Although constitutional amendments are ordinarily proposed by the Committee on the Judiciary, Norris was so determined to get his amendment before the Senate that he had it reported by the Committee on Agriculture and Forestry, of which he was chairman. On February 13, 1923, it passed the Senate by a large majority. The House of Representatives, under "lame duck" leadership, defeated the proposal, thus demonstrating a part of Norris's argument for the amendment. Interest in the amendment lagged, but Norris continued to fight for it at every session. He put it through the Senate several more times, each time to find it blocked by the House. The House finally gave up to Norris in 1932. It was ratified by the states a year later, and its author now styled himself "the father of the Twentieth Amendment."

For some decades a few professors and others have thought that there was no good reason and that there were several bad ones for the two-house state legislature which nearly everyone else thought was inseparable from any system of free political institutions. Some of the arguments which intelligent but conventional-minded men made in proving the necessity for this bicameral legislature would indicate that they were unconscious humorists. Long ago Norris examined the operation of the bicameral legislature and found it wanting. His principal arguments for a one-house legislature were that it would abolish the secret conference committee, the joint committee which really does the legislating on all important matters; that the one-house system would force the legislators to assume direct responsibility for their work, whereas the bicameral plan permitted the members of each house to hide behind the members of the other; and that lobbyists would find it much more difficult to confuse and mislead legislators. He would have the members of his legislature few in number, elected on non-partisan tickets, and paid adequate salaries.[31]

He did not press this idea upon Nebraskans at once, perhaps because he had seen the same idea presented in other states and turned down. In 1934, impressed by his success in finally securing the adoption of the "lame duck" amendment, many Nebraskans asked him to lead the movement for a unicameral legislature in their state. A constitutional amendment was drafted and placed on the ballot by petition. The campaign for its adoption did not start in earnest until the second week in October, when, returning from his vacation, Norris found that at least 430 of the state's 440 newspapers were opposed to the amendment and that it was commonly regarded as already defeated. He took the stump and went all over the state, giving attention particularly to the unrepresentative and secret work of the conference committee under the existing bicameral system. The people voted 286,086 for the amendment and 193,152 against it. Norris gives full credit to his faithful aides in this campaign and to the people full credit for their intelligence, but there is no doubt that the victory was very largely the work of the Senator.

Other political reforms to which Senator Norris has given his attention include the abolishment of the electoral college and the

[31] *New York Times*, January 28, 1923. On this subject see J. P. Senning, *The One-House Legislature*, New York, 1937.

spoils system and the democratization of the Supreme Court. His ungenerous designs on the archaic electoral college were originally tied up with his still more heartless plan of making "dead ducks" of "lame ducks." By dividing his project he achieved the second part of his objective. He continues to attack the electoral college from time to time. In 1934 his amendment for its oblivion failed to pass the Senate by just two votes.[32]

Norris has always detested the spoils system and spoilsmen, from the lowliest political henchman to the postmaster general. Above the clamor for spoils, his voice has been heard, over and over again, calling for merit. But it has seldom been heeded. It is a matter of great gratification to him that his Tennessee Valley Authority is relatively free from the baneful effects of spoils. A victory for the merit principle may be recorded here and there, but the Nebraskan has found that it is more difficult to separate the politician from his loaves and fishes than it is to bag "lame duck" Congressmen or make one house legislate where two houses legislated before.

Although standing in reverence of the people, Senator Norris does not stand in reverence or awe of the institutions which they have set up for their government. For a generation or more, the American symbol of governmental perfection has been the Supreme Court. It could do no wrong; it could commit no error. No impious hand should be laid upon it by statute or by constitutional amendment. Norris was one of a few senators who, in the Coolidge era, boldly proclaimed that the judges in this Court were human beings who were no more able to rise above their background, their training, their preconceptions than hundreds of thousands of other honest men. No violence was done to his views by the plank in the platform of the La Follette Progressives (1924) which called for the abolishment of the power of the Court to nullify acts of Congress and an elective judiciary. His criticisms of the Court were intensified by its decisions against the New Deal. "Monopoly, special privilege, the interests of predatory selfishness have lost their old commanding influence at the White House and Capitol," he said in 1937. "They

[32] J. E. Kallenbach, "Recent Proposals to Reform the Electoral College System," *American Political Science Review*, XXX (1936), 924.

are making their last stand in the Federal Courts. There too often they still have their way." [33] He continues to say that a simple majority of the Supreme Court should not declare an act of Congress unconstitutional. It takes a unanimous verdict of a jury of twelve men to find a man guilty of murder, he says. Why should the Court find a statute of Congress "guilty" of unconstitutionality by less than a unanimous vote? He is willing, however, to let the Court void a statute by a 7 to 2 vote.[34] Another significant item in his program for Court reform is appointment of judges for a term of years instead of for life.

The great monument to the industry and pertinacity of Norris is the Tennessee Valley development. This is the triumph of his "economic radicalism," a state of mind which he acquired slowly and only after much conversation with La Follette and others of his school, many trips to power sites, and long periods of study and reflection. Before 1929, the Nebraska senator had earned the reputation for political liberalism and he had received much hate for opposing our entrance into the World War, but the public was only vaguely conscious of the growing "un-Americanism" of his economic thoughts, thoughts which could not be forgiven so quickly as his opposition to the war. Yet Norris had interested himself in the power question even before he had entered the Senate, and his estimate of the potentialities of hydroelectric power and his early concern that it be held by the government for the use of all the people are among his chief claims to the title of "major prophet."

In 1912, he stood for a long time by a roaring waterfall in eastern Washington. Near by was a town which had not felt more than the first current of the electric age. Norris wanted to know why the leaping cataract had not been harnessed for power. A native informed him that Jim Hill owned all the power sites in that vicinity. Norris frowned and puffed his cigar meditatively. In the days and months which came as he puffed many other cigars and pulled on his pipe, it seemed unjust, scandalous, monstrous to him that a man should own a segment of a river. He

[33] L. H. Robbins, "Norris Restates a Liberal's Credo," *New York Times Magazine*, May 30, 1937.
[34] *New York Times*, January 12, 1936.

started his campaign for government control of water power to the end that it be kept from the hands of private monopolies and be used for the benefit of the people to whom it had been given "by God-Almighty." He prophesied that the day would come when coal would be almost forgotten, when water power converted into electricity would furnish the greater part of our light, heat, and power.[35]

The World War left the United States government in possession of a giant plant at Muscle Shoals which had been used for the manufacture of nitrates for munitions. Republican victories in 1918 and 1920 placed Senator Norris at the head of the Agricultural Committee. Hardly had Norris taken over the chairmanship, when Henry Ford came forward with his offer to take Muscle Shoals off the government's hands, to take charge of its white elephant, to "get it out of business." This marks the real beginning of Norris's tremendous concern over hydroelectric power. The Ford offer, carrying a provision to manufacture nitrogen for fertilizer at not more than eight per cent profit, was very popular with the farmers. Radical Non-Partisan League farmers in North Dakota insisted that the Ford proposition be accepted without delay, and much less radical farmers and farm organizations, including those in Nebraska, joined in the demand. Norris studied the offer and announced his unqualified opposition to its acceptance. He said that the magic name of Henry Ford (in 1921 he was even being boosted for the presidency) had dulled the farmers' senses, and he denounced their Washington lobbyists. Reporting on the Ford offer,[36] Norris's Committee stated that it was the "most wonderful real estate speculation since Adam and Eve lost title to the Garden of Eden," and inquired "why a warranty deed to the Capitol at Washington is not included in the great transfer of government property to this wonderful corporation." A combination of forces prevented the acceptance of the Ford offer, but the most decisive force was Senator Norris. In 1924, Ford withdrew his proposal.

Norris, of course, proposed government operation of Muscle Shoals, but the Underwood bill, having the support of President

[35] Neuberger and Kahn, *op. cit.*, pp. 202-4.
[36] July 20, 1922.

Coolidge, was brought forward as a substitute for the Norris proposal. By its terms, Muscle Shoals was to have been privately operated. Norris fought this proposal at every step. Speaking in the Senate on December 17, 1924, he said that he had recently had five or six short investigations going on and that he was led to the belief "that today there is not in the United States a place where this mighty power trust does not have its hold. You can trace the electric light in Omaha and the electric light in the South, and they both wind up in Wall Street." He showed the connection between the Alabama Power Company, the Electric Bond and Share Company, and the General Electric Company, and he concluded, "we are in the grip of the water-power trust." The Underwood bill actually passed both Houses of Congress, but not with identical stipulations. Consequently it was referred to a conference committee. It was assumed, however, that the bill was as good as passed, and *Current History* for March, 1925, announced that "the conference committee came to an agreement on February 5 and the bill was sent to the President." [37]   Norris knew that the conference report would have to be approved by the two Houses before the bill could be sent to the President, and it was at this point in the procedure that he turned defeat into victory. He attacked the committee's report on a point of order, the point of order being that the committee had placed an entirely new provision in the bill, one that was in neither the House bill nor the Senate bill. "Mr. President," said Norris earnestly, with only a minute left to speak: "I appeal to Senators. We are about to vote on something that will go down in history. . . . This is the most important point of order I have heard raised in the Senate of the United States, and the real question is, Are we to permit legislation in behalf of 110,000,000 free people to be made in secret, in conference, or are we going to insist that it be made in the House and the Senate." [38] The Senate voted to send the bill back to conference, where it remained. Muscle Shoals continued to be government property. Thus Norris, who had been able to rout the forces of Cannon when they had raised a point of order against his resolution to deprive the Speaker of the

[37] P. 923.
[38] *Congressional Record*, 68th Congress, 2nd Session, p. 4403.

House of his power to appoint the Committee on Rules, won a great battle for government operation of Muscle Shoals by raising a point of order on a measure which would have put the Shoals in private hands. If Norris had not distinguished himself along so many other lines, we might be referring to him as a very skillful parliamentarian.

With both the Norris and Underwood bills defeated, Congress decided to pass the "Alabama Ghost" on to a commission for investigation and report. A conservative commission was appointed and $100,000 was appropriated for its work. Norris, ever ready with his shafts of ridicule, said that he knew exactly what the report would contain, word for word. "I could write that report in just a few hours and have it all ready for the commission," he declared. Then he said he was going to have a little time on his hands during the summer, and he "wouldn't mind getting a little of that $100,000 that the President was going to spend to find out about Muscle Shoals." [39]

Norris had won many members of Congress to his side on the Shoals question and he continued to make progress, but New Englanders and conservative southerners (the overwhelming majority of southerners) remained firm foes of his plan. It goes without saying that private utilities were his most active opponents. Yet, in 1928, Norris was able to put through Congress by almost a 2 to 1 vote a resolution for federal operation of Muscle Shoals. President Coolidge disposed of this measure as quietly as possible by means of the pocket veto.

The Senator continued to study the power question, to study it first hand with engineers and by knocking at the doors of users of electricity, both urban and rural, both in the United States and in Canada. Whenever there was a fight between private and government power interests, Norris entered on the side of the latter. He kept his issue very much alive by presenting comparisons between private and public rates. During Hoover's term of office, Norris again put through Congress his resolution for government operation of Muscle Shoals. The President said that this was an engineering problem and that he would base his decision for or against the bill on engineering facts. He referred

[39] *New York Times*, April 2, 1925.

the matter to the heads of the executive departments. Norris had a word on this procedure: "The great engineer is asking advice on an 'engineering project' from those who are not engineers, and when those who are not engineers tell the engineer what to do with an 'engineering project,' the engineer will know whether to sign or veto the bill." [40] Norris was sure that Hoover believed the bill needed careful study and a vigorous veto! In due time the veto message was written.

But in these days the Boulder Canyon project was moving forward, the Federal Trade Commission was exposing the propaganda activities of the power industry, and, most significant of all, the steady accumulation of economic disasters was causing the great body of American people to lose some of their old faith in "individualism" and listen to Norris's "socialistic schemes" with much less horror than formerly. Then came 1932 and Roosevelt, whom Norris had been watching approvingly on the power issue for several years. Norris supported him "before Chicago" and in the campaign gave him every ounce of strength his seventy-one years could muster. After the election, he stood with the President-elect at Wilson Dam and through tears of happiness saw his dreams coming true.

Together the two men sat down and planned the great project. The President's message to Congress advocating the establishment of the Tennessee Valley Authority was the official approval of Norris's twelve-year dream. If the Tennessee Valley development is the most successful of all New Deal experiments, it is largely because the President has constantly sought the advice of George Norris, who from long years of study is familiar with every phase of the problem. Plans for other TVA's are taking shape, rural electrification goes forward and Norris takes his place as the statesman of the electric age, a place certainly as high as that occupied by technical experimenters who have demonstrated the uses of electric energy.

In the character of George William Norris are combined the democracy of Jefferson, the humanity of Lincoln and Bryan, and the courage of Cleveland and the elder La Follette. In his simplicity and modesty Norris most resembles Lincoln, but he lacks

[40] Neuberger and Kahn, *op. cit.*, p. 221.

something of the tolerant and forgiving spirit of the Emancipator. The sardonic, caustic humor which Norris uses as a weapon in debate contrasts with the mellow, conversational humor of Lincoln. There is a suggestion of Lincoln in the Nebraskan's melancholy expression. Norris is as honest as Lincoln or any other man who has made a place in American history. One is not likely to refer to Norris as "Honest" George Norris, for that might possibly convey the impression that his honesty had at one time been questioned.

More suspicious and bitter than his near-progressive friend, William E. Borah, Norris is less plagued by these qualities than was his friend La Follette. The Wisconsin senator knew no compromise; Norris can yield a point if it does not endanger his program. Borah and Norris often saw eye to eye with La Follette on human rights, but the Idaho lawyer sometimes balked when a problem required a little pioneering on legal or constitutional lines. Borah goes back to the Fathers on the subject of states' rights; Norris considers states' rights a theory which serves no purpose other than to block necessary action on the part of the national government. Borah wins easily in an oratorical contest with Norris, but the Nebraskan is as effective as the Silver-Tongued Orator of Boise in presenting an issue to the plain people. Borah is lofty and impersonal in his speeches; Norris is often "hammer and tongs," and he does not mind singeing beards.

Few if any men in public life study more than Norris. He is patient, persistent, and indefatigable. A master of the intricacies of parliamentary procedure, he watches and waits for his opportunities, the greater number of which did not come until he had spent thirty years in Congress.

If it is possible (and there are those who think it is) for one to oppose large standing armies, compulsory military training in schools, and big navies, and still be a patriot, Norris is a patriot.[41] He is a patriot in that he believes in America, in her duty to maintain peace and make possible the good life for all her citizens.

The miracle of Norris may be in his absolute independence of political parties. We search the pages of American history in vain

[41] Norris, having no faith in dictators, yielded some ground to the big navy people in 1938.—*United States News*, March 28, 1938.

for his equal. Borah has often been independent, but he admits that he has been a regular Republican from time to time. La Follette was independent, but he was simply independent of the Republican party. He actually believed in political parties and went so far as to run for president on a third party ticket. Norris scorns all parties. It may be that the American people are not as much interested in parties and party regularity as the politicians think they are. Of the Republicans who survived the elections of 1932-1936 a very large per cent had regularly flirted with Democrats and ardently courted independent voters.

There is some temptation to say that Norris has continued in public life because of his independence, honesty, and courage. No doubt these traits have endeared him to the voters with the passing of the years, but they were not as much appreciated in the middle-aged Senator as they are in the Nebraska Institution in his septuagenarian years. Norris has had some luck. He was first elected judge by the narrowest margin and several times he just missed being defeated for Congress.

Norris has never been a radical, unless that term should be applied to anyone who opposes the status quo. He was not even a good progressive until he was near the half-century mark. After thirty years of warfare he is still a progressive. Familiar figures are the conservative old men who were radical in youth and liberal in middle age. Some of them still imagine themselves to be crusaders. What has happened, of course, is that the world has passed by and left them where they were a generation before. Many of the progressives of 1910 were quite through "progressing" in 1918 or 1920. Norris has never wearied. He has continued to find new progressive solutions for new problems. As Brandeis the statesman-jurist has been able to write judicial opinions to fit the changing order from 1916 to 1937, so Norris has presented his legislative proposals in harmony with the new demands. His concrete proposals change, but they all partake of the spirit of the La Follette-Lane-Norris combination of 1913-1917. He has "preserved the aspirations of youth" as he has "accumulated the wisdom of years" and he "stands forth as the very perfect, gentle knight of American progressive ideals." [42]

[42] Franklin D. Roosevelt, quoted in Neuberger and Kahn, *op. cit.*, pp. 301, 326.

5

ROBERT F. WAGNER:
PILOT OF THE NEW DEAL

By John C. O'Brien

I

ROBERT F. WAGNER MAY BE APTLY CALLED THE LEGISLATIVE pilot of the New Deal. He has fathered the major enactments giving effect to the Roosevelt conception of social security. The short-lived blue eagle was born in the pages of an act that bore his name. A half dozen new federal agencies owe their origin to his labors. In short, his name is written in bolder letters across the legislative record of the last five and one half years than that of any other member of Congress. Yet he himself remains a blurred and shadowy figure. He is extolled by liberals and leaders of labor as a champion of the common man second only to President Roosevelt himself; yet a score of public men who have contributed little, if anything, to the permanent record of the current social transformation live more vividly in the public mind. Visitors to the Senate galleries in Washington are more curious about the "pink whiskers" of Senator J. Ham Lewis than about the legislative godfather of the NRA, the low-cost housing program, the labor relations act, and unemployment insurance and old age pensions.

The truth is that Wagner does not put on a good show. An unassuming man, sincere and unaffected, he has neither the desire nor the talent for self-exploitation. He lacks utterly the flair for showmanship that enables some men to project their personalities constantly on the retina of the public eye. He is the reverse of a Huey Long. His sober speeches never make flaming headlines. He capitalizes no eccentricities. He never plays to the galleries. He abhors the tawdry insincerities of the vote-catcher. Not even his severest critics call him a demagogue. Furious controversy rages over the measures he advocates, but the barbs seldom touch him. He has never felt the sting of personal attack, either in the Senate

or in other forums where his ideas have been assailed. Newspapers, opposed to everything he stands for, refrain from impugn-
ing his motives. Sometimes, it is true, his friends deplore his
"gullibility." Such sad head-shaking over his "unwitting" lapse
into socialism amuses him.

"Think of it," he said to a friend recently. "A good Tammany
Democrat like me turning socialist! What's socialistic in limiting
hours of labor to give workers more leisure and to raise their
standard of living?"

A core of consistency runs throughout Wagner's political career.
He has always defended the cause of the "forgotten man." Although many of those who support the New Deal have little heart
for the Roosevelt program, Wagner is one of the dwindling band
who actually believe in the New Deal. He believes with Roosevelt that the New Deal is engaged in the task of preserving democracy in the midst of a world-wide collapse of that institution. He
is impatient with those who say that the supporters of the Roosevelt policies are parties to a conspiracy to overthrow the established
economic order and the American form of government. It may
be conceded that his own social philosophy has been broadened
by contact with Roosevelt's sweeping conception of a new day for
the "submerged one-third." But it would be a mistake to assume
that he is merely a legislative instrument for giving statutory form
to Roosevelt's program. The architecture of many of Wagner's
measures betrays the hand of the President and of the little group
of advisers derisively called the "brain trust." Nevertheless, the
underlying ideas had been running through Wagner's mind long
before Roosevelt nailed the New Deal banner to the White House
flag mast. In the Hoover administration, for example, Wagner
was crying like a prophet in the wilderness for a planned public
works program to take up the slack in employment during business recessions—the forerunner of the Public Works Administration. In 1932, he urged Congress to appropriate a large sum for
public construction. As early as 1911, he made a speech in the
State Senate in Albany, advocating unemployment insurance. He
was thinking about the problem of unemployment long before
the debacle of 1929 brought that problem to the foreground. He
was preaching greater security for the working classes twenty years

WIDE WORLD PHOTOS

ROBERT F. WAGNER

"His dexterity in riding two mounts headed in opposite directions has stirred the admiration of seasoned politicians and astonished politically inexperienced liberals."

before Roosevelt unfolded his comprehensive security program in messages to Congress. Wagner cannot be grouped with other sycophantic officeholders who have beaten the New Deal drum to keep up with the procession. Throughout thirty years of public life he has been a consistent advocate of most of the objectives now proclaimed from every New Deal pulpit.

When Roosevelt moved into the White House in the panicky March of 1933, Wagner was beginning his second term as United States senator from New York. In origin, early environment, and political background two men could not have been more dissimilar. Roosevelt was well born, his ancestral line on his father's side running back to the days when New York was a Dutch trading post and on the distaff side to an even earlier date. Wagner was the immigrant son of immigrant parents. Roosevelt had had a sheltered upbringing, had never rubbed elbows with the poor. Wagner was of the poor and had passed his youth among them. Roosevelt never knew privation. Wagner contended with poverty until after he reached manhood. Roosevelt began his political career fighting Tammany Hall, and, save for brief periods of temporizing for the sake of political expediency, continued to fight it. Wagner was cradled in Tammany and continued steadfastly loyal.

A conviction that it is the duty of government to assert the rights of the average man was the common ground on which the descendant of early settlers and the immigrant's son could meet. How Roosevelt, who was born to privilege, came by this belief has been variously explained by his biographers. One writer names Jeffersonian democracy, the progressivism of Theodore Roosevelt, and the New Freedom of Woodrow Wilson as the sources of the President's own political philosophy.[1] In Wagner's case, it is not necessary to look for any such academic influences. Wagner's efforts to improve the condition of the common man have been motivated by a vivid recollection of the hardships of his own youth, the privation, the poverty and the suffering that were the lot of his family and his family's neighbors. He remembers long weeks in his boyhood when he scarcely ever saw his parents save on Sundays, for on weekdays he was up in the morn-

[1] Ernest K. Lindley, *The Roosevelt Revolution* (New York, 1933), p. 7.

ing and away selling newspapers before his parents were awake
and he was still shouting "Extra!" in the evening long after
they had retired. In Wagner's own words, "My boyhood was a
pretty rough passage. It left its mark, and when I found myself
in a position to influence legislation, the thought of the social injustice I had seen all around me and still see all around me impelled
me to work for the passage of every measure that I thought would
ameliorate such conditions."

Wagner's working alliance with Roosevelt has been close and
unbroken. To some of Wagner's admirers this is a source of constant bewilderment. They cannot reconcile his New Dealish liberalism with his unshaken loyalty to Tammany Hall. His dexterity
in riding two mounts headed in opposite directions has stirred the
admiration of seasoned politicians and astonished politically inexperienced liberals. But no question of conflicting loyalties has ever
troubled Wagner's mind. Strange as it may seem to those who
have formed their opinion of Tammany from repeated exposés
of corruption in its administration of the affairs of New York
City, Wagner thinks of Tammany as "the cradle of modern
liberalism." [2] He will tell you he joined Tammany, nearly forty
years ago, because Tammany was the Democratic organization in
New York and he looked upon the Democratic Party as the party
of liberalism, the champion of the common man against the interests. Perplexing though it may be, the fact remains that Wagner
did erect a considerable edifice of progressive legislation while he
was Tammany floor leader in the state legislature and utterly dependent on Tammany's support.

In his relations with the Tammany leadership since the election
of Roosevelt, Wagner has shown extraordinary political sagacity.
Tammany, it will be remembered, supported Governor Alfred E.
Smith for the Democratic nomination for president in 1932 in a
fit of pique over Roosevelt's firm handling of removal proceedings against James J. Walker, Tammany mayor of New York.[3]
After his election, Roosevelt evened the score by keeping Tammany's fingers out of the patronage pie. This put Wagner in a

[2] From a speech delivered in New York on July 5, 1937, and reported in the *New York
Herald Tribune* and the *New York Times* of July 6.

[3] Mayor Walker resigned in September, 1932, while defending himself in removal proceedings instituted by Roosevelt, who then was governor of New York.

difficult position. He could not follow his colleague, Senator Royal S. Copeland, in openly siding with Tammany without foregoing the opportunity to collaborate with the President in the achievement of objectives in which he believed passionately. A politician less shrewd might have joined hands with Roosevelt in an attempt to overthrow the Tammany leadership. Wagner decided to ride out the storm. He remained strictly neutral but regular. Subsequent events proved the soundness of his judgment. In the 1933 mayoralty campaign, Tammany lost control of the city administration to Fiorello H. La Guardia, who benefited from a split in the Tammany ranks engineered (so Tammany believes) by the President. Wagner was inactive in the campaign but he gave nominal support to the regular Tammany nominee and thus retained his standing with the organization. Four years later Tammany joined with the Democratic leaders of the other four boroughs in Greater New York in an attempt to draft Wagner as the Democratic candidate for mayor.[4] Paradoxically, it was Wagner's New Dealism that prompted the Tammany leadership to select him to oppose La Guardia, who had solidified himself with labor by running the affairs of New York on the New Deal model. Wagner declined to run; he wanted to remain in the Senate and complete his unfinished legislative program.

In other branches of political strategy Wagner has not had to prove himself. His skill as a campaigner and vote-getter has never been put to a difficult test. Where a political machine is as impregnable as Tammany was in New York City when Wagner entered politics, a candidate does not have to give much thought to building or retaining majorities. It used to be Tammany's boast that a Chinaman running under the star [5] was bound to be elected. A candidate's only concern was to keep in the good graces of the organization. If he could persuade the leaders to give him a nomination, he did not have to worry about getting out the vote. The organization took care of that. It was not until Wagner bucked the Republican-dominated upstate hinterland as a candidate for the United States Senate that he ever experienced uncertainty

---

[4] The nomination for mayor was offered to Wagner in July, 1937, in anticipation of the fall mayoralty election.

[5] The star is the emblem which appears at the head of the Democratic ballot.

about the outcome of an election. But neither his first nor his second senatorial campaign was a personal triumph. A defection of 300,000 dry Republicans from the regular Republican nominee gave him his first victory by a narrow margin, and six years later he had the surging sweep of the first Roosevelt landslide behind him.

But Wagner need no longer rely on luck or machine-delivered votes to keep in office. If he should not seek renomination for a third term, his party leaders would draft him, for they need the strength he would bring to insure victory of the state ticket. No other candidate now in sight could command at once the elements of support so essential to victory in an industrial state like New York—the indorsement of President Roosevelt and the good will of organized labor. Both of these Wagner has earned by his zeal for labor and welfare legislation on the floor of the Senate.

Wagner's chief assets as a politician, aside from fundamental honesty and sincerity, are a rugged constitution, an easy, urbane manner, a memory for names and faces, and vast capacity for work. In stature he is under medium height and stocky, a solid but unimpressive figure. A firm mouth and strong chin would suggest a contentious nature if the heavy-lidded blue eyes were not so mild and friendly. Wagner's liking for people is indubitably genuine. His cordiality is not the feigned cordiality of the professional politician. He carries the dignity of high office lightly. He never went "high hat," the unpardonable political sin. He still lives in the Assembly district (an unfashionable neighborhood) which elected him to his first public office. When he returns to New York for week-ends, he never fails to drop around to chat with the "boys," the district leader, and the election captains, at his old Tammany clubhouse. Every Fourth of July, when Tammany celebrates its birthday jointly with that of the Republic, he makes a point of being on hand and usually he makes a speech extolling the organization.

A virtue often linked with sincerity is humility. It is one of Wagner's most engaging traits. He will tell you that his achievements, such as they are, were won by "plodding." If plodding is a synonym for persistence, Wagner may be called a plodder. He never scatters his fire. It is frequently remarked in the Senate press gallery that "Wagner always comes through with one or two big bills each session." Opposition does not discourage him. He began agitating for unemployment insurance in his first term and kept everlastingly at it until he got the social security bill passed in the session of 1936. He labored three years to bring his low-cost housing bill to a vote. A practical realist, he is always ready to compromise, to take half a loaf if he cannot get a whole loaf. He relies on his persuasiveness in the cloak room more than on debate on the floor to win support for his measures. Early in his first term he abandoned the idea that the way to be effective was to make two or three speeches a week. The passage of a bill, he discovered, seldom turns on oratory. On the few occasions when he does take the floor, he speaks in the manner of a lawyer arguing from a brief. His voice is of medium pitch and he holds it to an even key. He avoids personalities; neither invective nor flippancy is part of his oratorical method. His colleagues always give him a respectful hearing, but he has never been known to pack the galleries.

Although he is one of the hardest workers in the Senate, Wagner spends little time on the floor. In the early days of NRA, he assumed, in addition to his duties as a lawmaker, the arduous task of serving as chairman of the National Labor Board. Throughout the incredibly hot summer of 1933, he divided his time between the sessions of the Senate and hearings on wage disputes. Often the telephone would ring in the midst of the drafting of a wage agreement and he would dash back to the Capitol for a roll-call vote. He squanders time and energy in the preparation of bills and speeches, for he has a Teutonic passion for thoroughness. He is willing and eager to learn from anyone who knows more about a subject than he does; he calls constantly on departmental experts for information and reads reams of official reports. No member of Congress makes more frequent use of the research facilities of the Brookings Institution.

Some of Wagner's critics deny him any claim to political courage or independence. They say he has played up to labor with an eye to capturing the labor vote. They accuse him of slavish subservience to the New Deal.

The same, of course, may be said of many politicians, whether justly or not, it is difficult to say, for it is no easy matter to pass judgment upon the motives of a man in public life. Wagner voted against the Supreme Court reorganization and the government reorganization bills, the passage of which was ardently desired by the President and by labor. Such independence hardly supports the charge of slavish subservience, but who can say whether it was aversion to the measures or a shrewd appraisal of public feeling back home which dictated the votes? There is no question, however, that Wagner mistrusted the Court reorganization plan.

When we come to Wagner's support of labor and welfare measures, the burden of proof falls upon those who charge that he has been moved solely by political considerations. Wagner is no recent convert to labor's cause. He began to work for a greater measure of social justice long before labor had become a powerful political entity, and for twenty years he has steadfastly pursued that objective.

II

It has been said that Wagner's efforts to improve the condition of the common man were motivated by a recollection of the hardships of his own youth. He was born in Nastetten, Province of Hessen-Nassau, Germany, on June 8, 1877. When he was eight years old, his parents, Reinhardt and Helen Wagner, emigrated to the United States. They were humble laboring folk of the sturdy type who came to American shores in great numbers about that time. Arriving in Castle Garden, New York, on Christmas Day, 1885, the Wagners were met by an elder son, August, who had come over from Germany several years earlier. August supported the family until Reinhardt Wagner got a job as janitor of a tenement house in East 106th Street, at the northern edge of a section on the upper East Side called Yorkville, where the population was predominantly German.

The family income that first year was the meager sum of $15 a month, the cash Reinhardt Wagner received in addition to the use of a basement apartment. To eke out the slender family purse, young Robert sold newspapers before and after school hours. At first he earned only a few cents a day, for the competition in that neighborhood was keen. One day his brother took him to the amusement park at Coney Island for an outing. As they were waiting for the train at Brooklyn Bridge, Robert cast an appraising eye at the throngs boarding and leaving the elevated trains and decided that this would be a lucrative stand for a newsboy. The next day he moved in, just as another East Side lad, who was later to become governor of New York, moved out. That lad, Alfred E. Smith, had just got his first full-time job.

Young Wagner's ambition at that moment was to earn enough money to buy a suit of store clothes. Up till then he had worn castoffs of his father's, cut to his measure by his mother. Of all his youthful trials this was the hardest to bear, for he always set great store on his appearance and is today one of the neatest dressers in the Senate. It was a red letter Saturday afternoon when he took in the large sum of $3.18 and was able to make the coveted purchase.

After he had passed through the elementary schools, it was de-cided, after many family conferences, that Robert should enter the College of the City of New York, a tax-supported institution where there was no tuition to pay. To help out at home while pursuing his studies, Robert worked nights as a bellhop in the New York Athletic Club. His brother August, who was a second cook in the club kitchen, got him the job. Some of the club mem-bers for whom Robert ran errands subsequently became profes-sional associates. Many years later, the president of the club, Barstow Weeks, sat with Wagner on the Supreme Court bench of the state. A quick student, Wagner won scholastic honors, was admitted to the Phi Beta Kappa Society, and in 1898 was grad-uated with the degree of Bachelor of Science. That same summer he obtained a teacher's certificate and started to teach summer classes. He probably would have continued to teach but for one of his professors at City College who persistently urged him to quit teaching and study law. With borrowed money, he put him-self through New York Law School, receiving his LL.B. degree in 1900.

In the fall of 1898, the year Wagner was graduated from col-lege, New York was in the midst of an exciting gubernatorial campaign. Richard Croker was fighting his last battle as leader of

Tammany Hall. The Republicans had nominated Theodore Roosevelt. Croker, ignoring the advice of his shrewdest lieutenants, had forced the Democratic state convention to nominate August Van Wyck, brother of Robert A. Van Wyck, the Tammany mayor of New York. At the height of the campaign Wagner went around to the Algonquin Club, the Tammany headquarters in Yorkville, and offered his services as a speaker for Van Wyck. He recalls that he rehearsed his maiden speech for two days before a mirror, committing every word to memory. What impelled him to enlist for that campaign was a youthful ambition to try out his oratorical powers. He had debated a good deal in college and had always been on the winning side. Twice he had carried off prizes. But the Van Wyck-Roosevelt debate went against him. Roosevelt was elected.

Shortly after this defeat, the Tammany leadership passed from Croker to Charles F. Murphy. Croker left the organization in such ill repute that Murphy decided to clean house. His first move was to send abler and younger men to the state legislature. Wagner's term came in 1904. In the Assembly, the lower house, Wagner first met Al Smith, another protégé of Murphy's. They became fast friends and lived together during the sessions in an unpretentious hotel in Albany known as "The Tub." The rule had been that Tammany freshmen were to vote as the floor leaders dictated and leave the introduction of bills to the experienced members. But Murphy gave his fledglings a freer hand. Without waiting to serve an apprenticeship, Wagner stepped forward with a bill to reduce the fare on the Brooklyn elevated lines from ten to five cents. Ten cents, he argued, was more than working men could afford to pay. Such impudence stunned the old guard, who held public utilities in awe, but they voted for the bill when they learned to their astonishment that Wagner had Murphy's backing. The young assemblyman's elation over his first legislative victory was short-lived; a few days later the bill was vetoed by the Republican governor—the present Chief Justice of the United States Supreme Court, Charles Evans Hughes.

After serving three years in the lower house, Wagner was promoted to the state Senate, and two years later, in 1911, Murphy had him made Democratic floor leader. A newcomer who voted in the Democratic caucus to ratify Murphy's choice was Franklin D. Roosevelt, who had been elected from an upstate district comprising three Hudson River counties, of which Dutchess, the seat of the Roosevelt ancestral estate, was one. In a few weeks the Tammany floor leader and the young Dutchess county squire were at war.

As Murphy's field marshal, Wagner was trying to force the election of William F. (Blue-eyed Billy) Sheehan, a corporation lawyer, as United States senator to succeed the Republican incumbent, Chauncey M. Depew.[6] Roosevelt promptly raised the issue of "bossism." Murphy, he argued, had no right to dictate whom the legislature should elect. He corralled a bloc of votes sufficient in number to block the election and served notice on Wagner that he and his associates (upstate Democrats like himself) would absent themselves from party caucuses until Sheehan's name was withdrawn. The battle raged for weeks. Wagner held out for Sheehan until he realized the Dutchess county insurgent could not be moved. Then he advised compromise and Murphy and Roosevelt finally agreed on James A. O'Gorman, a Supreme Court justice from New York.

Roosevelt continued on the outs with Murphy, but he quickly made friends with Wagner, whom he had grown to respect. A year after the Sheehan row, he was vigorously supporting a factory code that Wagner was sponsoring in the Senate. That code had its inception in a legislative investigation conducted by Wagner in the summer of 1911. In March of that year, one hundred and forty girls had lost their lives in a fire that razed the Triangle Shirtwaist Factory in New York City. Wagner promptly introduced a resolution, which was adopted by both houses of the legislature, creating a commission to investigate factory conditions throughout the state. A young social worker had been one of the horrified spectators at the scene of the holocaust. Wagner gave her a job as an investigator for the commission. That started the public career of Frances Perkins, the present secretary of labor.

At the next session, Wagner presented fifty-six bills drafted by his legislative commission. All the bills were enacted, and they form the basis of New York's present factory code, which ranks

[6] In 1911 United States senators were elected by state legislatures.

among the most enlightened labor codes in the country. Before he left the Senate, Wagner added to the statute books a workman's compensation act, an act regulating the wages and hours of women and children in industry, and a widow's pension law.

While he was serving in the legislature, Wagner was also building up a law practice in New York City. His firm handled the usual run of refereeships and receiverships that come to faithful organization lawyers by assignment from Tammany justices on the bench. But Wagner himself made a specialty of labor law. His most celebrated case was one involving the legality of the so-called "yellow-dog" labor contract. As counsel for the American Federation of Labor, he challenged the legality of a contract the Interborough Rapid Transit Company had made with its employees, precluding them from affiliating with the Federation. Wagner's brief in the appeal to the highest court of the state attracted wide notice and is now used extensively as a text on labor law in law schools. It was quoted extensively in the debate in the United States Senate preceding the rejection of President Hoover's nominee for the United States Supreme Court, Judge John J. Parker, of North Carolina. Labor, it will be remembered, opposed Judge Parker because of injunction orders he had issued in labor disputes.

In 1918, when he was only forty-one years old, Wagner was elected to the Supreme Court.[7] He thought his life's ambition had been achieved and he looked forward to spending his remaining active years in the courtroom. He had won all the honors he could hope for in the legislature. For a few months, following the impeachment of Governor William Sulzer in 1914, he had been acting lieutenant governor. He had turned down an appointment as postmaster of New York City which was sent to the United States Senate in 1916 (without his knowledge) by President Wilson. He coveted no other political preferment. In decisions in cases involving public policy, Wagner, as a judge, continued to assert the rights of the common man. He affirmed the constitutionality of wartime emergency acts of the legislature prohibiting the boosting of rents and denying landlords the right to

[7] In New York the Supreme Court is not an appellate court but a court of original jurisdiction.

dispossess tenants for refusal to pay increased rents. He granted the first injunction in favor of a labor union, restraining an employer from interfering with union activities.

In due time Wagner might have advanced to the highest bench in the state, the Court of Appeals (he had been designated to sit on an intermediate appeals court, the Appellate Division of the Supreme Court), but in 1926 Tammany and the other Democratic leaders of the state insisted that he resign and run for the United States Senate. Wagner consented reluctantly. A Democrat had not been elected to the United States Senate from New York in a long time; moreover, Wagner was contented on the bench. Normally he would have been defeated. But his Republican opponent, Senator James W. Wadsworth, had incurred the enmity of two powerful groups within his own party. An outspoken advocate of repeal of the Eighteenth Amendment and a foe of suffrage for women, he offended both the drys and the women who wanted the vote. The drys alone swung enough votes in the strongly Republican upstate counties to a Prohibition candidate to elect Wagner by a narrow margin.

When Wagner took his seat in the Senate, the country was careening on the crest of the business boom that carried profits and prices to the dizzy pinnacle from which they crashed in the fall of 1929. Such prosperity had never been known anywhere. But Wagner thought he detected warnings of catastrophe around the corner. He undertook an exhaustive study of business recessions in relation to unemployment and came to the conclusion that employment was not keeping pace with the rapid increase in production. In the session of 1928, he brought forth a program which, he thought, would soften the blow if a recession did come. He urged an amendment to the general census law to permit an enumeration of the unemployed. He offered a bill authorizing the Department of Labor to collect and publish labor statistics. He proposed the creation of two new federal agencies—a stabilization board to plan a public construction program six years in advance and a Federal Employment Agency to facilitate the transfer of surplus labor to places where it might be needed. The bill for the collection of labor statistics became law in 1930. The plan for a six-year public construction program was enacted by Congress but died on the desk of President Hoover, who refused to sign it. During his first term Wagner also advocated measures to exempt from income taxes funds set aside by corporations for relief expenditures; to commit the federal government to relief contributions equivalent to one third of the amounts appropriated by the states, and to create a congressional commission to study unemployment insurance in this country and abroad. He assisted in framing the law creating the Reconstruction Finance Corporation. He was instrumental in enacting the 1932 Emergency Relief and Construction Act, which made available $325,000,000 for federal construction to provide jobs for the unemployed and another $1,500,000,000 to the RFC for the stimulation of self-liquidating construction work and low-cost housing for families of low income.

But Wagner's big chance did not come until the Roosevelt administration came into power. With a president who saw eye-to-eye with him and an overwhelming Democratic majority in each House, Wagner's effectiveness increased steadily. His bill to create a Federal Employment Agency went through without opposition. He was able to get an additional $500,000,000 in relief funds in 1933, and in the same year he put through the National Recovery Act, bringing to industry unprecedented control and planning and to labor new safeguards and something approaching equality of bargaining power with employers. The same act made available $3,300,000,000 for public works construction.

In subsequent sessions Congress enacted three bills which Wagner considers a new bill of rights for the workers of the country. These were the railway pension act, setting up a system of retirement pensions for railway workers; the Social Security Act, embracing some 25,000,000 wage earners and providing retirement pensions and unemployment insurance; and the National Labor Relations act, perhaps the most widely discussed of all of Wagner's measures, which assures labor the right to organize and bargain collectively with employers. Eventually these measures, Wagner is convinced, will serve to stabilize the economic order by bringing about a more equitable distribution of the national income, which, in turn, would maintain purchasing power at a firmer level than the country has ever known. But wage earners will not have attained a reasonable measure of security, in Wagner's opinion, until the federal government assists in the substitution of decent low-cost living quarters for slums and sets up a system of health insurance. Wagner's $3,000,000,000 housing bill is now before Congress [8] and a health insurance measure is the next order of business on his legislative calendar.

Fear of raising up overpowering opposition to the housing bill kept Wagner out of the historic battle over President Roosevelt's proposal for reorganization of the United States Supreme Court. Rather than incur the resentment of foes of the Court reorganization bill, Wagner refrained from taking a stand publicly, although he had given the administration his word privately that he would support the compromise bill, the shadow of the original which was finally called up for consideration but which was consigned to the Judiciary Committee's storage vaults after the death of Senator Joseph T. Robinson, of Arkansas.

In other fields than labor legislation, Wagner has been consistently on the liberal side. Before he went to Washington, he supported in the state legislature at Albany, a direct primary law and a corrupt practices act limiting campaign expenditures, and he voted for ratification of the constitutional amendment giving the vote to women. He sponsored jointly with Senator Frederick C. Van Nuys, of Indiana, the federal anti-lynching bill which threatens to split wide open the Senate Democratic majority. In short, there has been in Wagner's time in Congress no roll call on a major progressive measure in which he did not stand in the liberal column. He has been, indeed, to the New Deal legislative ship both pilot and deck hand—this son of Tammany Hall, "the cradle of modern liberalism."

[8] The housing bill has since been passed.

6

MILLARD E. TYDINGS:
THE MAN FROM MARYLAND

By Holmes Alexander

I

No one present at the Democratic Convention of June, 1936, could have dubbed that gathering a League of Contented Men. The late Joe Robinson, wielding the chairman's gavel, looked lonesome for his Arkansas mudbanks and his Democratic Principals. Bennett Clark, head of the committee that changed the two-thirds rule, had the southern lion by the tail and was plainly disturbed. The ancient Carter Glass could not decide whether to go home or stay put. Even Jim Farley was being pestered by requests to send Al Smith a special message to come down from New York and make up.

But it would have been difficult in all that harassed assembly to find a man as obviously confused and dejected as the senior senator from Maryland. This lean, red-haired six-footer, generally so jolly on these occasions, had the air of one attending a wake. The long, jutting jaw, which could wag so entertainingly in private and so eloquently in public, was set and grim. In the committee rooms, in the corridors, in his seat on the floor, Millard Evelyn Tydings was a gloom—no less.

Those who knew him understood how it was. For the two years then past not even the fork-tongued Carter Glass or Huey Long, the Louisana hog-caller, had more sulphurously assailed the New Deal and most of its works. Less than a twelvemonth prior to the Convention Tydings had cut loose at the "alphabetical monstrosities"; at the policy of "trying to run the government on hot air"; on expenditures which "are nothing less than bloodmoney —eventually to be wrung out of the backs of the working men and women of America."

These tirades, however, all dated from 1935. As the presidential year advanced, the Senator was seen to be pulling his punches. On March 5, 1936, he addressed a large rally in Baltimore:

"Some of the policies of the Roosevelt administration are not popular . . . What can be done about it? . . . We can support the Democratic ticket; we can support the Republican ticket, or we can take a walk. . . . I do not propose to take a walk."

So that was the mood in which he arrived at Philadelphia. He was for the party and against the administration, but he could hardly desert one without hurting the other. Also he had an election of his own coming up in '38, and "I don't propose to let anyone drive me out of the party by playing into the hands of the opponents." It was not a unique dilemma. Other men in Philadelphia had the same problem, and each reacted according to his nature. Tydings reacted according to his. He scornfully refused his place on the Platform Committee. He let it be known that he would make no seconding speech for the President's renomination.

Had he held out in this position the gesture would have been sublime. Perhaps it was too much to ask of political flesh and blood. At the eleventh hour, with Mr. Farley in a dudgeon and seconding speeching already on the floor, Tydings retreated. At least he relented. In a crabbed, half-hearted cantation of 169 lack-lustre words he said he was for Roosevelt's re-election.

It is descriptive of the man to say that people who knew and liked him best were genuinely shocked at this surrender. To be sure, nearly everyone else in office was doing the same thing. But Tydings, people felt, was different.

"If I can't vote my sentiments here—to hell with the job!" Thus in a characteristic moment he once expressed himself on the Senate floor. He is a man of that kidney—explosive, forthright, blunt—and samples of it are legion. There was the time, in a heated debate, when he abandoned oratory and began throwing left and right hooks at an opponent. Or again: taunted with having cast an indecent vote, he yelled out: "I could lick the liar who said that." Or still again: the occasion when he flew into a tantrum and threatened to resign from the Senate in order to take his argument direct to the people.

These are some of the things he might have done at the Convention. Looking back, he may be wishing that he had done them, for neither Mr. Roosevelt's gratitude nor the Senator's tolerance of his chief has lasted out the two years. If Mr. Tydings wins re-election to the Senate this November, it will be because he has beaten, not only the Republicans, but the New Deal.

II

He was born April 6, 1890. His father's line reached Maryland direct from England; the O'Neills, the distaff side, came there from Ireland via the Valley of Virginia. Like many Maryland families, this one was divided in the Civil War. One of the Senator's kin was wounded at Antietam; another died at the Wilderness. But before that, and since, there were soldiers in the family. Ensign John O'Neill received a handsome sword from the citizens of Philadelphia for his single-handed defense of Havre de Grace in the War of 1812. The Ensign's daughter, Matilda, was a soldier too. She boldly boarded the British flagship to plead for her father's life, and Admiral Cockburn gave her his own gold snuffbox as a token of esteem. More than a century later this same Ensign's great-great-grandson would earn two more military trophies—the Distinguished Service Medal and the Distinguished Cross—for valor under fire.

The Tydings were good Democrats from the time Thomas Jefferson first organized the Democratic-Republican party. One of them, following the custom of the day, was named Millard Fillmore after the thirteenth president. This man became a marine engineer and eventually arrived at Aberdeen in Harford County, the seat of the O'Neills, where he was superintendent of water transportation at the United States Proving Ground there. He married Miss Mary O'Neill and named their son Millard Evelyn.

It was natural for the boy to try out his father's profession. The future senator attended public grade and high schools at Havre de Grace. He applied for appointment to the Naval Academy and, failing that, took his Bachelor of Science degree at the State Agricultural College in 1910. He joined the engineering staff of the Baltimore and Ohio Railroad, which was tunneling the mountains of West Virginia. Somehow the work lacked an inner ring of satisfaction. Young Tydings was tall, redheaded, and restless. There

UNDERWOOD AND UNDERWOOD

MILLARD E. TYDINGS

" 'I do not propose to take a walk.' "

may have been a literary or an artistic bug biting him, for later he would write some books and paint some pictures. At any rate, he came home after a year to study law at the University of Maryland.

His return coincided with one of America's minor revolutions. Since the Civil War just one Democrat had sat in the White House. After the downfall of Grover Cleveland the party had drifted into a stupor which could produce nothing better than the muddle-headed William Jennings Bryan as its perpetual presidential nominee. Few thinking Democrats took the Great Commoner seriously, but with the approach of 1912 a new figure loomed on the skyline. Woodrow Wilson, with his promise of the New Freedom, the idealist and the intellectual combined, was just the candidate to catch a young man's fancy.

"I was the original Wilson man in my county," says Millard Tydings. "I first became interested in politics at the time of his contest for the presidency."

Moreover: "Some of us first voters organized a Democratic Club up at Havre de Grace. I had no idea at all of running for office, but when it was announced that, anyhow, young Millard Tydings couldn't go to the Legislature, I just naturally had to go and get myself elected."

He went to the House of Delegates at twenty-six, returned after the War—Mexico as well as France—to become speaker at the age of thirty. After that things rolled along: 1920, the State Senate; 1922 and 1924, the House of Representatives; 1926 and 1932, the United States Senate.

III

A man can rise in politics without being much of credit to himself or his country. If he steps warily around controversial subjects, if he plays ball with the bosses, if he can remember names and sound off at intervals with patriotic platitudes, then—given some luck—he can become an American lawgiver and remain one to the end of his mortal days. Indeed there is more truth than flippancy in the maxim that the men with the longest records in Congress are those with the softest brains and most pliant backbones.

Millard Tydings is no political hack, but he is every inch a political realist. He will risk the lightning when he has to, though he prefers not to defy it for bravado. He bucked the American Legion, of which he is a member, on Soldier Bonus. He sassed the wet nurses of the Working Man so impudently that the Maryland Federation of Labor demanded his immediate resignation. But he knows his way around. He helped to squelch the Court Plan, but did not publicly join the opposition till thirty-two other senators were on record. He used patronage, dumped in his lap after March, '33, to build up a potent political machine. He is a cheery first-name caller. He is a joiner of the Masons, Odd Fellows, Elks, Moose, Rotary Club. He is not above using his brilliant war record to facilitate an election.

This last, in fact, was a contributing factor to his first arrival in Congress. There had been a wild party in an Annapolis hotel and the Anti-Saloon League had its snoopers on hand to smell out a scandal. Candidate Tydings was not a whole-hog Wet at the time. He favored local town-and-county option, but that did not suit the League. "If I had become its tool, instead of using what little sense I have, I should have had its unqualified support." Instead he had its unqualified anger. On the testimony of one Horace Davis, the League accused Tydings of having been publicly and disgracefully drunk. The candidate retorted by suing for libel and by unfurling the Stars and Stripes in the well-known manner of the 1920's:

"When the superintendent of the Maryland Anti-Saloon League was sitting in a swivel chair with his feet upon his desk drawing his salary . . . I was standing in the muddy trenches of France . . . upholding the Constitution of my country."

There is more than flag-waving here. It illustrates the approved Tydings method of taking the aggressive away from an opponent. The salvo which he saved for the informer also shows that he can sling mud for mud:

"I want to ask Mr. Davis in the columns of your paper this question. 'Were you ever intoxicated in Worcester County, and if so, how many times? And, secondly, did you not have a fist fight . . . and what was your condition as to sobriety at the time?'"

Millard Tydings has never lost an election. On his way to the House and Senate he unseated Republican incumbents in normally

Republican years. He has everything it takes to make his own way. His physical vitality carries him over the long grind of campaigning without a sign of fatigue. His striking figure, his pugnacious thrust-out jaw with the mobile features above, his energetic stance on a platform, his sabre-like forefinger cutting the air above his head—it all gives him a dashing and gallant air.

Always he is best on the attack. Thus his forays against Hoover in '28 and '32 were much above anything he produced in defending Roosevelt in '36. Spontaneity flows free. "Almost always I speak extemporaneously, often over the radio, and vary this rule only on occasions where extemporaneous speaking must be limited to a given time or some outstanding occasion."

He likes to act out his oratory, and his wit is often deadlier than his anger. Once in the Senate, attacking an idiotic waterways bill, he wiped imaginary tears from his cheeks while picturing the need of dikes to keep the Atlantic Ocean out of Vermont. He can go into wild extravaganza or delicate satire. At the Victory Dinner in Raleigh, North Carolina, he audaciously pinked the President's Court Plan by speaking on the virtues of a "tripod Government" —and by meticulously neglecting to mention the name of Roosevelt. The Tarheels scarcely recognized the subtle burlesque till it was over. They had had no chance to cheer the Great White Father in Washington.

"I listened in vain," complained Ex-Governor Ehringhaus, "to hear the name of the great general who has led us to the victory we are celebrating. . . . It was like the play *Hamlet* with Hamlet left out."

To see Tydings in action on a platform is to doubt his statement that "I am not fond of speaking but simply employ it only as a means to an end." The whole impression is that of a man having the time of his life. His legal training—he has been at the Maryland bar since 1913—shows itself in his methods. He pounces upon factual evidence with which to accuse an opponent. He leads his enemy into ambush. He falls into personal discourse, asks leading questions, turns the audience into a packed jury. He was probably the first to use Mr. Hoover's unfortunate remark about a chicken in every pot. Some of his set-to's with prohibitionists were so masterful that the irreconcilable William D. Upshaw pronounced him "the smartest wet I have ever locked horns with," and actually campaigned for Tydings, preferring him "to wet-pussyfooting Republicans." As a well-rounded example of how the Senator can lump fact-citing, satire, aggressiveness like a prosecuting attorney, this is how he shillalahed his opponent in the congressional campaign of 1922:

"Sir—I find that you have never made a speech in Congress . . . that you have introduced but fifteen bills, three of which donate captured cannon to towns in your district and the other twelve for relief—possibly pensions—of approximately thirteen persons in your district. . . . In one hundred and fifty roll calls on important subjects I find that you have voted but eighty-six times and sixty-four times were either absent or not voting.

"My object in calling these matters to your attention is to challenge you to a debate."

IV

In the business of getting himself elected, a politician unavoidably leads a double life. He has the relations with his public—speeches, appearances, issues. He has also the backstage existence where bosses pull strings and swap favors. The naïve explanation that he ran for the legislature on a dare does not entirely cover the beginnings of Millard Tydings. Actually the young man arrived at Annapolis tied to the coattails of an adroit factional leader, the late James J. Archer, who stood that term for the State Senate. Archer was a wing commander of the forces of Senator Blair Lee which were engaged in a boss-battle with Governor John Walter Smith.

Had the young candidate been gifted with prophetic foresight, he might have enjoyed seeing how elements of his future were piecing themselves together. He himself would one day be general-in-chief of boss battles. And the very figures who would fight for and against him were being formed under his very nose. The year Tydings went to Congress, Albert C. Ritchie was going into the second of his four terms as governor. And another man, Howard W. Jackson, began the first of his three terms as mayor of Baltimore. In years ahead these three—Ritchie, Jackson, Tydings—would be the triumvirate of Maryland politics.

Of the trio Tydings had less desire and less aptitude for boss-hood. He was ambitious but not acquisitive. He was the ideal boss's candidate, a vivid personality, a clever speaker with no inconvenient ideals about reform. While Ritchie and Jackson were putting their separate organizations together, Millard Tydings kept his hands in his pockets. Having no machine of his own, he was quite willing to hitchhike to new conquests on theirs.

He rode the Ritchie locomotive first. It was what took him to the United States Senate. Ritchie's second term still had a year to run in 1926. He liked the governorship well enough to stay there indefinitely, but it was well to have an alternate berth just in case. So he chose Millard Tydings, as the saying went around Balti-more, "to keep a seat warm for him in the Senate."

The Democracy of the Free State gagged a little over this pill. Congressman Tydings, all agreed, was a good man in his place. He was making a name for himself in the House. One commenta-tor at Washington had told how "Observers saw this tall, lean, sandy-haired youngster . . . defending states' rights and handing verbal wallops at prohibitionists . . . He radiated sincerity; he shunned demagoguery; he never spoke unless he had something to say." That was all very well, but it did not prove that Millard Tydings had the class to make a senator. The Baltimore *Sunpapers*, which exert a stern moral influence on Democratic affairs, were quite peeved when he got the nomination without having to fight through a primary.

"The *Sun* does not believe that Mr. Tydings is the best material that the Democratic Party of Maryland could offer. We feel that there are older men in the Democratic Party who would have taken front rank among the intellectual leaders of the Senate."

Nevertheless, finding him to be "industrious and shrewd, cou-rageous and attractive," the *Sunpapers* supported Millard Tydings against the Republican incumbent, O. E. Weller, and saw him win in characteristic style. Colonel the Honorable Millard E. Tydings, as he was formally addressed, moved across the Capitol hall to be-come (people thought) a seat-warmer. Meanwhile Ritchie went on

being governor, and, by the next senatorial election, it was plain
that the substitute had won a regular place from which he was not
to be ousted. Tydings paid his debt of gratitude by a rousing nomination speech for Ritchie at the Chicago Convention of '32. But
the impact he made on the national consciousness inadvertently did
more for himself than for his nominee. The boot had changed feet.
If there were to be any more kicking of persons upstairs, then
Tydings, not Ritchie, was going to do it.

v

Aside from any larger aspect the arrival in the White House of
Mr. Roosevelt worked a mighty change in the political life of
Millard Tydings. He who had virtually kept hands off patronage
now found a huge load of it dumped in his lap. The spring and
summer of '33 was the breaking of a drought for the unemployed.
Millard Tydings saw to it that all the manna he could control fell
on Free State soil.

"I'll venture the assertion," he said, "that more people from
Maryland have found employment with the Federal Government
since March Fourth, with the possible exception of New York, than
from any State in the Union."

It was the truth. In all sincerity the Senator was using his opportunity to bestow relief jobs regardless of political connections. It
could not continue that way long. Soon he was learning things he
had known only by indirection. Whether he liked it or not, boss-
hood was being thrust upon him. He hated the whole idea. He
broke out in violent denunciation of the dirty work he had to do
when the political appointments came along.

"In the making of recommendations I have been moved at times
between amusement, pity, and disgust. One leader endorsed thirteen men for the same job. Only one could be named, yet the other
twelve believed they would have gotten it, had I followed the leader's recommendation."

His indignation at such everyday procedure is proof enough of
the sheltered life he had lived for twelve years in active politics.
But he soon learned how to gear those multitudes of little cogs to
his own needs. The hour was at hand when he could use the knowl-

edge. The rivalry between Governor and Mayor had become acute. The former had overstayed his welcome at the Executive Mansion. The latter's yen to be governor had become practically a neurotic obsession after fifteen years of waiting for Ritchie to retire. The break came in 1934 when Ritchie, against the advice of every sincere friend, came out for a fifth term after Jackson had already filed for the nomination.

The boss-battle broke in earnest now. Aside from taking a ship for the Philippines, as he started to do, Senator Tydings had no possible way to avoid the fracas. The junior senatorship was open that year, but Ritchie refused to accept promotion at the hands of his former apprentice. Tydings offered to resign and be reappointed to the junior rank, if Ritchie would take the senior title. Still Ritchie refused. He was strong enough to force Jackson out of the primaries and take his fifth consecutive nomination. Tydings strengthened himself by sending his friend, George L. Radcliffe, after the senatorial opening.

What happened in Maryland at the general election of '34 was startling enough to make national news. Every single Democrat on the state and national ticket won—except Albert C. Ritchie. In certain Democratic sections the Governor ran thousands of votes behind his own slate. The result was so freakish that the *New York Times*, usually impervious to such local trivialities, was moved to give it editorial space. "It looks like a game of cut-throat politics, the revenge and opportunity of disappointed rivals."

"I never felt that the *Times* article was directed at me," said the Senator, "and I believe few people in Maryland consider it so."

Nevertheless it was a bad spot for all concerned. Hardly a well-posted person in the state but believed that Ritchie had been knifed in the back. There is no evidence against Tydings, and his character is stronger than any slander against it; but he has been accused probably oftener than he knows. With Ritchie's removal Tydings became undisputed boss of the Free State, according to the *Sunpapers*, "the only factional figure with a genuine statewide organisation of his own . . . an army that spreads through every ward and every county."

No doubt it is a position with much pomp and circumstance, and, since there must be bosses, Tydings is better than the average. Yet the people who admire him most wish he had left bosshood alone. It is simply not his game.

VI

But a game he does have and it is statesmanship.

"If I may say so without sounding like a demagogue or a prig, the science of government is my study. I spend most of my time reading, for every year I realize how much there is to learn and how little I know."

In that spirit of humility and inquiry he approached his task as a maiden senator. He presently discovered, if he did not know already, that all of his time could not be his own.

"The member of Congress soon has to decide whether he is going to be a glorified office boy, attending with great punctiliousness to his mail, calling on departments for little favors for his constituents, or whether he is going to be a Legislator. He cannot be both."

Tydings is eminently the legislator. His natural affability makes him the target of favor-seekers, and Maryland is too close to Washington for the Senator's liking. Notwithstanding, when he is busy, he lets callers know it. A great deal of his work is seeing after the rights of the Free State, of which the University of Maryland recently picked him as the best all-round representative. If the government insists on building bridges, then Tydings wants one over the Chesapeake Bay. If it builds airports, then he presses Baltimore's advantages as a depot. The Maryland crab and wild duck get his protection through legislation, just as the Maryland merchant is looked after by his Fair Trade Bill.

For the rest, he is always full of ideas. He suggested legalizing a sub-alcoholic beer for taxation purposes, long before Mr. Roosevelt got credit for the 3.2 variety. He proposed sending a commission to the USSR to study trade relations, long before Secretary Hull reopened diplomatic and commercial relationship. He got busy freeing the Philippines when no one thought it could be done. As chairman of the Committee on Territorial and Insular Affairs, he is now doing the same for other sore spots on the imperial outpost.

It is habitual to use Thomas Jefferson as the yardstick on all claimants to Democratic statesmanship. Actually the party saint set his seal rather casually on the Marylander's brow. Jefferson favored states' rights, and it is Tydings' first commandment. Jefferson believed in simplified systems of government, and Tydings once suggested reducing the House to a membership of three hundred. Jefferson was against the government's going into business, and Tydings' first major joust was a one-man filibuster against the Muscle Shoals project.

But with these primary tenets accepted, Tydings pulls off on some sharp tangents. Jefferson said rather picturesquely that the blood of the revolutionist was the "manure" for fertilizing freedom. He hoped America would never be twenty-five years without an active rebellion. Tydings is no such bug on the civil liberties. Recently the Negro institution at Washington, Howard University, allowed members of the Communist Party to make some speeches there. Tydings was so horrified that he called out the G-Men to investigate this nest of radicalism. He was asked, and he refused, to do something for Tom Mooney. He sponsored the War Department's famous Defection Bill, which proposed an arbitrary censorship on a free press and free speech. It is a commentary on the Senator's special blind spot that he failed to see any menace in this bill, which even lesser minds in the House recognized as a "brash piece of Hitlerite Fascism." Yet he took a leading part in the mock trial of *Der Führer* at Madison Square Garden.

VII

For nine years Millard Tydings was known as the most eligible bachelor in the Senate. He was well off, for his law business was profitable and his only extravagance was, now and then, an ocean trip. He was said to be handsome, but this was a tribute to his clean-cut, vigorous masculinity. He is not good looking as movie heroes go. The Merchant Tailors Designing Association picked him, with Peter Arno and Fred Astaire, among the Sixteen Best Dressed Men in America. This was a compliment to his quiet good taste. He never goes in for sartorial extremes. For exercise he golfed and tennised and swam. For sport he went duck-shooting and motor-boating. For relaxation he liked football and baseball games, the opera and the theatre. He admired John Galsworthy's novels and Maxwell Anderson's plays. He rigged up a studio in the attic of his Georgetown apartment and did some oil sketches— "for pastime rather than as works of art." He confessed a submerged ambition:

"I should like some time to try my hand at playwriting, feeling it is the best vehicle with which to present a problem and entertain at one and the same time. If I were out of politics and law, I should certainly devote considerable time to playwriting."

Capital society he found "amusing and diverting in moderation. I do not move in society enough to be bored, finding too many other things to take my time."

Then on December 27, 1935, at forty-six, he married. His wife is the former Mrs. Eleanor Davies Cheeseborough, daughter of our present ambassador to Belgium, very beautiful and accomplished, who brought him two stepchildren. He bought a manorial country seat, Oakington Farms, a twenty-room colonial house on Swan Creek, upper Chesapeake Bay. He went in for gentleman farming, cultivating part of six hundred acres, pasturing the rest with blooded cattle. Mrs. Tydings soon made plain her attitude about her husband's career. She already knew how to entertain at women's political clubs. She also learned how to make speeches at them.

In the past few years, Millard Tydings has taken on solidity. A man of property and habitation, in the prime of his powers, he becomes a recognizable product of his era. In some other Democratic period—Cleveland's or Wilson's—he would have been a driving liberal force. In the present regime he finds himself hemmed in by all the contradictions and confusions of the day. A self-styled "moderate progressive," he is outstripped by radicals in his own party. A stubborn idealist, he is intellectually compelled to oppose the Great Humanitarian. Potentially a constructive thinker, he dissipates his powers in guerrilla warfare against his own political kin.

It is not necessary to exaggerate the man's abilities in order to understand his importance. He is one, among a handful of others, who will bear the brunt of New Deal vindictiveness in the autumn primaries. The party label and caution for his own future caused Tydings to tolerate Mr. Roosevelt in '36, but there is no equivocation in the record. Tydings has voted against the NRA; the AAA; the TVA; the first Guffey Coal Bill; the Wagner Labor Act; the

Court Plan; the Reorganization Plan. At this writing he is being opposed, openly and in secret, by the administration. His opponent has received presidential benediction. His patronage is being diverted. He is boss in name only. Asked about his chances, the Senator gives a shrug.

"Whether I win or lose the election, I can truthfully say I have not lost my patriotic soul. Where the country finally goes is the thing. My greatest ambition is to have been found consistently on the side of what is ultimately best for the United States."

Quite the usual thing, that last sentence. A patriotic platitude, perhaps. But the point is that it comes from an unusual man. Millard Tydings really means it.

7

ROBERT M. LA FOLLETTE, JR.

By Wallace S. Sayre

ROBERT M. LA FOLLETTE, SR., WAS BORN IN A LOG CABIN ON THE Wisconsin frontier in 1855, the son of a family which had long been moving with the frontier, from the Delaware Valley pre-Revolution frontier to the Kentucky frontier, to the Indiana frontier, to the Wisconsin frontier. And though at the age of twenty La Follette turned his back upon the frontier, came up to the University at Madison, became a lawyer, went to Washington for three terms as congressman, and returned to Wisconsin to lead a political movement of great national significance, he continued throughout his life to resist the emerging industrial order with the political beliefs of the frontier.

When Robert M. La Follette, Jr., was born in Madison, February 6, 1895, his father was at the beginning of his crusade to free Wisconsin from the control of the railroad and lumber barons. Before Young Bob's sixth birthday his father had become governor of Wisconsin and was in the midst of his long struggle to control the corporations and "return the government to the people." Young Bob's earliest memories are of the governor's mansion and the dramatic figure of his father, who made it frequently the center of national attention. He grew up in a world dominated by the political revolution which his father was leading in the state, and his earliest education was less in the Madison schools than in the absorbing political discussions between his father, his calm, even-tempered mother, and the other leaders of the Progressive movement who met in frequent council at the governor's mansion. The regulation of railroads, the control of corporations, the direct primary election, the income tax, the merit system—these were familiar to Young Bob before he learned the multiplication table.[1]

[1] Ray Tucker and Frederick R. Barkley, "La Follette," in *Sons of the Wild Jackass* (Boston, 1932), Chap. VII, pp. 148-71; Francis Brown, "La Follette: Ten Years a Senator," *Current History*, XLII (August, 1935), 475-80.

When his father came to Washington as senator in 1906, Young Bob's education was transferred not merely to the Washington schools but to national political issues as well. The La Follette family custom of including the children in the discussions of political questions, begun in Madison, was continued in Washington. Thus Young Bob saw two years of "T.R." at close range, particularly during his father's struggles to widen Roosevelt's "Square Deal" into a program which would include his own Wisconsin ideas on railroad legislation and the control of the "Money Power." He saw even more closely, as his interests increased and his association with his father became more intimate, the social and economic forces reflected in the Taft administration. His father's prolonged and bitter struggle with the Republican leadership over the Payne-Aldrich tariff and over railroad legislation sharpened his understanding of political institutions. He was seventeen, and more interested in political issues than in schools, when his father made his almost successful bid for the presidential nomination in 1912. The disappointment in the family was great, but Young Bob had seen at first hand the forces which dominated national party politics and the methods which they used. During the next two years he watched the inauguration of Wilson's "New Freedom," and saw many of his father's proposals adopted by an administration which left him in relative isolation.

Then, for a brief interlude, he went back to the University at Madison. Here, while Europe plunged into war and his father began his opposition to Wilsonian foreign policies, he found formal education none too absorbing. At the end of his second year in Madison, he contracted a serious illness from which he did not recover for many months. His father sat at his bedside throughout the months of denunciation which followed the elder La Follette's vote against the declaration of war. Upon his recovery, Young Bob did not return to the University. He went instead into his father's office as his secretary. Here, at his father's right hand, he learned, in the intensive La Follette manner, about the complicated postwar issues: Peace and the League, taxes, railroads, monopoly, and prices. He learned, too, the way in which the Senate worked. In 1920 he had reached sufficient political maturity to be, with Gilbert E. Roe, his father's agent at the National Farmer-Labor convention. When Harding and his Ohio gang came into power, Young Bob sat beside his father as he planned the exposés of the oil scandals, attacked Harding railroad policies, the Fordney-McCumber tariff, and the Mellon tax reductions. The ascension of Coolidge and his acquisition of the Republican nomination in 1924 precipitated the final insurgency of the elder La Follette—his campaign in 1924 as an independent candidate for the presidency. Young Bob was in the middle of it. He was his father's spokesman at the Cleveland convention of independents, and then participated in the management of his father's campaign.

When his father died in 1925, Young Bob had had an unusual, if not unique, political education for his thirty years. He had had more than twenty years of intimate contact with insurgent politics. He had learned his politics from intimate association with the dominant figure of midwestern political revolt. He knew the Senate at first hand. He knew the machinery and the issues of national politics.

Despite all this, Young Bob's selection for the Senate was fortuitous. He had not deliberately planned a political career, but instead had inclined toward journalism. But when his mother, perhaps acting with that calm foresight which characterized her role in the Progressive movement, declined to be senator in her husband's place, he was the only member of the family eligible. It was agreed that a La Follette was essential. Confronted with the proposal, Young Bob showed no reluctance. He was easily victorious in the campaign which followed.[2]

He entered a Senate dominated by Watson of Indiana, Smoot of Utah, Reed of Pennsylvania—a Senate smug with the easy political triumphs of Coolidge and with the Coolidge era of prosperity. Its conservative leaders could look back upon six years of success: the protective tariff restored, income taxes reduced, the Supreme Court made safe, railroads returned to private owners with subsidy, a strong arm in the Caribbean, subsidies for business, liberal policies with oil and land, labor disciplined, the Federal Trade Commission neutralized. Business was in the saddle, and all opposition was silenced by prosperity and Coolidge taciturnity.

[2] *New York Times*, September 30, 1925.

"The youngest senator since Henry Clay" took his seat in this atmosphere with typical La Follette insurgency. He had been told, indirectly of course, that if he wished to moderate his position he might have choice committee assignments. His reply was that he was and would continue to be a Progressive as his father had been. The result was a threat to deprive him of all committee posts— then a surrender by Watson and Massachusetts' Butler.[3] The committees to which he was assigned were relatively unimportant, but it was hardly a period for committee work. He did not follow his father's example and immediately challenge the Senate leadership in debate. Instead he kept silent for the most part during his first year, preparing for future participation by reading extensively in political biography and political science.[4] He did, however, raise his voice from time to time on subjects which he was later to make his specialties; he asked for an investigation of the monopolistic character of the anthracite coal corporations and of their income; he asked for an inquiry into the Passaic textile strike; he introduced resolutions condemning the high food prices and the alleged monopoly of the Ward food companies; he attacked the further tax reductions proposed by the Treasury under Andrew Mellon.[5]

When he returned to the short session of 1926–27, he was ready to launch his career of insurgency more actively. The tenderest spot of the opposition was the question of the presidential succession. Was Coolidge to have a third term or were all the presidential aspirants in the party to begin competition for the nomination? La Follette thought conservative leadership would be most disrupted by blocking the third-term proposal. Accordingly he prepared a resolution which condemned third-term proponents for flouting American traditions and praised Coolidge for his adherence to tradition in his "I do not choose to run" declaration. The conservatives, pleased at the prospects of continued Coolidge rule, were nonplussed. They could not oppose a resolution which took the President's statement at its face value and praised him for his

[3] New York Times, December 15, 16, 1925; Frank R. Kent, "Little Bob Wins," Nation, CXXI (December 30, 1925), 758.
[4] O. G. Villard, "Robert M. La Follette, Jr.," Nation, CXXXIX (August 8, 1934), 147.
[5] New York Times, February 17, March 17, 1926; Congressional Record, 69th Congress, 1st Session, pp. 3677-83, 4491.

principles. After parliamentary delays had been exhausted, the resolution passed.[6]

In the next session, La Follette took a further step. To demonstrate the artificial character of the Coolidge boom, he began to develop into legislative form two of the issues which have been peculiarly his during the last ten years. The first was his determination to build a national tax system which would be based upon the principle of ability to pay and which would supply the national government with the funds necessary for the broad planning and service program in which he believes it should be engaged. His 1928 fight centered around his championship of publicity provisions for income tax returns which he made the focal point for a discussion and statement of a progressive national tax policy. The second was his attempt to draw the attention of the Senate and of the nation to the unemployment problem. This required courage and foresight in 1928, when the attention of the nation was upon the stock market and the "New Era" economists were revising their textbooks to eliminate all references to business cycles and depressions. Throughout the spring of 1928, however, Young Bob insisted upon a study of unemployment. To an indifferent and disbelieving Senate he patiently set forth the extent of unemployment in the midst of prosperity, excoriated the economic system which was responsible, and demanded that the problem be studied and a report be submitted to the Senate. The Senate could not believe that it was serious enough to require attention.[7] The Senate was equally indifferent to his proposal that the Federal Reserve Board be required to curb speculative loans.

This opposition to the Coolidge regime brought him national attention as the national parties organized their forces for the 1928 presidential campaign. There was the usual talk of a third party, but when Young Bob was asked to be one of its leaders, he said the time was not ripe for it. He continued in his hopes that the Republican party might be made the vehicle for progressivism—and he was certain that it had to be the vehicle of his own re-election in Wisconsin. He went to the Republican National Convention as

[6] Brown, *loc. cit.*

[7] O. G. Villard, "Robert M. La Follette, Jr.," *Forum*, XCVI (August, 1936), 87–91; *Congressional Record*, 70th Congress, 1st Session, pp. 7243, 7591.

chairman of the Wisconsin delegation, and to the delegates who had just heard in boredom the majority report on the party platform he presented a minority report which urged farm relief, public ownership of utilities, higher income taxes, the St. Lawrence waterway, the prohibition of injunctions in labor disputes, the curbing of stock market inflation. The delegates cheered him, but their votes went for the majority report.[8] La Follette later attacked the Republican platform as reactionary, ignored the Republican candidate, Herbert Hoover, and concentrated his attention upon his own campaign in Wisconsin. In November he was easily elected to a full six-year term. He now stood, not in his father's place, but as senator in his own right. There was an almost immediate growth in confidence.

With the Hoover administration La Follette was immediately out of tune. His first attack was upon the Hoover nomination of Irvine L. Lenroot, one-time Wisconsin Progressive and later Coolidge reactionary, to the Court of Customs and Patent Appeals. It had always been the custom of the Senate to vote upon nominations in executive session and to regard the vote as secret. The custom had long been honored in the breach whenever it suited the convenience of the leaders of the Senate, but when the United Press published the vote upon the Lenroot nomination, Senators Moses and Reed, among others, were so incensed that they sought to bar the offending reporter from the floor. La Follette came to his defense so effectively that the Senate, rather than discipline the reporter, abolished the rule of secrecy.[9]

His second and more important attack upon Hoover policies centered around the Smoot-Hawley tariff bill. He was the parliamentary leader of the coalition Progressives and Democrats who fought the conservative Senate leadership to a standstill for weeks. He took for himself the complex chemical schedule, and his searching exposition and analysis of the chemical tariff rates is one of the landmarks of his senatorial career. It was a factually exhaustive, brilliant exposure of the special favors in the tariff system. It was so unanswerable that he won substantial reductions from the embarrassed and disarmed Senate leaders. As the tariff battle contin-

[8] Brown, *loc. cit.*
[9] Tucker and Barkley, *op. cit.*, pp. 164-67.

ued, he persisted in his claims for the consumer, attaching the schedules as devices for price increases.[10]

When the widespread economic depression engulfed the Hoover administration in the winter of 1930 La Follette had completed his apprenticeship in the Senate. He had indeed securely established himself among the leaders of the increasingly powerful insurgent bloc. George W. Norris, Fiorello H. La Guardia, Robert F. Wagner, Burton K. Wheeler, Edward P. Costigan, Smith W. Brookhart, James Couzens, William E. Borah, and others, accepted him not merely as the son of his father but as a colleague. Norris more and more frequently referred to him as his successor in the leadership of the Progressive movement. This recognition had not been won by oratorical brilliance, for he had almost none. He lacked, too, his father's highly developed sense of theater. (For the elder La Follette's skill with voice and drama, attention was now turned to Wisconsin, where a second son had just become governor.) Young Bob's position of influence in the Senate had been won by his industry in committee and on the floor, by his intelligent approach to public questions, by his mastery of the subjects which he rose to discuss, by his consistency, by his agreeable nature, and by his fairness in debate. To these traits, with which he had by 1930 won the respect of his opponents as well as the admiration of his fellow insurgents, there is also to be added a high degree of parliamentary skill, the fruit of long service as his father's floor manager and of a deep interest in parliamentary techniques.

By 1930, then, La Follette was ready to turn from free-lance insurgency to the development of major public policies. Since that time he has devoted most of his energies to the analysis and solution of three major problems: unemployment, taxation, labor relations. Around these three issues most of his senatorial career has been built, and in his handling of each are to be seen his basic political beliefs and techniques.

His interest in unemployment dates from the Senate debates of 1928 when he began to challenge the pretensions of Coolidge prosperity. The collapse of 1929–30 substantiated his charges and his fears. He thereupon began the marshaling of facts which has be-

[10] *Congressional Record*, 71st Congress, 1st Session, 4617; 2nd Session, pp. 1854, 4698, 5976-78.

ROBERT M. LA FOLLETTE, JR.

*"He has political seasoning and skill, the respect and
loyalty of a regional, even a national, following, and
he has earned the stature of competent statesmanship."*

come the characteristic preliminary to all his proposals. During the autumn months of 1930 he sent out questionnaires to the mayors of all cities with more than 5,000 population asking for estimates of the unemployed. He asked the American Federation of Labor to furnish estimates of unemployment from the central labor boards throughout the country. With this impressive array of facts before him he led the questioning of Hoover administration spokesmen before the Senate Appropriations Committee, and when the administration declined to act he took the floor in the Senate to declare his belief that the federal government had a responsibility which it could not evade. Congress adjourned without action, but La Follette continued his independent investigation through the months preceding the reconvening of Congress in December, 1931. When Congress met, La Follette and Senator Costigan introduced separate bills for federal relief. La Follette, as chairman of the Committee on Manufactures, immediately began public hearings of which Senator Johnson later remarked: "No more intelligent hearings, in my opinion, were ever conducted by a Senate committee." At the conclusion of the hearings, the La Follette and Costigan bills were merged and were reported to the Senate. Debate was bitter and continued for two weeks, during which La Follette spoke once for five hours. On February 16, 1932, the bill was defeated by a vote of 48 to 35. La Follette had forced the realities of the unemployment problem upon the Hoover administration, however, and in July the Wagner substitute providing for loans rather than grants was accepted.[11] La Follette continued the fight for federal grants in the last "lame duck" session of 1933, but it was not until the arrival of the "New Deal" that his policies were enacted into law. President Roosevelt then and later conferred with him on relief policies, and he has continued to be influential in the various stages of national unemployment legislation.

His role in this field under the New Deal has inevitably been a subordinate one, but more than any other national leader he is responsible for laying the groundwork of national unemployment relief policies. He had the foresight to perceive the problem before

[11] "The Story of Bob LaFollette's . . . Fight for Relief," *Capital Times* (Madison, Wisconsin), April 15, 1933, p. 10; Mauritz A. Hallgren, "Young Bob LaFollette," *Nation*, CXXXII (March 4, 1931), 235-37.

the depression. He alone at first grasped the enormity of the problem. He was almost singly responsible for developing the facts of
unemployment while the Hoover administration insisted that prosperity was just around the corner.

La Follette's work in the field of taxation has resulted in the
most completely developed legislative program of his career. His
thinking has followed the principles established by his father in
Wisconsin and in the Senate, but he has also traveled a long distance on his own. Taxation was one of his first interests in the Senate. He had sat there for but two months when in February, 1926,
the Republican and Democratic leaders agreed upon a revenue bill
which La Follette attacked as "a bill to untax wealth." He worked
with Norris in a vain attempt to amend the bill to provide for publicity of returns, but his most important effort was against the repeal of the estate tax. During the next few years he continued to
resist the Coolidge and Hoover policies of tax reduction. As the depression intensified his interest in the problem of unemployment,
he became an advocate of governmental expenditure to halt the
downward spiral. This conviction, in turn, led him to advocate the
adoption of a national tax plan which would provide adequate revenues. Taxes must be levied, he declares, upon those who have the
ability to pay and in terms of their ability to pay. When taxes are
so collected, he believes, we shall have an important weapon against
the concentration of wealth which threatens democratic institutions,
we shall restore purchasing power to the masses, and we shall have
aided the establishment of economic stability.[12]

La Follette developed the outlines of his tax plan during the
Senate discussions which marked the final months of the Hoover
administration, but the Senate leaders were committed to economy
and to sales taxes. With the advent of the New Deal, La Follette
found a friendlier audience. Publicity was restored to the statutes
(but was repealed in a later session) and there was a disposition to
adopt the "soak the rich" features of the La Follette tax plan. But,
though he once persuaded his colleagues on the Finance Committee to adopt the main features of his program, his plan has been delayed by New Deal expediency. He has been an effective critic of

[12] Robert M. La Follette, "Taxes Needed by U.S.," National Broadcasting Company,
April 9, 1934.

New Deal borrowing, and his revenue program remains the magnet toward which the present administration's policies are drawn.

His interest in the problems arising out of labor disputes also goes back to his father's career as a labor champion in the Senate. He joined with his progressive colleagues during the Coolidge era in protests against anti-labor injunctions by federal courts. He was one of the leaders in the drive for the Norris-La Guardia anti-injunction act. His most prominent role, however, began in 1936 when he became chairman of a Senate subcommittee to investigate abuses of civil liberties and denials of the right of labor to bargain collectively. With the aid of Senator Thomas of Utah, he has set a new record in his already distinctive career of managing committee investigations and public hearings. He has probed deeply into the hitherto mysterious business of strikebreaking detective agencies, he has paraded *agents provocateurs* before the committee and before the country, he has laid bare the social and economic oligarchy of Harlan County, Kentucky, and he has put into the record the organization, personnel, and methods of the country's vigilante organizations. All these, however, have tended to be overshadowed by his dramatic and yet painstaking case history of the "Chicago Memorial Day Incident," in which the Chicago police dispersed with brutality and fatalities a group of steel workers who were on strike at the Republic steel plant.[13] Observers have described the development of evidence in this investigation as excelling all previous committee investigations.

La Follette's work with this committee has furnished the data upon which national and state labor legislation has been based, and, perhaps even more directly, the facts which have guided administrative practice in labor relations. The final report of the committee has not yet been made, but it is likely to guide future legislation and to make La Follette even more clearly an important friend of organized labor.

Each of these problems has revealed La Follette's scientific, almost scholarly, temperament, his respect for facts, his determination to know the theoretical boundaries of his subject, his preference for information rather than denunciation. His handling of

[13] 75th Congress, 1st Session, Report No. 46, parts 1 and 2. See also: Hearings of Senate Committee on Education and Labor, pursuant to S. Res. 266 (74th Congress).

each has demonstrated his keen awareness of the industrial order and his advance beyond the domain of his father's thought. Each has demonstrated his superior capacity for concentration upon the job at hand, his common-sense perspective, his skill at using experts. Through these qualities he has won stature in the Senate and in the nation.

La Follette is not a politician in the popular sense of the term. He has never been interested in the game of patronage, nor does he take readily to the intrigue with which conventional politics is associated. He is realistic enough to accept certain inevitabilities in the political process, and even to participate in them when they seem essential to the advancement of the program in which he is absorbed. But his political role has been one primarily associated with issues rather than organization.

He is effective in personal relationships. He has successfully appeased the jealousies of rival leaders in Wisconsin, and he has slowly won status in his own right in a Senate at first inclined to contrast him unfavorably with his father. Both in Wisconsin and in the Senate his methods have been cautious and deliberate, avoiding the *coups de théâtre* characteristic of his father. He has capitalized upon the traits of sincerity, common sense, modesty, and alertness.

He now occupies a highly strategic position in the present-day dynamic party politics. He shares with his brother, Governor Philip, the leadership of the Progressive party in Wisconsin, a party which they have slowly and carefully built out of the insurgent movement which their father led within the nominal structure of the Republican party.[14] They enjoy, further, a fairly secure regional leadership in the upper Mississippi valley, a region which has been the pivot of New Deal victories and which will continue to determine the direction of national politics as the mediator between agriculture and industry. This region, and with it La Follette, are indispensable to a continuance of the New Deal political structure. They are equally indispensable to the oft-proposed realignment of forces which would build a national farmer-labor party.

La Follette's career in the Senate and his strategic position in the

[14] Harold M. Groves, "Wisconsin's New Party," *Nation*, CXXXIX (August 1, 1934), 122-24; Wallace S. Sayre, "Left Turn in Wisconsin," *New Republic*, October 24, 1934.

party system have led to repeated prophecies that he will one day sit in the White House. The possibility is not too remote. He will, in 1940, be forty-five years of age, perhaps at the crest of his career. He has political seasoning and skill, the respect and loyalty of a regional, even a national, following, and he has earned the stature of competent statesmanship. He has demonstrated his grasp of the problems of twentieth-century America. The capture of the presidency is the greatest of our political gambles, but Robert M. La Follette, Jr., does not need the presidency to assure himself of a profoundly influential future in American politics.

8

ONE OF THE FOUR HUNDRED AND THIRTY-FIVE: MAURY MAVERICK, OF TEXAS

By Robert C. Brooks

"WHO WON THE SAN FRANCISCO EARTHQUAKE?" THIS QUEStion, truculently put by the gentleman from Texas, ended summarily a rather pointless performance on the part of a fellow member of the Military Affairs Committee of the House. True to his warlike instincts the latter had engaged at length and loudly in browbeating a witness before the Committee, Jeanette Rankin, herself a former representative, now one of the most effective advocates of peace in the United States. Climaxing a patriotic flight the gentleman shouted at the lady: "Who won the World War?" And received the above classic answer to his question in the form of another question, itself in a way as devastating as an earthquake. To make the irony of the affair more complete the Honorable Maury Maverick, who thus closed the incident, comes from the bustling city of San Antonio, Texas, which happens to be one of the greatest military centers in the world, if indeed it is not the greatest.

On another occasion when the news of Hitler's burning of the books was still fresh, Charles A. Beard, dean of American historians, was being interrogated before the same Committee, although the word "heckled" would describe the process more accurately. Because of his partial deafness the eminent scholar was at a marked disadvantage. Scenting an easy kill, one of the more militaristic members of the Committee started in full cry, his eyes gleaming, his nostrils quivering. And the object of his relentless pursuit? Ah, my friends, it was COMMUNISTIC LITERATURE, nothing less—and nothing more definite, either. He wanted to know all about it; in fact he clamored—and yammered—at great length for knowledge, meanwhile doing his utmost to browbeat the witness.

Most of all he craved to learn in what libraries such dastardly literature was concealed. Whether or not the Professor grasped this particular question, his mild answer was: "In all of them, I should think." To which Maury Maverick added, again ending the séance: "No doubt there's plenty of it in our own library, the Congressional Library. Does the honorable gentleman desire to have it burned down also?"

Unquestionably, given a good cause, the gentleman from Texas dearly loves to upset the apple-cart. And nothing affords him more joy, holy or unholy, than to deflate stuffed shirts, especially when enveloped in military uniforms, as sometimes happens to be the case. In so doing, of course, Maverick runs the risk of gaining the reputation of an *enfant terrible,* or, worse still, of a recognized congressional wit. The latter is, perhaps, the saddest of all legislative fates, as the career of "Sunset" Cox demonstrated a generation ago. That the gentleman from Texas has escaped such a nemesis is not due to any lack of humor, mordant or otherwise. It is due to the fact that he does not stop with the outburst of ready laughter. Attack with words, whether humorous or with "tough, hard, mean words"—to use his own expression—is always backed up by serried masses of facts, laboriously collected, meticulously ordered. And facts are also "tough, hard, mean" things. To illustrate and at the same time to revert to the two incidents narrated above, Maverick kept up the fight until he had killed the Military Disaffection Bill. He is still prouder of that success than of anything else he has accomplished in Washington. And that in spite of many notable achievements which bulk much larger as matters of public business and which have reverberated resoundingly through the press of the country as a whole. For example, his fights for the conservation of natural resources—the matter which is always foremost in his thought, for housing and slum clearance, for the TVA, for mandatory neutrality legislation, and more recently for the reform of the Supreme Court are not likely soon to be forgotten.

Maverick was born at San Antonio, Texas, October 23, 1895, the eleventh and youngest son of Albert and Jane (Maury) Maverick. English, Scotch-Irish, and French Huguenot stocks—a strong and typically American mixture—are all represented in his ancestry. It is impossible to talk to the Congressman for any length of time without discovering that he is enormously interested in the history of his family, a trait which, by the way, is abundantly manifested in his recent book, *A Maverick American*. At first sight it would seem to indicate that the gentleman from Texas shares the aristocratic outlook supposedly cherished by all members of "fine old Southern families." Twitted on this score, so incongruous with his extreme democratic outlook, Maverick defends himself with a certain show of indignation. He assures you that he is "an ordinary man with ordinary ideas" (which, with all due regard to his sincerity, is simply not the case); further, that so far as he can discover all his ancestors were of the same type. In other words, all the Mavericks were mavericks, i.e., commonplace men and women more or less astray in the midst of the social and economic forces of their time. Regardless of the tie of blood the Congressman assures you that he can see their vices and failures just as clearly as he sees their virtues and successes. Finally—and make no mistake about it —he studies their past struggles not because of any aristocratic feeling but solely for his own guidance amid the dominant forces of the here and now.

An ingenious theory, this, to dispose of the charge of ancestor worship. Nor can it be dismissed out of hand as rationalization, pure and simple. Still it is apparent that Maverick admires his forbears as a whole, particularly those who were on the popular side in the political conflicts of their day. Unquestionably also he takes a certain sinful pride in their fighting qualities, regardless of the side on which they fought. Chalking up this minor demerit—if demerit it be—against the Congressman, it must be admitted in his favor that his extended genealogical researches have given him an unusual knowledge of the history of the country and particularly of the South as seen from the viewpoint of human mavericks. Whether his ancestors were conservatives or radicals—mostly they were the latter—it is true that he studies them always from the point of view of the problems he is trying to solve today. One of the most characteristic features of *A Maverick American* is the way in which the author after describing *briefly* the exploits of some colonial or revolutionary ancestor, proceeds to apply *at length* the lessons thus learned to the matters he has now in hand, for example, to soil conservation, militarism, taxation, poor relief, and the like. Decidedly Maury Maverick is a much more effective and a much more down-to-the-minute political leader because he has forgathered so extensively and so intimately with his forbears.

In his political career the Congressman is under particular obligation—as will appear later—to his grandfather, Samuel Augustus Maverick. It was because of this gentleman's easy-going management of his ranch that the name "maverick" came to be applied to unbranded, roaming cattle. To his father and mother, however, Maury's indebtedness is beyond all computation. They seem to have been ideally fitted for parenthood; moreover they had had plenty of practical experience in child psychology before the birth of their eleventh and last child. In the charming picture which the son paints of their life together, characteristically using political colors, the mother is portrayed as a shrewd and active prime minister, the father as a quiet and kindly constitutional monarch. Tolerance reigned in their household; frankness and fearlessness were the order of the day. Here the twig was bent; so the tree is inclined.

Educational life on the whole proved much less satisfactory than family life. Young Maury came up through the public grade schools and the High School of San Antonio; for some reason undisclosed he notes: "did not graduate from the latter." Indeed he seems to have made a specialty, then and later, of dodging graduation. Which, of course, now leaves him wide open to the offer of an honorary degree. (Which, probably, he would decline.) There was a rather ineffectual year at Virginia Military Institute; after that, three "wasted" years at the University of Texas, where he enrolled for journalism. Again the notation: "did not graduate." This time the reason was that Maury found himself overpowered by a desire to practice law, probably with some thought of politics in the offing. As a result he set himself the strenuous task of doing the three years' work of the law school in one year. And a third time he "did not graduate." However, he won admittance to the local bar and threw himself into practice with the ardor characteristic of him when he is really interested in what he is doing.

One of the commonest obsessions of college men who have reached middle life is that during their undergraduate years they were regular hellicats. As a moral equivalent or sublimation for raising Cain after the time for that sort of amusement is over and done, this trick of memory probably has a certain ethical value. Curious, however, that a man so shrewd as Maverick should be subject to it. As foundation for the delusion he adduces nothing more conclusive than the usual catalogue of student sins—cutting, activities, college politics, membership in an organization known as the Campus Buzzards, drinking, brawling and disorders on the campus, run-ins with the deans, and so on, and so on. (No mention of "fussing." Why not? Texas was coeducational.) On the other hand, Maverick admits that during his high school and college years he was an omnivorous reader, particularly of "banned" books. As this was before the days when sex was discovered apparently these latter were for the most part treatises on ethics, philosophy, and sociology of which professors disapproved. Or *said* they disapproved. Experienced college instructors will recognize the device, which is at least several centuries older than Machiavelli. As they well know, nothing so whets the curiosity of an undergraduate as to tell him that he ought not read a certain book. Whether so intended or not in the present case, young Maury swatted up vigorously all prohibited literature; thus even when in college his education was largely self-administered. Evidently his intellectual curiosity was insatiable. Given a really understanding tutor he would have forged ahead at a tremendous intellectual pace. As things were, he did indeed make direct use of the instruction given him in journalism. On the other hand, he took no courses in economics or political science. Owing to his prejudice against professors Maverick is rather loath to admit being influenced by any of that tribe. Under pressure, however, he does pay handsome tribute to Edwin DuBois Shurter, now retired, whose instruction in public speaking, particularly in the matter of logical and effective presentation, has been of the greatest possible utility to him throughout his political career. And in general Maverick acknowledges the value of university training even if most of the courses in his time were dull and tiresome. One detail of his educational experience is not without distinct political significance. Since the University was located at Austin, students had an excellent opportunity to observe state government in action; also to meet personally the present and prospective leaders in Texas affairs. As a piquant detail he notes that many members of the legislature were attending the law school, adding "so we frequently attended the State Legislature."

It is by no means certain that Maverick was predestined to politics, highly gifted for that pursuit as he has shown himself particularly since entering Congress. Various other alternatives were first explored and eliminated. Thus he might readily have gone on with journalism for which he was trained at the University of Texas and in which undoubtedly he would have been brilliantly successful. Already at the age of eighteen he had secured a temporary job as city editor of the *Amarillo News* which he enjoyed hugely. After completing his work at the University he made rapid progress as a lawyer and was elected, partly as a result of his popularity among younger members of the profession, partly because of some shrewd political maneuvers, president of the San Antonio Bar Association at the age of twenty-four. It is clear, however, that the detail of legal practice is as repellent to him as it was to the young Theodore Roosevelt, whom he resembles in many other respects. Moreover he did not like the idea of prosecuting criminals; he "always felt sorry for the defendant." One other profession to which he devoted himself temporarily, that of the soldier, would have proved impossible in the long run. For an individual so wholly dedicated to the love of liberty as Maverick is, life under military discipline is unthinkable. Nevertheless he enlisted promptly after our entry into the World War, served with distinction as lieutenant of infantry in France until desperately wounded, October 4, 1918, and was awarded the Silver Star and the Purple Heart medals for gallantry in action. Of this experience, to which he devotes thirty of the most poignant and brilliantly written pages of *A Maverick American,* the principal results were the knowledge of war and the hatred of it which are the strongest of his intellectual and emotional drives to the present day.

Following his excursion into legal practice Maverick discovered, somewhat to his own surprise, that he was a business man of sorts. He made money hand over fist in lumber and building; indeed his conscience troubled him not a little at the ease with which he could run up jerry-built houses for $800 or $1000 and then sell them out of hand for twice as much. Quite apart from such scruples, however, it is clear that wealth makes little appeal to him. From his

successful building business experience, however, Maverick did de-
rive one result of permanent political value, namely a thorough
practical knowledge of the housing problem in the United States.
And that problem has ranked high among his preoccupations as a
public man ever since.

Considering the number of vocational bypaths Maverick explored, one may well ask: "Why, then, the ultimate decision to
enter politics?" Partly, as we have seen, because of ancestral tradition. It cannot be maintained, however, that immediate family environment predetermined his choice. True the Mavericks had the
advantage of being "old settlers"; moreover it is not without political significance that the Congressman himself has maintained a
residence in the San Antonio district throughout his entire forty-
two years, and in his present residence for ten years. Of living
relatives, however, only one, an uncle by marriage, had been a
congressman. There was, of course, the glowing memory of the
grandfather, Samuel of cattle fame, as a signer of the Texan Declaration of Independence back in 1836. While other more distant
relatives had held local offices on up to a governorship or two, still
the great majority of them had been soldiers, sea captains, merchants, and plantation owners.

As to the dawn of political consciousness Maverick is quite definite. It occurred at the age of six when President McKinley visited
his home, evidently making a tremendous impression on the boy.
Subsequently he was to meet Bryan under his father's roof, and
elsewhere La Follette, Victor Berger, and Eugene Debs, all of
whom he admired apparently in proportion to their radicalism and
forthrightness. And, of course, he met many Texas worthies including "Pa" Ferguson, who despite his demagogy "had a heart"
and also the guts to fight the fire of the K. K. K. with an even
hotter backfire; also George C. Butte, professor at the law school
of the University, whom Maverick was to support some years later
in his candidacy against Ferguson. Undoubtedly this range of
political acquaintance, extremely wide for one so young, was potent
in turning his thoughts toward a public career.

If the young Texan was predestined to politics it was, however,
neither family, nor education, nor acquaintance which decided the
matter. Rather he was driven by his social consciousness, or, to

PHOTO BY MC AVOY

MAURY MAVERICK

" 'Who won the San Francisco earthquake?' "

avoid professorial words abhorrent to the Congressman, let us say
he was overpowered by the true maverick spirit, namely by deep
sympathy with the multitude of those who were astray and neglected. The most distinctive thing in his whole earlier life was his
assumption of the role of a hobo during the last years of the
Hoover regime when there was no relief and when, as a result,
thousands of "transients"—human beings, not lost cattle—were
drifting aimlessly and in dire misery through the vast reaches of
Texas. To study their plight he dressed the part, not a hard job
for him; he lived with them in "jungles" and flophouses and on
the open road, incidentally becoming lousy in the process. But
he did not stop with the mere accumulation of sociological data.
Acting on what he had learned at first hand, he established a
co-operative colony for transients at the edge of San Antonio
which did excellent work until government relief began. In itself this experience may have been of minor importance. But it
is vastly significant as to the springs of action which move Maverick. In times of profound distress a man with his deep humane
feeling simply must leave all else and go into politics in the
effort to set things right.

Second only to this fundamental emotional drive, Maverick
had to go into politics because of the urgings of his intellect.
Nourished by ceaseless reading of economics and political science
he *knows* that he can set things right, some things at least, if
power be given him. And he means to do all that is in him to
that end regardless of opposition and objurgation. Those mistake
the man utterly who point to his alleged demagogy as a basic
trait of character. "I may demagogue," he observed, using the
word as a verb after a fashion coming into vogue in Washington,
"but never on any matter of importance." Really all that it
means to him is nothing more than an occasional resort to sensa-
tionalism in order to arouse interest and secure support. Back of
all such superficial manifestations there is a cool, disciplined, and
informed intelligence of the highest order. Also an inflexible
determination to tell the truth and shame the devil, regardless
of the cost to his own political career.

No doubt it will grieve the Congressman sadly, but it must be
said that, much as he affects to deride professors, he possesses

many traits of that species. True he does not speak their "jargon"; that would never do since he has to run for office from time to time. But he does read their books continually, translating them into bills, also into speeches for both congressional and popular consumption.[1] He does work the Congressional Library overtime, particularly the Research Division. He does write book reviews, even publishing them in the *Congressional Record*. He does contribute frequently to such high-brow journals of opinion as *The Nation* and *The New Republic*. He does call continually upon braintrusters for research assistance, sometimes putting two of them at work, unknown to each other, on the same problem in order to compare their findings. He does annotate his short, short speeches with long, long footnotes full of details, a professorial habit if there ever was one. He does make the damaging admission in *A Maverick American* that "the march of the professor is the greatest advance in the history of our government." Finally, as the Swarthmore address showed, he does love to talk to students. It was, in fact, a typical academic lecture even to the characteristic fault of such discourses, the effort to cover too much ground. Also Maverick sent several thousand public documents to the College beforehand, asking that they be distributed to students in preparation for his speech. In other words, professorial words, "collateral reading" if you please.

Although he had interested himself in civic affairs for several years Maverick's actual entry into politics did not occur until 1929, when he ran for the office of tax collector. To the surprise of the wiseacres he was successful against a city-county machine previously considered impregnable. Two years later he won his re-election against the same opposition. It is rare indeed that the personal popularity of tax collectors increases during their term of office. Nevertheless in 1934 Maverick was elected to Congress after two bitter Democratic primary campaigns in which he defeated the Mayor of San Antonio. Again in the primaries of 1936—final elections being virtually uncontested south of the

---

[1] For example, his H. R. 7325, 75th Congress, 1st Session, introduced June 1, 1937, providing for the creation of an Industrial Expansion Board and other Federal agencies, represents a painstaking effort to create the administrative machinery necessary for the carrying out of the principles of Mordecai Ezekiel's profoundly significant book entitled *$2500 a Year*.

Mason and Dixon line—Maverick received a vote nearly equal to that of his two opponents combined (Maverick, 21,703; Seeligson, 14,378; Menefee, 7,606), and a plurality twice as large as that by which he had won the nomination two years earlier. These figures are the more remarkable because the San Antonio district, unlike the overwhelming majority of those in the South, has been carried by Republicans at least half the time during recent decades.[2]

Maverick's campaign for the congressional nomination in 1934 took all the money for expenses that he could lay his hands on up to the legal limit of $2,500. Doubtless also friends spent something in behalf of his candidacy, how much he does not know. In his second campaign expenses were negligible. While contributions were made both in 1934 and 1936 by well-wishers and relatives, none were received from corporations. As noted above there is seldom much of a contest down South in final elections; hence the Federal Corrupt Practices Act is of even less importance there than elsewhere. In general Maverick believes that it is either not strong enough or not sufficiently supported by public opinion to insure absolute enforcement.

One incident of the first campaign for Congress is decidedly worth recording. As a result of the severe injury to the back and spinal cord which he received in France, Maverick had been in and out of hospitals more or less for sixteen years. On various occasions when supposed to be unconscious he had overheard surgeons predict his early death. Often he suffered from acute pains which made him unsteady on his legs. Although he was then on the water wagon it was perhaps only natural under the circumstances that his opponents should denounce him as a drunkard. Maverick did not deny the charge, believing it would do him less harm than a true statement concerning his precarious physical condition.

Whatever else may be alleged against him Maverick is anything but a machine politician. Asked to state in writing the importance

[2] In the primary of July 26, 1938, Maverick was defeated for renomination to Congress by an eyelash, his vote being 23,584 to 24,059 for his opponent. Perhaps the most striking feature of his campaign was the large amount of publicity it received throughout the country. It is seldom indeed that a mere congressional primary is thus treated as a matter of national interest. Maverick made a strenuous fight and took his defeat philosophically. To him it was merely the end of a round, not the end of the battle. Given his ability and energy one may confidently expect him, after a brief, well-earned rest, to resume his activities upon the stage of national politics.

he attaches to party committees—state, congressional, county, city, and ward—his answers were five straight "None's." Nor is he a member of any such committee. On the contrary, as we have just seen, he was opposed solidly by them, as well as by all the newspapers of the district, every time he ran for office. Also by the majority of big business men, especially the crooked oil operators; by all bankers save one; by "carpetbaggers," who are now of the corporate rather than of the old-time political variety; finally by nearly all those who because of wealth or prominence think themselves "big-shots," with or without foundation in actual personal achievement. On the whole a rather formidable opposition. As against it Maverick has the backing of a powerful Citizens League which he was instrumental in organizing. Further he has the support of a small number of big business men—big, that is, not only in amount of capital invested but even more so in the breadth of their social and economic vision. Of the manufacturers he estimates that some thirty per cent are for him; also a large proportion of the grocerymen, druggists, and small tradesmen and middle classes generally; and a still larger proportion of the poorer voters. Finally it is a matter of common knowledge that the masses of Mexicans of the San Antonio district swear by him. Evidently Maverick is as fond of them as they are devoted to him. Contrary to the practice of many politicians who think it a shrewd vote-getting device to address naturalized constituents in their own tongue, the Congressman, although fluent enough in Spanish, has always made it a point to talk to his friends from below the Rio Grande in English and to treat them in every way as full-fledged American citizens. Reckoning up all the friendly forces listed above, Maverick estimates that from thirty-five to forty per cent of the voters of his district are for him in spite of hell and high water. His task in campaigns, therefore, is to rally the additional ten to fifteen per cent necessary to victory.

Nor is Maverick much more interested in patronage than he is in other aspects of machine politics. After all, getting jobs is the business of lordly senators rather than of mere representatives. If Civil Service examinations stand in the way of applicants Maverick is heartily glad of it. He has asked for very few political appointments, and these chiefly for constituents who were in dire need.

And he is much more deeply interested in remedying economic conditions so that there will be jobs for all than he is in spoils of any sort.

Nor, finally, is Maverick a "joiner." Membership in the Masons or Moose, in the Eagles or Owls, does not allure him. Quite apart from the ethics of the case, he regards the mixing of secret societies and politics, i.e., peanut politics, as not worth the trouble involved. While an undergraduate at the University of Texas he did join a fraternity; now, however, he is inclined to believe that, because of their inherent snobbishness, such organizations might well be abolished. Curiously enough considering his strong anti-militarist views, he has retained membership in the American Legion and the Veterans of Foreign Wars, largely, he explains, "for sentimental reasons." But he has been an active, fighting member, from conviction, of the American Civil Liberties Union ever since his return from France in 1919. Perhaps as a result of the survival of the boy in him he belongs also to the Circus Fans of America and is a director of the San Antonio Zoological Society.

Emphatically Maverick does not belong to that school of statesmen who take the weight of public opinion by piling telegrams, pro and con, in separate stacks and voting according to whichever turns out to be the higher. Contrary to the insinuations of Washington newspaper men, it is doubtful whether any congressmen follow this procedure habitually. A certain justification might, however, be found for stacking telegrams—in the wastebasket—on occasions when public utility corporations have kept the wires to Washington hot with thousands of messages manufactured to order in their own interest. However this may be, Maverick devotes a considerable part of his time to keeping in touch with his constituents. Thus when the Supreme Court fight was at its hottest a pile of clippings fresh from the newspapers of the Twentieth Texas District was constantly before him. One bundle bore the following comment from a local observer: " 'Great Mass Meeting' last night. Fathered, mothered, and sistered by A—— B——, X—— Y——, and a few other 'Jeffersonian Democrats.' Attended by less than two hundred, half of whom were curiosity seekers."

Further, as part of the process of keeping in touch with constituents Maverick gives the most careful attention to his correspondence. He admits that its volume is ungodly; he receives requests continually for advice on subjects ranging all the way from obstetrics to theology from men and women in every walk of life. Notwithstanding the amount of letter writing involved the Congressman enjoys it, particularly when controversial in character. An early masterpiece of his along the latter line achieved national publicity and caused a country-wide roar of laughter. To a particularly stupid, abusive and long-winded correspondent he replied on official stationery, in full form with address and signature. However, the body of the letter consisted of one word only, *viz.*, "Ph-h-h-h-t"!

"A soft answer turneth away wrath" but it is not news. On the other hand, while "grievous words stir up anger" they often make the front page. The Congressman realizes this keenly, as the most cursory study of his correspondence reveals. To a "gentleman" in a remote city who had written calling him "an ass," his speeches "hooey," and his legislative activities "mere hocus-pocus," Maverick replied: "Your thoughtfulness, your kind-heartedness, and particularly your courage in writing me from such a distance, overwhelm me."

A persistent epistolary heckler from Amarillo, arguing the matter of soil conservation in what Sir Henry Maine once described as "weak generalities and strong personalities," denounced all congressmen as "opportunist politicos full of fanciful notions," whom "we pay $10,000 a year for being wooden Indians and messenger boys instead of statesmen"; adding sundry other chunks of verbal garbage too noisome and too numerous for quotation. Firing back at this human stinkpot Maverick wrote: "I thought that I had insulted you enough in my last letter. Why waste time on me? I am afraid you will find me hopeless as I know you are. . . . Please go out and jump in a dust cloud around Amarillo and get choked. As for me I shall continue to be for soil conservation, and for the elimination of dust clouds—after you have been choked."

On one hilarious occasion a postal card arrived from San Antonio bearing openly upon its obverse such genial epithets regarding the Congressman's stand on the Supreme Court as the following: "mean and abject," "viper-like trespasser," "traitorous bid for personal patronage from the hand of one usurping the leadership of the Democratic party for a Fascist cause." To which Maverick re-

plied in part: "You use language wholly improper for a gentleman
—hysterical, even insane. In sending language which amounts to
open libel and slander on a postal card you have committed a Federal felony for which you could be sent to the penitentiary. . . .
You will regret mailing the card, not on my account but your own,
for I shall do nothing and say no more about the matter. *You are
at liberty to show this letter to your friends.*" As the italicized sentence indicates, the Congressman is well aware that a red-hot re-
joinder is seldom exhibited to others by the recipient.

It would be quite misleading, however, to rest the epistolary
character of the gentleman from Texas upon the above bouquet of
thistle blossoms. In the nature of the case answering a fool according to his folly is futile, albeit good clean fun—and sometimes
news. The fact is, however, as any extended study of the Congressman's correspondence will show, that he answers each letter according to the nature of its content. To those who address him
courteously, no matter how strong their opposition, he replies with
courtesy, broad tolerance, and complete good humor. Always the
replies are forceful, clearly expressed, and entirely unafraid. There
are occasional stylistic slips such as occur in all dictated statements
but, taken as a whole, they make it clear that Maverick regards
letter writing to constituents as a fine art, practicing it not only
skillfully but also with that restraint which is the first sign of the
master.

"I should have lost," wrote Edmund Burke to his electors in the
City of Bristol, "the only thing that can make such abilities as mine
of any use in the world now or hereafter: I mean that authority
which is derived from an opinion that a member speaks the language of truth and sincerity, and that he is not ready to take up or
lay down a great political system for the convenience of the hour,
that he is in Parliament to support his opinion of the public good,
and does not form his opinion to get into Parliament, or to continue in it." Doubtless Maverick would find these sonorous words
somewhat egotistical and stilted, even professorial. Ever since they
were written, however, politicians and political scientists as well
have been mulling over the question: "Whom should a representative represent?" It is doubtful if the gentleman from Texas has
gone into the philosophy of the matter at all deeply, but on the

basis of his own experience he has worked out a quite definite and practical answer which is fully in accord with the principles set down by the great English statesman. However, Maverick adds certain corollaries of his own. He holds himself bound to act on mandate as to things definitely pledged during a campaign. On the other hand, he does not consider himself bound in matters of fundamental national interest, nor in cases of sudden emotion or of mob violence which might occur in his district. "A man must have guts enough to fall out even with his friends." If a new political issue comes up Maverick considers himself free to take sides as his convictions dictate. In any event he holds that he was not elected to be a rubber stamp. Finally he is convinced that "the only way to play politics is not to play politics."

In his various campaigns Maverick has made abundant use of handbills but not of placards. It is his stump speeches, however, that are most effective; they are racy, pungent, humorous, argumentative, straight-from-the-shoulder affairs that carry conviction to the hearts of his hearers. Apparently they cost him little effort; not so, however, the speeches which he makes in the House. As part of the Congressman's "record" the latter are prepared with meticulous care. Braintrusters may be called in for research and verification. But Maverick himself writes out and revises every word he is to pronounce on the floor of Congress; afterwards he goes over the printer's proofs painstakingly two or more times. He is particularly effective in his opening words which are designed to outline what is to follow or to strike a keynote or simply to catch the attention of his colleagues. For example, on the Judicial Reform Bill, February 22, 1937, he began crisply as follows: "Mr. Speaker, I rise today to make one statement, two observations, and one conclusion." He kept his word exactly and, having good terminal facilities, finished in exactly four minutes' speaking time. If details are important he adds them under leave to print in the form of notes which often show wide reading and careful collection of data.

Again speaking for the Gavagan anti-lynching bill before the House in Committee of the Whole, April 15, 1937, Maverick began: "Mr. Chairman, I am from the South, and I never knew a Republican was white until I was twenty-one years old." Humorous claptrap perhaps, but it brought a laugh, captured attention, and was followed two seconds later by words the like of which are seldom heard on southern lips and which went direct to the heart of the issue: "I am in favor of an anti-lynching bill. I am not in favor of any Federal bill that takes over local law enforcement. But I am in favor of a bill which guarantees constitutional rights of all American citizens within the United States of America."

Maverick is as careful about the ordering as he is of the selection of his material. Here his newspaper training stands him in good stead. He seeks always to put his case first in the smallest possible number of words so that he who runs may read. Afterwards a more detailed argument is presented for the benefit of those who have the time and are more deeply interested in the subject. He avoids the arrangement of materials in those long, unbroken columns of fine print which make the *Congressional Record* so arid and repellent. Each text published by the Congressman is carefully subdivided; all the subdivisions are provided with captions, often striking in phraseology, which enable the reader to pick and choose at will. It would be difficult to find a better arrangement of printed material anywhere than in Maverick's brief report on the military disaffection bill. In addition he made a dozen speeches on the subject but it was this smashing report, widely publicized, that killed the bill.

While careful in all matters of form Maverick does not hesitate to resort to innovations. Brevity ranks high among them. People may once have had time to listen to speeches as long as Andy Smith's famous prayer but that day is past. Younger members of the House are lucky if they get ten minutes—and a very good thing that is, too, in Maverick's opinion. Reports should not be allowed to run to two volumes; eighty, ninety, or at the outside one hundred and fifty pages should suffice. Nominating speeches of the old-time variety which went on and on and on, without mentioning the candidate, and then attempted to reach a climax at the end with the naming of the "gr-r-r-eat leader" are particularly obnoxious to the Congressman. Nobody is ever surprised or thrilled and everybody is exhausted and exasperated when the wind-up—usually a sad anti-climax—is reached. If the gentleman from Texas has an introduction to make he names the man at once, briefly recites his qualifications—and sits down.

One of the most striking of Maverick's innovations was the publication of numerous book reviews in the sacred but abysmally dull pages of the *Congressional Record*. He was a trifle truculent in prefacing this device: "If I should call this an oration—and take five or ten pages of the *Congressional Record*, it would meet with the approval of everyone, because no one would read it. Hence if I choose to call what I put in the *Record* 'a book review,' that is my constitutional right, and not even a unanimous decision of the Supreme Court can take it away from me." Naturally with so large a chip on his shoulder someone was certain to make a pass at it. In the course of the next few days a certain well known writer on the *Chicago Times* observed that: "the jolly old *Congressional Record* has at last stooped to folly in its most verbose form—three columns of masterly literary criticism by the Hon. Maury Maverick of Texas on a government report entitled *The Future of the Great Plains*." Maverick responded by reprinting the criticism in full in the *Record*, and having thus used the publicity of the affair for all it was worth, continued calmly with the publication of further book reviews. In the opinion of the writer, who is not without experience along this line, they are, while somewhat given to unconventional turns of phrase, fair in judgment, admirably written, full of verve and humor, and certainly far above the average of the common run of stuff printed in the *Congressional Record*. Incidentally they have served to give publicity and wide distribution to several important government reports which otherwise would have rotted in the basement of some public building in Washington.

First elected to Congress, November, 1934, Maverick came to Washington the following spring merely as one of the 435 members of the House. Within a year he was nationally known, figuring largely in the news reports of the country as a whole. The *New York Times*, for example, devoted seventeen articles to his activities between March and September of his first year as a representative. How did he thus manage to emerge from the obscurity which envelops the doings of the average congressman? So many of them remain immersed in trivia, notables perhaps in their own districts but little known to the world outside.

In part the answer has been indicated already. Maverick possesses gifts of brain and heart that would make him a leader in any social group. Fundamental to the understanding of his career as these qualities are, still certain other details are not without significance. One may ask: "What's in a name?" with the usual scornful intonation given to that question, but it must be admitted that Grandfather Samuel Augustus helped considerably on this score. Maverick is a quaint enough cognomen in and for itself, but it is also one which, thanks to the said ancestor, had passed into general use as a common noun. Since the new member of the House who bore it hailed from Texas he must, of course, be "picturesque"; doubtless he wore chaps, spurs, bandanna and a ten-gallon hat; doubtless also he was full of the tall tales so characteristic of the wild and woolly Southwest. Deluded by these stereotypes, which by the way nauseate Maverick and all other good San Antonians, reporters and press photographers descended in a body upon the new congressman immediately after his arrival in Washington. They saw a somewhat stodgy person in conventional and none-too-good attire; but they did *not* get the tall tales they were after. As for the expected cock-and-bull stories about pioneers, about the fall of the Alamo, about deeds of derring-do in the great open spaces where men are men and all that sort of antiquarian rot, there was absolutely nothing doing. Instead they got the cold, unvarnished truth. One reporter more intelligent than the rest—at least he knew something about the importance of San Antonio as a military center—asked Maverick for his views on war. The answer to that question was NEWS; it was so forceful, so wholly unexpected. Subsequently reporters have always received the same frank treatment at the hands of the Congressman. It is evident that they like him personally; in particular they like his habit of laying all the cards on the table, faces up. Perhaps also they feel him to be one of themselves as a result of his journalistic training and experience.

More important even than his facility in relations with the press were Maverick's affiliations with like-minded younger members of the House. Shortly after he arrived in Washington they came together for the formulation of common principles and policies, adopting a vigorous and comprehensive sixteen-point program dealing with labor, agriculture, taxation, public works, monopolies, war, education, revision of the rules of the House, free speech and free press, and with sickness, old age and unemployment benefits.[3] Since that time these independent younger members, reinforced by several veterans of the House, have held together, fighting pertinaciously for the ends they have in view.[4]

Now these independents, judging by the impression they have made in national affairs, "have what it takes." They do not care a tinker's damn what they are called, regarding the use of epithets as very old-fashioned reactionary technique. Just the same if any misguided opponent so far forgets himself as to dub one of them a demagogue, the honorable gentleman concerned is quite likely to demagogue him right back as a "Country Club Communist," adding sufficient detail to keep the said misguided opponent busy explaining to his constituents that he is nothing of the sort for a month or more. Nor do the members of the younger congressional group waste any time finding names ending in "ism" for their movement. "Liberalism"? In their bright lexicon that means too much—or perhaps nothing. "Radicalism"? They have broken with the old timers of that school who were forever shouting denunciations of Wall Street and never doing anything about it. "Socialism"? No; they regard the doctrines of Saviour Marx and Apostle Lenin as little relevant to the American scene. Congressmen of the new type are inclined to laugh at the soap-box rabble-rouser who always signs himself "Yours for the Revolution." They are convinced that the problems now before the country are not going to be solved by physical force; they have a deep underlying faith in scientific research and in democratic processes. On the other hand, they will tell you frankly that they regard the Constitution as having been made to meet human needs, and hence requiring amendment as conditions change. Rigidity they regard as the one most

[3] For a more detailed statement of these sixteen points see the *New York Times,* March 17, 1935.

[4] Among other members of the group the following may be mentioned: Jerry Voorhis, Charles Colden, Ed V. Izac and Byron N. Scott of California; John A. Martin of Colorado; Kent E. Keller and Frank W. Fries of Illinois; E. C. Eicher of Iowa; John Luecke of Michigan; John T. Bernard of Minnesota; Herbert S. Bigelow of Ohio; Sam Massingale of Oklahoma; Robert G. Allen, Michael J. Bradley and Charles Eckert of Pennsylvania; Fred H. Hildebrandt of South Dakota; W. D. McFarlane and Lyndon B. Johnson of Texas; John M. Coffee, Knute Hill and Charles H. Leavy of Washington; and George J. Schneider of Wisconsin.

dangerous political condition. They have not the slightest intention to confiscate wealth but *they do mean to distribute property rights widely.* If this be treason—or Radicalism, or Socialism, or demagogy, or what have you?—very well, then, you can make the most of it.

Maverick's attainment of national prominence within a year after he came to Washington was not due to work on his part toward that specific end. Rather it came about because he just worked, to the full limit of his forces, for the things which he knew needed to be done. There is, however, an essential logic in the nation-wide distinction he has gained. Essentially he is neither the local nor state type, not even the sectional type, of politician. He approaches issues from the point of view of the country as a whole; hence his actions and utterances make an appeal everywhere. Considering that the Congressman comes from below the Mason and Dixon line the absence of sectionalism from his make-up is particularly noteworthy. As a matter of detail in this connection, even his alleged southern intonation is only faintly if at all perceptible. It is not that he lacks interest in the problems of the South. On the contrary he is acutely conscious of them, particularly in such matters as soil reclamation and conservation, wages and wage differentials, housing, and the like. What he aims at, however, is not sectional welfare *per se* but rather to raise his section together with the country as a whole out of depressed conditions. As a corollary of this realistic national approach to southern problems Maverick loathes the old-time, moonlit, romantic, chivalric, dear-old-black-Mammy, magnolia-and-honeysuckle-blossom, so-red-the-rose-gone-with-the-wind type of fiction. One exception may be noted: the Congressman admits a certain regard for the honeysuckle. Not based either on scent or sentiment, heaven forbid, but solely on the fact that soil conservationists have found it "an effective gully control plant."

No attempt to account for the achievements already to Maverick's credit would be complete without mention of the fact that on May 22, 1920, he married Terrell Louise Dobbs of Groesbeck, Texas. "We are still together," he remarks somewhat whimsically in his autobiography; still, when one recalls what happened to so many marriages contracted in the tangoing twenties, perhaps such a fact does need to be recorded. Very much "together" also, judging by his wife's activity as helpmeet. Both as gracious hostess in their home and as efficient assistant in his office during occasional rush periods, Mrs. Maverick has contributed greatly to her husband's popularity. They have been joined by a son, Maury, Jr., born in 1921, and by a daughter, Terrell Fontaine, born in 1926.

As to physique one does not have to be an astrologer to read in the stars that Maverick was born under the sign of Taurus. Nor a genealogist to perceive that he possesses the bodily traits implied by his family name. There is a tremendous latent strength, slow-moving but persistent, in the man. Height, a trifle under five feet, eight inches; avoirdupois, perhaps the less said the better, however he does fall within the famous dictum sponsored by former Speaker Thomas B. Reed, *viz.*: "No gentleman ever weighs more than two hundred pounds." If there is too much adipose tissue especially around the girth, the result of sedentary life and lack of exercise, there is also plenty of bone and sinew. Maverick's shoulders are well set and powerfully muscled; arms long and brawny; hands—democratic hands with short, stubby fingers but capable of a tremendous grip; legs short and massive—one fancies them slightly bowed from interminable hours in the saddle during boyhood. Despite the burden carried the Congressman's gait is jaunty enough.

Cartoonists dealing with Maverick's head seize instinctively upon the heavy tousled thatch of wiry, dull-black hair. It can be made to lie flat at the back and sides but toward the front it shapes itself naturally into rebellious, wave-like rolls which bend first forward, then upward and back, the one immediately over the forehead especially protruding and giving the effect of a small plume. The brow is broad rather than high. Nose a sharply defined equilateral triangle, not the long, thin nose of a philosopher but fleshy and with a pronounced thrust *en avant*, inquisitive, penetrating, and pugnacious. Eyes slightly protruding and gray with a scarcely perceptible greenish glint; they look out on the world for the most part in a rather cool and speculative manner. Mouth firm and well rounded; full lips often puckered in thought; aggressive, fighting chin. On the whole a good poker face; but Maverick has never played the game, "too busy ever since I was born," and does not know one card from another—thus one more cherished illusion about Texas is shattered! In spite of his ordinarily serious expression the Congressman is quite capable of an engagingly boyish grin over an amusing episode or story.

As to dress, careless comfort and quiet colors seem to be the ends aimed at although it is doubtful whether Maverick ever gives the subject a thought. To say that "he looks as if he slept in his clothes" is putting it too strongly. His manner as a rule is almost Quakerlike; when strongly aroused, however, there is no lack of animation. Standing before a fireplace discoursing on the Supreme Court he sweeps all the Nine Old Men from the high stone mantel to the floor with a single vigorous gesture. His voice is always well controlled; in conversation it is low-pitched, unemotional but persuasive; in public addresses he can use it to meet any mood on the part of his audience and to fill resonantly any hall, no matter how large.

The general physical impression, that of a steady uprush of inexhaustible energy, is verified by Maverick's capacity to put in day after day of grueling labor, eighteen hours out of the twenty-four, for months on end. Obviously this is a pace that cannot be kept up indefinitely. It is true that political work is always fascinating and frequently amusing to the Congressman; in a sense he makes play out of it. On the other hand, the word "recreation" is simply not in his vocabulary, a dangerous oversight; he even seems embarrassed when it is mentioned and seeks to excuse himself by saying that, when not busy in Washington, he enjoys making field-surveys of his dearly beloved reclamation schemes, of housing projects, of the TVA dams and power-plants, and of government works generally. (At this point, feeling that his self-justification is complete, he remarks that it would do the justices of the Supreme Court a world of good if they were to follow his example, thus learning something about American life as it is actually lived, instead of slumbering away four long months each summer in various pleasant country retreats.) When the Congressman's attention is once more drawn tactfully to the fact that field-surveys are also work and that he has not so far put in evidence any real recreation on his own part, he mumbles something rather sheepishly about his small farm with its street car home perched on the hills above San Antonio. There at rare and all too brief intervals he potters around, looks after his fruit trees, escaping the sun in their grateful shade —and lets the world go hang. It is a curious quirk of the man, however, that while he himself scarcely ever stops working he is profoundly convinced that "America must learn how to use its leisure time."

Maverick's office, Room 101 of the Old House Office Building, is a favorite port of call not only for politicians but for all the news-hawks of Washington as well. It is essentially a man's workshop; there is nothing sissified about it, no spick-and-span furnishings, no flowers on the desk, no lady secretaries *à la mode* to do the honors and give a tone of refinement to the place. Chairs, tables, and book-cases are heavy and serviceable. There are, ahem, one or two brass cuspidors on the floor—solely for the use of certain visitors; other-wise, of course, it would not be a real politician's office. On the walls a motley array of maps, plans, photographs, and engravings. Among Presidents, Jefferson, Jackson, Lincoln, and Johnson look down upon the busy scene; in a place of special honor there is a photograph of Franklin D. Roosevelt warmly inscribed to the Honorable Maury Maverick. Interspersed with the foregoing there are cartoons dealing with recent political happenings, drawings which present realistically the life and labor of the very poor, a wall map showing the WPA in action, engineering plans of great national reclamation projects. An incongruous note is supplied by the picture of a squadron of military airplanes in flight among the clouds. However, it is balanced by a reproduction of Constantine's gruesome painting, "Battle's End," which shows a young soldier, wounded and mud-stained, who has dragged himself to die in the midst of a graveyard. Close by one sees a small blackboard on which are noted the days and hours of Maverick's engagements at the House Gymnasium, most of these followed by a zero to indi-cate that he had cut class. Books, books, books, among them many presentation copies, stacked on tables, desks, and shelves, the great majority being recent publications in economics and political sci-ence, precisely the sort of reading on which college professors of these subjects are now engaged. On the floor in various places, convenient or inconvenient, great piles of public documents for consultation or for mailing out to constituents. Decidedly this is an office which reflects the character of its occupant.

On the basis of Professor Charles E. Merriam's analysis of the qualities most frequently exhibited by political leaders, it is evident that Maverick would receive a grade—if one may speak in that professorial jargon which he abominates—of "A" or at least of "A—." [5] Unquestionably the gentleman from the Twentieth Texas District possesses unusual sensitiveness to the strength and direction of social and industrial tendencies, always, however, with particular reference to their effect upon the underdog. He is politically inventive and quick in putting his inventions to work. In group combinations and compromise his success at Washington has been noteworthy, although here perhaps he is more inclined to belligerency than to caution. As to political diplomacy in ideas, policies, and spoils, the first two rate an "A+," but the third must be marked "D—," although this is everlastingly to his credit. Maverick possesses marked gifts in making personal contacts, also facility of the highest possible order in dramatizing the sentiments and interests of large classes of voters. As to "courage with a dash of luck" the former is his in superabundant degree; regarding the latter he opines that he is indeed lucky since he just missed getting killed several times in battle and later in a number of the automobile accidents of peace time. To the objection that this is a rather negative conception of what constitutes good fortune his reply is: "Never got anything worth having by luck; always by hard work and plenty of it."

With so much already achieved, what of the future? If he cherishes ambitions Maverick does not worry about them. What he wants is to do a good job now. Granted that, the future can safely be left to care for itself. In any event he wishes no preferment which would inhibit his personal independence. Certainly Maverick is not one of the type of politicians classified by Professor Merriam as "power-hungry." On the contrary there is nothing of the pride of place in his demeanor: to use a homely phrase he is "as easy as an old shoe." One can imagine his raucous laughter over the pretentious, know-it-all "statesmen" still so common in Washington. Of an essentially combative nature, to Maverick the fight's the thing in large part, victory or defeat mere incidents of slight consequence. Yet he rejects Nietzsche's dictum that " a good

[5] See Charles E. Merriam, *American Party System* (rev. ed., New York, 1929), p. 48.

fight hallows any cause." Rather he holds a draconic conviction of the justice of his cause and hence of its ultimate prevalence. Above all, his profound sympathy with the poor and underprivileged and his even more profound belief in the possibility of social meliorism through democratic processes are the prime motors of his every action. He knows the world is out of joint but thinks it no cursed spite that he has been called, so far as his powers avail, to set it right. On the contrary, this should be the highest duty and privilege of all men who are strong and intelligent not only, but humane as well. To a very large degree Maverick painted his own portrait when he inserted in the *Congressional Record* the stirring words of Louis Untermeyer's "Prayer":

> Ever insurgent let me be,
>   Make me more daring than devout;
> From sleek contentment keep me free,
>   And fill me with a buoyant doubt.
>
> From compromise and things half done,
>   Keep me with stern and stubborn pride;
> And when at last the fight is won,
>   God, keep me still unsatisfied.

9

"HAPPY" CHANDLER:
A KENTUCKY EPIC

By J. B. Shannon

"WHEN I ENTERED TRANSYLVANIA COLLEGE I HAD ONLY A RED sweater, a five dollar bill, and a smile," repeated a soft, southern voice 816 different times from May to November, 1935, as a novel Personality emerged on the political stage of Kentucky. "Happy" Chandler, dubbed by his opposition "sappy" and "playboy," was riding to victory in the state's bitterest gubernatorial primary of this century. Both disgusted and amused by the four-year struggle between aged, "tracksore" Governor Ruby Laffoon and boyish Lieutenant Governor Chandler, ardent partisans disputed, and filling station philosophers applauded or cussed the strange antics of "Ruby" and "Happy."

Who was this David challenging Goliath, the most powerful political machine in Kentucky's history? Few knew the Lieutenant Governor by any name but "Happy." Subsequently, friends and foes alike were somewhat startled when the youthful Governor signed his full name, Albert Benjamin Chandler. People almost instinctively greet "Happy" instead of Governor Chandler because of the popularity of this familiar political shorthand. A college chum, two decades ago, had fixed this label on the cheerful lad whose smile was spontaneous and warm—a label worth hundreds if not thousands of votes in the electoral cash register—the ballot box.

The dazzling career of Kentucky's second young governor is cast in the mold of authentic American political myth. The story of the humble boy, who against almost insurmountable odds of poverty clambers to the top of the heap of power, is interwoven in the warp and woof of American political folklore. The overtones vary somewhat, but the theme is ever the same—the inevitable triumph of honest virtue, pluck, persistence, good will, and hard work. Were Horatio Alger writing the Governor's biography he would doubtless entitle it, "Happy Chandler, from Newsboy to Governor's Mansion." On July 18, 1898, in a village of Western Kentucky, Corydon, population 1,000, a son was born in the home of Joe Chandler, the town's handy man. Half orphaned at five by his mother's voluntary departure, young Chandler did not see her for thirty years. The Lieutenant Governor's discovery of his mother in Florida and her visit to his home won nation-wide attention as a human interest story. Life was not easy for the youth, but he was a "good boy," a boy scout, a newsboy, an athlete, and a likable fellow. The Governor recalls that he was never out later than nine o'clock at night before he was seventeen or eighteen. His early habit of long hours of sound sleep has been of tremendous value to him when making five or six speeches a day. "In sleeping," says the Governor, "I about set the record." "Seven or eight hours?" he was asked. "Nine or ten if they'll let me."

High school completed, young Chandler chose a higher education instead of a job, despite parental opposition, and in college, following his own inclinations, refused to study for the ministry as his father wished. Smilingly, the Governor confesses that his father is now well pleased with his son. Entering Transylvania College without funds, his smile and energy speedily got him two jobs. Shortly the boy with the tenor voice whose favorite song was "When Irish Eyes are Smiling," was dubbed first "Irish," and then "Happy." He carried newspapers, waited on tables, pitched baseball, was quarterback on the football squad, played running guard on the basketball five, participated in track, sang in the glee club and choir, drilled with the S.A.T.C. ("Saturday Afternoon Tea Club"), and played minor parts in the dramatic organization. The leading roles, smiles the Governor, went to "Walter," his roommate and present secretary.

Scholastically, there were a few A's, some D's, an average near B. An instructor describes Chandler as too busy with activities to be a hard student, though his naturally attentive mind absorbed a great deal in classes. His chief interest lay in history though he had a fondness for poetry. Today he recalls no favorite poet though he likes Poe, Shelley, and Keats. Sociology, economics, and education were included in his chosen studies. He became a member of Pi Kappa Alpha social fraternity after an unpleasant episode in which he was black-balled by a ministerial snob whose graduation permitted Chandler's initiation. He held no offices, being "too busy," he relates, to attend class meetings. Fellow students remember his "yodelling," and athletes recollect his visits to the lockers of opposing teams where he shook hands with the coach and players, making friends widely. The constant reminder of Transylvania's great heroes, Henry Clay, Jefferson Davis, and Champ Clark did not influence him toward politics, says Chandler, for becoming governor has "always seemed natural" to him.

His A.B. attained, Chandler's ambition led him to the Harvard law school, "the incubator of greatness," but the road was tough with expenses to earn by coaching in addition to his legal studies. He finished his last two years of law at the University of Kentucky paying his way by teaching and coaching. Locating in a small Bluegrass town, the young lawyer taught history, coached, and played baseball, this last activity taking him over most of the state, widening the circle of his acquaintance. He married Mildred Watkins, a teacher in a local Episcopal school. The marriage, laughs Chandler, was performed by a "Christian preacher in a Baptist church with an Episcopalian ceremony." He became a Mason, a Shriner, a Knight Templar, a legionnaire, a member of the Forty and Eight, an Optimist, and finally chairman of the Democratic County Committee. "Happy" describes this period of his life as one of making a living and "starting a family."

In 1929 his candidacy for the state Senate, his initial plunge in politics, attracted wide attention on account of his youth and his frequent singing of "Sonny Boy" and other popular songs. Despite the scoffing of skeptics, Chandler's majority was greater than his predecessor's. In the Senate he further widened his acquaintance, met and observed older and more experienced politicians, and saw the forces which made Kentucky's political machine go.

The elements which were to make him lieutenant governor and subsequently governor had begun to shape themselves. In 1931, Chandler was given second place on a ticket with Ruby Laffoon, chosen in the first Democratic nominating convention in thirty years. Swept into office in the midst of the depression by a large majority, Laffoon, hard pressed for revenue, proposed a two per cent general sales tax. The Lieutenant Governor, at the crossroads of his career, joined his young political friend, John Y. Brown, speaker of the House, defied the Governor, and defeated the unpopular sales tax in a legislative deadlock which left the state with insufficient revenue to function. Continued operation of schools was endangered and the Governor threatened to open the doors of the penitentiary. The two young college men were subjected to withering criticism. Finally, after repeated special sessions, a combination of Laffoon Democrats and Republicans stripped the Lieutenant Governor of his powers, leaving him the most helpless presiding officer in the history of the state. Subsequently, a three per cent general sales tax measure was driven through by the narrow margin of one vote in each house. "Happy" was definitely "down" but had established a reputation among his colleagues of being able "to take it and smile."

Chandler's ambition to be governor seemed hopeless when the year 1935 opened, for the Laffoon administration, through its control of the Democratic State Central Committee, adopted the convention method of nomination over the eloquent opposition of Senator Barkley, who carried a blessing from President Roosevelt. The nomination of Thomas S. Rhea, chairman of Laffoon's State Highway Commission, was a foregone conclusion.

Then came a lucky moment in "Happy's" life. Laffoon went to Washington leaving Chandler legally governor. "Happy" moved swiftly and dramatically in the most daring act of his career. Laffoon had scarcely reached Washington before Chandler convoked the General Assembly into special session to enact a compulsory primary law. He captured the limelight, broadened his popular appeal, and grabbed the offensive. Even enemies began to speak of him as "smart." The Democratic masses overwhelmingly favored a primary, and this support, together with the sentiment opposed to the sales tax, was now canalized in Chandler's favor. The fight was on. Laffoon hastened back into the state secretly (to avoid service of an injunction prohibiting revocation) and revoked the special call. Chandler legislators assembled, but adjourned, lacking a quorum, since Laffoon members refused to attend. The situation was tense.

ALBERT BENJAMIN CHANDLER

" 'From Newsboy to Governor's Mansion.' "

Thrown into the courts, a local circuit judge, then under consideration for appointment to the federal bench, and subsequently selected on Senator Barkley's recommendation, invalidated Laffoon's action. The Court of Appeals divided 4 to 3 (rejecting a 4 to 3 Nebraska precedent) holding that the governor's legislative powers were exhausted by the original call. "Happy" had won his first skirmish.

A primary law was inevitable; so the Laffoon-Rhea faction staked all on a double primary bill, hoping to produce a deadlock between the pro-Chandler Senate and the pro-Rhea House which would entitle the Governor constitutionally to adjourn the Assembly. Further, Rhea men believed a first primary would exhaust the enthusiasm of the voters so that the machine would win in the second contest. Confronted with two primaries or none, Chandler yielded and is reported to have roguishly told the Governor, "I hope this bill gives you as much pleasure as it does me!" Chandler had won a battle.

The Lieutenant Governor entered the race supported by ex-Senator Beckham, who, attracted by Chandler's youth which recalled the days when he and his young wife lived in the mansion, found in "Happy" compensation in a measure for the recent poignant loss of his own young son. Opening his campaign in the center of the fiercest opposition to the sales tax, the youthful candidate advocated its complete repeal. His attack was vigorous; the offensive was his. Employing the sound-truck device for the first time in a gubernatorial contest in Kentucky, "Happy" set a breath-taking pace, making four or five speeches a day. Chandler's excellent health and his unusual ability to sleep stood him in good stead. After a speech in one town he slept in the rear seat of his automobile while his faithful bodyguard, chauffeur, and masseur drove him to the next. Strengthened by singing, his voice and throat never weakened.

The Governor described with a chuckle a meeting with one of his contenders whose voice was exhausted. With a twinkle in his eye Chandler shouted, "Hello, Governor!" The candidate muttered, "H-e-l-l-o!" "How are you, Governor?" cried Chandler. Lowering his tone the Governor perfectly imitates the feeble voice of his opponent. "Y-o-u-'-v-e k-i-l-l-e-d m-e!" was the weakly whispered response. Laughing his merry "ha-ha-hah," the Governor adds, "He is a fine fellow."

"Governor, did you feel you were going to win all the time?" "Oh, yes," he replied quickly; then grinning, "The other fellows began losing their tempers and getting mad, so I figured I must be going along fine." The grueling campaign ran on through the hot summer with stronger forces piling up behind the younger man. The Lieutenant Governor was altering the technique of campaigning. Conscious of modern dislike of long harangues, he deliberately cut his speeches to fifteen or thirty minutes, while he devoted the remainder of his time to shaking hands with the boys, former baseball teammates, old friends, and all comers. A veteran of many campaigns pleasantly recalls at least one episode in the contest. After speaking, the candidate kissed a baby who was handed him. "Immediately," says the observer, "all the fond mothers began passing their babies to the front and," concluding with unadulterated admiration, "he kissed babies for thirty minutes without stopping. I tell you he is a 'natural.'"

His speeches, frequently containing the phrase "with a song in my heart and a smile on my lips," a sort of theme song with him, were good-humored, though filled with pungent cracks at his opponents. He attempted no fine oratorical flourishes but stood with his hands in the side pockets of his coat, his gaze fixed straight on his audience, his feet planted squarely on the platform. There were no roseate word pictures, no hand laid across chest with eyes rolling heavenward. His few gestures were a mechanical lifting of his arms and hands. An attack on the Laffoon administration, denunciation of the sales tax, and the simple story of his early hardships were the substance of his plea. People listened: men and women; aged and young; farmers and business men. He told coal miners that his election would mean that any boy of theirs might attain the governorship. "Ah, I tell you," asserts a former football teammate, "those mothers were sitting on the edge of their seats with tears in their eyes as 'Hap' told them of his youthful hardships. His boyish face and slightly tousled hair struck straight to their mothers' hearts. I swear he had them eatin' out of his hand." Doubtless a certain plaintive timbre in his voice, a sort of sup-

pressed sob in his tone, gave catching quality to his politically unconventional addresses.

The August primary surprised political prophets, for Chandler
was only 13,000 votes behind the leader. In the run-off two of his
rivals supported Chandler as did several powerful political chiefs.
His following included a queer assortment of fighting factions and
hostile leaders, some of whom had been bitter foes for forty years.
As the run-off drew to a close the Lieutenant Governor, riding the
crest of a wave of popularity, invited everybody "to get on the
bandwagon for the tail gate is down." Troops sent to Harlan
County on Laffoon's orders failed to discourage voting, for the
second primary drew a larger vote than the first, not only in Harlan
but throughout the state. The run-off primary had made "Happy"
the Democratic nominee by 26,000 majority.

After a brief rest the Democratic leader plunged into the final
campaign. He took full advantage of the contrast between his own
amiable personality and the sterner exterior of his opponent, Judge
King Swope, whose smiles lacked the spontaneity of "Happy's"
and whose reputation as a severe judge gave him less popular
appeal. Represented as irritable, high-tempered, and autocratic,
"King" Swope became "his majesty." Chandler's greatest task was
to rally the bitterly divided ranks of his party. He joined quickly
with the nominee for lieutenant governor, a representative of the
opposing element, to close party wounds. Overtures of President
Roosevelt to bring both factions aboard his special train were rejected by the losers, who finally supported Swope but in vain, for
Chandler was elected by 95,000, the largest majority in the state's
history.

Jubilant over his victory the Governor-elect declared the inauguration would be simple, the "people's" affair, with no silk hats or
other formal attire. It was. Thousands came to celebrate. Never in
the history of inaugurations was there a more severe contrast between incoming and outgoing governors. The angular features of
the aged, dour, and gloomy Laffoon threw into bold relief the
genial smile of the youthful "Happy."

But what kind of governor would the singer of "Sonny Boy"
make? The answer was soon forthcoming. Swiftly he required the

resignations of all appointive officials, offering in explanation that his promised reorganization would be hindered by lobbying boards seeking to perpetuate themselves. The state payrolls were purged of thousands "without creating a vacancy." A near riot at the penitentiary and the escape of a few convicts brought charges of inadequate personnel. Boldly the Governor addressed the convicts in person, promised them fair treatment, and personally directed the recapture of those who had fled. Within a few days he left the state, invited the Lieutenant Governor to the mansion, sent roses to his desk, thereby pointing out the contrast, with the preceding administration.

Manfully the Governor undertook to bring the state's expenses within its income. He appointed a group of representative citizens to a non-paid commission, headed by former Governor Beckham, who prepared measures for the legislature. Soon Chandler presented a unique type of legislative strategy, unprecedented in Kentucky, and perhaps unparalleled in American legislative history. This session, in part, resembled the first hundred days of the New Deal. Knowing from his own experience that the sixty-day sessions always ended in a legislative jam where lobbyist groups combined to kill hostile bills, especially revenue measures, the Governor induced the Democratic caucus to pledge adjournment at the end of thirty-nine days. The Governor promised to call special sessions which were constitutionally limited to such legislation as the executive specified. Swiftly and by large majorities, the Assembly repealed the sales tax, passed a compulsory single primary, enacted a state-wide registration law, provided for old age pensions, and adjourned. In consecutive special sessions the Governor successfully piloted to enactment a budget and a reorganization bill which concentrated administrative control in his hands. But his thorniest problem remained—where to get the money? Leaning heavily upon the advice of experts, the Governor proposed and the Assembly adopted taxes on the new distilling industry, increased inheritance levies, and set up the state's first income tax.

The young Governor now faced his toughest fight—a proposed tax on cigarettes. Since production of cigarette tobacco is one of the chief industries of the Bluegrass region, the Governor was courting the fierce antagonism of his own people who have for years protested federal taxes on their product, notwithstanding reiterations of economists that such taxes do not injure the producer. While the Governor was out of the state the legislature heeded the protests of huge crowds of "farmers" and defeated the tax overwhelmingly. Returning home to find his enemies gloating, the Governor predicted the triumphant passage of his bill, warning that "he had never run away from a fight yet." He tells proudly how a bill was introduced to cut sharply the charges of tobacco warehousemen whom he considered responsible for the hostile demonstration. "I decided to show them who was the farmers' real friend and they soon cleared out." The cigarette tax was passed, a political miracle in Kentucky.

The Governor had become a parliamentary leader who answered questions and defended his measures on the floor of both houses. In a subsequent session members of the lower house criticized the Governor on his invitation. "Those who can't stand the gaff shouldn't play the game," he explained. A Republican legislator says some members resented the Executive's action at first but warmed to his frankness. Chandler made no comment when it was suggested that his legislative technique resembled that of a British prime minister but agreed that his coaching experience had been helpful. The acid test of Chandler's legislative leadership was the ratification of the child labor amendment in 1937 despite two previous overwhelming defeats.

What manner of man is "Happy" Chandler? First, he is thoroughly virile, a man's man. Sturdily built, he seems stocky at a distance, yet stands five feet ten and a half inches in height, most of his 190 pounds the brawn of the athlete, though his waist has started to thicken. Agile, the Governor walks with a swift springy step and mounts the mansion stairs two or three at a time without loss of breath. His arms are muscular, especially his right, a result of baseball pitching. His fingers are short, yet long enough to clasp a hand in a firm, almost crushing grip. In a crowd his right hand is cocked, always ready for a greeting.

The Governor's broad shoulders are starting to round. His head, with firmly set jaw and evenly cut lips, is well placed on a short but not heavy neck. He has a straight, pointed nose, beneath heavy brows, and blue eyes with steel-gray glint. At a distance, his eyes appear to squint as if facing the sun, perhaps a hangover from base-ball pitching. Close up the Governor's countenance is open and frank, his gaze steady. When he is intensely interested in conver-sation, his eyes glow as he fixes an intent look upon his listener. Mr. Chandler's dark complexion appears darker because of his thick crown of brownish black hair, parted in the middle and combed slightly backward from his high forehead.

Boundless energy and good health are clearly written on the Governor's person. Never seriously ill, though disturbed by an oc-casional cold, good health is undoubtedly a great asset. It enabled him personally to direct removal of prisoners from a flooded re-formatory filled with rioting convicts, as well as to wear down his political opposition. Ordinarily it keeps him in good humor but sometimes he may be testy. For example, he has given public evi-dence of his displeasure on at least two occasions, once when critics severely condemned the additional salary paid his highway engi-neer by private persons. The press quoted him as saying it was "no-body's damn business." When accused of being the tool of another, Chandler invited his audience to come to Frankfort and find out "damned quick who is governor."

An intimate associate notes that the Governor is usually in ac-tion, playing with a child, toying with a strap, or in some manner always in motion. Speeding along in an automobile, he explains his highway program, emphasizing each point by a sort of open-handed pounding on his companion's leg while his eyes move swiftly as he directs his colored chauffeur where to cut through traffic with the "buggy." Simultaneously he is telling enthusiastically how he re-financed the state's debt. Despite dynamic tension when traveling the Governor is in complete repose in conversation. "See," said he, raising his hand, "I am not at all nervous."

The most unpleasant relation connected with the governorship is the "lack of privacy." Curious tourists drive rapidly around the mansion and endanger the lives of his growing children. Pointing out a young girl who was taking a snapshot of her sweetheart on the mansion lawn, he said, "I don't mind people like those, they won't do any harm, but reckless drivers do." After a long day of "constant pounding" at the office, people come "pounding" at his door at night, "wanting a road or a job." It is distressing, he says, that he cannot see everybody, especially people who do not know how to get an interview, many of whom he wants to see badly. "Some persons," continued the Governor, "say that the mansion belongs to the people, and that is right, yet it is the only home I have and the only place to raise my children." He is proud of his home, shows visitors the drawing room, turns on lights and points out boyishly the beauty of the remodeled mansion. He took his guest to his "quarters," including his bedroom, his shower bath, and an air-conditioned room where the family sleeps when heat is excessive. He welcomed warmly an old college chum who came in, and directed Mrs. Chandler to show him the mansion and his offices.

A political associate telephoned. "Oh, how are you, old boy?" greeted the Governor. "I am conferrin'," he replied to a query. "I have a distinguished visitor with me," he went on, giving a sly wink. Concerning his baseball "tryout" with the Cincinnati Reds in Ohio the previous day, "Ah, I enjoyed it fine." A pause. "Yes, but I told them I might be running in their territory next time, ha-ha!" Turning to politics, Mr. Chandler continued, "You are not going to give me a bad attorney general for a good one are you?" "That's fine, old 'hoss,' that's fine." "Ah, that senatorial race? Opposition at the last minute! Well, we'll see what we can do for him, old fellow." In this easy manner the conversation continued.

A former Republican federal judge, a bitter anti-New Dealer, exchanges pleasantries concerning Louisville politics with his host during lunch. All was not light and gay, for Mr. Chandler appeared to be deeply grieved by the death of the daughter of his next door neighbor in his home town. He hurried through lunch to attend the funeral. "What is the 'bessert,' George?" inquired the Governor, speaking the language of his baby son.

"Keep him there and throw away the keys," commanded the Governor to a state policeman who had just jailed a drunken driver. His police force was short, some having been suspended for drinking, with which their chief has little patience. "I don't see why the boys will do that." He described firing a drunken highway official who after reminding him of their long friendship, begged him "to keep in mind his wife and family." "I asked him," said the Governor, "if he expected me to think more of them than he did. He promised to do better but I doubt if he will." Chandler himself never drinks liquor in any form or smokes, he confides, because he does not like either.

Speaking of the manager of his numerous campaigns, his commissioner of finance, assailed by political enemies as "dictator" and maker of the Governor, Mr. Chandler said simply and loyally, "Dan Talbott is an honorable man. He is a druggist who never had any money and probably never will." The Governor expressed no hostility towards "the critics." There is no need to answer them since false stories will be boomerangs. To illustrate he mentioned the newspaper which had printed unfounded rumors of many convicts drowned during the great flood of 1937. Asked about a story that he had struck down a convict who had hit at him, he answered, "Not a word of truth in it. We had no trouble at all."

Towards his political foes he manifested no animosity, though one was characterized as an ignorant "blackguard." His sharpest remark concerned a Republican senator who, after voting for an early adjournment of the legislature to save expenses, changed his vote when it proved to be decisive. "You can't get along with a fellow like that," he exclaimed. The senator feared the judge in whose jurisdiction he practiced law, but "I am not afraid of him," mused the Governor, "nor do I remember ever being afraid of anyone.[1] I don't want people to be afraid of me. I like them to talk back to me if they disagree." Some people fear him because he is governor, but, "After all, I am just another fellow."

Though his political philosophy has never been systematically outlined, Chandler optimistically believes better people are going into politics—the quality of persons in public life equaling or surpassing that in business. His experience in politics has not made him cynical about human nature.

A careful examination of the evidence had convinced him of the guilt of Harlan County miners convicted in the Evarts killing. Tried before an impartial judge through a change of venue by a jury living far from the scene of the crime their conviction had been affirmed by the Court of Appeals. Many people do not understand the depression background in Harlan County, he stated, and union organizers receive fees for organizing. The United Mine

[1] "I am not afraid of a buzz saw," he cried in a recent speech.

Workers did not support him in primary contests, "But they didn't tell the La Follette Committee that." He took from his finger a diamond ring which the United Mine Workers had presented him, as a token of appreciation. In lawyer fashion, he contended that the sit-down strike interfered with possession of property. "A man who has a little property is more likely to be law-abiding than one who does not," he affirmed. In the preliminaries of his campaign for the Democratic nomination for United States senator Chandler's opposition to the sit-down strike device became increasingly evident. It is to be remembered, of course, that his appeal was directed to Kentuckians, who are to a large extent farm owners in whom the property impulses are well developed.

Passing upon executions is a very trying experience especially since "you realize that if you sign this paper a man will live, but if you sign another he will die." He has to accept a duty imposed upon him by the people.

With little time to read himself, Mrs. Chandler reads to the Governor and calls matters of general cultural interest to his attention. "She has been a great help to me," he added. Greeting "Milly" with an affectionate kiss and good-husbandly hug, he explained to her that his visitor was going to "write up somebody you know along with 'Rosy' and a lot of other fellows." The mother of four young children and mistress of the mansion, Mrs. Chandler has an arduous task since Kentucky fails to provide a housekeeper for its mansion. She facetiously remarked that her husband's reputation as a Shylock in collecting taxes gave her little hope.

What are "Happy" Chandler's peculiar characteristics of mind and temperament? First, an enormous energy driven by great ambition carries him over many obstacles. A close friend and admirer speaks of him as a "consummate egotist." The Governor reads flattering editorials and letters with more zest than official documents, says an associate. But the same "ego drive" gives him great pride in accomplishment. He is proud of having been elected to three public offices by greater majorities than his predecessors and of his record as governor. He tells with elation how he "persuaded" all other state schools to abandon graduate work and concentrate it in the state university, though "I was told I couldn't do it. We'll have a great graduate institution in the future." He is gratified by a favorable comment in a national newspaper on Kentucky's increased per capita expenditure for schools. He boasts that he has a new kind of private secretary, one who is not a "wirepuller." It gives him satisfaction that the prisoners are now working and have gained fourteen pounds per man and will soon work on a 2,184-acre state-owned penal farm. He enjoys telling that he has "the best road engineer in the country." Self-confident, he looks to the future. "There will be a new president in this country someday and I have as good a chance as anybody," he tells his homefolks.[2]

During the early months of 1938 the direction of the Governor's ambition became apparent. A Kentucky legislature under his control passed a resolution endorsing Senator Logan for the vacancy left by the resignation of Justice Sutherland. If Logan had stepped aside Chandler's way to the Senate was clear. The judicial appointment went to another Kentuckian, Solicitor General Stanley Reed. This fact did not improve the relations between majority Senate leader Alben W. Barkley and the ambitious young Governor. Another vacancy on the bench, this time on the United States Circuit Court of Appeals, afforded another opportunity to remove Logan and permit Chandler to take his place. It was at this time that Chandler's intention to challenge Barkley became clear. The Governor visited the White House only to discover that the President was loyally behind "dear Alben." On his return Chandler reported that "that fellow" (the President) had urged him to wait his turn, but the Governor replied that Mr. Roosevelt had never waited "to pop the question."

Soon thereafter, Chandler entered the lists against Mr. Barkley. Chandler took this action after conferring with a number of southern senators, including Senator Byrd of Virginia, whom the Governor had taken as a political idol several years ago. Speaking of his own prospects for the Democratic nomination in 1940 with increasing frequency, at the same time directing criticism at Barkley's support of President Roosevelt's spending policy while emphasizing the balanced budget of Kentucky and the declining debt, he indicated his intention to become the spearhead of a southern right-wing effort to capture the leadership of the party nationally by attacking Senator Barkley, the leading exponent in the South of New

[2] Lexington *Herald*, July 25, 1937.

Deal liberal policies. A defeat of Barkley would have been a stunning blow to President Roosevelt's prestige and might have given an aggressive, vigorous, vote-getting personality like Chandler's a nomination despite the handicaps of Kentucky's being a southern state and having a small electoral vote. He took as his campaign slogan "A man of action, not of words."

The Governor's bold challenge placed Kentucky Democrats on the horns of a painful dilemma. They were forced to make a choice between a "good" Governor and an "able" Senator. Chandler's ambitions were met with derision by some voters who said that the Governor had not "grown" but merely "swelled," while others admired his ambition. A slightly inebriated voter, while shouting loudly his opposition to Chandler and describing him in obscene language, at the same time vociferated his profound admiration for Chandler's "guts" in trying to get ahead. The Governor's greatest opportunity lay in his becoming the symbol of the "little man" who achieves all things by grit and determination. Frequent charges are made, however, that the Governor had violated the politician's code of honor and has proved "disloyal" to friends. His break with his Damon and Pythias friend and former political ally, John Young Brown, now a leader of the C.I.O. forces and potential candidate for governor of Chandler's opponents in 1939, is cited as the principal example.

The Governor's ill-advised campaign for the Senate in 1938 attracted nation-wide attention. To Kentucky came President Roosevelt, the Prince of Smiles, to match smiles with the youthful Governor as he gave his historic endorsement to Senator Barkley. A too optimistic faith in his destiny probably induced Chandler to reject the warnings of his more seasoned advisers. His robust health failed him in the midst of the campaign, and the question whether the ice water he drank was poisoned remains as yet undetermined. With no popular issue to employ against Barkley, who was supported by a powerful national administration, the organized farmers, and all branches of organized labor, the merry Governor and his engaging personality went down to overwhelming defeat before the sixty-year old but still "iron man" Barkley.

A man of strong emotions, "Happy" makes people feel that he genuinely likes them. A farmer (a former football teammate)

comes up to shake hands. Chandler presents his wife, "the com-
mander-in-chief." In the midst of a busy campaign he delights his
former associate by personally replying to a letter. "They were all
for me, weren't they?" he exults, speaking of his old college acquaintances. To a crowd, he conveys a personal touch. In a big
rally he tenderly describes his little son bringing him the morning's paper crying, "Daddy, here's your picture!" When a shrill
voice shouted, "Happy," in the midst of a formal speech, Chandler
stopped, laughed infectiously, the huge crowd joining with him,
even as forty thousand people united with Franklin Roosevelt in
hilarious laughter at fumbling old Ruby Laffoon, who mumbled
before the microphone that he had the wrong speech!

The Governor has a sense of humor. Attending a commencement he publicly congratulates a personal friend who is getting his
doctorate, adding, "I tell him I got mine first [referring to an
LL.D.] but he tells me he earned his." Addressing a summer session with the usual formal salutation, "Members of the faculty,
students, ladies and gentlemen," he grins, "not that there is any
difference." His crowd laughs with him.

"Happy" Chandler is a perfect extrovert, handicapped by no
embarrassing self-consciousness. He sings "Carry Me Back to Old
Virginny" with a college audience and improvises when his memory is hazy. He leads the mountain laurel festival in singing "My
Old Kentucky Home," and kisses the brow of the queen deco-
rously. At a college festival he stops in the parade to pat the blond
head of a five-year-old boy. He does it easily, unaffectedly, naturally. Between halves he rushes up to a microphone to describe a
football game between his alma mater and a rival institution. He
has announced basketball games at state tournaments. He likes to
sit on the bench with the players. In the excitement of one basketball game he is reported to have given the back of the dignified
and distinguished president of the University of Kentucky several
resounding wallops. He leaves lunch with his cabinet to get the
score in the world series. Governor of the state, he sings to his legislature, "Home on the Range," accompanied by a hillbilly band,
and entertains a crowd of racing fans with "There is a Gold Mine
in the Sky." He lives heartily, buoyantly, happily—apparently he
seldom indulges in the melancholy diversions of a Hamlet. Nei-

ther does he spend hours in lonely darkness, engaging in the Sisyphean task of the "intellectual," who rolls his thoughts up the hill so that they may tumble down again. Life is real and earnest—but full of fun. His brow is unfurrowed by premature lines, and no strand of white mingles with the black of his hair, as silver streaks the distinguished head of Phil La Follette.

Full of zest for living, dynamic, and magnetic, "Happy" Chandler epitomizes the always unrealized but never forgotten urge of humanity to live and to live enthusiastically. He symbolizes the grit and determination of a civilization yet young which believes that God's still in his heaven whether or not all's right with the world.

10

JOHN L. LEWIS

By Philip Taft

JOHN L. LEWIS IS THE FIRST AMERICAN LABOR LEADER TO ACHIEVE an important political position. Lewis is not a political boss. He has no jobs or contracts or projects with which to reward his political followers. Yet he is the spokesman for thousands, and possibly millions of wage earners. No man of labor has been able to muster as large a political constituency, and the feat has been accomplished in the face of the opposition of seasoned veterans of the craft union sections of organized labor.

Does Lewis's constituency represent an ephemeral following ready to scatter as soon as the novelty of his leadership has worn thin; or is Lewis the activizing element who has stimulated the latent dissatisfaction and hope of labor into a potent political force? People fond of analogies hopefully proclaim that his rise parallels the skyrocketing of Huey Long, the "saintly" Coughlin, and the other assorted political medicine men washed up by the depression; and that Lewis must inevitably slide the same toboggan to political impotence. Only time can vindicate their dire prophecies; but, meanwhile, attention to the differences in the constituencies of purely political leaders like Long and Coughlin and the following of John L. Lewis might induce them to postpone their post-mortems. No one writing on the subject of Lewis can ignore the pronouncements that his present activity on the economic and political fronts is nothing but a drive for personal power. We need not entirely deny that one of the ingredients of successful leadership is the desire for position, but there are more reasonable and rational explanations for Lewis's activity than the mere seeking for power and glory.

The role of the individual in history is a subject of intriguing and perennial discussion. The several schools of determinists are ready with other answers, but at no time has the great personality theory been lacking in advocates. Social and economic conditions prepare the ground and the basis of activity; but the outstanding individual is the catalytic agent promoting and stimulating forces that are latent in society. We may, therefore, at the outset concede the ability, drive, and leadership of Lewis, but his present conduct can be best understood by studying his activity in relation to the problems and needs of the United Mine Workers of America, in whose service he has spent the largest part of his official life.

Lewis's personal life need not long detain us. Born in Lucas, Iowa, in 1880, of Welsh parents, he spent his early life around Lucas and Des Moines, Iowa. Upon leaving school he went to work in the coal mines. Soon after, he left home and began roaming about the country, returning to Lucas, where he married the daughter of a local physician in 1907. He then moved to Panama, Illinois, where his career as a union officer was launched in 1909. He was elected to the Illinois Miners' legislative committee and also as a delegate to the convention of the United Mine Workers. He resigned two years later to become a lobbyist and organizer for the American Federation of Labor in the Southwest.

His own local at Panama continued to send him as a delegate to the international conventions of his union. Lewis did not take the floor frequently, and in most matters he was aligned with the conservatives. In 1911 he had occasion to come to the defense of William Green, who had just been elected to the Ohio Senate on the Democratic ticket. The Socialists, who were at the time a not insignificant minority, charged that Green's election unfitted him to sit as a delegate at a miners' convention and demanded that his seat be denied him. Lewis rose to his defense and made the motion to seat the Honorable Gentleman from Ohio, and after a bitter debate the motion was finally carried. Lewis's importance was on the increase, and in 1916 he was chosen to represent Illinois in the negotiations of the Central Competitive Field Agreement. In the same year he showed his skill as a parliamentarian when he presided during the debate on the most tempestuous issue of a hectic convention. In 1911 the president of District 14 was accused of accepting a bribe to use his influence on behalf of the Southwest coal operators. It was subsequently proved that it was a plot to destroy an honest union official, and the officer against whom the charge was leveled was vindicated in the courts. He was, however, dissatisfied with the aid and attitude of the national administration in the affair, and he now came to the national convention, the highest body in the union, to demand justice. Feeling ran high, but Lewis managed to steer the debate without arousing the animus of either side.

By 1916 Lewis was a man of national importance in the union, and in February, 1917, he was appointed International statistician. Shortly thereafter, John P. White, the International president, was asked to join the Fuel Administration, thus placing Frank J. Hayes, the present lieutenant governor of Colorado, in the chief executive's post. Although Hayes had at one time been a Socialist and Lewis was a conservative, the men were friendly and each respected the other's ability. Lewis was appointed to the International vice-presidency in October, 1917. He later defeated Thomas Kennedy, then president of District 7 in the anthracite and now secretary-treasurer of the miners' union and lieutenant governor of Pennsylvania. Hayes did not serve long as president. He became ill in the early months of 1919, and the job of chief executive fell on Lewis in the most critical period in the history of the United Mine Workers of America.

Under his regime the membership declined to the lowest point since the strike of 1897, and then rose to the greatest number in the history of the union. During his leadership the Central Competitive Field fell to pieces; but upon its ruins he built a greater and more inclusive one, the Appalachian. In addition, it was he who took the first step to clean up the forgotten sectors of American industry and bring their workers under the hegemony of organized labor. With the aid of a few other progressive labor leaders he launched the most extensive organizing drive in the history of American labor. With the help of these men he also has initiated an active political movement which may soon become an important factor in bringing about the long discussed realignment in American politics.

The mine workers' organization developed in a climate different from that of other sections of the labor movement. The isolation of mining communities and the nature of their work has developed a strong sense of labor solidarity among the mine workers.

Their willingness to sacrifice transcends their own group, and strug-
gling workers everywhere have always been able to find sympathy
and support among them. As a result of their wider interest in the
problems of labor, the conventions of the miners' union have been
great forums for the discussion of labor policies and programs. An
active minority has always frowned upon the laggard conservatism
of the American Federation of Labor. A conservative in the mine
workers was, moreover, never a reactionary. The United Mine
Workers of America espoused the cause of industrial unionism, and
frequently it went on record in favor of independent political action. One of Lewis's predecessors, John Mitchel, one of the great
labor leaders of his day, led the fight for industrial unionism in the
convention of the American Federation of Labor in 1912; and to
Mitchel, as to Lewis, conservatism did not mean stultification, nor
undeviating acceptance of the status quo.

For many years the Socialists were a leavening influence in the
organization. These men were perennial advocates of independent
political action, and they always took the lead in fighting for
broader policies. The Federation's political line was anathema to
these men, but they also objected to the general indifference of the
Federation leadership to the problems of the unskilled and unorganized. Leaders who developed in such a milieu could not avoid
being influenced by the broader policies advocated by the mother
union. That this group was no insignificant minority can be seen
from their insistence in 1912 that the United Mine Workers of
America withdraw from the American Federation of Labor because
of the latter's neglect of the unorganized. The resolution was defeated, but the miners never agreed with the narrow policies of the
Federation.

There is, in addition, a more fundamental reason for Lewis's
turn towards politics. The miners' organization had not, until the
NRA, completed the unionization of the bituminous coal industry.
The Central Competitive Agreement which followed the strike of
1897 was never extended to the southern coal regions. A number
of attempts to bring that growing coal area under the hegemony of
the union failed because of the unrelenting opposition of the operators. The heroic Mother Jones led organizing expeditions in
1904, and again in 1912, but Mother and her boys were either

thrown into stockades or run out of the district. Other organizers were even less fortunate, and their bullet-riddled bodies were frequently given decent burial as a reward for their unionizing attempts in the southern fields. The union faced a magnified Harlan County, with no Wagner Act on the statute books or La Follette committees to protect its rights to organize.

The constant increase in non-union tonnage perennially placed the question of West Virginia and the non-union areas at the head of the union's convention agenda. All the leaders recognized the ominous importance of the non-union outpost, but none could devise a technique for surmounting the barrier. Until the World War, West Virginia and the other non-union areas represented only a threat to the future, but the far-sighted leaders could read the handwriting on the wall. The World War intensified the problem, as it brought a tremendous expansion in non-union tonnage, and soon after the armistice a new attempt was launched to organize the region. The attempt was frustrated by the inability of the union to break through the ring of steel erected around the five non-union counties.

Lewis took the helm at a time when the union's position was being increasingly threatened by the inroads of the non-union producers upon the union markets. There were, however, more immediate problems pressing for solution. Dissatisfaction was rampant throughout the coal areas, and the workers demanded action from their officials. A contract negotiated during the war had failed to keep wages parallel to an ever-rising cost of living. Another serious grievance crying for correction was the penalty clause, which fined the miner a dollar for every day he remained away from work in violation of the joint agreement. It was a difficult situation faced by the new executive, but Lewis rode out the first storm with flying colors.

In addition, Lewis was confronted with a vigorous opposition from inside of his union. Some of the more powerful district presidents were casting envious eyes in his direction. Many of them felt that a man who had never served the usual apprenticeship in the form of a district presidency or secretaryship should not be rewarded with the highest office in the union. The fates seemed almost to conspire against him in the first months of his long administration. Soon after he took over the job of president, he was called

UNDERWOOD AND UNDERWOOD

JOHN L. LEWIS

*"Spokesman for thousands, and possibly millions, of
wage earners. . . . A middle western American raised
on simple American political fare."*

upon to authorize the revocation of the charters of twenty-four locals whose members had gone on strike in violation of the agreement. This action did not sit well with many of the more radical members in the union, but the convention subsequently supported his action overwhelmingly. This action revealed a trait in Lewis's makeup which was to cause him considerable trouble later in his administration. From the beginning of his career as president, Lewis would not tolerate breaches in the agreement, and, come what may, he would insist upon obedience and use the full power of his office to punish violators.

Opposition to "illegal" strikes did not mean that Lewis was a believer in quietism. In the first months of his administration, he called for the abrogation of the Washington agreement, and proposed a set of demands for presentation to the bituminous coal operators which demonstrated that he was determined to utilize the full power of his union to eliminate grievances and improve the conditions of the coal diggers. His recommendations aroused a storm of indignation in the camp of the operators. Lewis proposed the abolition of the penalty clause; the six-hour day and the five-day week; and a two-year contract to run concurrently in all bituminous fields. The latter proposal was a great step forward and one which had long been advocated by the progressive elements in the union. It meant that all the bituminous coal diggers would act as a unit in bargaining with the operators, instead of each district making its agreement separately.

The operators rejected the Lewis-inspired terms, and the most extensive strike in the history of coal unionism followed on November 30, 1919. The country was in the midst of a red-baiting campaign, one of the unhappy legacies of the war, and an attempt was immediately made to label the strike as a revolution. An effort to smother the strike by an injunction followed. Attorney General A. Mitchell Palmer appeared before Judge Albert B. Anderson, of the Indiana District Court, and asked that the strike be curbed. The Judge obligingly issued the most sweeping injunction in the history of labor warfare. The officers were forbidden to engage in any activities tending to encourage or support the strike. No strike relief could be paid, and even a letter appealing for the support of the walkout was in violation of the decree. Lewis faced a serious dilemma. Surrendering to the order of the court would not only mean sacrificing the opportunity to rectify the rightful grievance of 350,000 miners, but it might have led to a serious rift in the organization. On the other hand, open defiance might lead to results almost as serious. The union's funds might be impounded and its leaders thrown into jail for contempt. The national and district leaders met in what was the most critical session in the organization's quarter of a century of existence. A small minority advocated open defiance of the judicial ukase. They were overruled. Instead, Lewis announced cryptically: "We can't fight the government." Nominally the strike was over, but no union man came near the pits. It was an interesting demonstration of the old adage of the horse and the water. Injunctions could prevent strikes, but they could not mine coal. In sending out the notices for a return to work to the locals, the seal of the International union had been inadvertently left off the order; and the strict constructionists among the miners would never honor a document unadorned by the official insignia. The walkout continued for another month, and it was settled by the intervention of President Wilson, who appointed a commission to settle the controversy. The ultimate settlement aroused scant enthusiasm, and was in fact disapproved by the miners' representative on the commission, but the union did demonstrate that it would not be intimidated by a judicial decree.

It was the first real test of Lewis's leadership, and he piloted the organization through a difficult journey with considerable credit. None of his predecessors had been called upon to meet a similar situation. It is true Mitchel was once sentenced for contempt of court, but this had no relation to the affairs of his union and was an outgrowth of a boycott campaign. Lewis had maintained a strike in the teeth of an injunction and had forced concessions despite the judicial interference. He had demonstrated the ability to meet an external opponent, but he was soon confronted by an opposition of a different order. In a controversy with the operators, all groups in the union could be depended upon to unite for common action. In an internal struggle the situation was changed. The presidents of the important districts had always acted to a large degree like independent feudal barons. With their district treasuries and district membership as support, they could frequently defy the International officers. The most powerful of the district officers, Frank Farrington of Illinois, was a bitter personal and political enemy of Lewis. Farrington was an intelligent and shrewd fighter and political manipulator and commanded a membership of more than 90,-000 miners. Himself a conservative, he was ready to combine with any group out to get Lewis. An able leader and capable negotiator, he lacked the stubborn tenacity and basic integrity of his opponent. It was the absence of these qualities which finally enabled Lewis to destroy him completely as a political factor in the miners' union, and reduce him to an impotent sniper on the fringe of the labor movement.

Farrington attempted to raise one of his henchmen into the presidency of the United Mine Workers of America by supporting Alexander Howat, the fighting president of Kansas District 14. After the national coal strike, Governor Henry J. Allen, of that state, devised what he regarded as a solution for strikes and lockouts. The Industrial Relations Court was established and compulsory arbitration introduced. Howat fought the law with tooth and nail. He was a determined and courageous leader, and he demonstrated that the Governor's panacea brought industrial strife instead of peace to the coal fields. His open defiance discouraged the spread of the Governor's innovation. While opposed to the Industrial Relations Court Act, the International did not countenance the "illegal" strikes in the Kansas district. No action was taken, however, until a strike was called against one of the largest coal producers in District 14 over the introduction of automatic hoisting machinery. Howat contended that these changes were forbidden by the terms of the agreement. The operators denied his claim and finally the Southwestern Coal Operators' Association appealed to Lewis to end the illegal walkout and force obedience of the agreement. Lewis upheld the position of the operators, and he ordered Howat to end the strike. Howat repeated his original contention. A commission was dispatched by the International office to investigate. They upheld the position of Lewis, who again ordered obedience of the terms of the contract. Refusal this time led Lewis to revoke the charters of the thirty-three locals involved. Howat still refused to change his policy and was consequently suspended from office and the district charter revoked. A provisional officer took command, and an attempt by Howat to have the suspension set aside by the courts led to his expulsion from the union, on the ground that the United Mine Workers forbade appeal to the courts on organization issues. He was later reinstated and remained a constant thorn in the side of Lewis.

Lewis's character and policy as revealed by this episode should be borne in mind, especially by those who are loud in proclaiming him a radical. From the beginning of his official leadership he has always insisted upon a meticulous observance of contracts, and it required courage and strong conviction to challenge an important district leader with a wide appeal and strong support on this question. Not only did Howat have the unanimous support of the Illinois district, but out of a total convention vote of 4,028, Lewis was upheld by a majority of only 118. Defeat on this issue would have meant political death, but the maintenance of agreements was regarded as so important that Lewis was willing to run the risk of political destruction rather than countenance or overlook a persistent violation. The fight was won for the time being, but for the next ten years Lewis was confronted by the powerful and unyielding opposition of the Illinois district officers.

The following year Lewis decided to tackle bigger game. Within the American Federation of Labor considerable opposition had developed to the unbending conservatism of Samuel Gompers. His attitude on such questions as government ownership of railroads did not sit well with the railroad bloc and other progressive unionists. Gompers had not been seriously challenged since 1894, when he met his only defeat at the hands of another miner, John McBride, and was given a "Sabbatical." Gompers possessed a well-oiled and smooth-functioning machine capable of bowling over almost any opposition. In addition, he knew all the arts of rabble-rousing and political maneuvering, and was considered by his followers as the Grand Old Man of Labor. He had then served the American Federation of Labor for four decades, and many delegates regarded him with deep affection. Lewis, undeterred by the popularity of Gompers, entered the lists as a candidate supported by the railroad bloc and the majority of progressives. He was defeated, but he made a creditable showing and forced the Gompers machine to make a few bargains to carry the election.

In the next few years the situation in the coal industry engaged his complete attention. Serious internal problems were facing the union. With the Illinois district as a center, Lewis's political opponents kept up an unceasing warfare against him. He was not the man to take it lying down, and he returned the blows of his opponents with interest. Even more serious than the internal difficulties was the trend of production in favor of the unorganized districts. For the time being the union was in no danger, but the alarming increase in non-union tonnage was a portent which boded ill for the future. In 1922 the internal problem was complicated by the intrusion of the Communists into union affairs. Excepting some of the red-baiting building trades, labor unions have generally taken the position that a worker's political or religious opinions are his own affair. As Lewis has recently expressed it, "the employer chooses the membership of the union." This view is possible and desirable as long as a political group does not meddle in union affairs. The Communists had other hopes in the early twenties. They organized the Trade Union Educational League, which was designed to capture the trade unions and utilize them for the advancement of Communist policy. Against this program Lewis reacted with all his power. Those found guilty of Communist connections were summarily expelled from the organization. Charges of dictatorship and despotic rule filled the liberal weeklies, but unless Lewis was ready to hand over his organization to a left-wing caucus no alternative was open to him. The United Mine Workers of America, in common with most organizations of labor, has always allowed discussion of policies and opposition to the administration. As long as the opposition is not organized on the principle of capturing the movement and using it for the advancement of political purposes, no objection has ever been raised against it. There are dozens of men in important posts in the United Mine Workers of America and in the C.I.O. who have differed and fought with Lewis on organization policies. That has always been and is today considered a legitimate exercise of democratic rights guaranteed by the organization.

The Communists were this time not the only opposition to Lewis within the union. He was being blamed for the loss of union tonnage, a tendency which had been developing for more than three decades. The convention proceedings and union bulletins contain hundreds of pages of discussion of this growing menace. John L. Lewis was not only acquainted with the situation through secondary sources, but he had been active in organization work in the non-union area prior to becoming International vice-president. There were some in the union who advocated the acceptance of wage cuts by the organized miners to enable the union producers to meet the competition of the unorganized fields. This advice was rejected by Lewis for two reasons: First, internal political conditions would not enable an officer to survive politically who carried out such policy. The most important reason was that the non-union regions could always improve upon the union's attempt to salvage its position by wage cuts, as the absence of the organization's restraining influence would enable them to cut wages at their pleasure. The Jacksonville agreement signed in 1924 accentuated the differences between costs in the union and non-union districts. Soon after its signing, rebellion and contract-repudiation swept the organized areas, but Lewis advised against a downward revision of wages. Instead he hoisted the slogan of "No Backward Step" and fought with all of his resources the attempt to beat down the scale. The union was fighting a losing battle, and the deunionization of the organized districts brought with it widespread dissatisfaction. "Save the Union" committees sprang up throughout the coal fields. In 1926 the opposition challenged the policies of the administration by nominating a full slate against Lewis and his group. The opposition candidate was John Brophy, at that time president of District Two. In many ways Brophy resembles the English type of labor leader. He is quiet and thoughtful, and always has been progressive in his views of trade unionism. His differences with Lewis were not political. He advocated the boycotting of the northern properties of those coal producers who also operated in the southern fields, and who refused to deal with the union in both sections, until such time as the operators in question would recognize the union in all of their properties. Lewis did not regard that program as feasible, as he feared that the operators would counter such a movement by shutting down their union properties, and thus it would only accentuate the difficulty oppressing the organization. An attempt has since been made to describe Brophy as a Communist. Brophy happens to be a devout Catholic, and naturally is out of sympathy with the materialistic determinism of the Communists. What is more, Brophy's Catholicism is not something he uses for display, but it is a deeply held conviction. His son, Philip Noel, is studying for the priesthood at St. Meinrad's Seminary in Indiana, and he and all the members of his family are devout and conscientious churchgoers. Brophy fought on a union issue, and as soon as the Save the Union committee showed dual union tendencies, he hurriedly disassociated himself from it.

In 1928 the control of the union was gone in all of its old strongholds except Illinois. The destruction of the United Mine Workers in a large section of the bituminous coal fields did not solve the problems of the industry. If anything, the absence of any check upon wage-cutting intensified its illness. Price- and wage-cutting failed to restore vitality to an industry suffering from anarchic individualism. More than anything the bituminous coal industry needed regulation. This function had been performed by the union for many years through an elaborate system of differentials, but this control broke down as a result of the increase in non-union tonnage. Lewis saw that the problem of assuring a fair return to capital and labor in the coal industry depended upon government intervention. Only then could order and profit for capital and a living wage for the workers in the industry be restored. It was at his request that Senator James Watson, Republican leader of Indiana, introduced the first bill to regulate the coal industry. The country was, however, not yet ready for such innovations, and the bill was not taken too seriously.

In 1929 Lewis faced another serious internal situation. The organization had been able to maintain its position in the Illinois district throughout the trying period following the Jacksonville agreement. Illinois had nurtured a powerful opposition movement from the beginning of his administration. Farrington, its old leader, had been forced out of office, after he had accepted a $75,000 retainer to act as adviser for the Peabody Coal Company, but the old animus persisted. A powerful secession movement arose when Lewis suspended one of the local officers for being involved in a shady real estate deal in the purchase of a union headquarters. Lewis was charged with interfering in the affairs of the district, and a revolt flared when he insisted upon his right to intervene. The district officers entered the fray and charged that Lewis and his group were no longer the rightful United Mine Workers of America, as the constitution had lapsed. A vindictive struggle followed, with both sides claiming to be the real miners' union. Injunctions and counter-injunctions were requested, and finally an arrangement was worked out which gave the Illinois district complete autonomy, with Lewis agreeing to accept terms barring him from interfering in the district's affairs. The majority of the members outside of Illinois sided with Lewis, and even in Illinois he was not without followers.

Shortly after the settlement, the district officers were pleading with Lewis to help them out of a serious dilemma. The Illinois operators found it difficult to hold their markets in the face of the lower wage scales in the unorganized areas. They pleaded for a readjustment of wages, beginning April 1, 1932. The unorganized districts, enjoying a wage differential, were destroying the Illinois market and making it impossible to mine coal profitably. The district officers, who were aware of the situation, encouraged resistance, for political reasons. A strike was called, and after three months a contract embodying a substantial wage cut was accepted by the district officers. It was overwhelmingly rejected by the membership. At this stage Lewis's enemies invited him to attempt a settlement. He had been kept out of the Illinois district by the terms of the settlement of the union controversy. With the situation desperate, he was invited to come in and try his hand at bringing an end to a costly strike. Another referendum on the operators' terms was held, but the ballots were mysteriously stolen; the union officers were charged with having engineered this maneuver. An emergency was declared and the operators' terms accepted. The entire affair was bungled by the district officers, and they appealed to Lewis only when they had got themselves into a difficult mess by proclaiming that there would not be a wage cut, when they knew, or should have known, that the Illinois operators could not survive without one. The revolt against the terms resulted in the formation of the Progressive Miners of America. Lewis is not without blame for the development of the unfortunate situation in the Illinois coal fields, as he was very likely aware of the intentions of the district officers to settle the strike regardless of the wishes of the membership. No doubt a settlement was imperative if the union were to be maintained. However, the recognition that the essence of democratic unionism is the right of the membership to make costly mistakes was evidently without influence upon Lewis or the district officers.

With most of the bituminous coal territory deunionized and its old stronghold in turmoil, the outlook for a revival of the United Mine Workers did not appear promising. It became customary to blame the defeats of the organization upon Lewis. Actually these developments were inevitable, and they had been predicted by the leaders of the organization, unless the union managed to bring the southern fields under its jurisdiction.

Lewis became more convinced that the problems of the industry could be solved only with the aid of government intervention. The destruction of the union had not brought with it an increase in prosperity or profits. On the contrary, the cut-throat competition had only carried increased demoralization to an overdeveloped industry. Order could be restored by union-management co-operation, but restraining influence upon the large non-union area would be necessary so that this section might be brought under control. The Kelley-Davis bill, sponsored by the miners' union, was introduced in Congress, but the country was still addicted to rugged individualism.

While keeping watch on the political situation, Lewis kept in close touch with his organizers and leading union members, always hopeful that a favorable opportunity to re-establish the organization would arise. The chance came in the early months of the NRA. Lewis knew that unionism comes almost naturally to the coal digger. It is not wages and hours alone which the union protects; but honest weight, proper deductions, and payment for dead work, which are of great importance to the miner and which only a union can guarantee. While the NRA was still being considered, Lewis summoned his active organizers to a conference and instructed them that the right to organize would be protected by the government, upon the passage of the new legislation. All the financial reserves at the disposal of the union were utilized, and money was even borrowed to meet the expense of organizing. The union people swept through the unorganized regions, signing up miners by the thousands. For the first time in the history of the United Mine Workers, the non-union southern fields were brought under the organization's control, and a feat which had baffled all the leaders from John Mitchel to Frank Hayes was accomplished by John L. Lewis.

The NRA also gave Lewis an opportunity in another direction. The recognition of labor's right to organize, coupled with the disillusionment of the depression, created a strong demand for organization among workers heretofore deaf to the appeals of unionism. Large groups of workers in the mass production industries were among those now seeking admittance into the family of organized labor. Largely made up of semi-skilled and unskilled workers, operating in industries where craft lines were blurred, they felt that the industrial form of organization would be the most natural and effective type of union. This desire ran counter to the claims of the craft unions, who insisted that their jurisdictional rights, which gave them the authority to organize certain types of workers regardless of industry, be respected. The workers in the mass production industries, largely neglected by the craft unions and unacquainted with technical jurisdictional claims, naturally insisted that they be allowed to form the type of organization more suited to their needs.

The craft unions were, however, not ready to surrender their technically-held domain without a struggle. A fight for the splitting of the membership of the newly-organized industrial unions among the crafts was launched. In the face of the threats to dismember the young organizations, the progressive unions in the American Federation of Labor did not remain quiescent. Led by Lewis and the United Mine Workers, the progressives demanded that concessions allowing the workers in the mass production industries to form industrial unions be granted. Lewis's leadership in this fight was not a mere historical accident. The miners' union, which he led, was largely made up of semi-skilled workers, who had organized on an industrial union basis. Even their enemies could not contest the excellence of the coal diggers as fighters for the cause of unionism. Moreover, the miners had never accepted the pseudo-scientific theory that the semi-skilled and unskilled were poor organization material. The great miners' leader of another day, John Mitchel, had led a fight against the craft union policies of the Federation in 1912, when he charged that something must be done to draw the unorganized and unskilled under the banner of organized labor. His prescription was the same as Lewis's is today. The irony of the situation is that William Green signed that industrial union resolution.

Not only was the espousal of industrial unionism in keeping with the traditions of the miners' union, but Lewis and his associates felt that unless the workers in the mass production industries were organized, the miners' union would never be safe from attack. Only by organizing the mass production industries could the political climate in which organized labor operated be changed. Employers must be taught that organized labor is a normal and natural co-partner in industry, and not an intruder to be extirpated at the first opportunity. This goal could be achieved only through granting the workers in the mass production industries the right to form unions on an industrial basis. It was, therefore, natural for Lewis to lead the fight of the workers in the basic industries at the conventions of the American Federation of Labor in 1934 and 1935. It was of no avail; the craft unionists were adamant to all pleas and refused to make concessions. Then, with the aid of Charles Howard of the printers, Sidney Hillman of the men's clothing workers, David Dubinsky of the ladies' garment workers, and the heads of several other unions, he launched the Committee for Industrial Organization, which was to help bring about the organization of the mass production industries on an industrial union basis. Attacks, suspension, and now virtual expulsion have forced the C.I.O. to become in fact another labor movement.

An organization which attempts to storm the battlements of the mass production industries faces tremendous obstacles. Industrial groups with millions at their disposal, with private armies of guards and company unions, confront the organizers. The old tactics of political neutrality are under such conditions impossible, and in some cases of direct aid to the enemy. Against such powerful combinations labor must have the aid of government, and Lewis's entry into the political field was a logical and practical corollary of his experience with the problems of his own union and the desire to organize the mass production industries. There are some who are puzzled by the fact that Lewis, who had been a Republican most of his life and who had faithfully followed the political policies of the American Federation of Labor, has become active in promoting a strong political movement of wage earners. In the main politics is, for Lewis, the extension of trade union activity to another plane. It was to protect his flanks from attack that he first entered the political arena, and that important factor will compel him to remain an active participant in that field. The need of a favorable administration to bring his organizing campaigns to a successful fruition and the growing importance of government in the economic sphere forced him and his co-workers to embark upon widespread political activity and lead in forming Labor's Non-Partisan League.

The associates of Lewis are, in the main, leaders of semi-skilled workers, who face the same difficulties of maintaining their unions in the face of their industries shifting to rural communities. These men recognize, as does Lewis, that government must come to the aid of the labor movement. The unskilled and semi-skilled lack the resources and the strategic position to compel the employer to come to terms. In a measure this repeats the experience of the English labor movement, which after its great organizing successes in the unskilled trades in 1886, turned increasingly towards independent political action.

Having led a large section of the labor movement down the political road, what are Lewis's present aims and purposes? It must be remembered that Lewis is not a utopian or a builder of political air castles. To him political action only supplements the economic activity of the organized workers of the trade union movement. He is not interested in blueprints of the new society, nor does he exhibit any burning passion for its reorganization according to the prophetic insights of the Marxists. His aims are more direct and immediate; organization of the workers in the mass production industries, the right of the worker to a voice in the determination of the terms of his employment, which he calls industrial democracy, and the raising of the living standards of the workers and an increasing amount of security, both on the job and through old age and unemployment insurance schemes. Lewis's political philosophy is very simple. It is based on the principle that the workers should have a greater part of the social income, but there is no trace of anti-capitalism in his views. He believes in group bargaining rather than in class struggle. He rejects both the spirit and philosophy of revolutionary labor. His mind does not operate in terms of the historical destiny of the working class. Unlike Gompers, he has not been an assiduous student of European revolutionary movements. Gompers was brought up in New York City, where the socialism of his day found a large following and had many active disciples among labor men. Lewis, on the other hand, is a middle western American raised on simple American political fare. The classics and the Bible are his intellectual and spiritual mainstays, though he is a man of wide and varied reading. In his speeches he is more apt to quote a Shakespearean soliloquy or a couplet from Tennyson than the wisdom of Marx and Lenin. His speeches are singularly free from "foreignisms" or reference to oppressed classes. His constituents are "my people." Organization is necessary so that the workers will be able to bargain equally with the employer. His appeal has scant traces of demagoguery, regardless of how this term is interpreted. He never appeals to hate, and his speeches are free from vituperative reference to any social group. Even the most belligerent employers are only denounced for being unreasonable, and not as parasites who have no place in industry.

Those with their eyes turned to Europe are afraid of all strong men. There are many who honestly look upon the development of a strong man with a large following with considerable trepidation. Lewis to them represents a threat of the "Leader," who might at a propitious moment sweep our democratic liberties into the dustbin of history. Those who honestly believe that Lewis represents this danger point to his love of power and his handling of opposition within his own union. There is, however, not a single instance in which he acted without warrant in the laws and customs of his union, and in no case was his conduct different from most other labor leaders under analogous circumstances. The American labor movement has fostered the development of the strong executive. Perhaps this is a reflection of the general political set-up in the United States. It is the executive as represented by the governor of a state or the president of the nation who occupies the most important political positions in their province. Similarly in the trade unions, the national or international president is the dominant personality. He is the officer who is called upon to enforce discipline and carry out the rules and resolutions of the conventions. Interference in the affairs of the local organizations—especially in the event of irregularities, or contract violations—is normal in American trade unions. Only recently the president of the typographical union threatened to revoke the charter of a mailers' local unless it obeyed his orders. The same action has recently been taken by the chief executive of the printing pressmen, teamsters, machinists, and others. Similarly with Lewis, it has been his job to discipline recalcitrant locals that failed to carry out the orders of conventions.

Lewis talks and thinks in democratic terms. He has no mystic appeal and does not ask for blind obedience from his constituents. He does not single out one group as the cause of all of our social and economic ills, nor is his philosophy based on the repression of any section of the American populace. He is an opportunist; that is, he lacks a blueprint which charts the future, but he follows a consistent policy of constantly trying to raise the standards of the wage earners. Moreover, Lewis has been raised in the trade union movement. His entire life has been devoted to its advancement. It is therefore hardly likely that he would set in motion forces which would inevitably curb its activities, or subvert them for their own ends.

Another group fears the rise of Lewis's political power because it would mean an increase in the influence of the wage earner upon government. A man able to collect large sums for a political campaign may be powerful enough to undermine the foundations of democracy and reduce the elected official into a pliant and willing tool. It should be remembered that the contributions made by Lewis's organization were authorized by the convention. Moreover, they only matched the sums contributed by a single family in the last campaign to one of the political parties. There is no more reason to assume that a large collective contribution made by hundreds of thousands of workers is more subversive than an equal sum made by a half-dozen people. In most countries workers have even gone beyond donations to political parties, and have organized independent political organizations of their own, and the political parties supported by the trade unions have always been the sturdiest defenders of the democratic principle.

Another pertinent question in any analysis of Lewis's political activity is, How important and permanent is his influence? To a large extent this will be determined by the ability of the new unions to consolidate their positions. Should the new unions overcome their infantile ailments, they will be able to exercise considerable influence in determining the political trend of the next decade. It will mean that the Republican party will not be able to count upon the certain adherence of the industrial workers. The factors that have made the formerly-sure Republican state of Pennsylvania into fighting territory will operate in the majority of industrial states. It is, however, too early to predict a political realignment, for Lewis and his close co-workers, being essentially union leaders, are accustomed to bargaining. They are not wedded to any compulsive theory which would lead them to gamble all on the certainty that history endowed them with a great mission. They are pragmatists, who will demand concessions for their constituents as the price of support. These concessions would in no way include any basic attack upon the rights of private property, as Lewis and his close co-workers are essentially of conservative outlook.

More vigorous political activity by labor cannot be regarded as an unmixed blessing. It exposes the labor movement to a number of serious risks which only an adroit and idealistic leadership will be able to circumvent. Intensified political action may easily lead to the diverting of a large share of labor's limited human and financial resources from economic to political channels. The road of politics appears very attractive, and it is easy to overemphasize the more spectacular electioneering activities, especially when the gaining of economic concessions becomes difficult. Moreover, the leaders of labor may develop an appetite for public officeholding and thereby subordinate their interest in a legislative program to the "spoils of office," leading to the slow transformation of economic organizations into disguised political parties.

Another danger is that the Lewis-led political movement of labor may isolate itself from other progressive groups in the community. Undoubtedly Lewis cannot be held responsible for every local difficulty, but unless he can steer his movement from isolationism, a duplication of its experiences in the Detroit and Seattle municipal election is inevitable. The above elections seemed to show that a slate offered by a "semi-class" party cannot normally win. The evidence also demonstrates that Lewis's constituents are not unworthy allies in a political campaign. The mayoralty election in New York confirmed the view that under intelligent and shrewd leadership the new labor political consciousness, stimulated largely by Lewis, can be effectively utilized.

The Pennsylvania primary in which Lewis's old associate, Thomas Kennedy, was defeated for the governorship partially confirms the results of Detroit and Seattle. The indications are that a candidate closely identified with a section of organized labor may have difficulty winning election to a major office. The charge that a candidate is the representative of a particular class may be sufficient to defeat a worthy aspirant. The Lewis-led section of organized labor has, however, demonstrated that a progressive candidate cannot win without its support, in many sections of the country. This places it in a favorable bargaining position with those political groups seeking its support.

Lewis is, of course, only the spokesman of those workers who either belong or who are sympathetic to the Committee for Industrial Organization. In fact, President Green has announced that the chief aim of the American Federation of Labor, on the political field, will be to defeat the candidates endorsed by Lewis and his followers. The efforts of Mr. Green will undoubtedly affect the power of Lewis's movement, but not too seriously. The American Federation of Labor has seldom conducted vigorous political campaigns. Moreover, the members of the American Federation of Labor are, on the whole, less politically-minded than the followers of Lewis. The majority of pre-Roosevelt unionists in the C.I.O. (miners and clothing workers) have frequently favored independent political action; while the new unionists, having had their rights to organize protected by the government, are naturally more sympathetic towards political action than the older union members organized in the skilled trades by the American Federation of Labor. The hostility to government intervention, which has been a part of the craft unionists' mentality, is alien to these workers. Lewis is therefore in a much more favorable position to exercise political influence in those sections where the unions affiliated with the C.I.O. have substantial memberships.

It is obvious that under Lewis's leadership forces have been set in motion which may mean that the organized industrial worker will, for the first time, become an important factor politically. With a permanent problem of relief and security, and the recognition of the increasingly important role of government, we should expect a heightened political consciousness among the wage earners. Recognition that it is a natural, and even a belated, development would do a great deal to calm those for whom any novelty or experiment is a harbinger of chaos and disorder. A more politically-minded wage earner is long overdue, and it seems to be a question whether the movement will be led by a reasonable pragmatist of the Lewis type, or by a doctrinaire theorist.

Lewis's pragmatic opportunism is, however, open to a very serious criticism. Though seeking wide influence and power, he has offered nothing but the vaguest sort of program, if his scattered pronouncements can be considered a program. Rightfully demanding a greater voice for labor in the affairs of government, he has offered no analysis of basic difficulties, nor any program for overcoming them. His avoidance of theorizing may impress some as typically American, but unless one diagnoses the nature of the disease, he is in no position to prescribe a remedy. Insistence upon the maintenance of wage rates, or even of wage increases is hardly an answer to the problem of unemployment. One who seeks power is obligated to inform his constituents and others of the solutions he proposes. An integrated and nationally-organized political movement must be considered more than a pressure group seeking special legislation. Lewis is therefore obligated to inform us of his views on power, agriculture, foreign trade, armaments, the revival of investment, and many other controversial questions. Only then would it be possible to make a fair estimate of his political statesmanship.

BIG JIM FARLEY

By Duncan Aikman

I

BIG JIM FARLEY IS RAPIDLY BECOMING A MEMBER OF THE RE-public's mythical pantheon. To his friends and co-partisans, he is the worker of political miracles—the man who organizes victories on a scale of astronomical digits, who makes deserts blossom in majorities, and converts factional wars into crusading enterprises of blood-brothers by the exorcisms of magic backslaps. If the age depended for its news on bards and folklore-makers, the legend would already be in the making that Big Jim had carried Mars and Venus for Roosevelt by getting a few precinct leaders on the tele-phone.

On the other hand, Big Jim to his enemies is the super-Van Buren of political slickeries, the super-Tweed of political corrup-tions. By "playing politics with human misery" he has "Tammany-ized" a continent. While you tie him to his bed in Washington and observe his innocent breathings under the fluoroscope, he will be stealing an election from you in Colorado. On grounds considerably less plausible, Loki was promoted from a village practical joker to a god.

Since, for better or worse, our unchurched times are a god-making and demonology-spawning era in which Hitlers are wor-shipped with Holy Roller orgies and Trotskyites invoked with black masses, little can be done about it except to remark in passing that most of the legends are heroin for emotionalists. Big Jim is neither a wonder-worker nor the son of a werewitch out of Beelze-bub. He is a passionately competitive, normally acquisitive Ameri-can with a commonplace mind steered by a phenomenal memory.

Big Jim shines in politics for only two reasons—neither of them in any sense esoteric. Most politicians are in the trade for reasons of vanity only. Being in public office or being the boss of officeholders satisfies a strain in the ego akin to an actor's lust for personal exhibitionism. Big Jim, who came into politics from the semi-pro baseball diamond rather than from the high school debating platform, has more than the average citizen's yearning for victory for "our side," but the typical politico's exhibitionist vanity simply is not in him. He approaches political problems and "contacts" with the acute self-interest of a good teamsman but with a virtually total lack of self-consciousness. Neither billingsgate nor disaster on minor fronts upsets his poise or his judgment, because touchy statesman's vanity just isn't there to be offended. He keeps his head and plays his best game in tight places, because he is immune—an almost incredible immunity in Washington—to tantrums of hurt feelings.

Big Jim's other unique point is a by-product of this extraordinary virtue. Politics on the whole is an institution conducted by people curiously incompetent at politics. They are backslappers or stuffed shirts or town characters primarily and professionally; amateur organizers of voters' support in their off hours. The average congressman—or the average city councilman and not a few average presidents—is the sort of man who, when three street-corner loafers have announced their intention to vote for him, shouts to the elevator boy that "it's in the bag" and either rushes home to bathe in the little wife's praise, or to the bar to gossip with his fellow statesmen about the spoils of victory. With great difficulty he can be controlled in these habits by diligent managers and made to do enough precinct and door-to-door work to push over a rival amateur in an election. He is in somewhat the same category with the salesman who doesn't feel it necessary to call on the customers because he is making so many friends on the golf course.

Big Jim lacks this congenital self-admirer's easy-going strain. With his passion for victory, he puts as much energy into politics as a business man with a passion for success would put into a campaign to sell every solvent male in the United States an electric razor. In a campaign to sell Democratic tickets to 50,000,000 voters, he leaves no routine job undone, no ruse untested, no plausible hunch untried. He neglects no charm appeals and strategies, he pulls no punches.

In short, Big Jim is a phenomenon, a folk hero, a G.O.P. household goblin, partly because of his glandular organization but mainly because of his setting. He has invaded a profession where efficiency is seldom allowed to interfere with the ego's perpetual reiteration of love crises, with the relatively simple talents of an expert sales-manager. In a field where loafers flourish, he really works at his job. In a field colored by the exploits of amateurs and disordered by their errors, he really is a professional.

If he is successful and powerful and increasingly glamorous to the public imagination, it is merely because he uses the straight American copy-book virtues and most of the vices which the sociologists attribute to the specialized competitive instinct, on a stage where they rarely have been seen before.

II

It is night in Big Jim's onyx-lustrous office in the Post Office Department Building in Washington. It is past ten o'clock, and the early-show moving picture theater audiences are beginning to drift home from the soda fountains. But Big Jim, who began his working day a few minutes before eight in the morning, is still going strong. Early in the afternoon he shifted from his work as postmaster general to the routine drive of his job as chairman of the Democratic National Committee. Now he is exclusively immersed in party organization matters.

He sits at his desk, a burly, bald, full-blooded athlete looking all of his fifty summers, but his posture is as erect, his movements as brisk as a twenty-two-year-old fullback's. Two stenographers of the day's third shift of half a dozen sit poised for action at his desk-side. The soft patter from the noiseless typewriters of the four others drifts in the quiet over the transom of an inner office. Numbers 67 to 82 of the day's grist of callers are waiting in a reception antechamber.

But at present Big Jim is ripping toward the bottom of the last of seven-foot-high piles of correspondence and is wholly concentrated on dictation. Now and then he slices the space between letters with a mild wisecrack for the stenographers' benefit. "They don't know out in Wyoming how much we suffer for 'em—do they, Miss Smith?" he chortles with mock pathos. The work pressure eases itself with a giggle. Always he keeps a friendly twinkle for the crew he is slaving with, as if the job were half sporting event. He is, as everybody who can keep the pace of the Farley office admits enthusiastically, a swell boss to work overtime with.

Nine tenths of the letter-writing is a matter of form letter citations. "Give Joe Doakes of Happy Valley, Kentucky, the regular one about party harmony," the cheerful voice crackles in rapid-fire syllables. "Then add this:

"It sure is tough to hear the boy missed the breaks in the West Point examination. Tell him for me I wish him better luck next time."

. . . "Give Al Jones in Ashtabula the regular one on we're doing everything we can for him. . . . Harry Robinson, Missoula: His job question's in the Commissioner's hands now, and from now on he'd better deal with that office. . . . Herbert Moran, Nashua: Tell him this job's all washed up but we appreciate his work for the party and want him to keep in touch. And don't forget to ask how the little girl's getting along with the measles. . . . Arthur Morgan, Minneapolis: Sorry, we can't transfer him, that's up to his bureau bosses. Same for Donald Acton, Seattle, Sidney Kidder, Cheyenne." The low, hurried voice rattles off the names of twenty importunates.

"Arthur de Quincey, Peoria: The regular one about not being able to speak at the State Elks' convention. Nope, not Art, call him 'dear Colonel.' He belongs to the old school. . . . Now, take a real one." And the voice gathers speed as it goes into the superscription, "Dear Mayor Smithers——"

It is a letter to the mayor of a middle-western state's second-largest city who is preferring charges of political perfidy against his United States Senator. "I have just gone over the whole situation with the Senator," Big Jim reassures him genially, "and have come to the conclusion that we're all together on the fundamentals. I think we can iron out the nonessentials if you can break away and come down here to talk it over with me. Phone me if it's urgent, and I'll make room for you on the appointment list any day you say."

Big Jim sifts to the bottom of the pile with quick instructions for a dozen different brands of "regular ones." It is one of his thousand-letter days, and when the last one is disposed of, he smiles neither wearily nor triumphantly, but gaily—like a man who has done something faintly humorous.

Mr. Farley, in fact, is rather whimsically proud of himself as the greatest writer in political—or possibly human—history. Every letter to Big Jim means a personal contact. And every personal contact, according to meticulous count of his political statisticians, means forty votes of the friends, henchmen, and relatives of a minor politician brought within the scope of his influence.

Forty thousand voters, then, have been drawn by the day's proceedings a little deeper within Mr. Farley's orbit. Forty thousand potential customers have been brought within personal-contact-once-removed, of the arch sales-manager's artifices. For even to the correspondents whom he has had to turn down flatly without hope of future favors, he has managed to convey a sense of intense interest in their personal affairs and welfare.

"Okay," he grins with morning briskness to the last stenographer. "Who's waiting?"

One by one, or in groups of two and three when they are on the same business, the callers enter. Seven of the fifteen are seeing the "big man" about jobs. He disposes of them in what might be described as seven lightning-flashes of friendliness.

"I've got it all fixed up," he tells the lucky ones eagerly. "You're to see the Commissioner—(or the Bureau Chief, or the Cabinet member)—tomorrow. Give him my thanks and if you run into any jams flash me the old S.O.S. signal."

"Now here's how it is," he confides in the gentlemen whose cases refused to be smoothed so readily. "We can't get you the place you're shooting for. But I think there's a spot or two in some of the other departments where they can use you. Give me twenty-four hours to think it over, and we'll see if there aren't some big shots in town we can talk business to. Ring me up day after tomorrow. Believe me, young fellow, after the work you've done for the ticket out in Kanbraska, if there's any good news we can stir up for you, you'll sure get it."

Even when deeper obstacles are involved, the assurances of helpfulness are persuasive. "We might as well be frank about it," Big Jim tells a real patronage problem. "You haven't got political

UNDERWOOD AND UNDERWOOD

JAMES A. FARLEY

"If the age depended for its news on bards and folk-lore-makers, the legend would already be in the making that Big Jim had carried Mars and Venus for Roosevelt by getting a few precinct leaders on the telephone."

clearance from your state committee yet, and we just can't turn a wheel for you here until you get it. But hold on a minute. I know what you've been worth to us in that situation out there, and you know how much I want to help you. See the boys down at headquarters tomorrow. Meanwhile I'll tell 'em you're coming. If there's anything we can do to straighten out your jam with the state chairman, we'll sure do it."

Two of them come to complain about the nefarious practices of a rival faction in southern state politics. Big Jim in slightly less than five minutes' conversation shows that he knows the situation and the personalities involved as intimately as the state chairman.

"Now let's have another meeting here the first of the week," he interrupts their flow of criminations genially, "with our friends of the opposition. Let 'em see how many fundamentals we can get together on for the good of the party, how many old sores we can scrap as bygones and then figure out how many things we've still got left to fight about. I'm not against fighting, you know, being a pretty good Democrat myself, but I just don't think we need to fight about anything that isn't important . . . What do you say about it? How about lunch next Monday?"

Another duet comes soliciting Big Jim's support in a primary contest and whispering dark charges that their prospective opponents are engaging in black treacheries against the Roosevelt administration and even against Big Jim himself. Big Jim listens with his expert "Gosh, I'm glad to know about this" air and soothes them with a flow of endearing inquiries about the health and personal fortunes of a complete company roster of their fellow factionalists.

So when he dismisses them, it is with an emotional flourish that sounds almost like a pledge of secret alliance. "Now you know how things are down here," he laments apologetically. "The national party organization just can't get itself into these state contests or it would have to spend all its time fighting other Democrats. . . . But I'll tell you what we'll do about it. I know, with a lot of regular guys like your crowd in this fight, it's going to be clean and aboveboard. So when it's over, no matter how it turns out, you come and see me. And if I can do anything for you then, you can bet your shirt I'll get busy and do it."

The final four are a group of controversialists called in to settle a patronage fight. They break out into clashing claims and mutual recriminations, and fail to settle it. Big Jim's own overtures about the apportionment of the two or three available offices are politely rejected. So for the first time in a thousand-letter and eighty-two-appointment day Big Jim turns faintly haughty.

"I can't stop you from disagreeing over this business, and being a fellow Democrat, I probably wouldn't if I knew how to," he admonishes them amiably. "But I can't, by the rules of this office, recommend anybody's man until he gets everybody's indorsement. So until you can all agree on what you want, there isn't much use coming back here. As things stand, much as I want to be helpful, we just can't do much business. . . ."

And Big Jim smiles and dismisses them with a flow of jocose personalities. Within a week, or perhaps within ten hours, as he diagnoses the symptoms, a telephone call will come announcing that one, if not both, of the irreconcilables is ready for concessions. The ultimatum has been put lightly and politely—almost in a tone of jovial banter. But few really practical politicians, Big Jim shrewdly realizes, will care to nourish a local patronage feud very long when it means not being on business-talking terms with their National Chairman.

Big Jim looks at the clock, which stands at five minutes past midnight. His thousand-letter, eighty-two-caller day is behind him, and he has just disposed of the last fifteen visitors, including three fairly ticklish conferences, in less than forty-five minutes. If he has any self-conscious thought at all as he heaves his 225-pound weight along toward the elevator with a stride that a small man would have to dog-trot to keep up with, it is probably that now he can eat.

A vainer and more typical politician, looking back on such a prodigious evening, might reflect with some swelling of the bosom that he had not sharpened a single animosity, left a single friendship unstrengthened, failed in a single tight place to make a plausible appeal to self-interest, or made a single promise that he couldn't keep. But with Big Jim all this smooth functioning is the normal routine—no more a matter for self-exaltation than the perfect digestion which keeps him at a razor edge of physical fitness on sixteen-hour work days and post-midnight dinners.

Big Jim would consider it memorable only if one of these errors had been committed.

III

There are more than a hundred days of this pattern of intensity in a normal Farley year. There are perhaps a hundred others when the pattern changes but not the intensity: The week ends when Big Jim visits New York and as chairman of the New York State Democratic Committee immerses himself in the affairs of his feudal principality; the days when he travels—probably two months of them each year on the average—making speeches and cultivating political fences in the Republic's hinterland. Big Jim, as a tripper, has less thousand-letter days than in Washington—though he may have one on an occasional Saturday when the exigencies of New York politics call for it—but he fills in the time gap by seeing more people. It is said of him that in an afternoon when he dedicates a new post office in a cow state hamlet, he can see, placate, enchant, organize, and confer with every Democrat worth seeing from every precinct in three kingdom-sized commonwealths. And on the junketing days when he has relays of stenographers meet his train at the metropolitan division points, the thousand-letter pace is only fractionally slackened.

There are, to be sure, periods when the great energizer definitely loafs. His annual vacations run longer than a month on the average, and he usually spends them in places where political conferences are difficult, if not impossible. He has spent them in Ireland, Italy, and Bermuda, and in winter resort clubs where he is effectively shielded from the intrusions of state committee chairmen and even United States senators. The story that he devoted an audience with the Pope several years ago to launching a program for forming a Democratic Students' Club in the College of Cardinals is almost certainly apocryphal. Then there are days when, by strictly relative standards, Big Jim takes things easily. One or two nights a week, he actually breaks away from the office before eight-thirty, and if there is no political or official dining out to be done, spends the evening with his family.

Big Jim rules an empire, in short, and rules it by three qualities:

a passion for personal contacts, an infinitely efficient care for details, and a boundless physical energy.

It is without any doubt numerically the most powerful political empire ever created in the United States by any expert in political management. It has produced the biggest and most crushing majorities, infected the enemy's front with a record maximum of discords, confusions, and despairs. Down through the 1936 election at least it functioned with a more far-reaching vote-mobilizing efficiency, a subtler coherence in appeal, and a swifter cohesion in action than any national political organization yet formed in America.

It has deep roots in political spoils, quite obviously, yet to call it, as Big Jim's envious critics do, an empire built on spoilsmanship is to miss the fundamental method behind Jim's achievement. Big Jim's spoilsmanship has been ruthless and as all-embracing as he could make it, and on occasion—as when he boosted an Oklahoma politician dying of alcoholism into an assistant attorney generalship or when hordes of faithful Democrats were encouraged to trap Republican "holdover" postmasters in technical service inefficiencies—it has been more than delicately tainted with scandal. But other and more ruthless spoilsmen—Mr. Harry Daugherty's Ohio gang, for instance—have built smaller and less stable empires. There are better reasons for the flourishing state of Big Jim's empire than that its builder has had a hand in parceling out somewhere between 200,000 and 300,000 federal jobs.

The empire exists because Big Jim manages to know every worker of the slightest local consequence in its deepest provincial structure and on its farthest frontiers; to keep informed about his personal and political problems and to keep the channels open for constant frank and friendly communication about new problems as they arise; and because he stands ready, with his sixteen-hour-a-day stamina and his expert conciliating talents, to help solve those problems as fast as human ingenuity can.

The empire is not a glorified organization chart which has taken on flesh and blood along with its hierarchical division but a myriad-stranded network of Big Jim's personal contacts. It is not a personal following in the sense that a glamorous leader like Theodore Roosevelt may fashion a crusading army out of hordes of personal worshippers. It is a personal empire built of days of a thousand letters signed "Sincerely, Jim," and of a hundred intimately friendly political conferences about trivial local affairs which a national chairman might not be expected to know about but does. It differs from the Theodore Roosevelt type of following chiefly in being more intimate.

Neither is it the sort of political empire which might be expected to grow up out of a great city machine organization like Tammany, with the big boss sitting alone in a center of mysterious and corrupt power, growling orders. Big Jim had a fair share of his growth under Tammany auspices and is no innocent about the crooked by-products of machine politics or occasional uses of corrupt political practices. But his touch is not the touch of Croker or Murphy or of the slicker Fordham-bred collegiates who have succeeded them.

It is the touch, in a word, of the epically efficient county chairman who gets out the vote, partly, to be sure, because he sees that the best campaign workers get jobs in the county courthouse, but even more because he knows every man, dog, child, and woman in the county on terms of hearty bucolic sociability, knows what they want and what they are thinking about in terms of their own language.

The smashing efficiency of New Deal politics is largely due, in short, to the fact that Big Jim has made himself county chairman of a continent.

IV

Jim's grass roots go back to a county chairman's environment. Forty miles up the west bank of the Hudson the last suburban color fades from the social habits of the Valley people and the country begins. (The color lasts a good thirty miles further on the east bank, where the commuting squirearchy rules, but this fact did not affect Jim's political education in the slightest.) Grassy Point, where Jim was born and grew up, is a suburb of Stony Point, which was barely big enough by the turn of the century to support a semi-rural union high school. Both are tributary to Haverstraw, but Haverstraw is no metropolis. Except for the fact that the women of the three communities do their bargain-hunting in Macy's basement and the young men know places in New York where they can take their girls to dinner without benefit of cover charges, life is as provincial and as socially self-contained as in Bucyrus, Ohio, or Chibley, Georgia. The people you know are the school contemporaries you were born and grew up with, the people in your two- or three-block neighborhood, and the people you meet every day or two in typical small town business operations. A young man with an impulse for broadening his acquaintance realizes his ambition not by cultivating casual transients from Denver and Miami and visiting prep school friends in Wisconsin, but by the simple expedient of loafing around in centers where he meets more of "the folks" from Rockland County.

Jim had the impulse—unquestionably less out of political guile than out of a healthy youngster's tastes for indiscriminate sociability, to begin with—and fate presented him with unusual opportunities for satisfying it. He was tall, strong, athletic, and good-tempered and the best marble-shooter in grammar school—efficient credentials for an almost hundred per cent acquaintance among Grassy Point boy circles. When he was eleven, his father, a former saloonkeeper retired into brickyard ownership, died of a horse's kick, and Jim went to work after school hours running errands and serving counter customers in his mother's corner grocery store. That meant that Jim began meeting the grown-ups of the community on a natural, give-and-take conversational basis while his contemporaries were still ducking up alleys to avoid tipping their hats to their mothers' sewing circle acquaintances.

A little later came baseball. "Stretch" Farley—nicknamed for his first baseman's reach after hot liners—traveling with the Stony Point High School Team met the "high school crowds" and the local sporting experts all over Rockland County and even beyond. When he graduated from high school and became a semi-pro on such adult organizations as the Stony Point Alphas, his friend-finding range increased. Before he was twenty he was earning a mild athletic celebrity for himself and making friends on a first-name basis all the way from Troy to Yonkers, from Binghamton on the west all the way to Danbury over the state line in Connecticut.

Between times, now that he had his man's strength and there were plenty of younger brothers to take care of his mother's store errands, he was working summer vacations in brickyards and ship-yards. Here he picked up hundreds of new first-name acquaintances in the Haverstraw-Stony Point labor world. When he sailed as an able cargo-handler on his uncle's brick schooner to New York, he penetrated socially into the slowly declining society of Hudson River roustabouts.

Even his favorite social diversion served as a contact-builder. During his late teens and early twenties, it was dancing. But Jim, perhaps because he did not belong to the Haverstraw elite, did not waste his talents on an intimate social set. Instead, nightly each summer he shared them impartially with the shop and factory girls who were the best tango and "boston" performers at the public dance halls up and down the river from Poughkeepsie to Yonkers. And since he seemed to regard dancing as a form of exercise rather than a prelude to amorous adventures, he made quite as many friends among his partners' boy friends as among the "working girl" population.

By the time the acquaintance-broadening habit became chronic, Jim was aiding it with a few deliberate ruses. When he met the Haverstraw bigwigs on the street, for instance, he would call them by their first names regardless of a prior lack of formal introductions. Some of the local magnates bristled at the first familiarities, but came eventually to the conclusion that the Farley youngster's "freshness" was due to nothing more subversive than an uncontrollable social exuberance. None, so far as the local traditions go, ever failed to acknowledge his greetings. Furthermore, Jim took over the job of rising before dawn and going down to the farmers' markets to act as the maternal grocery store's garden-truck buyer. It gave him a chance to talk with the farmers. It is also in the local tradition that some of the older of the farmers are the only people in Rockland County—or in the United States for that matter—whom Jim still calls "mister."

There were other points that fed his local celebrity. Among the young Catholic boys of the neighborhood, Jim was regarded as a moderate paragon because he had made a confirmation vow to his patron, St. Aloysius, to abstain from liquor and tobacco—no commitments were made to St. Aloysius about gum-chewing—and kept it. But since his paragonship accompanied such notable athletic prowess and his Catholicism was never obtrusive in interdenominational company, Protestant Sunday school teachers, pastors, and Y.M.C.A. leaders found a good deal to say in praise of it to the small fry in their own congregations. Jim in his early twenties was already being held up as a fairly glamorous model for the three towns' rising generation.

At any rate, after his high school days and a year at a New York business college, the paragon became a minor worker for the local politicians in the tri-town set-up. His early work, which was distinctly on a volunteer, unpaid basis, appears to have consisted largely of dropping in from time to time to report the gossip on what the local voters in their various sociological stratifications were thinking and whom they were favoring in the way of local candidates; and in a little doorbell electioneering in the local crises.

There is no evidence to show whether Jim got into precinct work by formally volunteering for it, or by solicitation of the local politicos. The probabilities are that he just drifted into it, through his already established habit of using small favors to strengthen his hold on a new group of acquaintances. Although he was not yet a voter, the ordinary embarrassing preliminaries for a neophyte seem to have been omitted. No politician in Rockland County needed to ask Jim after the age of eighteen, "What are your contacts?" They knew already that they were more numerous than the average county chairman's. Even so, if Jim had cared to boast of his list, it would have been impressive.

Yet the veteran politicians of the neighborhood were chiefly struck with the evidence that Jim, in spite of his merits, was impractical. He joined the Democratic organization, and the Democrats in Rockland County had had hard sledding since the Cleveland debacle following the panic of 1893. A young man with so many friends and so much horse sense, the Republican sages gossiped, ought to realize that his future lay with the majority.

They had yet to realize, as Jim did routine small-fry wheel-horse work in his spare hours during the Democratic defeat years between 1908 and 1911, what a young man could do with a county chairman's quota of contacts when he came out in the open for himself.

This happened in 1912—the first year of Democratic promise —when Jim announced himself for the Grassy Point town clerkship. He won by a curious expedient. Jim was out of town six days a week selling building materials on the road for the United States Gypsum Company, but he got around this hazard by sending the voters postcards. Every day two score or more of the Grassy Point franchise-holders got a line from Jim saying that he was having a swell time in Olean or Schenectady and wished they were with him; or that it was "great" to have had a chance to talk over that little sidewalk-fixing problem with them last week-end and he certainly hoped he'd see them again next Saturday.

Since Jim knew literally all of the Grassy Point voters, literally everyone was in on the correspondence. The upper brackets snickered mildly, but in the mail-boxes where personal communications were few, Jim was appreciated. A postal card was something you could carry around with you and brag or wisecrack about to the neighbors after a backslap had withered. Jim was elected hands down.

As an officeholder, Jim developed overnight a dominant operating principle. It was to the effect that in a small town where everybody knew you, all your acquaintances and especially the people who had worked and voted for you, would appreciate something in the way of special personal service. So Jim's first term was largely a search for favors to do. Were Grassy Point's young courting couples shy about running the gauntlet of loafers when they went to the town hall to get their marriage licenses? Very well. Jim would bring the license around to her house on the quiet this evening, and no extra charge except maybe they'd save him a slice of the wedding cake. Was a local hunter too busy or forgetful to get his license the day before the season opened? All right, Jim would bring it around to the house Sunday morning—before daybreak if he wanted to keep a sunrise rendezvous in a duck cove. Was a shipyard carpenter's boy having a little police trouble? Jim would spend hours in justice of peace and constable's offices arguing punitive-minded men into maximum leniency. Wouldn't the street-mending crew do anything about that mudhole in front of Bill Smith's house? Jim would fix it up with the supervisors even though he had to promise to do a little extra precinct-scouting for these worthies as a pay-off. After all, that was the beauty of politics. You started out to do one man a favor and you ended up by doing favors for three or four. It was like earning three hundred per cent dividends.

Jim at any rate worked practically as long hours tying Grassy Point to his fortunes with bonds of personal gratitude as he does today on his thousand-letter days in Washington. But it paid. Jim had three terms as town clerk and then two as Stony Point supervisor. Before the twenties began he went up to Albany as the Haverstraw district's representative in the Assembly. And betweenwhiles he moved into the place specifically grooved for his talents—the Rockland County Democratic chairmanship. A reliable Republican outpost since the Civil War except in years when Democrats flourished like grasshopper plagues, Rockland promptly went into the teetery column and remained in it even during the year of the Harding landslide. Jim's more intimately personal crew of Democratic officials survived even that holocaust.

But meanwhile in Albany Jim was busy with larger matters than county politics. If extra personal services could bind the Grassy Point voters to his enterprises, extra services could also bind the leaders of his party in the state. Assemblyman Farley set himself out energetically and specifically to cultivate the Democratic high command.

He voted with the Tammany faction often enough to qualify as an upstate regular. He found his way in and out of Governor Al Smith's office as a shrewd adviser on Hudson Valley patronage and organization problems. He voted for young Assemblyman Jimmy Walker's Boxing Commission bill, and became an expert in applying pressure to rustic legislators for Walker and Smith and Tammany enterprises generally. During these years he managed to function almost in the role of a dual personality. Tammany thought of him as one of its own and on his increasingly frequent trips to the metropolis took him deeper and deeper into its inner strategic confidences. Yet to the upstate politicians, with his friendly small town ways and his almost middle-western Haverstraw accent, he seemed charmingly devoid of Tammany's iniquities and haughty mannerisms. If he could talk practical strategies with the most beetle-browed of the Bowery chieftains he was also a Brother Elk to the legislators from Lockport and Canandaigua and could gossip

about crop prospects responsively, even with the G.O.P. moss-
backs from undiluted farm districts.

The quality of Jim's behind-the-scenes services to his superiors
rose with his experience. In 1922, for instance, Al Smith had been
two years out of office, following his defeat in the Harding landslide, and Tammany leader Charles F. Murphy had grave doubts
about nominating him for a "come-back" trial. Jim went straight to
Murphy, and in several hours of cogent argument convinced him
that a better upstate organization could be built up for Smith than
for any other Democrat. When Smith was nominated and elected,
Chairman Farley of Rockland was recognized by the inner circle
as one of the victory's personal authors.

Al Smith remembered it a year later when Jim, as a final extra
service, undertook what would have ranked in his baseball record as
a fairly glamorous "sacrifice." Smith wanted the Mullen-Gage state
prohibition enforcement act repealed, and, furthermore, wanted
upstate votes pointedly cast for its discard. In the face of a roaring
dry crusade in Rockland County, Jim, who had always stood in
with the "church crowd" previously because of his personal teeto-
talism, flung himself dramatically into the breach and cast the de-
ciding vote in the Assembly for the Smith program.

The outraged Volsteadians took Jim's seat away from him in the
1923 election. But Governor Smith paid off with the $5,000-a-year
wardmanship of the Port of New York, and a year later with a
place on the State Boxing Commission. By way of knowing everybody and doing favors for everybody who was worth knowing, Jim
was arriving where the big politics was made.

v

A beaming, bald-headed man, the *New York Times* described
his prize-ringside presence several years later, "always he sits in the
first row, and always men come and go from this place holding
short conferences. Most of the time he keeps his eye on the ring,
and frequently referees look anxiously at him."

Before he had been many months on the Boxing Commission,
however, Big Jim had many more types of people than referees

looking at him anxiously. Theoretically the Boxing Commission's range of authority was confined to a narrow professional sphere, almost a technical province, but Big Jim was shortly using it to blanket the whole state with his political influence and even to let it drift lightly in the direction of New Jersey and Pennsylvania.

He began by making himself Commission chairman. One day when Chairman Browder was absent he explained to his fellow commissioner, William Muldoon, that the time had come to rotate the office, and with his slightly superannuated colleague's co-operation a unanimous election took place. A year later, when Mr. Browder demanded the chairmanship back, Mr. Farley explained that it was not being rotated any longer. Mr. Browder was naturally displeased, but he was only a relatively unimportant Brooklyn politician, and Mr. Farley was interested in putting himself in a position where he could please the greatest number.

The way he adopted of spreading pleasure around was to enlarge the commission's list of powers. The more powers it had, the more exceptions and adjustments could be made, and the more adjustments, the more fight managers and subsidiary entrepreneurs in the fight industry who could be rendered grateful. There was the matter of fighters' trunks, for instance. The Commission in 1927 issued a ruling that pugilists must procure trunks of a certain pattern and high-expense quality from the Everlast Sporting Goods Company. The Everlast Sporting Goods Company and all the relatives and friends of its employees were naturally grateful, but when one Giuseppe Erario of the Ideal Sporting Company protested the discrimination, Big Jim rebuked Bert Stamp, the Commission's secretary, so harshly and publicly for issuing the original ruling that Mr. Erario and all his backers in the fight-fan section of Little Italy must have felt grateful, too. Meanwhile, sophisticated fight managers had had their tip that the Everlast Company had an "in" with the Commission; so no considerable feelings of revulsion toward Jim could have been aroused in that quarter.

Big Jim meanwhile was branching out as a regulator in more potent directions. He took charge of the affairs of fighting gymnasiums by requiring all gymnasiums which charged a fee for their facilities to take out a license with the Commission. It meant that all gymnasium proprietors, from Dunkirk to Staten Island, would have to come to Jim for permission to operate. He annexed all the wrestling promoters to his kingdom by requiring Commission approval for mat bouts. He put up a two-year fight for the Commission's wide power to license amateur boxing exhibitions, and finally won by a Supreme Court decision from Tammany judges who had probably experienced Jim's power to do favors on other political fronts.

When he eventually left the Commission to become postmaster general, he was engaged in a battle to establish the Commission's right to regulate fight broadcasting over the radio. Here was a field where there would be favors to trade and adjustments to make with advertisers and radio corporations whose entrapment in Mr. Farley's political spiderweb meant contacts hot with potential campaign contributions from some of the nation's biggest corporation treasuries.

From time to time, on the other hand, Jim relaxed a rule, when it suited his convenience. He allowed bouts between boxers of mixed weights, for instance, apparently because it gave him more fights to regulate. For several years he maintained a running feud with Madison Square Garden, slashing at ticket prices on a few notable occasions, interfering with the details of its manager contracts, and maintaining a stern anti-smoking rule in its amphitheater. News experts hinted at a dark personal vendetta with Tex Rickard, but the motive behind it more probably was simply that any attack on the Garden made Big Jim more popular with New York State's several thousand minor boxing-arena proprietors.

But Jim's main friendship-building agency during his commissionership was his use of free fight tickets. All over the state, Jim realized, there were thousands of good Democratic leaders and potential campaign contributors whom he had met on a friendly basis during his Albany activities, and who now would feel that a courtesy from the Commissioner was a charming recognition of their personal and political importance. And what form could courtesy take more appealing than a free ringside seat to a world-heralded pugilistic event with the Commissioner's own compliments?

Mr. Farley accordingly became one of the prize ring's prize patrons. At the Dempsey-Sharkey World Championship fight in

July, 1927, the three Commission members got 126 of the top priced, $27.50, as their personal complimentaries, and of these Mr. Farley managed to corral over 70. In addition, the purchase of 282 more was credited to his personal account at a cost of $9,024. Mr. Farley, in consequence, had somewhat more than 350 tickets to distribute to the Tammany worthies, Big Business acquaintances, and upstate county chairmen and bosses whose grateful remembrance was most worth having. The gifts were not rendered any less sweet by the fact that the commissioners' seats were considerably better than most of their occupants could have secured by waiting in line at the box office, and that a good many of them would have been worth $125 cash money purchased from speculators.

Generosity with tickets, however, by no means was confined to major fighting events. If the great whales of the Democratic hierarchy received the Commissioner's courtesies for the championship bouts, the minnows of precinct and local labors were equally showered with Mr. Farley's complimentary remembrances when the minor nose-punching spectacles occurred. Few back-of-the-barn professional fights, in fact, took place even in the second-rate rural county seats without a dozen or more of the locality's more eminent Democrats being reminded by a "Sincerely, Jim" epistle, and a pair of free pasteboards through the mails, that the great man had paused amid the labors of office and thought of them.

How Jim managed to pay for so many gift tickets in addition to the Commission's allotment of free complimentaries remains one of the great mysteries of politics. In one of the periodic uproars over the question, Jim's defenders insinuated that Jim was merely helping his friends to secure first-class seats at regular boxing office instead of speculators' prices and was being reimbursed for most of his investments. Another hint was to the effect that while the tickets were charged to Jim's account with the usual bookkeeping formalities, no serious efforts were ever made by intelligent fight impresarios to collect for them. Still another theory was that Jim, who had gone into the building supply business in New York soon after he had made the proper Tammany connections in Albany, was making so much money by now that he could afford the tickets as an investment in future advancement.

There probably was merit in all three deductions, but there was no question about the contributions of gift fight tickets to Jim's ascent as a careerist. When in the summer of 1928 he rather unexpectedly became a candidate for the powerful post of secretary of the Democratic State Committee, hardly a delegate was present in the Convention who was not moved by the recollection of one or more of Jim's ticket courtesies and whose gratitude, since it was manifest that Jim intended to keep the commissionership along with the secretaryship, was not stirred by the expectation of further favors to come. Jim, as it turned out, was elected without even a contest.

Big Jim had climbed into the higher rounds of state political management at last. But the state Democratic organization was the gainer by it. For Jim by this time was a walking allegorical figure of almost perfect preparedness. He knew more upstate Democratic workers intimately than possibly any other Democrat living and certainly more than any Democratic leader who was at the same time deep in Tammany's confidences. With his obliging disposition and his gift-ticket system, he had done favors for more Democrats in minor key positions than anyone in his generation, not even excluding the Governor who gave out the patronage. And Big Jim had not yet had to surmount the patronage-giver's enemy-making hazard of having to refuse favors.

Meanwhile, with his devouring energy, he was branching out more than tentatively into new fields of influence. He had attended every Democratic National Convention since 1920, and spent his leisure as a fairly inconspicuous delegate cultivating friendships with expert Party workers in remote parts of the continent as ardently as he cultivated Bronx B'nai Brith officers and Cattaraugus County Grange worthies. He followed up these acquaintances with his most faithful Grassy Point note-writing diligence, and now and then, more or less secretively, a pass to a championship bout went to a first-string visiting fireman from Oklahoma or Oregon.

Also on the continental stage he was building himself up as a professional Elk, of somewhat legendary proportions. He missed few, if any, national conventions of the Order during the 1920's, and while he shied away from national offices, which he could have had without opposition, he came away from each convention with notebooks bulging with new addresses for his correspondence system, and with a thousand shrewd ideas about political propaganda which he had absorbed by using the Elks as a listening post. It was a brother Elk, incidentally, who summed up the Boxing Commission Chairman's charm during this period in the aphorism that Jim could be more convivial over three dishes of ice cream than a Saturday night poker party over two gallons of bootleg.

All this time he was sharpening his already phenomenal memory. People in Rockland County had voted for him and worked for his candidates, he realized, because Jim knew all about them and never forgot to mention the things in their lives, from wedding anniversaries to children's tonsil operations, which they liked to have friendly outsiders notice. Gruff Tammany sachems and the third cousins of upstate ward-heelers, he was finding out in his wider activities, responded to exactly the same treatment. Now at the Elks' powwows and the national conventions he began practicing his individual applications of the "You are Addison Simms of Seattle" memory test system on a continental scale.

If Big Jim ever bothered to frame a success motto in his decade of political climbing, it was—"Don't forget what kind of a tree it was that little Johnny fell out of and which arm he broke."

VI

Mr. Farley had been in the state committee secretary's office slightly less than a year when the New York press began to publish intimations that he was actively laboring to supplant the state chairman. The news was substantially accurate. The chairman, one William Bray of Utica, was having a running controversy with Governor Roosevelt over the policies of the state organization's propaganda bureau, and Mr. Farley, with his ready gifts for winning new friendships, lost no time in putting himself on the Governor's side. He had had a casual acquaintance with the Governor for fully a decade, but public relations was a subject which Mr. Roosevelt took seriously, and now the relationship ripened fast into professional intimacy.

But Secretary Farley had learned suavity since the unique day when the Boxing Commission chairmanship was "rotated" and the later intrigue proceeded pro forma. He and the Governor took over the Press Bureau by slow stages, and when Mr. Farley was proposed for state chairman at the October, 1930, convention, Mr. Bray himself made the nominating speech. It was accompanied by a polite explanation from Governor Roosevelt himself that fully six months previously, Mr. Bray had confided to him that he would decline re-election. All the internal evidence suggests that he declined because Mr. Farley wouldn't let him have it.

Chairman Farley, in any case, was immediately immersed in his first big campaign job. It was a walk-away and he had only a month to show his mettle. He sat more or less continuously at Albany, Hyde Park, and New York City telephones conversing with up-state leaders who had been the beneficiaries of his fight-ticket courtesies and similar endearing artifices, advising them, out of his capacious memory, on the most intimate strategies in their baili-wicks. The results justified all this energy and demonstrated Chairman Farley's extraordinary grasp of details. Mr. Roosevelt was re-elected by 725,000—which put him automatically in the lead over all competing 1932 presidential aspirants—and proved himself to be the first statesman since the Civil War who could win a plurality for a Democratic ticket north of the Bronx.

Big Jim reacted to triumph in three ways. He instantly launched Mr. Roosevelt's presidential candidacy. He plunged into a campaign to recondition the Democratic party organization in the state which reached down into the lowliest rural precinct and was even more strenuous than the campaign he had just conducted to re-elect Governor Roosevelt. And he wrote thirty-eight thousand letters.

The letters went out to every Democratic campaign and election official of whatever degree, to every Democratic candidate for office, successful or unsuccessful, to practically everyone who during the autumn of 1930 had rung a doorbell for Democratic political purposes. They not only assured the recipients of Jim's formal gratitude and of the fact that he expected further prodigies of them, but with thirty-eight thousand intimate personal touches made it plain that their chairman was carrying their interests close to his heart.

Big Jim's reorganization scheme is especially important for the intimations it gave of his executive passion for thoroughness. He insisted that the localities where Republican majorities still prevailed be organized on a full-staff basis for aggressive operation as efficiently as old-line Democratic machine districts. He demanded that county chairmen go out and form Democratic clubs of young people and unemployed farm hands, if no others were available, in remote rural hamlets where no sizeable Democratic votes had been cast since the James Buchanan election.

By telephone and hotel-bedroom conferences from one end of the state to the other he prevailed upon local leaders to shunt old Party war horses with a fatalistic minority psychosis into the background and to enlist youngsters between twenty-one and thirty in the local organization key posts. Big Jim foresaw the revolt of an economically "lost" generation against Hoover and proposed to attach its vanguard to his fortunes before competitive bidding developed.

Finally, he launched out on a quiet but intensive purge of Democratic election officials, demanding that oldtimers who held their places through chivalrous connections with Republican majority rings be replaced by young and aggressive fighters. Jim not only declined to permit overnight rust to gather on his machine in the weeks after election, but before the year 1930 was out it was a far better machine than the one which had elected Mr. Roosevelt.

Meanwhile, he had flung Mr. Roosevelt's name into the presidential contest with what was substantially an election night broadcast. The *New York Times*, in fact, was all but horrified at such precipitancy. "Unless Governor Roosevelt puts his foot down promptly," it commented editorially early in November, "his Presidential boom will become prematurely active before next month." Mr. Roosevelt put nothing down, and the campaign unquestionably became active. But Mr. Farley's behavior, far from causing his chief embarrassment, betrayed the main outlines of a rather intelligent line of policy.

Mr. Roosevelt, it shortly developed, was to sit coyly in Hyde Park and Albany, conducting himself as if the pre-nomination campaign were some obscure intrigue of the Martians. Mr. Farley, on the other hand, quite evidently was commissioned to advertise Mr. Roosevelt, ridiculously and without dignity when the occasion seemed to demand it, and to take the blame, with a certain almost oafish impassivity, for such errors of taste as the arbiters of elegance might discern in his program. After all, a ward-heeler turned field marshal was not expected to know etiquette, and Mr. Roosevelt could hardly be blamed for the sins of a Boxing Commissioner so lately translated into political glory.

But the ward-heeler was also expected to win victories; and it is worth mentioning that along with the thirty-eight thousand letters to New York's faithful Democrats, close to ten thousand went out of the Farley office during the 1930–31 winter to brothers in Elkdom and National Convention fellowship. All of them, amid the winsome patter of personal greetings and recollections, stressed Mr. Roosevelt's extreme "electability."

As favorable answers came back from gentlemen of genuine political potency, Mr. Farley helpfully informed them of tasks they might do to build up Roosevelt sentiment in their respective regions and localities. Thereafter as reports flowed in of the progress of their work and observations the Farley correspondence with the hinterland took on a swifter pace. Indeed, by the early summer of 1931 an informal skeleton organization for a Roosevelt campaign had been set up in all but a handful of the forty-eight commonwealths, and when Mr. Farley journeyed to the Elks' national convention in Seattle in July, he traveled over ground which for the most part had been prepared by subtle but intensive gospel-sowing.

The Seattle junket, with its rounds of visits to nineteen of the twenty-two trans-Mississippi states, has gone down in Jim's mythical biography as a kind of lone-hand missionary exploit. Actually, it was thoroughly, not to say brilliantly, organized in advance. Jim saw the obvious state and western-city machine leaders by carefully prearranged appointments, and he met small-town bosses and semi-bosses and party sages from the rural hamlets in droves of hundreds and of thousands, because in each state capital or way station where he lingered, friendly Elks had contracted to bring the local political paladins to him. What the trip demonstrated was Jim's emotional capacity to get on terms of Grassy Point intimacy with a continent and his physical fitness to keep up with a man-killing schedule, rather than a provincial New Yorker's courage to go crusading among outland strangers and savages.

What was more to the point, however, was the fact that Jim on his return to New York numbered more Democratic politicians of a practical precinct-working quality among his acquaintances than any other national campaign organizer in history, and that his traveling bags were fat with new addresses. It was in this crucial period that Jim began hiring stenographers in relays. On his home-bound train, and for several weeks afterward, he kept them busy informing the regiments of new blood-brothers that that sure was a swell party you threw in Mankato; that it was great news that the little wife's pleurisy was better; that he was counting on fellows just like you everywhere to put Minnesota in the bag for Roosevelt.

Later in the year, Mr. Farley busied himself with similar exploits in the South and New England, and, meanwhile, with the prestige of a gentleman whose continental lines of contact were well established, he approached the bigwigs in Washington. Senators Hull and Burton K. Wheeler were quickly amenable, and Mr. Wheeler obliged with a statement saying precisely what Mr. Farley himself might have been expected to say against "favorite son" candidates and the dark corporation connections of Mr. Newton Diehl Baker. Less publicity was given to certain prolonged conferences with Mr. Joseph F. Guffey of Pennsylvania, but as a result of these mysterious *pourparlers* Mr. Guffey was observed bestirring himself to seduce disaffected Republican ward-heelers in Philadelphia and Pittsburgh into the Democratic service. Meanwhile members of the Smith-Raskob-Hemphill combination—which in the 1930 election had run up the first respectable Democratic minority vote in Pennsylvania within more than a generation—were suddenly dropped from posts of prominence in the state organization. From this and a few similar instances occurring simultaneously in the provinces, it was becoming evident that the Haverstraw Elks Club's best hand-shaker also knew how to steal a state away from under a rival organization's noses.

Between these operations Mr. Farley gave transient but shrewd attention to shaping the campaign's issues. Almost up to the eve of the 1932 convention, he dodged the extreme ferocities of the wet-dry controversy, mainly by bearing down hard on Mr. Hoover's failure to relieve the country's economic sufferings. "The issue is not what shall we do about something to drink, but what can we do about something to eat," he stated his position in a speech during the Seattle trek. And during the winter he publicly condemned a Raskob project to have a repeal resolution passed by the Democratic National Committee.

By the late spring of 1932 his sensitiveness to western opinion was so far advanced that he even disassociated himself faintly from Tammany. As the last Bible Belt states were entering upon their primary orgies, he commended Mr. Roosevelt to them as a statesman who could carry New York State while dispensing with the Tammany vote altogether. Jim was thinking of his water-tight upstate organization, no doubt, but also in the back of his mind was the thought that his boast would help to cover up certain embarrassments over the fact that Tammany was sending a split delegation to the Chicago convention more for Smith than for Roosevelt.

In its way, indeed, after all these intensive preliminaries, the Convention was mildly anticlimactic. More of the Roosevelt bloc's strategies were dictated from Albany than from Mr. Farley's hotel suite, and the great drama of the occasion, Mr. McAdoo's transfer of the Garner delegates to the band-wagon, appears to have been arranged without even the Roosevelt manager's knowledge. Big Jim was also disappointed that he did not name his man on the first ballot and passed not a few hours bemoaning the fact that he could not get Convention seats for all the visiting Elk and political brothers who asked for them.

But the triumph was no less great because unforeseen obstacles developed. What Big Jim had done was to build up a nation-wide organization against which even the most formidable sort of a "Stop Roosevelt" alliance was helpless. The anti-Roosevelt coalition cracked up from the moment it became apparent that Roosevelt and Big Jim, in the last analysis, would hold the power of the federal patronage.

Furthermore, on the crucial second and third ballots, Jim's emotional indoctrination of ten thousand leaders from everywhere had lasted. "Many states," the *New York Times* declared of him, "were carried by a telephone call or two. . . . Wherever he went rainbows flashed and quivered . . . Give him time and opportunity, and he will call everybody in the United States by his Christian

name except babies still anonymous. . . . But he appears more dex-
terous in the manipulation of small fry politicians than of whales."

There was a more profound compliment in this final observation
than the *Times*, perhaps, intended.

VII

In a sense, putting over Mr. Roosevelt was Jim's crucial achievement. Lurid as it can be made to appear through the eyes of his
enemies, the rest of his career mainly represents the application of
strategic principles already developed.

There was first and foremost the problem of keeping national
politics, Rockland County style, close to the grass roots. In the
election campaign which followed the Chicago Convention, Mr.
Farley, now national chairman, achieved it by revolutionizing the
traditional character of the Democratic national organization's
regional contacts. Instead of the conventional arrangement of two
or three regional headquarters directed by "big names" and more
or less chronically stuffed-shirt celebrities, and specializing in conflicting decisions, Jim ordained that regional advisers, and even
state liaison officers when the difficulties of the situation warranted
it, should be attached to his personal staff in New York. Consequently when discord broke out among the Pacific Coast chieftains
—as it somewhat continuously did—or apathy threatened to engulf
the Podunk precinct workers, Jim learned of it with a minimum
time loss from a trusted adviser who could put him in touch at once
with the most subtle complications in the situation's background.
The regional-adviser system, together with his voluminous correspondence and his capacious memory, made Jim a better expert on
the campaign's day-to-day local intricacies than many a state chairman on the problems of his own bailiwick.

And Jim took equal care to keep his lines of contact open with
"the sticks" from the moment the new administration took office
and he became its postmaster general and distributor of patronage.
The trick was done through a process which the bright young staff
officers with whom Jim surrounded himself in his new status,
promptly christened "political clearance." Political clearance meant
that before an applicant for a political appointment in any branch

of the federal service would even be considered by the patronage powers, he must secure the indorsement—or preferably the fervent backing—of his county and state chairman. In other words, political clearance meant that state and county chairmen from Aroostook to Point Loma would be constantly in touch with Jim's office about the problem nearest their hearts—jobs for their most potent satellites.

Jim, as a matter of fact, wanted the state and county chairmen to be the be-all and the end-all of political clearance. Then he would have had the party's local managers locked to him in a strategically perfect system of information and favor-trading, secure from interference from outsiders with personal and factional axes to grind. That was the way to keep the party organization on its toes and under control in every hamlet in the Union, Jim reasoned plausibly, and if the administration was out to hold the whip hand in legislative matters, that was the way to make or break congressmen and senators. It was only, indeed, after a controversy which had to be settled by the White House in the spring of 1933 that Jim accepted senators as co-ordinating indorsers of patronage applicants. He obviously suspected senators—and probably still does—of being more interested in their personal machines and private vanities than in building party efficiency, and of being prima donnas in their sense of what is going on among the voters.

In any event, it shortly became clear in the highways and even the byways of hinterland politics that while Jim would seldom go to bat for a senatorially recommended appointment candidate against a state or county chairman's lightest disapprobation, he would practically never fail to try to overcome a senator's objection when the party chieftains on the ground urged their man with genuine enthusiasm. The effects of this disposition upon political artisanship in the provinces were definitely electric. State and county leaders, accustomed to viewing themselves between elections as the "forgotten men" of politics, observed that they had a national chairman in Washington who was actually more concerned about their practical interests than in the patronage gossip of senatorial salons. To justify Jim's current favors and especially to deserve future ones, they began, in the spring and summer of 1933 as this news of the New Deal's more idyllic aspect began to penetrate to their fastnesses, refurbishing their local machines with almost as much zeal as Jim himself displayed in renovating the New York organization after his triumph of 1930.

A great deal of Jim's success in the 1934 and 1936 elections was due, in fact, to this inspiration he gave to the spirit of perpetual care for organization matters in the provinces. The newly lubricated state machines, moreover, were ready for emergencies as they might happen to develop between elections. In 1935, as an illuminating example, some three million men and women were hired by their federal government on the ostensibly non-political WPA payrolls.

It was not necessary, in these exhilarating circumstances, for Mr. Farley to seek any embarrassing conferences with Mr. Harry Hopkins, the WPA administrator, concerning the opportunities for the infiltration of deserving Democrats. In the forty-eight states and the District of Columbia scores of thousands of Mr. Farley's eager workers, functionaries, under their state and county chieftains, infiltrated into the WPA's straw-boss-ships and administrative posts as naturally as water seeks its level. In the 1936 election they unquestionably swelled Mr. Roosevelt's phenomenal majority by voting their charges' collateral in-laws, but no peculiarly gruesome conspiracy to play politics "with human misery" was involved in their maneuvers. The party took over the WPA to all practical intents and purposes save in a few laggard or incurably Republican areas, simply because Mr. Farley's policies toward the local leaders had built up between forty and forty-five state organizations capable of taking over any promising field of political activity that turned up.

Interwoven with the matter of grass-roots contacts was the problem of patronage. Contrary to certain widespread impressions, Jim did not consider jobs the natural rewards of his friendships. Jim, for one thing, by the time Mr. Roosevelt's election was won, had close to a million friends in all parts of the Republic and most of them, with their friends and their friends' friends, were potential candidates for office. The problem was manifestly too staggering for human arithmetic. It was simpler—and more efficient—to view jobs as agencies of party discipline.

Jim desires first of all to build up a party organization that will be responsive down to its lowliest outposts to his personal authority. So he ordained from the beginning that the bulk of the jobs should go to the elements he had learned how to work with and whose leaders in many cases were grateful to him for their present posts of eminence. So the FRBC—or for-Roosevelt-before-Chicago —cohorts got the preference.

But there were important exceptions. Senator McAdoo and Mr. Garner had stopped the "Stop Roosevelt" movement at Chicago; so Mr. Garner's brand of Texans were shunted toward the front rank in Mr. Farley's waiting lines, and Senator McAdoo got some of the richest patronage the administration had to offer long before the original Roosevelt elements in California got even a smell of it. Mayor Frank Hague of Jersey City had shouted at Chicago the convention's supreme insult—that Governor Roosevelt would be a "push-over" for Mr. Hoover. But he recanted the instant the nomination was made and worked loyally for the ticket. So Mr. Hague was recognized as patronage boss for New Jersey. As time went on, conciliating tidbits were tossed to numerous factions which had been originally hostile or standoffish toward Roosevelt—provided, that is, that they reconciled themselves to the absolute supremacy of the Roosevelt leaders in their provinces.

For those that remained standoffish, punishments were sure, regardless of ancient friendships. Tammany is the classical example of Jim's steady punitive vengeance. Tammany intrigued for Al Smith at Chicago, covertly opposed the Roosevelt-Farley 1932 program to name Lieutenant Governor Lehman for the governorship, tried to unseat Postmaster General and National Chairman Farley as New York State chairman, and through its congressmen ranged itself in 1933 against several of the crucial New Deal legislative measures. Tammany as a result got no patronage in 1933 at all. Even in 1935, after Sachem Jim had utilized its defeat in the La Guardia mayoralty campaign to bring about the ousting of John F. Curry and the selection of the friendly James J. Dooling as leader, it had received only three major local patronage offices and a very thin sprinkling of small-fry appointments. Dooling, it had developed, had been unable to bring the anti-Roosevelt leaders into line; so Tammany continued to pay the penalty.

Jim, according to intimate testimony, regards the whole Tammany fiasco with the utmost philosophy. If the Tammany leaders insist on fighting the administration and among themselves, he accepts it, after five years, as a matter of incurable temperamental instability. But the organization must pay for its privileges of inner dissension in an almost total lack of consideration from its federal government. Jim would like to be helpful if he could, but circumstances have compelled him to starve Tammany into the position of a relatively impotent Manhattan faction increasingly at the mercy of the Democratic organizations which he has helped to build up under dependably pro-Roosevelt leaders in the more populous Bronx and Brooklyn sections. The power of the patronage is, in other words, the power to isolate, and Jim, from the strictest amoral motives, has done more, perhaps, to sap the Tiger's vital forces than all the fusion reform heroes in history.

Above and beyond rewards and punishments and problems of strengthening the right machines at the right places, there was the question of finding enough jobs to go around. On this point the gentleman who invented home delivery service in marriage and hunting licenses was no man to refuse to turn fast corners. Mr. Farley frankly kept the New Deal emergency agencies free from civil service classification, fought its extension all along the line in the permanent departments, and lobbied to have it removed from all classes of federal employees where there was the slightest pretext for doubting the immaculacy with which it had been bestowed by the Republicans. In the Post Office Department he revived the Postmaster General's long-discarded prerogative of choosing postmasters from the three highest candidates on the examination lists, and devised an intricate system of provisional appointments and repetitive examinations which made it possible to boost his—or a Farley congressman's—man into the eligible trinity if it took all summer. He shortened the terms of scores of Republican "holdover" postmasters by encouraging local agents to report signs of "offensive political activity" in their conduct and postal inspectors to check their efficiency records with microscopes.

Through these expedients Jim created down to the 1936 election a total of nearly 300,000 available patronage appointments where under the government's pre-New Deal status he would have been confined to a bare 150,000. To the best of his ability, he awarded these jobs on the principle declared in an early 1933 patronage conference with Democratic congressmen, that "there are 200 Republican appointees riding horses down along the Mexican border and I know 200 Democrats who can ride a horse just as well." Within limits, and with due consideration for the intimate problems of his local satraps, he has tried to pick the better brands of Democratic horsemen. But the principle back of his spoilsmanship is the same one which he found effective on the New York State Boxing Commission: Every extension of your lines of authority ties more practical politicians to your fortunes in the bonds of fear and favor.

VIII

Jim stands on his pedestal today as America's supreme political pragmatist. There have been errors in the record, of course, but none of the errors has counted. Once he manufactured close to half a million dollars' worth of stamps deliberately botched for collectors' purposes and gave them away, or permitted their face value sale, to friends near and dear to him in Democracy. But what did the indignation of a million philatelists mean to him when not one stamp-collector in ten thousand has political influence even on his own block? None of the politically influential beneficiaries of Mr. Farley's thoughtfulness was noticeably cooled by his generosity. The gift-stamp scandal will probably not be repeated, but the net effects, as far as they went, were quite as satisfactory as those of Commissioner Farley's free fight-ticket system.

Again, a great hubbub was raised in the spring of 1935—mainly by the late Senator Huey Long—about the contacts between Mr. Farley's building supply firm in New York and contractors doing business with the government. But the Senate, having even more important business matters to discuss with Mr. Farley, voted down an investigation, and the probable final result of the disturbance was to advise hinterland contractors who had never heard of it before, that the administration's premier political fixer was in the building supply business.

Sitting in the center of his far-flung lines of communication with the provinces, Big Jim can afford to treat these occasional personal embarrassments lightly. His continental machine operates above and around them as trunk highway traffic flows past a minor accident.

His major patronage problems are behind him, and the day's grist of new ones can be taken care of by his smoothly-oiled clearance system. The organization of his empire is complete except for occasional minor adjustments which he can make with the practiced hand of a gentleman who keeps all the details in his mind. The New Deal's conflicts of programs and philosophies do not unsettle him. For one thing, he has excellent ghost-writers. Even more, as Mr. Robert Duffus once said of him, he is practically devoid of either radicalism or conservatism and is purely a politician. If his conscience ever troubles him for his feats of super-spoilsmanship, his shrewd sense of the main chance tells him that he has done no more than any normally competitive business entrepreneur would do to introduce his products into the provinces and to undermine rival sales managers.

Doubtless he recognizes in his darker moments that Mr. Roosevelt or some future president could destroy him by taking away his power of the patronage. But he is equally entitled to the reflection that a statesman who chose to destroy Mr. Farley might not long continue to be president.

For Big Jim has not been so short-sighted as to devise a self-operating machine for winning political victories. What he has done more expertly than any political machinist in our history is to organize himself as a power house.

NORMAN THOMAS

By Don D. Lescohier

Norman Thomas is a prophet who condemns profits. His clarion voice is calling America to a new social order. He believes that Socialism will make ours a land where exploitation, poverty, and war will be no more. Capitalism he sees as a civilization based upon greed and exploitation, floundering toward its inevitable doom; Socialism as the final stage of social evolution.

Mr. Thomas is one of the significant figures on the American political stage. He is chairman of the National Executive Committee of the Socialist party and was its candidate for president in 1928, 1932, and 1936. The hopelessness of the candidacy was of no importance to him. His eye was fixed on the future, and each campaign was an educational process intended to bring the American people closer to Socialism. Since he differs from the typical politician in being devoted solely to a cause rather than to the advancement of his personal fortunes, the campaign rather than the office was the important matter.

Whether he is a John the Baptist foretelling the coming of a new social order or only a vigorous critic of the present one the future alone can reveal. His untiring advocacy of the replacement of Capitalism by Socialism keeps the minds of millions turned toward the future; while his stinging criticisms of the southern share-cropper system, his vigorous advocacy of the cause of labor, and his relentless exposure of evils in both our economic and our political systems call men to reform the present order.

The combination of Thomas Socialism and Thomas's reform activities fits the realities of American life and the psychology of the American people better than the program of any other American Socialist leader. Though the present writer is not a Socialist, it appears to him that Mr. Thomas in *The Choice Before Us*[1] has depicted a Socialist order which conceivably might be worked out in the United States.

Thomas believes that the nation's land and natural resources should be the common possession of all the people and managed for the common welfare; likewise all tools and equipment that must be operated by specialized groups and cannot reasonably be owned by the individuals who use them. The basic initiative of this socialized state would be that of engineers and administrators rather than of profit seekers. Starting with the resources, equipment, technology, education, and trained population which is already existent in the United States, the American Socialist state would not have to go through the scarcity era which has been necessary in Russia. Each industry would be operated under a board of directors chosen from the industry by the workers in the industry and by the consuming public, not under a politician like the Postmaster General.[2]

Thomas is a middle-class leader. He came from a family of Presbyterian preachers and was himself a minister for eleven years. He was born in Marion, Ohio, November 20, 1884, of Celtic and Anglo-Saxon stock. His father was the Rev. Welling E. Thomas; his mother, Emma Mattoon. One grandfather was a minister, the other a missionary. His childhood home was characterized by unaffected devotion to a stern Calvinistic creed. It was a home in which spiritual rather than material values dominated. It was a home which put an ineradicable stamp upon the character of Norman Thomas. In it he learned the winsomeness of righteousness, justice, and human kindness; that right is right and wrong is wrong; and that no compromise with wrong can solve man's problems.

Thomas's boyhood was essentially normal. His family had modest, but adequate, resources. He lived in a typical midwestern city, participated in the sports and other activities of middle western boyhood, and read avidly. His mother, as well as his father, was a leader in the community and intellectually stimulating to her six

---

[1] Norman Thomas, *The Choice Before Us*, New York, The Macmillan Co., 1934. The writer is calling the readers' attention to this particular book because he considers it very representative of Mr. Thomas's ideas and preferable to scattered citations of his writings in this short account of his life. *The Choice Before Us* gives a consistent and comprehensive statement of his current analysis of our socio-economic problems.

[2] For more details, see Norman Thomas, *op. cit.*, Chap. IX.

children. They believed, likewise, in work, and—strange irony of fate—Norman Thomas in his boyhood peddled the *Daily Star*, Warren G. Harding's newspaper.

He revealed an alert, eager mind at an early age. With a brilliant high school record behind him he went to Bucknell College for a year and then to Princeton, where he was a student of Woodrow Wilson. It was at Princeton that his interest in politics and economics became definite and his skill in and enjoyment of debating was revealed. In later years, after being refused for six years the right to speak on the Princeton campus, he was granted the honorary degree of Doctor of Letters by Princeton in 1932.

He was graduated from Princeton in 1905 and spent two years in a settlement house in the slums of New York City. This experience directed his attention to the disastrous moral, intellectual, and physical effects of poverty, furnished abundant object lessons in human exploitation, and intensified his interest in the politico-economic maladjustments of current society. A trip around the world which followed laid the foundations for the interest in world problems which has been one of his outstanding characteristics. For Norman Thomas's interest was in mankind, regardless of nationality, race, religion, or social class. He had not yet become a Socialist.

When he returned from his trip around the world, he became assistant pastor of Christ Church Settlement, New York. There he met and married Frances Violet Stewart. They have a family of five children. He next became assistant to Dr. Henry Van Dyke at Brick Presbyterian Church on Fifth Avenue, New York. Meanwhile he was studying at the Union Theological Seminary. His work at the Seminary was marked by an increasingly critical attitude toward both the economic and theological concepts which were conventional. When he was examined for ordination, the newspapers made front page copy of the fact that the Presbytery spent an entire afternoon questioning this independently-minded, but obviously able, young man concerning his dissenting views.

That was in 1911. He now left Fifth Avenue and went back to the poor. He was pastor for the next six years of East Harlem Presbyterian Church, New York. This church was a part of the American Parish, a group of Presbyterian churches and settlement houses on the upper east side. Thomas was chairman of the Parish.

Here he was surrounded by immigrants, especially Italians, Hungarians, and Swedes, which strengthened his internationalism. More important, he saw unemployment in its stark realities, poverty-stricken old age, what sickness means to the poor, the depredations of loan sharks, the ravages wrought by the parasites who prey on youth, and municipal corruption in the raw. He saw that neither settlement houses nor churches could grapple with the evils of the nation's East Harlems, for too many of their evils were inherent in the nation's social institutions.

During these years he was reading widely and thinking deeply. The Socialist writers became familiar to him. His religious and economic ideas were recast. When the World War broke out he found himself unable to endorse it. To him the war was a test of Christianity and social intelligence. The spectacle of ministers of all nations using the Scriptures to justify mass murder sickened him. "I have not yet seen in recent years," wrote one of his friends, "any of that depth of despair into which he fell during the period of the World War and its aftermath, when he was, for a time, genuinely bitter through and through—having enlisted for what he thought was to be a life work in the Christian Church, and having seen the betrayal of religion by a war-mad clergy." [3]

His attitude toward the war strained his relations with his church. When he supported Morris Hillquit, a Socialist, for mayor, retention of his pastorate became impossible. He resigned in 1917, joined the Socialist party and immediately became one of its crusaders.

"What I like about Norman," said a leading Socialist, "is that he came to us when everybody else was running away." For Thomas joined the Socialist party when the war situation, with its hysteria of nationalism, had made both the pacifism and the internationalism of the Socialists anathema, and many formerly active Socialists either had dropped out of the party or became inactive. Thomas quickly breathed new life into disheartened men and women, won back many of the discouraged, and turned their eyes again toward the future.

Aided by a few friends he next started publication of *The New World* (later *The World Tomorrow*). His relentless criticisms of

[3] Letter of DeVere Allen to the present writer under date of August 19, 1937.

alleged brutal treatment of "conscientious objectors" in federal prisons brought upon him the wrath of the government. Department of Justice agents trailed him, tapped his wires, questioned him. Postmaster Burleson tried to suppress *The World Tomorrow*. But the paper continued and Thomas edited it until 1921, when he resigned to become an associate editor of *The Nation*.

Two organizations founded during these years have proved to be major vehicles for Thomas's activities. With Roger Baldwin he founded the National Civil Liberties League to defend the constitutional rights of citizens, and with Harry Laidler he reorganized in 1921 the old Intercollegiate Socialist Society into the League for Industrial Democracy. His life since has been closely identified with these two organizations, both devoted to fighting for the underdog; the one for such liberties as freedom of speech and assemblage, the other for economic justice. For Thomas is a man who cannot let wrong go unchallenged anywhere he sees it.

These activities have brought him into frequent conflict with local authorities. When the sheriff announced during the textile strikes in Passaic in 1926 that no more public meetings could be held, Thomas immediately made a test case. He was arrested and spent the night in jail. But the incident made the front page in the nation's press and there was little difficulty in proving the arrest illegal. At Terre Haute he defied martial law in 1935. In the same year he gave Tampa brain-storms after the murder of Joseph Shoemaker, leader of the unemployed. Two years later the Shoemaker case was still a live issue as a result of his activities. In 1938 he was battling Mayor Hague of Jersey City for labor's right to freedom of assembly, of speech, and of organization.

In scores of cities he has backed up the picket lines of strikers, fought for free speech, and defended racial, political, or economic minorities. But always and everywhere his battles over special situations have been characterized by unceasing efforts to educate in fundamental Socialist principles those with whom he worked and to tie those principles into the facts of the particular situation. Whether fighting political corruption, bad housing, racial persecution, the maladministration of justice, a Jimmy Walker, the Du Ponts, or Franklin D. Roosevelt, he is the evangelist of Socialism.

Since the death of Debs, no Socialist or radical leader has been so completely immersed in the problems of trade unionism. His New York office has been for years the haven of workingmen and trade unionists seeking advice and aid in their campaigns for better working conditions. Through his Emergency Committee for Strikers' Relief he has aided more than a million unionists and strikers and raised over $400,000 for their relief. Thomas believes in industrial rather than craft unionism, and long before the Committee on Industrial Organization had forced the issue he declared that the American Federation of Labor unions should be organized on an industrial basis; that unionism *in general* should finance the organizing of each particular industry and not throw the whole burden on the union in that industry; that it was time to reduce the power of union executives and develop a more democratic situation; and that the color line should be wiped out in the labor movement.

A large part of his time has been given to fighting for exploited share-croppers in the South and for labor groups like the southern textile workers or West Virginia coal miners—social groups which have been economically exploited and politically controlled by machines in the hands of employers. His championship of the cause of the share-croppers has made the nation aware of the plight of a group hitherto unnoticed and without outside sympathy and aid. To reconcile his genial, kindly personality with his readiness for any fight for the oppressed, one has to take account of the intense hatred of injustice which he derived from his heredity and early life, religion's focusing of his moral earnestness far into his adult life, the intensity of his nature, and his extensive contact with the unrighteousnesses of the current social order.

The political career of Thomas has been a series of defeats which have increased his reputation more than victory does that of most political candidates. In 1924 he was the Socialist party's candidate for governor of New York; in 1925 for mayor of New York; in 1926 for the state Senate of New York; in 1927 for alderman in New York; in 1928 for president of the United States; in 1929 for mayor of New York; and in 1932 and 1936 for president of the United States. There is only one logic underlying this running for office continually (and for offices ranging from president down to city alderman)—each campaign gives him an opportunity to expose relentlessly current political and economic wrongs and to

UNDERWOOD AND UNDERWOOD

NORMAN THOMAS

"In debate he is fiery, alert, dynamic."

preach Socialism. A political campaign gives him a hearing by the nation; and, though defeated, his campaigns have yielded gains; in 1928, as Socialist candidate for president, he polled some 250,-000 votes; in 1932 approximately 880,000. In 1936 his vote fell off to about 200,000 when Franklin D. Roosevelt captured the imagination and votes of liberals generally.

His campaigns for mayor of New York City in 1925 and 1929 increased his reputation more than any other political activity. For he revealed an intimate knowledge of what was wrong in New York's government and advocated specific immediate programs to improve the situation in the public interest. It was this essentially practical aspect of his campaign that made the Citizen's Union, the *World Telegram,* and the *New York World* support him.[4] His demand for municipal ownership of public utilities was one that thousands of non-Socialists could support enthusiastically; his exposure of political rottenness met a response from thousands of his fellow citizens.

In his presidential campaigns he has stressed particularly the inadequacy of the conventional programs of the old parties to solve the nation's economic problems, and has contended that only thorough-going Socialism could end business depressions, properly control the money system, enable the economic system to produce to its maximum capacity, provide economic security, and abolish economic exploitation.

Thomas's campaigns have been financed partly by money raised by subscription directly by the party. But his popularity as a speaker has been so great that the party locals in the various cities have eagerly raised considerable sums in order to get a Thomas date. These local honorariums have been paid into the national party treasury, and Thomas has refused to accept a salary out of them, though in 1932 his campaign tour netted the party over $3,000. Incidentally, it may be mentioned that the Socialist party has not been a source of income for Mr. Thomas. He has supported himself by writing and lecturing, and received only his expenses when speaking at Socialist party meetings or during campaigns.

Thomas has played an important, but not a dictatorial, part in the determination of party policies. His convention speeches have

---

[4] These papers were merged at a subsequent date.

frequently swung opponents into line. In the meetings of the National Executive Committee he has exercised a major influence. It would be difficult, of course, for a personality as strong as his to avoid dominating to a considerable extent the councils of any organization. It is the testimony of other members of the National Executive Committee, however, that "he has often leaned over backwards to avoid that result" and that "in some cases he should have exerted himself more" to control the situation. He has matured politically during the last decade and has assumed a more active and consistent part in molding party policy, but has demonstrated a capacity to accept the decisions of the majority even when those decisions did not seem wise to him.

He has shown a remarkable capacity to get along with a great diversity of people in the party, many of them living under high tension and many "possessed of the personality characteristics which most observers have come to associate with ardent radicals." [5] Overworked, and a very intense person, his temper sometimes breaks through, particularly at petty snipers within or without the party. But, said one of his associates to the writer, "He has probably had to bear more disappointments and take a greater spiritual punishment than any individual I know, and yet through it all, he bobs up with an incredible degree of humor and philosophical insight."

Within the party there has been a faction which has resented the middle-class characteristics of Thomas, particularly his friendship and alliances with "liberals" and "progressives" of the non-Socialist variety. James Oneal, for instance, contends that the "Socialist party is a party of the working class." "The Socialist movement is primarily a movement of the working people, a class that needs no neglected geniuses of the academic and professional world to lead it; a class that must select and educate its leaders from its own ranks." [6]

"We cannot neglect the task of winning deflated sections of the middle and professional classes, the intellectuals and students for whom capitalism holds out little or no hope; but to direct our work with the view of placing all responsible party posts in the hands of collegiates and intellectuals is to assume that bourgeois educational

[5] Statement of a member of the National Executive Committee to the writer.

[6] James Oneal, *Some Pages of Party History*, pp. 10, 27. This pamphlet illustrates the Oneal faction's point of view.

institutions are training schools for party leadership. . . . Let us turn to the task of ending play-boy revolution." [7]

The widespread popularity of Mr. Thomas among the middle classes and students has been due not to his Socialist ideas but to his essential character and his dramatic platform techniques. In the first place, he has an idealistic philosophy of which Claude Fuess said: "His spiritual kinship is with St. Francis of Assisi, with Tolstoy, and with Gandhi." In the second place, he believes profoundly that sound ideas will, in the long run, profoundly influence human conduct. Thomas himself considers this to be the most important difference between himself and Socialism on the one hand, and such men as Franklin D. Roosevelt and the New Dealers on the other. The New Dealers, he said, are "reluctant to give us a philosophy. Instead they rather exult in a pragmatism of an opportunistic sort. They will increase social control, they will protect the underdog, they will stabilize business, and yet somehow or other preserve individual initiative, private profit, and the rights of the little man." They have "not given the masses of the people any fanatic faith to sustain them or any new philosophy to guide them in a wilderness." Roosevelt's "liberal aspirations are meaningless except as he gets results"; "the road which the New Deal has opened will not reach any distant horizon without sharp detours to the right or the left." [8]

Thomas's philosophy is a part of his personality. He is a gentleman in the best sense of the term. His physical appearance immediately registers the fact. Tall, slender, and slightly stooped in the shoulders; conventional in dress, dignified and thoughtful; he looks to be what students call "a gentleman and a scholar." His quiet, reserved face is lighted frequently by an attractive smile. His eyes are blue-gray, nostrils sensitive, and features sharply chiseled.

In debate the man is transformed. Now he is fiery, alert, dynamic. His logic is reinforced constantly by telling illustrations; his platform manner replete with flashes of fire, humor, and sarcasm, and with clever, laugh-provoking phrases. But these illumi-

[7] *Ibid.*, p. 28.
[8] Norman Thomas, *The Choice Before Us.* All quotations in this paragraph from pp. 164, 165. Quotations by permission of The Macmillan Co., publishers.

nate without softening the tremendous earnestness of his attacks on capitalism, nationalism, communism, and fascism and the intensity of his faith in Socialism. Indeed, both on the platform and in his writings he depends somewhat too much upon cleverness and these aptly turned phrases, too little upon the careful assemblage of facts and well-integrated argument. His appeal is to emotion and idealism rather than cold reason. The hearer is inspired and motivated more than instructed. Nevertheless his writings include much solid reasoning which impresses the reader with the feeling that Mr. Thomas has raised issues which cannot be lightly brushed aside.

One or two illustrations of his technique may serve to clarify the point. In *The Choice Before Us* he says, "By and large, if one were to draw up a list of great fortunes in America and then try to answer the question, 'What have their possessors done to deserve such wealth?', the adequate reply would be 'They have done us.' " [9] Again, referring to the steps taken by Mr. Roosevelt in 1933 to rehabilitate the banking system, Thomas said, "He could have nationalized banking with the public behind him." . . . But he "did nothing of the sort. He patched up the system and gave it back to the bankers to see if they could ruin it again." [10] After "he had driven the money changers out of the temple, he had soon let them back, washed a bit behind the ears, wearing for a time at least their Sabbath raiment, and watched more carefully. But back they were, some of them in the choir, for a time at least, singing praises to their savior." [11]

These statements, humorous, dramatic, and effective as they are, are allowed to stand unsupported by documentary, statistical, or other evidence of their truth. This is, perhaps, the greatest weakness in his writings, and to a less significant extent, of his speeches. But a large part of the public, judging from the popularity of his pronouncements, prefer these bonbons to meat.

There are four "isms" which bear the brunt of Thomas's attacks —nationalism, capitalism, communism, and fascism. Space does not permit a detailed exposition of his arguments against them.[12] But the point must be emphasized that he believes America (and the

[9] P. 21.   [10] P. 89.   [11] Pp. 89-90.
[12] His criticisms of all four are summarized in *The Choice Before Us*, Chaps. I-VI.

world) is fast coming to a point where a choice must be made among them. That choice, he believes, cannot be a turning back to a past state of society; it must be a moving forward to a new situation. He declares that ever since the Great War a large section of public opinion, especially here in America, has been talking about returning to something or recovering something. The Republicans were going to return to normalcy; the Democratic policies were headed by a "National Recovery Act." "The first condition of a desirable revolution is that we should recognize that we are not recovering something but gaining something. True prosperity is what great masses of human beings have never had. They may win it, they can not recover it." [13]

But he constantly reminds the Socialists that a better world must be achieved. It will not come of itself. "There is no destiny which determines man's fate utterly without his power to dream and act. We ourselves help to make our fate." "But the field in which men may choose is limited." "If our analysis has been correct we ought at this point to decide what roads are open to us and where they are likely to lead." [14] "The myths which justified and supported the Coolidge epoch have been made ridiculous in the eyes of the masses. If they are to be cowed and kept in some sort of subjection it must be by new myths, new illusions, new fears, new hopes, however false." [15] But, as he observes in another place, Italian and German fascism shows "that men can be coerced or cajoled into accepting pathetically little in a world which might give them abundance, provided the dictator can give them such emotional satisfactions as come from their personal identification with the glory of their nation and the grandeur of their race." [16]

"What is the newest and most significant in fascism . . . is the extent to which it has driven the notion of the sovereignty of the national state, exercised under a party dictatorship. Ever since the French Revolution nationalism has been the religion of Western man. It helped to drive him into the hell of 1914 to 1918 and sustained him in it. It remained for Fascism to develop a concept of the totalitarian state which would absorb not only in war but in peace the loyalty, the energy, and the conscience of men." [17] Ob-

[13] *Ibid.*, pp. 11-12.
[14] *Ibid.*, p. 162.
[15] *Ibid.*, p. 163.
[16] *Ibid.*, p. 48.

viously, in Thomas's view, Socialism is not the only type of society which might emerge in America if the present economic and political order should crumble or be wrecked. Socialism, if it comes, must be brought about by a carefully planned, well organized revolution, followed by a well thought out, constructive social reorganization.

Norman Thomas believes that the least desirable type of revolution is one involving violence and bloodshed. "No violence promises us anything better than a deeper descent into a hell of our own making, unless, as Reinhold Niebuhr has suggested, it bears some resemblance to the violence of a surgical operation rather than of wholesale butchery, a violence limited in duration and extent, so that the healing processes can soon begin. The less the violence and the hate, the more secure will be the co-operative commonwealth which shall arise." [18]

On the other hand, he is not willing to wait for "endless elections" to whittle a little off the old order here, put patches on there, and hope that sometime mankind will muddle through to a better world.

Instead he urges Socialists to push forward to the earliest possible seizure of political power, and advances his belief that it is at least as likely that the capture of the state can be the achievement of a workers' democracy as of any sort of dictatorship. "And the more we can keep of civil liberty and the tolerance that has been associated with democracy, the happier will be the transition period and the surer its victories. Nevertheless our struggle must be for the capture of all power." [19]

He warns the Socialists that "In practice we shall deal not with the purely economic effects of capitalism, but with them plus their psychological and political consequences and accompaniments. In particular we shall deal with capitalism far more definitely bound to the service of the national state than before the Great War," ... "the rampant nationalism which set nations to fight one another with tariffs and with struggles for the possession of gold," and the preparation for war.[20] Consequently the task of reconstructing the social order involves far more than the mere reorganization of the management of industry, commerce, finance and transportation.

[17] *Ibid.*, pp. 48-49.
[18] *Ibid.*, p. 207.
[19] *Ibid.*, p. 222.
[20] *Ibid.*, p. 25.

"We shall make the greatest mistake of all if we think that man, the individual, will be satisfied to have any state or commonwealth become forever his mind and his conscience—even if, by chance, in such a society he and his fellows are reasonably well fed and entertained." [21]

To accomplish a social revolution with little or no bloodshed, followed by a constructive and acceptable program of reconstruction of the economic and political order and with democratic processes of social control, Thomas sees that other classes than the manual laborers must be a vital part of the revolution. Consequently he stresses the importance of the Socialists' winning all classes of workers, both hand and brain, including the white-collar workers, engineers, and other technicians, and not limiting their appeal to wage workers (and overall workers at that). He contends that the Socialists must also win farmer support and assistance for their movement. He declares that the farmers, white-collar workers, the technicians . . . "must be definitely won to Socialism if Socialism anywhere in the world is to be the alternative to chaos or Fascism." [22]

Mr. Thomas, obviously, is playing a unique role on the American political stage. His objectives involve a rather complete reconstruction of the nation's political and economic structure and far-reaching changes in social relationships, conditions, and practices. His campaigns are not for the purpose of obtaining public office but of obtaining a nation-wide hearing for his doctrine. Meanwhile, he works unceasingly for the current amelioration of the lot of the masses; fights injustice wherever he sees it; defends human liberties on every front.

POSTSCRIPT

A friend who read this chapter before it was sent to press said: "Your chapter is an appreciation of Thomas. Perhaps there should be more of criticism." I am moved to a personal word on the subject. My acquaintance with Norman Thomas began in 1931 when I debated him at the Adelphi Theater, Chicago. I never saw him until that occasion. The following winter I participated in a series of triangular debates with Thomas and Scott Nearing, at Chicago,

[21] *Ibid.*, p. 41. [22] *Ibid.*, p. 78.

Toledo, Milwaukee, and Madison, Wisconsin. Peculiarly enough, I have never met him personally except upon occasions when we have been opponents. But I have read many of his books and magazine articles, watched his career with deep interest, and had opportunity to talk with many persons who know him and his work. I believe that what I have written above is a realistic picture of Norman Thomas. I do not feel the need to criticize further, for such criticism would necessarily have to emphasize minor points or else my differences of opinion with Thomas. He is too big a personality to deserve captious criticism, while his opinions have just as good a chance of being judged correct (in the long run) as mine have. He has enough critics—bitter, merciless enemies, many of them. Though I can not subscribe to his philosophy, what I have written above expresses my personal concepts of Norman Thomas, the man and the politician.

13

DAN HOAN, MAYOR OF MILWAUKEE

By Lindsay Hoben

I

SOMEONE THREW A BOMB! FIRING STARTED FROM BOTH SIDES. Eight policemen fell writhing in death. Sixty-eight more were wounded. Nobody counted the dead workers.

Chicago's Haymarket Square riot was over. Finally the crowd dispersed. It was May 4, 1886. Warrants were issued immediately for the arrest of the demonstration's leaders, but none could be found.

A few weeks later little Danny Hoan—he was then five—ran into the kitchen of the Hoan house near the end of West Main Street, where it sloped down to the Fox River in Waukesha, Wisconsin.

"Dad," he piped, "there's another tramp out in the barn." He knew, as everyone in Waukesha knew, that old Dan Hoan—the town radical—never turned away a tramp.

This tramp stayed for seven weeks. He called himself Jackson. He worked for old Dan as a carpenter. Then the summer waned. The Middle West buzzed about the thousands of dollars of rewards which had been offered for the arrest of the accused in the Haymarket riot.

Townsfolk in Waukesha wanted to burn in effigy one of the accused men.

"Better not let old Dan see you," the more cautious whispered along Main Street.

At the Hoan house "the tramp" could stand it no longer. "You've helped me," he said to old Dan, "but it's no use. Take me down to Chicago and give me up; you might as well have the money."

Old Dan was furious. He wouldn't, he exploded, do such a thing if he were starving. He believed that the accused men in the Haymarket riot were innocent victims in the labor struggle and that they were being railroaded.

But "the tramp" went to Chicago, anyway, and gave himself up. He was Albert R. Parsons, editor of the *Alarm*, which had praised dynamite as "the beautiful stuff" for the workers to use to win freedom.

The next fall, with three others—Louis Lingg, in his cell, had blown his own head off with a dynamite cap—Parsons stood on the gallows. As he shouted, "Let the voice of the people be heard. Oh—" they hanged him!

Little Dan Hoan always remembered Albert Parsons. He didn't know whether Parsons had been a good man or a bad man, guilty or not guilty, but the whole affair made the youngster acutely aware of labor's upward struggle. Radicals wanted an eight-hour day and labor unions. This *was* revolution in the eighties. The *New York World* commented: "The American laborer must make up his mind, henceforth, not to be so much better off than the European laborer. Men must be content to work for low wages. In this the workingman will be nearer to the station in life to which it has pleased God to call him."

Such was the atmosphere of struggle in which Dan Hoan grew up—little knowing that he was destined to reign as Milwaukee's mayor for a quarter-century. He was a quiet lad, and hard working. He had to be, for he was the youngest of four children (another sister [1] was buried the day before Dan was born) and there was little time for play. When there was, old-timers in Waukesha still recall as they pause in their checkers in the veterinary's office on West Main, "he used to play with the niggers down on 'smokey row.' And his dad—old Dan Hoan . . ." The anecdotes are endless. Old Dan, it seems, was quite a hand with the ladies. He was, the reminiscent relates with a wink, a "Mormon."

When Dan was eight, his mother left home. From that time on, old Dan was father and mother to his youngest. They were inseparable. But six years later the father died leaving the lad of fourteen in charge of the household. The oldest brother [2] was

---

[1] Ella.

[2] William, died November 26, 1937. He had no visible means of support; was sometimes helped by the Mayor, whom he disliked, or, at least, pretended to.

away. The other, physically handicapped, remained at home,[3] as did a sister.[4]

Dan managed to put up a brave front and arranged for the funeral. But, as he walked homeward from the cemetery, Dan felt as though his very heart were torn out. He was suddenly overcome with helplessness. "My father's dead, my father's dead," he repeated to himself. For five years afterward scarcely a night passed that Dan didn't dream of his father. They had never been more than a day apart.

The neighbors gave young Dan advice. "Put away your father's radical theories," they told him. "You can't get anywhere as a Populist or a Socialist. Those ideas will handicap you. Go into business."

This sounded like good counsel to Dan; so he crammed two years' schooling into one and went to work, first as a waiter, then as a cook. He was a serious boy, studied much, and never entered into the social life of the young people, because he felt that he was a misfit. The unhappiness of his home life, culminating in his mother's leaving, and a sense of isolation in being the son of a man who held "queer" ideas, contributed to this. It was years before Dan overcame this feeling of inner awkwardness. But neighbors with that prophetic vision (which they recall later, if they are right, and forget, if wrong) were already saying: "You watch that boy; he'll be famous some day."

Dan moved to Milwaukee and sought new kitchens to conquer. He soon worked at the best hotels and restaurants in town. Meanwhile he mixed much study with his soup.

He was seventeen and a half when on a brisk November night —shades of Dick Whittington—he stood in the square by the City Hall and listened to speakers at an outdoor political rally. Dan was beneath the very windows of the mayor's office which he was destined to occupy longer than any mayor of a big American city.

A Populist began to talk—of public ownership, of exploitation of the laboring masses. Dan's heart quickened. Here was a man running for public office who expounded the beliefs of Dan's

[3] George, hanged himself September 21, 1931, under the Mayor's back steps. He was jobless, despondent, had $1,200 in the bank, which he left to the Mayor's son.

[4] Gertrude (Mrs. Henry Losey) died April 16, 1938.

father. At this rally Dan became politically conscious. The fires of his father's ideas were rekindled. The young man visited the head-quarters of the three workingmen's parties—Populist, Socialist, Social Democrats. He joined the last. (Three years later a merger of the last two resulted in the Socialist party of today.)

When Dan was twenty-one, encouraged by a customer who liked to debate socialism with him, he decided to go to the University of Wisconsin as a special student. In four years he covered an entire high school and college course and earned his own living. His one attempt at athletics was blighted under mysterious circumstances. Hoan wanted to make good at football, as any youth would who stood six feet and weighed 205 pounds. But, most important, the football squad was fed free for the season. To Dan, who had cooked for a living for many years, this was an inviting prospect. But the manager of the football squad was the manager of the Kappa Sigma fraternity, for which Hoan cooked. Hoan was kicked off the squad, and to this day he wonders whether his athletic demise was because he was a bad football player or because he was a good cook.

At the University Hoan discovered that he was a good debater and he spent many hours in this extracurricular pastime. He founded the first Socialist club at the University and, incidentally, refused to work for the La Follette organization. Not until thirty-five years later did Dan Hoan play political ball with the La Follettes, and then it was half-heartedly in the loosely knit Farmer-Labor Progressive Federation.

Hoan learned how to organize his thought and how to gather material for his endless disputation. He had, in debates, an almost peasant directness, a homely and incisive humor, and a fine sense of logic. This more than made up for his rasping, unpleasant nasal voice and his sometimes unorthodox grammar. In all of these things, the Hoan of today is the Hoan of three decades ago. The deadliness of Hoan's repartee—since learned by many an adversary—was well illustrated when he was challenged by a conservative and well-to-do student to debate: "Resolved: That Socialism is a Cure for All the Evils Growing Out of the Capitalistic System." "Delighted," responded Hoan, but would the challenger be so kind as to furnish a bill of particulars listing the evils of capitalism so that the Socialists could prepare their answers? The debate ended right there.

By the time Hoan graduated from the University, president of his class of 450, he was as self-possessed as he had always been self-reliant. It is interesting that the 1906 *Badger*—the year-book of the University—after listing his oratorical and debating activities, says: "A bluff old brother at the bowl, a welcome guest in hall and bower, he tells a story—then another—to while away the weary hour." He still spins a salty yarn. But he is fundamentally a serious person, as he was then. Indeed, Hoan's thesis was: "The tendencies of court decisions in labor disputes."

From the University, Hoan went down to Chicago to work in a law office for $6 a week—the lowest wage he had ever had—and to attend the Kent College of Law, a night school. He completed his entire law course in nine months and passed the bar examinations in both Wisconsin and Illinois among the three highest in rank. Hoan wanted to be a labor lawyer and he was making a start when, in 1908, a delegation of Milwaukee Socialists, inspired by Victor Berger, induced him to come back to Milwaukee. They promised that Hoan would not be asked to run for office, but only to work for the welfare of the growing Socialist party. Hoan had already been a member for ten years and always an active one. He continued to work hard in the party and to seek practice as a labor lawyer. Within six months of his arrival in Milwaukee he was attorney for the Wisconsin State Federation of Labor.

Then the Socialist party, despite its promises, decided that Hoan must run for city attorney in the 1910 election. It was a routine affair, they told him. The Socialists did not have a chance even though their power had been growing steadily for eight years. Everybody knew that the then acknowledgedly corrupt local Republican and Democratic machines had things well in control. Still, the Socialists wanted to have a full ticket. Hoan demurred. He did so want to be a labor lawyer and he was having a hard time scraping up practice. He shuddered at the mere thought of the names he would be called when the political mud-slinging started. It would ruin his practice. But Hoan was called before the vigilance committee and told that he had to run. Reluctantly he acquiesced.

The campaign had no more than started when the worst happened. The city attorney, running for re-election, uttered a few blasts at this young "red flag carpet-bagger from Chicago" who dared to aspire to the city attorneyship. Candidate Hoan replied with a prosaic attack on the city attorney's indifference to the need for an adequate boiler inspection ordinance (an explosion a few weeks before having killed several men in a brewery). Hoan also, by luck and ridicule, cast his opponent in such a comic role that the workers began to sing him down when he tried to speak. But the chief reason for the city's beginning to swing toward the Socialists was a kind of civic nausea over the so-called Democratic regime of the putrid Dave Rose machine and over the feeble shadow-boxing of the Republican opposition.

Milwaukee's municipal affairs smelled far past the limits of the city. But whatever the cause, sentiment began to shift. The motormen and conductors on the street cars—the surest barometers, since they talked with everyone—began to say: "It looks like Seidel and the Socialist ticket." They were right. When the ballots were counted, it was a landslide. Milwaukee had its first Socialist mayor —Emil Seidel—with the Republican and the Democrat trailing far behind. All the elected city officials were Socialists. They controlled the common council and even the county board—*neither of which bodies have they ever, incidentally, controlled since.* For so frightened were the old-line parties that they scampered out to Madison and rushed through a bill creating a so-called nonpartisan election system in Milwaukee. What this meant, and still means, is that the Socialists run against the field. (The Socialist Party selects its candidates for office without struggle in the primary; the Nonpartisans —there are no Republicans or Democrats in Milwaukee politics— select their candidates in the primary. Thus the race usually is run between one Socialist and one Nonpartisan for each office. Divisions in the common council are between Socialists and Nonpartisans.)

All of the city officials had two-year terms except the city attorney. For some occult reason the law had recently been changed to make the city attorney's term four years. This accident probably gave Dan Hoan the chance to start his career in municipal government which is now known from coast to coast—and in many cities of Europe. The four-year term saved young Hoan in 1912 when the other Socialists had to run for re-election and were swept out of office by the Nonpartisan fusion forces, even though ten per cent more people voted for Socialist Seidel in 1912 than had voted for him in 1910.

But four years was enough for fighting Dan Hoan to make a start in Milwaukee.

II

In Hoan's own words, the city "was in the grasp of the sinister and slimy hand of special interests, dive-keepers, crooked contractors, petty racketeers, and political bosses. The city was then as graft-ridden as any other." [5] *Collier's Weekly Magazine* twenty years afterwards said: "The machine of David Rose, prior to 1910, was one of the crookedest political machines in the nation." Young Hoan had plenty to do. First he started a fight on the local electric utility, a fight that developed into a feud which has never ended. The new city attorney discovered that the franchise terms were not being observed by the street railway. It was not paving the street between its rails at its own cost. It was not sprinkling this area. It was not removing from the streets the snow it swept off its tracks. All these things the street railway was required to do by its franchise. Hoan decided to enforce the franchise terms. He went to court. He won. His action here has saved Milwaukee between five and six million dollars.

The young city attorney believed that street railway fares, telephone, gas and electric rates were all too high. He fought for reductions and won. Next he turned to the problem of grade crossings within the city where accidents frequently killed persons. This Hoan still considers to be his greatest legal victory. He believes that at least two members of the commission before which he fought the grade separation case were under heavy obligation to the railways. There were three different hearings. Finally the young city attorney won. The railways had to elevate their tracks and bear eighty per cent of the cost.

What this all meant was that young Hoan was making an impression on Milwaukee, not just on the Socialists, but on the vast

[5] Introductory note to Hoan's book, *City Government*, New York, 1935.

number of citizens who are always apathetic to party labels. In 1914, Hoan ran for re-election as city attorney. It was a bitter campaign full of unrestrained language. Gerhard A. Bading, later minister to Ecuador, was running for re-election as mayor, backed by fusion forces. "There are only two issues in this campaign," he said, and then outlined them as Americanism versus Socialism and a business administration versus a "repetition of the worst administration [Emil Seidel's, 1910–12] the city ever had." It was, Mayor Bading continued, an issue of the Constitution against a "propaganda organization despised in every civilized country in the world," an organization—the Socialists, of course—which had given Milwaukee "a black eye throughout the country."

Before election day, the press shrieked in eight-column editorials at the tops of the front pages that Milwaukee must be saved from the Socialists—"the most bitter, intolerant and fanatical kind of party rule."

Then came the counting of the votes. It was a clean sweep for the fusionists—except for city attorney; Daniel Webster Hoan had squeezed in by 354 votes, running far ahead of the Socialist ticket. So he was in for another four-year term, though the other city offices were still two-year terms. Hoan continued to fight the big interests. Some of them had had pretty much their own way for decades, and there is little doubt that many aldermen and other city officials had been corrupted with bribes from time to time. At one period the friends of the city officials used to greet them: "Hello, John, been indicted yet?"

Then came 1916 and the Socialists were again confronted with the choosing of a slate. They drafted Hoan to run for mayor, though he had two years left to serve as city attorney. It was war time, but one newspaper preserved enough balance to print both sides of the campaign. This was the last word in political tolerance in Milwaukee.

But the betting odds were for Bading. From 5 to 4 they shifted to 5 to 3 the day before election. Mayor Bading said that the Socialists were "liars, indecent, un-American red-flaggers, not fit for office, Anarchists and political pirates." Bading continued as follows:

"The fang of the viper is ready to suck Milwaukee's life blood.

Socialism, with all its heresies and un-American ideas, is knocking at the door. Will you . . . never again allow the Red Flag to replace the Stars and Stripes on the flagpole of the City Hall."

The fusionists coined slogans to save the city: "Join the nearest anti-Red club, young man," "Either Socialism or the American government must perish."

Dan Hoan went forth to battle. He accused his opponents of dirtying the American flag themselves by dragging it into a municipal campaign. Then he said:

"The main issue of this campaign is whether the flag of the street car company will float over the City Hall instead of the Stars and Stripes left there by Mayor Emil Seidel, former Socialist mayor. I refuse to believe it necessary to sell out the City Hall to the street car company and its black flag of monopolistic piracy in order to be American citizens."

Clever, this young fellow; perhaps not so un-American after all. The voters took notice. Hoan pounded away on simple municipal matters. He showed pieces of corroded water pipe ruined by electrolysis from current escaping from the utility. He still campaigns in the same "earthy" way, talking about garbage and ash collection, water supply and sewers. He never waves Marx and Engels in the voters' faces.

There was a light vote in the 1916 election. Hoan ran 5,000 ahead of the rest of the Socialist ticket and beat Bading by 1,500 votes in a total of 66,000 cast for both candidates. No other Socialist city official was elected and only a few aldermen. The "capitalist" reporters joshed Hoan. "Tell us," they said, "how it was that you rose from the kitchen to the chief office in the City Hall?"

"I was a good cook," replied their quarry, simply— "and I shall try to be a good mayor."

Thus began the reign of Dan Hoan as mayor of Milwaukee, a reign probably unprecedented in American cities. The gaunt lawyer walked into the office under the tower of Milwaukee's City Hall. He looked out of the windows, set in massive walls, to the square below. Eighteen years before he had stood there listening to campaign speeches that had crystallized his own political philosophy.

That political philosophy now brought difficult days for the Mayor in the period of war hysteria. Because of the Socialist party's staunch stand against the war, Hoan was branded as a traitor. "Patriots" shrieked for his removal. In the 1918 election a lively barrage was laid down against his loyalty. "We shall all know Wednesday," one newspaper editorialized the day before election, "whether Milwaukee is an American city."

By this newspaper's criteria it was not. The Mayor won. He polled more votes than any Socialist ever had and he increased his lead over his opponent. Needless to say, Milwaukee did its part in the war—and more—and the Mayor performed the tasks that fell upon him. But he never failed to voice his disbelief in the war, and feeling ran so high that when the soldiers returned after the Armistice the Mayor was booed at a municipal reception and a captain irately arose, "in the name of the cause for which the boys fought," to bid the Mayor stop trying to speak.

Still Hoan increased his vote in the 1920 elections and in the 1924 elections—all city officials' terms by that time having been made four years. In 1928 and 1932 the Mayor swept everything before him, in the latter election carrying even the prosperous "gold coast" wards and being blessed by the city's leading newspaper. Two other Socialist city officials were carried into office and enough Socialist aldermen so that, with the occasional aid of two Nonpartisan straddlers (to whom political largess was generously distributed) the Socialists sometimes had control of the common council. In 1936, despite a bitter old-fashioned campaign, the Mayor was re-elected because 112,061 persons preferred him to the able incumbent sheriff who, when asked whether it was true that he never got past the fourth grade in school, replied: "I am still going to school." He was the choice of 96,897 citizens.

But all other Socialist city officials or candidates were defeated in 1936, as well as many aldermen. Milwaukee fell back on its usual formula: Always elect Hoan, never support him.

III

What kind of man is this, who, when his present term expires in 1940, will have been mayor of America's twelfth city for nearly a quarter-century, seven times elected and twice victor in recall movements, head of one of the best-governed and most solvent

MILWAUKEE JOURNAL PHOTO

DANIEL WEBSTER HOAN

"Mayor Hoan believes . . . that municipal government,
'next to the family itself,' . . . is the very foundation
of the nation."

cities in the nation? Why does Milwaukee consistently elect Dan Hoan and as consistently repudiate his party, and some of his dearest projects?

Now you've started something, and there is no undisputed answer. But first let us look at the man.

If blood means anything, Hoan is a sort of League of Nations. His father was born of Irish parentage in St. Sylvester near Quebec and the name was Horan. Young Daniel Webster Horan—strange that an American statesman should have appealed so strongly to Irish parents in French Canada—was soon orphaned. An uncle took him to Boston and, thinking to Americanize the name, dropped the "r". This man married Margaret A. Hood, a Waukesha County (Wisconsin) farm girl of English and German parentage whose ancestors had been in America since 1732. To them was born Daniel Webster Hoan who became mayor. (The Mayor's son bears the same name for the third generation.) There was no political tradition in the Hoan or Horan family, although one distant antecedent had been a member of the Canadian parliament.

Mayor Hoan's family life has been as placid as his father's was tumultuous. The year after Hoan came to Milwaukee he married Agnes Magner, whom he had met in Chicago. Despite the fact that Mrs. Hoan is a devout Catholic and the mayor has no church affiliation, harmony has reigned in the Hoan home. Mrs. Hoan is a simple woman, untouched by the political Furies that blow about her husband, except that she is incensed sometimes when "Dad"—she always calls him that—is bitterly denounced. He calls her "Mother."

The Hoans live modestly and always have; they've been twenty-one years in the same frame house in Milwaukee's socially unstylish west side. They distinctly are never in what is called "society," but you may find them, particularly the mayor, at many a meeting or festival of middle-class or working folk. The Hoans have two children, Daniel Webster (the third) and Agnes, both college students. The Mayor, radical in politics, is conservative in most personal matters. He is, for instance, driving the sixth automobile of the same make (Studebaker). He has a commonplace summer home in northern Wisconsin where he spends five to eight

weeks—always subject to call from his office. He has no extrava-
gances, unless it be the overuse of tobacco. Despite his gauntness,
he is a doughty drinker when the steins are passed around; yet no
one has ever accused him of excess.

He is a personable fellow. Face to face you can't help liking him.
He has a remarkable ability to talk specifically to his hearer with a
warmth and friendliness that can be intoxicating. Usually the vivid-
ness of what he says makes one forgetful of the odd grammar and
the crude phrases—whether consciously cultivated or accidental—
that carry a thought directly to any listener, be he a scholar or an
untutored workman. Sometimes the Mayor talks bunk (the Communists used to call him Mayor Hokum) or he carefully skirts an
issue, but you tend to forget that he is doing so. More often he
plunges directly into his subject.

He dramatizes everything. He can't talk more than a few minutes without getting up and stalking back and forth while he
impersonates a crowd, a lobbyist, a street car, or whatever is necessary to his story. He does the same thing in public. Your neck tires
following him. His arms wave—he has Ichabod Craneish angles,
if you catch him just right—and his argument or description comes
rasping forth. Outside of the heavy doors to his office, at such
times, a secretary smiles indulgently and says: "You can hear hiz-
zoner's horn going today." He is notoriously inaccurate in details concerning names and figures; his enemies say he is "half-
cocked"; his friends say he simply can't be bothered and that his
point of view is always sound.

The office of the Mayor of Milwaukee has something about it
of the stability of the town; there's nothing flashy to it. A huge
table sprawls in the middle of the room, an ancient roll-top desk
fills a corner. In a long-outmoded office chair sits the Mayor. His
clothes are nondescript; the truth is he is unconscious of them.
Sometimes his suit is shiny. He wears a colored shirt with stripes,
without distinction. His wrinkled necktie is of uncertain color. A
mop of his unruly black hair, now graying, dangles above one eye.
The lines about his mouth are deep, but pleasant; the face is spar-
klingly animated. Always there lies near by a half-consumed cigar
or smouldering pipe—or both. The odds are heavy that you find
the Mayor in his shirt sleeves with unlovely but utilitarian sus-

penders showing in the armholes of his vest. His feet go up on the table when comfort demands, but never as a pose. Naturalness describes the Mayor.

On the wall hang pictures—Abraham Lincoln, Victor Berger, Emil Seidel, a drawing of Mrs. Hoan, an oil painting of the Mayor, and a mounted fish. A model of the ocean liner, "Milwaukee," tops the desk. In another painting a Hungarian peasant stares forlornly at a pittance in his hand—one week's pay for three years' corn.

When the mayor makes a fine point, he doodles with his inkwell, or paper weight, moving it precisely a quarter-inch this way and five-eighths that. He spices his conversation with occasional profanity—neither gifted nor picturesque—just ordinary proletarian profanity. In reminiscing of college days, he corrects himself—"No, I didn't swear like that, then."

There are no back stairs to Dan Hoan's office. This always slightly shocks visiting reporters—especially from the big cities. If there were, it is Dan's boast that the special entrance would be for working people. Perhaps this is histrionic, but the fact is that anyone may see the mayor for any good reason and sometimes the reason doesn't have to be good. One does not find hangers-on roosting in the outer office. The general impression is one of sleepiness. One is met without affectation by the secretaries or the patrolman-clerk; there is neither pomp nor obsequiousness.

One of the first things that Hoan did when he became mayor was to open the door to his office to break what he calls the Sicilian blackhand gangs in Milwaukee's large Italian population. He found that the strength of the gang leaders was largely due to their political tie-up. They could deliver large blocks of votes; so they were given free rein by police and politicians. Hoan went directly to the Italian-American citizens. He told them they could get no favors through any gang leader, that they could always come directly to the City Hall with their problems and their pleas. Perhaps this is not the whole story, but the gangs disappeared.

Hoan isn't as much of a joiner as you might expect in a politician. For decades he was active in a Milwaukee social settlement; for fifteen years he was a member of the Knights of Pythias, for ten years of the Eagles and Elks clubs, but he is not active in them. So much for the Mayor in private.

In public the Mayor is no mean adversary. Most observers are sure that he carefully picks his spot before he blasts, that he knows where the rocks will fall, and that he will pry loose more votes than he will destroy.

One time in prohibition when the W.C.T.U. demanded that Mayor Hoan shut saloons "openly violating the law" he replied: "More temperance can be accomplished by the open sale of beer and light wines." So the reformers dubbed the Mayor a traitor to his nation's laws, a wrecker of youth, and a destroyer of homes, as one friend put it.

When, in 1932, Hoan refused to attend the Los Angeles meeting of the American Association of Port Authorities, he said: "I won't enter California as long as Tom Mooney is held in jail."

In Chicago, irked by reporters he said: "So you're from the press? Well, your newspapers can all go to hell. You lied yesterday and you're getting ready to lie again today. Go climb down my back." He was irritated at reports that he was going to bolt the Socialist party.

Hoan's first verbal explosion to ring round the nation—if not the world—was his now famous remark when it was suggested in 1919 that he invite King Albert of the Belgians to Milwaukee. "I stand by the man who works," he retorted, "to hell with kings!"

The press of the nation panted with rage.

"How long," asked the Baltimore *Sun*, "will even Milwaukee stand for such blatant and long-eared demagogues?" The *Sun* called him a "boor" and continued to describe Milwaukee as "that sweet-scented city of Socialism and disloyalty . . . famous not only for beer and Berger . . ." and then suggested that, since Hoan was a good cook, Milwaukee "send him back to his pots and pans."

The stately *Public Ledger* in Philadelphia commented: "He talks in this profane and loud-mouthed fashion not because of any passionate sincerity of his convictions, but because he thinks it will make a hit with the crowd and be widely quoted to his glory." The *Record* in Philadelphia called Hoan one of the "American Bolsheviki" and hinted that Albert was more of a worker than the Mayor who made Milwaukee infamous. The Wichita (Kansas) *Beacon* frothed, but could not bring itself to print the nasty word in "to —— with kings."

The historian is amused to discover that, thirteen years later, the *Sun* and the *Public Ledger*—and a good many other American newspapers—were pleased to ask "the long-eared and boorish demagogue" to tell them why Milwaukee was America's best-governed city, particularly why it was solvent. (The Mayor, incidentally, does not claim that Milwaukee is better governed than, say, Cincinnati.)

Hoan's bluntness is illustrated by his refusal after the war to send a telegram of congratulation to General Pershing and by his subsequent refusal to sign a resolution of the common council conveying condolences to Mrs. Woodrow Wilson on the death of her husband. The resolution contained the words "great American."

"I do not," Hoan told the council, "and never did think Wilson was a great American and I will not be a hypocrite by signing and subscribing to such a resolution."

Similar outspokenness is found in his reply to the National Army and Navy Preparedness Committee, which had asked him to appoint three local members to it. "I know of nothing," he said, "that will be more likely to lead this country into the war than organization of the group in which you are engaged." He refused a request to set aside a Navy Day in Milwaukee, calling it "propaganda to increase the size of the navy."

Even in the most hysterical red-baiting days just after the war, when many otherwise sane persons saw Bolsheviks under every bed, the Mayor did not curb his tongue. In November, 1919, a group of ex-service men took upon themselves to raid an I.W.W. office using the same strong-arm methods since popularized by Hitler's and Mussolini's henchmen. They smashed furnishings, burned books and papers. The Mayor characterized this as "anarchy and a blotch on our record as a law-abiding community." He demanded that the police arrest the raiders and prosecute the case. In 1919 this was intestinal fortitude, perhaps something more, when you consider the atmosphere. He said that failure to agree with the I.W.W. did not mean that its members were deprived of their constitutional rights. He added that if their literature were illegal the United States Department of Justice (perhaps he had his tongue in his cheek) would undoubtedly seize it.

Time and again the Mayor has clashed with the American Legion. The most dramatic encounter was over the police horses. The Mayor had consistently vetoed appropriations for feed for Milwaukee's six police horses, partly on grounds of economy, largely because it was politically expedient to do so. Radical orators had an embarrassing way of referring to the mounted policemen as "Cossacks used only to crack workers over the head." The Legion headed the horses' advocates, took collections to feed them, but finally the horse war culminated in a referendum. In November, 1936, Milwaukee (along with choosing a president of the United States) voted 120,914 to 92,147 for the horses. It was the first time, wisecracked many Milwaukeeans, that they had been given the opportunity to vote for complete horses.

For Mayor Hoan's chronic adversary, the local electric utility—controlled by one of the nation's major holding companies—choice words are always found. During thirty years now, Dan Hoan has sparred with this corporation. He likes to remind people, particularly when they talk about "taxes" and governmental extravagance, that "the salary paid to the president of the Milwaukee street railway (in 1931) was $96,000—more than the total of the salaries paid the Mayor and the thirty-two department heads of the city of Milwaukee." The mayor draws $12,000 a year, but he started at a paltry $4,000, plus expenses, and had to "work up" to his present stipend. A sample of the truly touching relationship between Hoan and the utility is found in the Mayor's reply to a letter from the president of the company to the city during the street car strike in June, 1934. The president had "notified" the city that he would hold it liable for any damage that might occur to the company's equipment or employees because of mob action or riot.

The Mayor then let fly. His friends think he was courageous; his opponents say he was playing to the rabble whom he knew to be overwhelmingly against the utility. Anyway, he said: "I now notify you and through you the most powerful trust the world has ever known, which you represent, that you alone are solely responsible for the riots that have so far blotched the good name of this city. . . . Your attitude toward your employees, our people, our city, our federal government, is more arrogant than that of any ruler in the world. Not since the days of King George III of England has any such ruler successfully defied our nation. But you as impudently refuse to comply with the reasonable request of the representatives of the United States government until Uncle Sam himself has been compelled to rebuke the insolence by removing your Blue Eagle."

In the summer of 1937 six insurance companies which paid amounts to the electric company for damage in the 1934 riots sued the city, charging that the city had not adequately protected the company's property. The Mayor pointed out that the utility had tried to import a gang of Pearl Bergoff's notorious strikebreakers (which had been summarily arrested and run out of town by the police) and then, from the witness stand, he said that the public "considered the electric company an absolute lawbreaker which shouldn't be dealt with any better than bootleggers." The strikebreakers had been imported after the riot in question and these references were ruled out. A jury found quickly for the city, but the insurance companies appealed and won a reversal.

On the whole, the Mayor stays out of strike controversies, unless drawn in—as in the street car strike. He did, however, speak at a rally—early in the Hoover depression—of automobile body workers. He did say, some years ago, after bombs were thrown in a clothing factory dispute that investigations showed provocateurs to have been responsible, that the police could handle the situation but would not co-operate with "unprincipled undercover men." He did reply tartly when one strike-ridden firm threatened to leave Milwaukee: "I am not so sure that other communities will be so happy to receive you when they learn that their taxpayers must help to keep your working men alive." He referred to "pitiably low" wages. Out of this controversy grew the Boncel ordinance allowing the mayor or chief of police under certain conditions, advised by a mixed board, to close a factory to prevent strike rioting when its management refused to bargain collectively. The ordinance caused a furious political storm and was quickly repealed by the next (hostile) common council.

What *is* Mayor Hoan's political philosophy? Is he really a

Socialist? These are the first questions the visitor always asks about Milwaukee's mayor.

One writer called him one-tenth Socialist and nine-tenths lawyer and business man—and a good one. Socialists, some nationally known, from other cities have asked the writer, confidentially, whether Mayor Hoan has ever read Karl Marx's writings or any other Socialist works. One of them said that he frequently made up his mind that Hoan knew nothing of Socialism and then, suddenly, the Mayor would bring up—as though from his past—some Socialist remark or argument and dust it off. The late Morris Hillquit scoffingly called Hoan's politics "sewer socialism." The Mayor is probably proud of this accusation. He is far more interested in the sewers of Milwaukee and such practical municipal problems than in theoretical socialism. He is almost untouched by the international quality of socialism and frequently has opposed foreign undertakings within the Socialist party. One cannot imagine Dan Hoan raising the clenched fist and passionately shouting: "Workers of the world unite! You have nothing to lose but your chains! You have a world to gain!" Yet Hoan quotes in capital letters what he calls this "immortal message of Karl Marx" in the climax of a pamphlet which he (Hoan) wrote entitled: "Abraham Lincoln, A Real American," and the Mayor has written in his own book, *City Government*—concerning the economic theories of Socialism— "During the 26 years I have spent in the public service I have been guided wholly by these economic formulas as a foundation in effectuating policies and in promoting governmental measures." The Mayor is not so terse when he writes political science as when he campaigns to a Polish or Italian audience. He also states that he believes ultimately in the "co-operative commonwealth."

The truth of the matter is that the question of Daniel Webster Hoan's Socialism is as baffling to his party as it is to his non-party public. Those close to him will tell you that he thinks it absurd for Americans to rant in the European Socialist lingo about "Cossacks and tyrants." As one of them put it, "Of course, the workers' condition is far from perfect; but we do have civil rights and a basically democratic system of government in America."

Hoan is a remarkably shrewd politician, but he is guided by a strong idealism. He is an intensely practical man and has little use for abstract principles—whether of Socialism or anything else. Yet he lost many friends, and alienated the largest paper in Wisconsin which was momentarily friendly, by refusing to help unearth what turned out to be the worst scandal in years in the City Hall. The city treasurer, a Nonpartisan, was later indicted (he died before trial) on a charge of embezzling a half-million dollars in peculiar city fund dealings with a banker who was subsequently sent to the penitentiary. The Mayor and the Socialist party—though in no way implicated in this scandal—were conspicuously lacking in zeal to unearth it. The reason was that the crooked banker held notes of many leading Socialist politicians and also notes of the Socialist newspaper which was in financial difficulties. The Mayor's ardent supporters argue that his hands were politically tied in the alleged embezzlement matter; his enemies say he lacked moral strength.

Milwaukee is not the only place where Hoan is honored. Friends remind one that he has served three terms as president of the Wisconsin League of Municipalities, two terms (then honorary) as president of the United States Conference of Mayors, three terms as president of the Great Lakes Harbors Association, vice-president of the Alliance of Cities (an organization interested in getting natural gas for cities in several midwestern states), vice-president of the National Municipal League. These groups evidently do not consider Hoan a subversive force.

Within the Socialist party, Hoan was a member of the National Executive Committee from 1928 to 1937 when he refused re-election; was chairman of the party's committee for the adoption of the workers' rights amendment; president of the League Against Fascism [6] (a short-lived satellite Socialist organization); and chairman of the national Socialist presidential campaign committees in 1932 and 1936. The Mayor has consistently maintained that a man cannot remain in public life without a party behind him. He cites many a reform organization which has taken office in American cities only to be swept out in the next election. He acknowledges freely that the great non-party masses of Milwaukee elect him, but insists that the Socialist party is the nucleus, the organization that distributes the campaign literature, makes the door-to-door calls, collects money (to the annoyance of the press) from many city

[6] Not to be confused with the Communists' League Against War and Fascism.

employees. Nobody is forced to give, the foes of Hoan admit, but they claim that persons who don't give don't get along so well.

With all his acumen, Dan Hoan is known even among many of his friends as a sucker for cure-alls. He doesn't like the doctors, on the whole, usually refers to them as the "medical fraternity," and has given testimonials to healers and sellers of healing devices, some of whom have unfortunate police records in other cities.

For instance, Hoan wrote to Mayor Cermak of Chicago a testimonial in behalf of "Prof." John Hugh Lally, dealer in health-giving "love rays" who had been arrested in Miami, Winnipeg, and other places for practicing medicine without a license. When the Chicago police broke up a meeting of this protégé of Hoan, the "professor" was intoning to a group of customers—"Let the waves of love flow through you. They are coming from above, coursing through your brain, down past the duodenum and out through your feet into the earth. They are washing away the congestion in your brains, curing all of your ills, healing your cuts and driving away your pains. The waves of life will send you forth as different men and women; you who are poor will become rich; you who have frozen real estate will be able to sell [this was February, 1932]; you who are unemployed will find jobs!" Unbelievable! But the Mayor stood by his testimonial, claimed that the "professor" had helped his son's hearing.

The Mayor has long used a colored-light healing system which is blacklisted by the American Medical Association and by the Better Business Bureaus all over the United States. And for making a speech before the American Naturopathic Association, he was made a "doctor of natural philosophy" by President Benedict Lust and, according to his diploma, the Mayor is now entitled to practice the thirty-six sciences of naturopathy.

Some of the Mayor's enemies believe that this is the true Dan Hoan—a man who falls for cure-alls—in the field of politics as well as healing. Few, indeed, impugn the Mayor's personal honesty, though charges are sometimes whispered that appointees occasionally indulge in petty graft—or something that looks strangely like it. There is always grave doubt, however, whether the Mayor knows about these incidents.

Mayor Hoan believes in his job. He believes that to be mayor of a big city is infinitely harder than any governorship and is a public position exceeded in difficulty only by the presidency of the United States. He believes that municipal government "next to the family itself" (no red bugaboo of nationalized women here) is the very foundation of the nation. And he affects no modesty when he says that he believes he has done a good job. In fact, he has written a book on the subject, and he is more proud of this literary accomplishment than of any other single thing he has ever done.

Yet what a paradox is "Socialist" Milwaukee. Its virtues are the bourgeois virtues so anathematized by Marx and Engels. Its triumphs are in excellently managed capitalistic municipal finances (maturing bonds redeemed early, a rapidly growing amortization fund to make the city debt free by 1943,[7] skillfully devised negotiable tax redemption certificates to use as a sort of city currency), low fire and burglary insurance rates, and cheap ash and garbage collection. The latter, however, have recently gone from bad to worse. Milwaukee's story of clean municipal government is too long to tell here. Hoan claims it is because of the Socialists, and the non-Socialists insist it is because they usually control the common council and watch the Socialists. At any rate, there is no Socialism in Milwaukee, not even municipal ownership of the gas or electric utilities or the street railway—though the Mayor has pleaded with the populace through the decades. Whatever the red-baiters may have said for the last thirty years about Milwaukee under Socialism, the city stands today as a fine example of "good old American democracy."

And the man who is almost a part of its City Hall does not quote so much in a decade from German Karl Marx as he does in a year from an American politician, to whom he secretly loves to be compared—and whom he ever so slightly resembles, at least in physique and homely wit—Abraham Lincoln.

[7] Unless currently discussed borrowings for PWA projects upset the plan.

14

S. DAVIS WILSON,
MAYOR OF PHILADELPHIA

By T. Henry Walnut

SAMUEL DAVIS WILSON—HIS HONOR THE MAYOR—CAME TO Philadelphia from Boston, following the example set by a distinguished predecessor, one Benjamin Franklin, nearly two hundred years before. He brought with him a New England accent, the traces of which may still be detected, a Puritanical conscience for the sins of others, and a letter of introduction from the Watch and Ward Society of Boston which led him to the circle which revolved about D. Clarence Gibboney, secretary of the Law and Order Society.

Mr. Wilson was then about twenty-four years of age, of medium height, somewhat stout and short of neck. His hair was a light brown, his eyes a pale blue. Neither his personality nor his appearance was conspicuous.

He had, however, a quality not apparent from mere observation which marked him as different, perversely different, in fact, from any accepted Philadelphia model of a politician or a public officeholder. This quality was his own brand of imagination. With it he pictured himself as the public champion attacking and slaying evil dragons of corruption and special privilege. He had a great ambition for public office, and the route he was to follow was that of the knight errant performing his exploits singlehanded in the sight of the world, achieving acclaim and a high place at the Round Table. His mind was well stocked with information, much of it true, about a variety of evil creatures which existed in the town and which were fit subjects to go to work upon.

An imagination such as his, accompanied with a restless energy, made him an uneasy companion and set him apart during the many years that he played a minor role in the affairs of the town.

Very few understood the urge that was in him. Many thought that the creatures he wanted to attack were not really poisonous reptiles at all, and very few credited him with the talents needed for the fulfillment of his purpose. He had no particular oratorical ability —it was years before he became known as a public speaker—no peculiar capacity for writing, and he did not look like Sir Launcelot.

However, he clung fiercely to his image of himself, and some of the small parts that he played were developed in his telling into major ones. He could dilate upon his importance to the reform movement and could tell how the election of Woodrow Wilson was made possible through his efforts, how he prosecuted and convicted the tile dealers for violation of the Sherman Anti-Trust Law and how he prosecuted and convicted draft evaders and other offenders against the government during and after the war. In all these stories he was the center of the plot. All other actors faded into insignificance or disappeared, including chairmen of party committees, attorneys general and district attorneys. It was not only the story he was telling that seemed to concern him. He was insistent that his listeners understand that he, Wilson, was no ordinary man, that he struck mighty blows and was destined to strike more.

Another characteristic that can't be overlooked, that certainly is not overlooked by his enemies, is his erratic handling of his private finances. The story of his borrowings provides ammunition for his opponents in any campaign. These borrowings persisted even after his election as mayor, in which position his stated salary is $18,000 a year.

Finally, in this prologue it might be added, as anyone who has rubbed against him will testify, that he has a quick and adroit mind, a faith in himself that is almost sublime, and reactions to circumstances that are bafflingly unexpected and follow no code.

He is a combination so complex and uncertain as to make judgment upon him difficult. It is true that judgment is usually rendered by those who dislike him, and these are legion, in short swift sentences, with words that may refer slurringly to his mother, but fall short of explaining how he happens to be mayor. This latter phenomenon still has many of the men who voted for him puzzled. They have difficulty crediting it. Certainly for the first twenty-five years after his arrival in the town no one, with the possible exception of himself, suspected that he carried a mayor's baton in his knapsack.

The year of Mr. Wilson's arrival, 1905, was the year of the great political explosion over the renewal of the gas lease. The city had settled habits. It has had a gas works for a hundred years and for a hundred years it has been fighting over it, at first because the plant was run badly by the officials at City Hall and later, for the past half century, because of accusations that the private company which leases it is taking advantage of the city. The city also has had street cars, over the operation of which there has been continual dispute for the best part of a century. In 1905 the system was known as the Philadelphia Rapid Transit Company. These two matters, together with the perennial issue created by the "gang" at City Hall and its iniquities, were lively ones in 1905, and are equally lively today. Mr. Wilson was to have much to do with all of them.

The renewal of the gas lease in 1905 developed a smouldering reform movement, antedating Lincoln Steffens' story of "Philadelphia, Corrupt and Contented," into a conflagration which burned more or less fiercely until 1911 when Blankenburg was elected as a reform mayor. Thereafter it burned out. A militant and spectacular figure in this reform movement was D. Clarence Gibboney, whose work in the Law and Order Society was so dramatized by the newspapers that he became the perennial reform candidate and the perennially defeated one. At his office on Walnut Street there collected not only the staff of the Society, but a band of political soldiers of fortune.

In another quarter of the town committees of substantial business men met and passed resolutions against the corrupt and wasteful methods of the "gang" and contributed money to carry on the political campaigns and the investigation of various phases of the city government. Mr. Wilson became connected with one of the business committees as secretary and was a frequenter of and worked about the Gibboney headquarters.

The Republican organization at that time was as complete an institution of its sort as could be found anywhere in the country. Senator Boies Penrose had just taken over the state leadership. He was the guardian of the interests of the state and bestrode it like a colossus immersed in the smoke that hung over the mills of Pittsburgh and the factories of Philadelphia. His party organization in the latter city was made up of elected committeemen of each election division or precinct who constituted the ward committees, each of which elected a city committeeman. These men were the ward leaders, a tough, hard-bitten crew of warriors who knew their wards as a feudal lord might know his fief. With their retainers behind them they could deliver with uncanny accuracy a given number of votes to the ticket. McNichol was the chief city leader and lieutenant of Penrose. The Vares were then putting together a hegemony of wards in South Philadelphia, preparing to challenge the leadership of Penrose and McNichol.

The town itself, for whose political interest this elaborate machinery had been prepared, was prosperous and growing. It lay upon the great cross made by the intersection of Broad Street running north and south and Market Street running west from the Delaware River. City Hall spiked down the arms of the cross. It was a massive, gloomy building, the atmosphere of which was so permeated with "influence" that the place was made unreal to one who did not belong. It was the stronghold of the organization. To the citizens who during that reform period voted against the gang and were defeated, it seemed impregnable. When in 1911 it was known in the early morning hours following election day that Blankenburg had been elected, columns of shouting citizens marched upon the place, poured through the entrances shaking their fists at some of the still-lighted windows. The citadel had fallen. Mr. Wilson, though he participated in the campaign, did not then get a place in the Hall. That achievement was still fifteen years in the future.

Information as to the early history of the Mayor is entirely autobiographical. He speaks of his New England ancestors with reference to John and Priscilla Alden and of other ancient forebears whose habitat was Maine. His mother, for whom he shows great respect, was a graduate of Bates College. He was born August 31, 1881. His father died when he was five years of age and his mother when he was seventeen. He attributes to his mother not only his desire to succeed, but his choice of the means. He attended the Allen School at Newtown, Massachusetts, and Phillips Exeter

Academy. He says he was only a tolerably good student and took little interest in mathematics. This last is an interesting comment in view of the way he has bewildered the town by his mathematical calculations relative to its budget.

He spent a period in the law office of John D. Long, who was afterwards secretary of the Navy under Theodore Roosevelt, and he was also at this time secretary of the Boston Public School Association, a position which provided him with a chance for one of his public exploits, his first. The Association's candidates for school director had been defeated on the first returns. A recount was demanded. He as the secretary watched the recount with untiring vigilance. As a result the Association's candidates won.

Up to this point his story makes of him such a respectable and normal figure that most persons to whom it is told in Philadelphia scoff at it as untrue. They assert that a start like that could not turn out a Sam Wilson. Afterward he became what might be called a detective. Then came a two-year service with the United States Signal Corps, following which he went to Washington as secretary to Edward Everett Hale, the chaplain of the United States Senate. Immediately preceding his coming to Philadelphia, he was associated with the Independent Reform Bureau.

These several positions carried some indication of his qualifications and the course that he was ultimately to follow. In Philadelphia, after his service with the reformers and Gibboney, he became in 1912 secretary of the Republican Woodrow Wilson League, and was impressed peculiarly by his contact with Senator Penrose, with whom, according to Mr. Wilson, he dealt in order to assure the election of Woodrow Wilson and the defeat of Theodore Roosevelt. For many years this story appeared as a great exploit in Mr. Wilson's career. It did not, however, lead him to any prominent place in public office. Just what he did following 1912 is not clear, but in 1916 he went into the insurance business. This venture lasted less than a year. Then he formed a partnership and entered the business of selling tiles. This, too, was short-lived. He complains that there was an organization of tile dealers who saw to it that no one but themselves could get tiles. There at once arose in him the urge to correct this evil, and a prosecution of the Tile Dealers Association for conspiracy in restraint of trade resulted. Mr. Mitchell, assistant United States attorney general, afterwards to be Mr. Hoover's attorney general, handled the case for the government. There was a conviction and Mr. Wilson added this to his list of exploits, and later the firm of Gallagher and Wilson, tile dealers, brought civil suit for $100,000 damages, subsequently settling for $4,000. In the spring of 1918 after the conviction of the tile dealers, Mr. Wilson entered the United States Department of Justice as an agent of the Bureau of Investigation—this cumbersome title has since been abbreviated to "G-Man," and a number of new exploits were added to his catalogue.

In 1919 he was out of the Bureau and had moved to South Jersey, where he functioned as a justice of the peace for some years and likewise went into the business of making automobile bodies. The business came to a sudden termination and Mr. Wilson returned to Philadelphia with equal suddenness. Later, men who wanted to attack him, went to South Jersey and came back with statements about unpaid bills. These, however, were paid up ultimately.

For a year or so after his return to Philadelphia he did a series of odd jobs, of which the only one that received public notice was his engagement to secure information relative to violations of the Sunday law on the grounds of the Sesqui-Centennial Exposition. His pay for that work was $5.00 a day. This was in the summer of the year 1926.

Certainly at that time no one thought of him as an important figure either in the public or the business life of the town and he did not look like a mayor, but throughout he carried the conviction that he was not an ordinary man and that he needed but a chance to show it. He got that chance the beginning of the year 1927 when Will B. Hadley, city controller, took him into his office as a special assistant, afterwards as deputy.

The controller was an elective official who audited the books and accounts of the city and county departments. Theoretically, having been elected by the people he was independent of the other departments, but in practice the office had never disclosed any such quality. Whatever differences arose were settled under cover. Mr. Hadley himself was a quiet, retiring man who shrank from violent altercations. He was respected for his integrity and capacity as an accountant. He had been the deputy under a previous controller, and upon the death of that controller had been appointed by the governor to the office and subsequently had been placed among the slated Republican candidates for re-election in 1921 and 1925. To secure the appointment and to be slated for election required no little influence. Some powerful factor in the organization must have backed him. It was whispered about that Charley Hall had done it. He was leader of the Seventh Ward, a member, and afterwards president of City Council.

When the year 1927 opened W. Freeland Kendrick was mayor of the city of Philadelphia. It was the last year of his administration, which had had more money to spend and had spent it more freely than any other in the city's history. It was the period of the "new era." The Republican party controlled the city, the state, and the nation. Secretary of Commerce Hoover forecast the cheerful news as the year opened that there would be jobs for all and the business outlook was free from fear of commercial or financial cataclysm.

William S. Vare, the last of the three Vare brothers, was city leader and also United States senator-elect. The twenty-one members of Philadelphia's City Council maintained an accord with each other and with the Mayor. Many of them were ward leaders. They were all in close accord with the Republican City Committee. All city officials and party leaders swore fealty to their chief, Senator Vare, and loudly proclaimed themselves a band of brothers. The old reform party was dead, and it seemed as if the power and glory of the Republican organization was permanently fixed.

There were some difficulties on the horizon. The Philadelphia Rapid Transit Company had an agreement with the city dating back to 1907 whereby the city received certain payments and had a right to audit the traction company's books. This audit had been merely formal, but there was pressure for an independent audit. The Transit Company was dominated by Thomas E. Mitten, who had managed it well, but in the twenties had developed auxiliary plans. He created Mitten Men and Management, which took over the operation of the system for a fee represented by a percentage of gross receipts. He added a Mitten bank, Mitten Bank & Securities, and in 1926 an air service from Philadelphia to Washington. His was a great name in town. Small investors purchased Mitten securities and he wielded potent influence at City Hall. He did not favor an independent audit, but Council to satisfy the public appropriated a fund to the controller for the purpose of making one.

Another troublesome matter had arisen out of the Sesqui-Centennial Exposition held in 1926, which had not been successful and which had closed leaving behind it a buzzing swarm of unsatisfied creditors and $5,000,000 in claims against the city, payment of which had to be approved by the controller. But there was no fear of the controller or his office.

At the opening of the year, however, that official began to display a perverse quality. On January 3 there was a newspaper headline: "Hadley Fires Four Aids, Proteges of Mackey and Hall." In addition, there emanated from his office a threat to dynamite the Republican organization by an exposure of the Sesqui-Centennial claims. Mr. Hall was then president of City Council. Mr. Mackey was city treasurer, leader of the Forty-sixth Ward and a candidate for mayor to succeed Mr. Kendrick. He had been chairman of Vare's campaign committee in the senatorial fight of 1926. Both of them were potent leaders. The newspapers remarked that Mr. Mackey's law partner represented some four hundred of the Sesqui claimants in their efforts to secure approval of vouchers by the Controller in order that they might be paid by the Treasurer.

A few days later came the proposal to subpoena the Mayor to appear before the Controller with the Sesqui accounts. This proposal was both astonishing and impertinent. The Mayor was the tallest figure about City Hall. The picture of him descending from his ample second floor offices to the stuffy little office of the Controller on the first floor, south side, to be examined about a lot of petty book accounts was ridiculous. It didn't happen, but it drew attention to the Controller's office and created a buzz of excitement as to the unsuspected potentialities of that official. Within six months City Hall was full of gossip about this strange fellow, S. Davis Wilson, who had squeezed himself like a stout Caliban into the Controller's quarters and was busying himself at becoming a nuisance. One reporter commented, "City Hall, where the workers of the Republican organization hold jobs and draw their pay, is the housing place at present of an impenetrable mystery."

The story was headlined: "Meet Mr. Wilson, Man of Mystery at City Hall. Fashions Brick Bats for Controller."

Mr. Hall when interviewed brushed the whole matter aside stating that Mr. Wilson had no standing whatever. His place in the Controller's office had never been authorized by City Council and anyway he was "an unknown in politics."

This latter comment was the unkindest cut of all. The band of brothers regarded itself and its charmed circle highly. It was snobbish, and to be politically unknown was to be a nobody. Mr. Wilson cried out hotly: "I am not a mystery and I am not unknown!" He developed this answer through a letter by Mr. Hadley outlining his past achievements and his wide acquaintanceship with men and affairs. In any event, people marveled at Mr. Wilson's sudden "ascendancy to power at the right hand of the Controller and a place at conferences with the highest officials of the city." He was a rank outsider trying to jimmy his way into the charmed circle, and confidence was expressed that he would not be admitted and that shortly he would be "stepped on," and that would be the end of him.

Presently the wise fellows who lurk in the shadows of City Hall and who know so much about what "they"—the big fellows—are thinking and doing, were asserting with confidence that an investigation had been made of Mr. Wilson's past record and enough information secured to drive him out of town. There was great expectancy as to when the damning information would be revealed. It finally appeared in the form of whispers to the effect that his name was not Wilson but Waite, that he was a murderer and didn't pay his bills.

The first two charges arose out of that period in Mr. Wilson's life prior to his arrival at Philadelphia when he was a detective, or more accurately speaking a special under-cover investigator, for the state's attorney of Windsor County, Vermont, carried on the payroll as Samuel D. Waite. After the conviction of some law violator he became decidedly unpopular among the friends of the convict and according to the story was set upon by a gang who wanted his blood. A shooting occurred. A man was killed and Mr. Wilson was indicted for the killing, tried and acquitted. In the campaign for governor following the occurrence one of the candidates charged his opponent with importing murderers. A suit for slander was started in the federal court which after some vicissitudes resulted in a verdict for Mr. Wilson. This suit with a recital of the facts appears imbedded in the *Federal Reporter* under the title of "Wilson v. Clements."

The whispering about of this story apparently gave Mr. Wilson no concern whatever; rather it was an opportunity to recount with telling effect the fierce battle at the White River Junction House, and to shout, "Was the man who killed Dillinger a murderer?"

When Mr. Mackey became mayor in 1928 there were more matters for the Controller's office to cry out about. Mr. Mackey retired from his law firm, but his partner headed a bonding company and represented a nest of corporations dealing in supplies needed by the city and city contractors. Letters were sent out on the letterheads of the law firm with a thin black line through the Mayor's name soliciting business for the bonding company. Mr. Wilson reported that it was doing eight times the business of its nearest competitor.

A contract for fire hose and one for a certain make of steel were stopped. The articles covered were listed as patented and, therefore, outside the requirements for competitive bidding. Mr. Wilson reported that the patent on the first had expired and there never was one on the second and the materials provided were of dubious quality. He called certain persons liars, and the Mayor, who stepped into the controversy, was promptly labeled with the same title. Mr. Wilson announced that there were seven ways of evading competitive bidding and that the Controller was going to conduct "a probe of the contract system." Whereupon the Mayor promptly appointed a committee to investigate, made up of leading officials of the railroad companies, the utilities, and large industrial plants. Their names constituted a roster of business leaders. Mr. Wilson at once pointed out the contractual relations between the city and the companies represented by each of the individuals named, with the innuendo that they were chosen to apply whitewash. This was an impious thing to do, for in 1928 those individuals were the town's pedestaled figures, but it was like Mr. Wilson to do it. Certainly the committee's report, which appeared five months later, did not satisfy a public waiting for precise information as to particular instances of improper conduct.

These contract matters were only incidents in the Controller's activities. Demand was made for an inventory of city property, a city director was called to account for putting his private stenographer on the city payroll, an announcement was made that a judge had not paid his taxes for thirteen years. An audit of the Philadelphia Gas Company's books was started and a demand was made for access to the books of the Fairmount Park Commission and the Board of City Trusts. These last two were sacrosanct institutions, appointment to which was made by the common pleas judges and was the equivalent of knighthood. The Controller had never done such things before; it wasn't cricket. Most of all, he wanted to get at the books of the Philadelphia Rapid Transit Company, which, when the Controller's office had revealed its unexpected quality of perversity, had been withdrawn, and it took Mr. Wilson two years of insistence to get them returned.

During this period he was incredibly busy. The newspaper reporters haunted the obscure spot in City Hall which formerly had been the source of little or no news and now had become a veritable mine of good stories. The stout Mr. Wilson with pendulous chins would sit back of the Controller's desk, with a perpetual cigar, and talk about a vast array of iniquities that he knew about and was prepared to attack when he could get around to them, and he kept going round and round.

He would be carrying on fights with three or four officials of different institutions at one time. He personified all of his fights, and the language that was bandied about was simple and direct. The newspapermen remarked that the more fights he had the better he seemed to like it, and he was a tough opponent with an uncanny knack of picking the most sensitive part of his antagonist's anatomy.

Everybody about City Hall wondered what his game was, and they figured he must be crooked. They were always looking for the contact man, the man who could "fix it" with the controller's office.

By the time he got the books of the Philadelphia Rapid Transit

WIDE WORLD PHOTOS

S. DAVIS WILSON

"Usually he has a half dozen fights going at once, any one of which would be quite enough for an ordinary man."

Company the dominance of the magnificent Mitten was turning brown at the edges. In the fall of 1929 the Controller was ready to go into court with a suit attacking the Mitten Management. On October 1 the news was flashed that Thomas E. Mitten had been drowned in the lake on his Pocono estate. There was speculation as to whether it was an accident, suicide, or fake. Mr. Wilson's melodramatic mind inclined to the latter view. In any event, the suit went on with much battling over Mr. Wilson's right to appear in court representing the Controller. He was not a lawyer, but had an immense urge to be one. He forced his way in, and that famous law case with Mr. Wilson conducting it against a battery of the ablest lawyers in Philadelphia is still talked about. The case dragged as law cases will, but in about eighteen months the decision came down. It was headlined as a famous victory for the city and the end of Mitten Management judicially found to be permeated with fraud, but the Judge, not Wilson, drew the headlines and the plaudits.

Another function of the Controller's office was that of estimating the city's income in order that City Council might prepare a budget in November for the following year. This had been a formal matter, but Mr. Wilson had his own way of handling it. He would start in October with the prophecy that Council should be able to cut the tax rate for the next year. He would fire away at Charley Hall as a public menace and czar of Council and ask him to explain his relationship to the subway, the Sesqui-Centennial, and the City Hall Annex contracts. He would condemn the drones on the city payroll and refer to a ward leader drawing a fat salary, and list his kinsmen also drawing salaries. He would insist that if the drones were fired the pay of the policemen and firemen could be raised. These last were the picked troops, the palace guards of the organization, and he had the audacity to bid for them. Council would cry "bunk," "unfair," "misleading," and assert, "We are for an increase in the pay of the police and firemen as soon as it is possible."

Having prepared the atmosphere, he would come into Council or before its finance committee and a scene like this would be reported.

Mr. Hall: "Did you say that I told you that eighteen years ago I was an $1,800 sergeant-at-arms and now was worth two million?"

Mr. Wilson: "Yes, I said something like that."

Mr. Hall (very red in the neck): "Why should I tell a dirty rat like you my personal affairs?"

Mr. Wilson: "You're a dirty rat yourself."

Mr. Hall: "You're a bare-faced liar."

Mr. Wilson: "You're a liar."

There were frequent altercations with councilmen and others, where "liar" would be a term freely used, plus "blackguard" and "blatherskite," coupled with prophecies that the people of the city would soon get wise to this fellow, Wilson, but he kept on going. It was quite clear that Mr. Wilson at last had a job that was the breath of life to him. He lived for his job. He could not tear himself away from it. The more he worked and talked the bigger he seemed to grow. It offered the fulfillment of his ambitions to be a great public figure and a leader of men.

The extraordinary circumstances by which Mr. Wilson ultimately became controller in 1933 and Mr. Hadley was elected treasurer in the same year involve a story of local politics too intricate to be detailed. It is enough to say that when Senator Vare had a stroke on August 1, 1928, and was thought to be permanently incapacitated, the band of brothers split and a Grand Jury investigation of the police and of gangsters shook City Hall. In the confusion Mr. Hadley was slated by both factions and renominated in 1929. He was, of course, re-elected and Mr. Wilson continued as his deputy. Four years later in 1933 Mr. Wilson ran as a candidate for controller and Mr. Hadley as a candidate for treasurer. They were nominated by the Democrats and elected with the help of what was known as the Town Meeting Party. So in November of 1933 S. Davis Wilson, controller-elect, appeared as a conquering hero before City Council in its deliberations on budget making, where a few years before he had come as a despised trouble-maker and a temporary nuisance. The councilmen had not been up for election that year. They were all Republicans greatly disturbed by the discovery that the rock upon which they had stood so firmly, the Republican organization, had crumbled under them. Moreover, they were facing a financial crisis so acute that it looked as if there must be a fearful slaughter of City Hall employees. They were dependent upon the Controller's estimate of income. He saved them from their distress by adding millions to income to be derived from collections of delinquent taxes, from the sale of city-owned real estate, and from manipulation of the sinking fund. The newspaper comments represented him as a prestidigitator pulling white rabbits out of a plug hat. His attention was drawn to the fact that he was elected city controller, not city magician. Mr. Wilson predicted a rapid rise of real estate values under the New Deal and offered to resign if his calculations were not substantiated. That offer later was pointedly and persistently called to his attention, but without result.

The next year, 1934, was the great battle for United States senator and governor with Guffey and Earle heading the Democratic ticket. Wilson supported them, both in the primary and in the election, but in no very gracious mood. Nevertheless, his speeches were sufficiently emphatic. He urged the voters to support these two candidates in the primary "as true disciples of President Roosevelt and the Roosevelt New Deal." He again urged the voters to support them in the election. ". . . The special interests have persistently disregarded the rights of the citizens. . . . It is our chance to deliver a second crushing blow to the old out-moded Republican rule in Philadelphia."

Shortly after the election, he was working again with Council on the budget. The financial situation was, if anything, worse than that of the year before. But once again the Controller came through with a set of figures eagerly grasped by Council and referred to by the newspapers as another amazing sleight-of-hand performance. The councilmen were all to come up for re-election the following November. The Republican margin of victory in 1934 had been slight and many councilmanic districts had gone Democratic. The outlook was grave. A forced cut in the City Hall payroll might prevent their individual renomination and certainly promised to assure their defeat at the election. To raise the tax rate was out of the question. Mr. Wilson's magic not only preserved the payroll and the existing tax rate, but enabled Council to restore pay cuts to all city employees. It was a blessed deliverance, and the rumor passed that Wilson had his eye on the Republican nomination for mayor in 1935 and was making sure of councilmanic support. He denied the rumor, asserting that the acts of a public officer who was concerned solely with his public duty were being misconstrued.

Nevertheless, the following August the Republican party was divided between City Treasurer Hadley and City Controller Wilson as its choice for mayor—the outcasts were now sought as saviors. In the primary the City Controller won. He was now beginning to assume the proportions of a man of destiny, proportions that were confirmed as he went on to win the election. In the course of the final weeks of the election campaign, it was discovered that the national administration was an issue of importance. He dwelt upon that issue. A Democratic victory would be looked upon as an endorsement of the "economic fallacies and social vagaries of the New Deal—the New Deal must be utterly repudiated." Philadelphia should support the "sound and tried Republican policies that have made Pennsylvania the industrial capital of the nation."

He was sworn in at high noon on the first Monday of January, 1936. The ceremonies were most pretentious. They took place at Convention Hall, the largest meeting place in town, with thousands of citizens looking on, while Justice Maxey of the Supreme Court, a prominent political figure in the hard coal counties, administered the oath to Mr. Wilson, who was dressed unostentatiously in street clothes. It was a fine contrast—the imposing ceremonies and the homely figure, the recipient of the honors.

The night of his inauguration a dinner was given to the retiring president of Council, Mr. Cox. It was a Republican gathering replete with satisfaction over its recent victory and the conviction that the Democrats were on their way out. The new officers sworn in that day were catalogued as Republicans, but the Mayor was not referred to although he was present and spoke vigorously against the fallacies of the New Deal. No one seemed to care to tag him with a party label. Within a month he was in close co-operation with the leading Democrats, working with the Democratic National Committee at Washington and coming back in a triumphant blare of trumpets, announcing that the National Democratic Convention had been secured for Philadelphia.

When he entered the mayor's office he accelerated the pace he had set as controller. He seemed bursting with energy and enthusiasm. A half dozen major matters were kept continuously in the air, and he tossed in a new one every so often, with the dexterity of a juggler. A newspaper writer who helped write his speeches complained that they sometimes had as many as five to get out for a day, in addition to proclamations on a variety of subjects, and the clippers of news items would shake their heads and mutter, "Was there ever such a man? Three front page stories of a morning."

He kept that pace for two years. It was amazing how he did it. In January of 1938 he broke down and was confined to his home for some three weeks, during which he was pictured conducting business from his sick bed, his staff at his bedside. To the chagrin of many, he came back, though thinner and reduced in velocity. Perhaps he does not now get the same exuberant gratification out of driving down Broad Street behind a battery of motorcycle policemen with screaming sirens. In the early days of his administration he would do that, seated alone in the back seat of an open car, visible as a stout figure in a soft hat smoking a big cigar. During those first two years, being mayor was his vocation, his avocation, and his hobby.

The Philadelphia Rapid Transit Company arrived at the federal bankruptcy court, and the Mayor now sits as one of the operating trustees sharing the place once filled by Mr. Mitten. The renewal of the gas lease appeared on the schedule again in 1937. The Mayor had promised fifty-cent gas. No one appeared able to make good on that offer. Council approved of a new lease, but the Mayor refused to sign it. The matter is dragging in the courts.

Labor troubles reached a crescendo in August of 1937. Mayor Wilson constituted himself as chief settler of the strikes, established his own labor board and permitted the National Labor Relations Board to sit in if it chose. He claims that he settled some two hundred strikes. He purported to be both the friend of labor and the guardian of the common welfare. He handled the situation undoubtedly with an eye to the labor vote, more particularly the C.I.O., but when he was defied he struck with the police and struck hard.

Usually he has a half-dozen fights going at once, any one of which would be quite enough for an ordinary man. The School Board has for many years been labeled by the cagey politicians as untouchable, but the Mayor has attacked it headlong, criticized its expenditures, and thwarted its proposal to raise its tax rate. It is probable that the city is spending more on its schools than it can afford, but the school payroll carries better than ten thousand names and a cautious politician would hesitate before arousing that constituency.

The Fairmount Park Commission was discovered to have bank accounts that should have been paid into the city treasury. The members of the Commission flared hot at his meddling with their time-honored freedom, but turned the money over.

The Board of City Trusts, the most sacrosanct institution in the city, fought his efforts to pry into its affairs, but was finally forced to yield and reluctantly revealed transactions which should have caused the faces of its members to grow very red.

He fought with the Democratic governor and the chief local Democratic contractor and leader, with the chairman of the Republican City Committee, with the chief contributor to the Republican War Chest, with members of Council, with the gas company, the electric company, with the reform Committee of Seventy, with a judge or two, with the Republican district attorney, with anyone, in fact, that happened to stray across his path.

In the primary campaign of 1937, the Mayor disagreed with the Republican leaders on candidates. It was obvious he was headed back to the Democratic camp. On the day after the primary, the Republican district attorney, having discovered that racketeering had reached a pitch that required a Grand Jury investigation, filed a petition to that effect with the Court. Just nine years before, in 1928, a Grand Jury investigation had given the district attorney control over the police. What had happened once might happen again.

There had been persistent talk about the amount of "racket" money collected at City Hall, and in connection with that there was talk of the Mayor's financial dealings. One authenticated story related to a suit for $12,000 started just before the mayoralty election. The plaintiff was a lawyer who was reputed to act as a contact man for the utility interests. Shortly after the suit was brought, Mr. Wilson's Democratic opponent propounded some searching questions to Mr. Wilson asking him how he came to owe that money and how the lawyer came to lend it to him and why he was now being sued for it, and followed immediately thereafter with the question, "Mr. Wilson, how much money have you received from the utilities? Why was this money paid you?"

There were other searching questions as to money transactions and promissory notes.

No answer was filed to the suit, in the statement of which it was set forth that $1,700 had been advanced for the payment of income tax, rather a puzzling item since Mr. Wilson's public salary was exempt from tax. Ultimately the suit was marked settled.

"Racket" money is always a subject of gossip in the shadow of City Hall. Ten years before, when Mayor Mackey, then newly elected, had disbanded the special police units operating out of City Hall, he did so with the remark: "Even the children on the street know they are collecting."

In the legislative session of 1937 a committee had been created to investigate the judicial system of the Commonwealth. In July of that year a state policeman was arrested tapping the private telephone wire of Mr. Wilgarde, the Mayor's secretary. The Mayor exercised a long-disused function of his office and sat as a committing magistrate. The policeman was brought before him and held in $5,000 bail. Sitting judicially, the Mayor made a fervid speech in which he accused the Governor of an underhanded dastardly trick in furtherance of a scheme to drive him out of office, and he gave to the press a memorandum found in the possession of the arrested policeman which recited, "It is reputed the gamblers are paying for protection and the money is placed in a three-way pool (1) Wilgarde (2) Donoghue (3) Mayor Wilson." The Commonwealth must be saved from such vicious un-American espionage, and he would run for governor in order to save it. The state policeman was working for the legislative investigating committee. What Mr. Wilgarde's wire had to do with the judicial system was not explained. Nobody bothered much with the heavy verbal firing that went on between the Mayor and the Governor and the Chairman of the committee and nobody bothered about the young state policeman. The burning question was, "Have they got the goods on him?"

The proposal to conduct a Grand Jury investigation was generally considered to be another gunning expedition for the Mayor. Wilson opposed the proposal. The Court directed that the investi-

gation should proceed. The Mayor thereupon dashed to Harrisburg, the state capital, and strongly urged the Attorney General
to take control of the investigation himself. This was ultimately
done. The Attorney General was a candidate for governor. It was
announced in November that the Grand Jury would require six
months to complete its investigation. Those who were astute politically, quickly calculated that its presentment would be made
about May 1, just before the primary election. They commented
that if the Mayor could be burned at the stake he would make a
blaze so hot and brilliant that it would light up the Attorney General's candidacy so that every voter could see it.

In face of these concurrent investigations, neither of which was
ostensibly directed at the Mayor, but both of which were known
to be at his heels, he ran for the United States Senate on the
Guffey-Lewis slate in the Democratic primary. So from March
until the 17th of May the city was uncertain whether its Mayor
would be on his way to jail or to the United States Senate on the
18th of May.

He was beaten in the primary by Governor Earle, but he made
a whirling-dervish fight of it. He was the "hatchet man" for his
slate and put out the story of Governor Earle's borrowings from
the Democratic contractor, McCloskey. He had fought with both
of them before. Although he was defeated, his opponents are nurs-
ing a few wounds that will not heal readily.

How does he add up? The short, swift denunciation of those
who hate him isn't the answer nor is his own description of himself
as a crusader fighting for the right. If he was either he wouldn't
be mayor.

It was almost a year after the filing of the petition for the calling
of the special Grand Jury, a year in which arguments on street corners and over tables and bars persisted as to what the Grand Jury
had on the Mayor or did not have. Then a presentment was made
charging him with official misbehavior in failing to suppress gambling, in firing and demoting city employees without due respect
for the civil service laws and in interfering with the attendance of
witnesses before the special legislative committee. Indictments
have been returned based on these charges. The Mayor's answer
was, "Persecution." His attorneys filed a motion to quash. The

man on the street remarked, "Maybe so, but what the Hell?" and the Grand Jury went on investigating.

It may be well to list the charges against him. The old-time reformers, who have carried on as committees, investigating, compiling, advising, and criticizing, trying to be helpful and constructive, are gloomy about him. To them he represents the widest gap between headline and performance yet witnessed. He starts a great variety of things, but finishes nothing. He is a poor administrator and a juggler with figures. He can take the gas company figures, the transit company figures, the city budget figures and put them out in a way that makes them false and misleading. To those who believe in the sanctity of figures that is unpardonable.

To party politicians he presents a continual cause of complaint. He is devoid of party loyalty. He won't stick with any crowd. He can deal with individuals shrewdly enough to accomplish a purpose, but he creates no lasting bond. When the thing is done he is likely to explode unexpectedly in the face of his ally, and be accused bitterly of double-crossing. As a politician he is first and last a Wilson man, and he can have no one around who diverts the spotlight from himself.

The manufacturers will tell you that he turned the town over to the C.I.O. and gave it a free hand to sack and destroy. The only occasions when he came down with the police were when the A.F. of L. was underneath. There is evidence to support the charge.

Nevertheless, there are men of quiet, careful judgment who have worked with him in difficult situations who will not dismiss him in cursory fashion. They may admit he is an egotist and that they don't understand him, but they credit him with capacity, energy, and earnestness. Admiration has also been expressed for his attitude in the labor difficulties of 1937, which presented situations not easy of solution. He would spend twenty-four hours at a stretch trying to reconcile the irreconcilable, and when the time came to use the police he did it. It is true that when a result was secured, he wanted, even demanded, that his picture appear on the front page of the papers as the man who saved the town from anarchy, but in no small degree he deserved it.

What he has done in the way of uncovering iniquities cannot be dismissed with a mere statement that they represented self-serving stage play. Nobody ever before did such things in such an extensive way for Philadelphia. Some of his accusations were exaggerated and distorted, and when he had worried and mouthed a particular thing for a while he moved on to something else. He is criticized for providing no constructive remedy, as merely touching off explosions, but it may be queried whether there is any constructive remedy for the failings of mankind, and blasting serves a purpose.

His activities are so scattered and he moves from one to another so rapidly that he is given little credit for executive ability, and yet the arrangements made for the Democratic National Convention and for the Army-Navy football game, matters that the town could see, made friend and foe alike agree that that man Wilson was on top of his job.

Politically he can answer his critics by the assertion that when he got the Republican nomination he was giving as much as he took. He helped the party to victory and expected it to follow his lead, and when it followed the lead of the big contributions he was at liberty to leave it.

What has he done that is constructive? Who knows? The town does not know which way it is going or wants to go. It once believed in the protective tariff and the open shop as the base of its prosperity. These beliefs satisfied it for better than a half century; all others were "isms" and unAmerican. Now its convictions are a chaos.

He has counted his voting strength as coming from the small streets and has played up to it. When he was running for mayor he appeared at a rather dressy hotel dinner and suddenly blurted out in the course of his speech: "You don't like me, but the people in the little streets and the alleys—they are going to elect me. You're going to take me as your mayor and like it."

There was something of bitterness in his assertion and perhaps of adroitness too, for his outburst made the headline.

In fairness to him he should be given the last word and he probably would put his case somewhat like this:

"It has always been my ambition to hold public office. I wanted to be mayor. I want to be governor. I want to be a leader of men. I want to fight evil things to show up the big thieves and the little. Enemies? Sure, I've got them everywhere. They've been waiting like wolves to tear me to pieces. They have waited ten years, but they haven't got me and they won't get me. The Legislative Committee and the Grand Jury spent $300,000 and what have they got on me? Nothing. They can't understand me. They never did understand, but I showed them. I fought them all. I came through on my own, in my own way. I got public office in my way. I have served the people in my way. I have been a leader of men in my way. I have done it. I am the Mayor."

We have a belief in Philadelphia that the office of mayor is a four-year corridor with blazing lights and applause at the entrance, cold contempt and oblivion at the exit.

We rarely like our mayors after the first six months of their terms. Usually we have no faith in their integrity. When we admit their honesty we do so grudgingly as though it represented a mean, small-minded trait.

Mr. Wilson has shared with his predecessors the vicissitudes of his office. Whether he will survive its blight is a question that would ordinarily be answered, "No," but he has reversed so many traditions that he may reverse this one.

In any event, it may be said that in 1935 the old patterns of thought in the town had been washed out, and new ones had not yet formed. The town did not comprehend itself, and it elected its least-comprehended citizen as mayor.

15

SOL LEVITAN: THE PORTRAIT OF A CANDIDATE

By J. T. Salter

I

I FIRST SAW MR. LEVITAN IN 1930. I HAD ASKED AN OLD-TIME resident of Madison to give me the name of the most colorful politician in Wisconsin. Immediately the answer came, "Sol Levitan, the state treasurer, is the man you want." I called on Mr. Levitan in the Capitol, introduced myself, and explained that I wanted him to tell my political-party class about his experiences in politics. He threw up his hands and exclaimed, "Professor, I can't do that. I talked three times last week and I talk tonight, but I can't talk in a classroom." I said that if he could talk to the farmers and the other people of the state, he could talk to the students. "Oh, no, Professor, talking to the University students is different from talking to a lot of damn Eskimos." [1] I insisted that the same talk would do for both groups and added, "There will be a newspaperman there to get your speech." He said that he would come.

It was midwinter when he came. He left his great brown chinchilla-like overcoat and his gray felt hat in my office. Before we entered the classroom, I stopped to introduce him to several students standing near the doorway. As I pronounced the name of one of them—a Miss Goldberg—he held out his hand, smiled, and said, "That sounds like home cooking to me." When he entered the classroom, he first of all removed a large gray sweater coat that he was wearing over his coat. Underneath, another gray sweater coat was visible. And in the classroom, he lifted his glasses high on his head, looked at the seventy students, many of whom were Jewish, smiled and remarked, "I am glad to see so many of my cousins here." The class laughed their appreciation, and Mr. Levitan's

---

[1] I have substituted the word "Eskimos" for the name of a dominant nationality group in Wisconsin.

career as a University lecturer most auspiciously began. (Since that day he has failed in only one term to talk to each new class studying politics.)

He began with a smile, an inquiring eye, and a hand full of notes. The notes (in large print) were on strips of cardboard six or eight inches long and two inches wide. They were either briefest clews to paragraphs in his mind about his life story or collaborated passages on such important subjects as "You American people, the greatest educated people in this world. . . You hold in the palm of your hands the greatest treasure on earth—the ballot. If you have a man in office who votes and works against the people's interest, 'Raus Mit em.' You American people are broad-minded. You don't care where a man comes from, what congregation he belongs to if he is a real American. . . Now my dear people you are studying for the good of the country. Help the government by following the teaching of St. John, 'Love thy neighbor as thyself.' " (Sometimes when he uses this biblical quotation, he ingratiatingly adds, "Won't you give me credit that I don't quote Moses?") "Don't worry. Worry won't bring you anything. You can't change the world any more than you can change the planet. We all have to guess, and sometimes we guess wrong. The worst thing a man can do is to give advice and advice doesn't always work out. I said five per cent brains and ninety per cent luck. And I can illustrate this. In Europe we have lotteries. Nobody can be rich unless he buys a ticket. One man wanted No. 14. He got 14 and he won that million. Everybody wondered how he came to pick No. 14. He said that it was brains, but they knew it wasn't brains. They kept after him, and he told them that he had had a dream about the million. A great big six and a great big nine appeared to him. So he used his brains and figured out that 6 plus 9 was 14, and that is how he won."

His naturalness, charm, and wit in his spontaneously told life story were infectious and compelled attention; they carried him through the laborious reading of the rather stilted and impersonal parts. (However, in 1936, after the election, when he gave his campaign speech in the classroom, the speech was a unit and altogether delightful.) Moreover, the speaker was so finely attuned to the response of his audience that he dwelt on those ideas and stories that the class most appreciated, and briefly disposed of the others. The end product was a performance that every student abundantly enjoyed.

II

Here follow the most revealing incidents in the story of his life as he tells it to the student—and the voters too, for on election night when I was at Mr. Levitan's home as the returns were coming in over the radio, he suddenly smiled and said, "Professor, the speech I gave to your students so many times is the speech that elected me. I started on June 15th and spoke in sixty-nine counties, sometimes two or three times a day. It is now my one speech. It takes forty minutes or an hour to give."

Some of his observations and stories have such a unique and arresting turn that they are fascinating even without the presence of Sol himself. To understand his full appeal, however, one must have some picture of how he looks to the eye. He is only five feet five, but rather squarely built, and he bears himself well. He is at home with all the world; he is interested in everyone, and he assumes that everyone is interested in him. And nearly all of us are. He is, however, quaintly unique in both appearance, manner, and speech. His very uniqueness is appealing. The sight of him delivering a political address suggests for the briefest instant the foreigner, but only for the briefest instant, and only once, for after he begins to talk, a very different galaxy of figures strikes one. He may be the patriarch, or the mischevious Puck; or he may be the stern lawgiver protecting the public's interest, or the thrifty trader. Or again, he may have both the pitiful and lovable expression of a bird dog that is most anxious to please. But always he is the warm friendly human being who looks directly at you as he talks, and you forget his appearance and become sympathetic and absorbed in him. You think of him as somehow being connected with you, and many voters in Wisconsin would no more vote against him than they would refuse to support a member of their own family for public office. In atmosphere or personality, he is something like a Wisconsin Will Rogers or Mark Twain, or he brings to mind a comical and touching picture of one's own parents from Europe who had to struggle to make their way in America. There is something magnetic about him, with his fringe of rather long snow-white hair, his very close-cropped goatee, his round, and at times almost cherubic face that is pleasant, good-looking, and unmistakably Jewish, his dark eyes that seem to relish what they see, his variable⁄expressions, ranging from jovial friendliness and whimsicality to a look of concentrated seriousness. His voice has an expressive quality that wins his audience. His speech creates an emotional and physical response; it strikes somewhere lower down than the reason, although the reason accepts what he says. He seems to be life itself rather than a highly specialized detail of life. Thus he disarms criticism and wins support as the home baseball team wins the good will of the people in the community.

III

He was born in Taurrogen, Lithuania, on November 1, 1862, studied the five books of Moses at the age of six, Hebrew and Yiddish (his native tongue) and German at the age of eight, and at eleven he studied the Talmud. Later he earned money praying for the sick or writing letters for those unable to write. During these early years at school, he lived on rye bread and water (meat once a week), and mended his own clothes. "Our beds were the benches with straw for mattresses, and our overcoats for covering." At the age of sixteen he gave up the idea of a formal education and set out, without a dollar in his pocket, to see an uncle in the Crimea, many miles away. He remarked that people were kind to him, and much of the distance he traveled smuggled under benches of trains at night. One night at about 3:00 A.M. he was discovered and put off. A few hours later he met some pious Jews going to a synagogue. That same morning they introduced him to a ship captain, who took him to Kiev, another taking him to Krima Chug, and another to Yakatrine Slav. From there he took a train to the Crimea (hitch-hiking in the seventies). At first he was hired out to a grain merchant at $50 a year, the second year he was given "$85 with board and lickings free." Life looked good; he now had meat and white bread daily. He did not miss the absence of recreation in this life, for he never had had it.

A pogrom broke out in the Crimea in 1880. A Jewish woman was accused of throwing a bomb at the Czar. "Every Jewish business house was destroyed; no Jew was safe." His employer went out to search for his wife. A big soldier caught him by the neck and started choking him to death. Sol picked up an iron bar and hit the soldier on the arm; the soldier released the employer and started after Sol. The crowd laughed and taunted the big soldier, "What, can't even catch a little Jew."

His employer was so grateful that he offered Sol the choice of a modern education or a ticket to America. Sol reached Baltimore without five cents and unable to speak the English language. (His speech is still picturesque rather than grammatical.) He worked on a street-paving job, saved some money, and became a peddler with a pack on his back. (He hesitates as he says this, smiles, and then adds, "They call them bond salesmen today.") He peddled among the Pennsylvania Dutch for they could understand him. Often in the evenings at the farmhouses where he spent the nights, the children would help him to spell and pronounce English words. He would repay this and other kindnesses by doing chores around the house and barn, or by tending babies for the farmers' wives. He finally migrated to Wisconsin and settled permanently. A large number of the people that he went among were immigrants— Scandinavians, Germans, or Swiss. He felt at home and picked New Glarus as his "home town," a little town near Primrose, the home of La Follette. This was in 1881, and by 1887 he was able to open a store of his own.

One Saturday morning before his store-keeping days when he still had his pack on his back, he walked into a bank in a small Wisconsin town. He stopped, as he entered, to look at the bank president signing bank notes. The president was disturbed by the persistent stare. He abruptly asked, "What do you want?" Sol explained that he would like to know how long he would have to stay in this country before he, too, could put his name on money. At this the banker laughed so noisily that two clerks came up to see what the commotion was about. The banker pointed at Sol, and exclaimed, "This Jew peddler wants to know how long he will have to live in America before he can sign currency!" And then turning to Mr. Levitan he said, "Why you could live here forever and never sign a bank note."

Mr. Levitan adds, "I thanked him for the encouragement he had given me." And then, "Some years later when I was the president of the Commercial National Bank of Madison, a much larger bank than the one in the little town, I thought of this first bank president of my acquaintance. The first $10-bill that I signed I sent to him as my calling card. I wrote, 'See, I am now signing bank notes, and it did not take me half as long as you said it never would.' "

Another time he was walking along a country road, wondering more about his next meal than about the next sale. He came to a farmhouse, but there was a forbidding sign in the yard—No Peddlers Allowed—Mr. Levitan surveyed the sign for a moment, took a piece of chalk from his pocket, and wrote "Only Sol" underneath the word "allowed" in the sign. He then knocked on the door, was admitted, sold some goods, stayed for dinner, and was right in the midst of his meal when the man of the house returned from town. He, following an old-time custom of certain farmers, had been drinking, and when he discovered a peddler in his home, he shouted, "What are you doing here; can't you read my sign?" Mr. Levitan said that he could read a little, but not very much. The farmer then took him out to the sign and read it to him. Mr. Levitan pointed out the "only Sol" printed below and he exclaimed "I am Sol." The farmer was at first bewildered and then good-naturedly invited him to return and finish his dinner.

This was the first of a series of sales and dinners at this farmhouse. Years later, Mr. Levitan adds, the farmer confessed to him that when he put up that sign against peddlers he meant Sol too, "but you fooled me. So I fooled you. I heard that a Jew that eats pork never goes to heaven. I told my wife to cook pork chops covered with gravy every time you came to dinner. I told you it was veal, but it was always pork. Now you will go to hell." Mr. Levitan tells this story, as all of his stories, with an appreciative smile, and the audience always laughs with him.

He then described his chance meeting with the original Bob La Follette and the official start of his career in politics—(for, actually, he started in a form of politics when he first sought the favor of people. First he sold merchandise from his pack, then from his store, and finally he sold himself to the people).

"I happened to go down to a neighborhood near New Glarus. That is where Senior Bob La Follette was born, and I stayed around there and made my home with a man by the name of Eli Peterson, called Uncle Eli. One day when I had dinner, a nice appearing young man, very intelligent, came and right away Eli said, 'Bob, what brings you here?' 'Uncle, I am going to run for district attorney, and I want you to help me.' And they were talking politics; so all at once he turned and said, 'Bob, why don't you get together with the Jew peddler here? He knows all the farmers and can do you lots of good.' So he said, 'Bob, here is Sol; Sol, here is Bob.' We shook hands, and an honest-to-goodness handshake, not like here in Madison. I didn't know a darn thing about politics, so he instructed me, told me how I should talk to the farmers, and gave me some kind of cards to tell all about it. Well, after we got through talking, business is business with me, and I right away sold him a pair of suspenders, and I supported him the balance of his life."

In 1892 Mr. Levitan was elected to his first public office, that of justice of the peace, in the town of New Glarus. This was just five years after he had established himself as a storekeeper with a store of his own. "I didn't run. There was a town caucus that nominated me. I held the office four years and never made a cent." His knowledge of law was nil, but resourcefulness has always been one of his dominant characteristics. He "settled" the law suits out of court and sometimes made two friends where he had had one or none before. To quote him, "I was not educated enough to read the law. I didn't want to be embarrassed; so when a case came up before me, I would settle with them. I would say to them, 'Now you are neighbors. You don't want to have a fight; why not settle this out of court?' and I settled with them. Sometimes they had to apologize, sometimes one would pay with a keg of beer, and many times they would not settle, so I would pay it myself. If there was trouble between man and wife, I would ask the husband 'Are you sure that your next wife will be any better?' I would then turn to the wife, 'Are you sure that your next husband will be any better?'

Nobody could be sure, and I advised them to keep what they had. Later I was often thanked by both parties—in private."

His quick wit is revealed by the following story told one evening in his home. "One time I was at a meeting in New Glarus where delegates were chosen for a convention—it was before the direct primary. I was being suggested for a delegate when a Norwegian spoke out and said, 'Here, we have enough delegates of our own people. We don't need to go to Jerusalem for one.'"

I interrupted and asked Mr. Levitan how he answered the Norwegian. He had not intended to mention this part of the story, but he smiled and added, "He said, 'We have enough here to chose from and no need to go to Jerusalem for a delegate.' 'Well,' I said, 'you did once. Are you sorry?'"

His resourcefulness is suggested by the following. "In one early fight when La Follette was a candidate for governor, word was sent to me that the La Follette delegates must carry Green County—my county. I then had a store in New Glarus. One of the other merchants controlled some votes. I often had bargain sales that hurt this man, but this time I needed his votes, so I said, 'Albert, help me elect La Follette delegates, and I will never have a cut-price sale again.' He said, 'Can I trust you?' I said, 'Other people do,' and so he helped me.

"At the convention, I had all the La Follette delegates lined up, and I moved that we make the strongest one of our opponents, the leader of the opposition, chairman of the meeting."

I asked his motive. He answered, "Don't you see, if we had him up there on the platform as chairman, he couldn't work around among the delegates. He would be out of the way, and we might win the ones that weren't so sure."

Later he added, "When I was a candidate for treasurer, I used to get every vote but four in New Glarus, and every vote but three in Primrose."

He became a Progressive because he liked La Follette and his ideals, and also because he doubtless had the feeling that La Follette would be Wisconsin and Wisconsin would be La Follette's. To the students and to the voters he explains the matter in these words. (And now when he speaks, when he mentions the La Follette name and the Progressive cause, he grows tense, he stands erect, or leans forward and shakes his fist at the unseen foe of the people. His voice now has no faint undertone but thunders a defiant challenge at all who might be so rash as to question what the Progressives have done for the people.)

"Why am I a Progressive? When I moved to Madison, La Follette and I were neighbors. And he always said that people were not getting fair play and something should be done to change conditions. Naturally I liked his way, and Progressives have done considerable. Now they give you the Civil Service. Before it was only a few, those who had a little pull, could get a job. Now they have got Civil Service, and we all have the same chance. If you have good marks, you get a job. That's a step in the right direction.[2]

"Now they have got Workmen's Compensation. I remember when I was up north peddling in the lumber camp, when a man took sick, nothing to it, just took him off the payroll. When a horse took sick, they right away put him in the stable, and give him plenty of rest, and send for the doctor. They know if they lose that horse, they lose $100, but when they lose a man, they haven't lost nothing. Nobody paid any attention to the poor widow and orphans. Now Progressives made the law where they got the Workmen's Compensation, and the poor widow and orphans are taken care of.

"Now we have got Unemployment Insurance. A person can't kick a man right away after working for him. They have got to give him a certain amount of salary until he gets another job.

"Now we have got the primary election law. Before, it always was behind closed doors, four or five people tell you 'You will be

[2] But in 1937 when the legislature was considering a bill that would extend the merit system to the inspectors in the Beverage Tax Division then under Mr. Levitan's control, he worked against the measure. He was called upon to testify before a Senate committee. He launched into the story of his life, was interrupted and asked if he did, or did not, favor the Thompson (Merit System) Bill. Mr. Levitan paused an instant, smiled, looked at the man who had introduced the measure, and exclaimed, "Why, I have known Mr. Thompson for 25 years," and then with a twinkle, "and I have known his wife for 50 years." Everyone laughed, and Mr. Levitan was excused. Sol steadily opposed the application of the merit system to his own employees in spite of campaign speeches in its favor. He also opposed the transfer of governmental agencies from his department even though the transfer was most certain to mean improved efficiency in the public service. When the members of the Assembly were considering the question of transferring the Beverage Tax Division to another department, Sol said, "Gentlemen, don't take the Beverage Tax Division away from me. I'm an old man." Charles Perry, former speaker of the Assembly, said, "That is why we are taking it away from you."

governor, I will be lieutenant governor.' It is the primary where you, the people, decide who should be your officer.

"Now we have got unemployment pensions, mothers' pensions, old-age pensions."

In his successful re-election campaign for 1936, he made a particular appeal to the women in his audience. He asked the rhetorical question. "Who is it that brings up the American race?" And gave the answer, "The woman, she brings up the child from the time he is born until he votes. Say that a woman is not a politician? She is the greatest politician in the world. She plays politics to win her man. After she is married, she plays politics to keep him happy. I live in Madison. The women there are wonderful. Half of them have a university education. The other half make you think they have. The men could never get along without you. When we are young we love you. When we are middle-aged, we appreciate you; but when we are old, we are crazy about you."

And then to the voters he adds, "Let me tell you, my dear people, you don't have to be afraid of La Follette. It took courage to be a Progressive at one time. I remember in New Glarus the banker called me in and said, 'Sol, you are hollering too much for Bob. Now you owe us $1,000. When you pay us up you can holler for Bob. As long as you owe us, you don't holler for Bob.' Then $1,000 looked like a million. I decided I was going to borrow from my relatives. I soon discovered that the poorest place in the world to try to borrow money is from relatives. They know you too well. I borrowed that money, and I have been hollering for Bob all his life time, and I am supporting Phil La Follette for governor."

All of his life he has learned by doing—the way that more than ninety per cent of all politicians learn. He learned about people from people. People are to him the data that the surgeon finds in the hospital or the student of constitutional law in the Supreme Court reports—except that the physician and the lawyer have other sources of information too, but Sol has only one—people. The ballot box on election night tells him how well he understands his subject. He does a thing a certain way and if it meets with the right response, he does it again; if he fails to receive the desired result, he asks, "Now wherein was I wrong? How should this be done?" He gained wisdom from first-hand experience.

Mr. Levitan was first elected to county and state conventions and then in 1924 he was a delegate to a national convention—an alternate delegate in 1916 and 1920. "Once I was a presidential elector—in 1912." He first became a candidate for state treasurer in 1918. Some of the party leaders wanted him to try for the office of lieutenant governor instead, but he said, "Now you gentlemen know that I cannot preside over the Senate. I don't know Roberts' Rules of Order, but make me state treasurer. Give me something that I know. I can count your money in the dark and never lose a nickel."

The argument seemed as logical to the students as it does to their parents—the voters. However, in his 1918 campaign, and again in 1920, he was defeated. "I didn't campaign at all in these years. They told me to stay home—the less the people look at me, the more votes I have. I did use a campaign card. One of the leaders said I lost because my picture was on the card. But in 1922 I went out campaigning. Lieutenant Governor Comings, Mrs. Rosee, and Ada James went with me. La Follette was not there, but he told the people to vote for me. They told me how to make a speech, but each morning my speech was 'How much is the bill?' [the hotel bill where the campaigners had spent the night]. Then at Baraboo I did make a speech—because of luck. Mrs. James was talking about bacon and pork, the rich robbing the poor—how it was that bacon sells so high and yet the farmer gets so little for his pigs.

"A conductor in the crowd of farmers said, 'Let's hear what Sol has to say.' I hadn't my speech with me, but I started talking about the big packers in Chicago who buy the pigs at their own price. They form a monopoly and cheat the farmers. The conductor called out, 'What in hell does Sol know about pork chops?' Everyone laughed, and I knew what the people wanted in a speech."

However, he nearly lost the third try at the nomination. I quote Mr. Levitan. "In 1922, La Follette didn't want me. I'd tried twice and lost. He thought I couldn't make it. So he invited some leaders of the Progessives (Crownhart, Comings, Evjue, etc.) and says to them, 'Gentlemen, I brought you here. We need a state treasurer. Must have a Progressive. I feel friendly to Sol, but I feel he can't make it. I don't want to jeopardize the Progressive movement for any man.' La Follette asked each what they thought of me. Then Secretary of State Hall came into the discussion. La Follette told him, 'We want to make a strong ticket. We don't want to put any lemons there.' Hall asked, 'Who's the lemon?' 'Sol Levitan.' Hall said, 'Let him talk. A man who hears Sol will vote for him.' " La Follette was persuaded by the group to give Sol his support. Hall was right—the people that heard him talk voted for him. And since that time Sol's main ambition is to give the sovereign voter the opportunity to hear him talk.

(Later he told me in a personal conversation that he had learned much by his first speech. "I asked myself what must I do to get elected? What do people want? I decided that they don't want it all like going to church. They want jokes, so I studied what to do. I learned some German stories, some Norwegian stories, and told them in every speech. The press carried these stories, and I got much publicity.

"It gave me an idea—here I come in a country, don't know the language, the ways, but I sell them merchandise. Why, when I know English ways, don't I sell them myself? I studied what every kind of people want, tried to be humoristic.")

Then addressing the students, he said, "There was a man named Jensen that campaigned against me. He was Jensen when he talked before the Danes, but he was Johnson when he spoke to Norwegians. I would say, 'Suppose I tell you I am a Swede. You look at me and say "Langte fra" (Far from it!). I could change my name, what good would it do me the minute that you look at my Irish face?" Then he glanced at a most beautiful girl with classic features and fairest color, sitting in the first row. He pointed at her. "Of course I would like to have a pretty face like that too, if I could." It was a direct hit with all the students. Sol had scored again! He had made each one in the class feel that he was just a little better than Sol. For in that class as in every other advanced university class or in every community outside of the university as well, there are people who feel inferior, or who are afraid that they never will quite reach the mark, or achieve the success on which they had earlier counted. They naturally associate correct English with superiority. Now they behold a man speaking what seems to be broken English with a foreign tang. His accent, his double negative, his slurring of words cause these people, many of whom are uncertain about such intricate questions as the plural subject and plural verb present, to feel superior—even patronizingly so. Sol inflates the ego of the student and the voter; they recognize this new feeling of power that comes to them as they listen to him jest at himself or at his race. They show their appreciation by their vote.

IV

I spoke truly when I first told Mr. Levitan that the students would like him as well as the voters did. They did and do. (After a politician visits my class to speak about his actual life in politics, each student writes a paper on the traits or characteristics of the speaker that might account for his success in getting elected to public office.) The comments from the students, not only from this first group in 1930, but from each succeeding class as well, indicate that Mr. Levitan is the student's choice as well as the people's choice. Almost unanimously the students express their unqualified surprise, delight in, and approval of the man. After his appearance in 1936, when he gave the class of 105 students his campaign address, all the reports were favorable except three, and these three recognized the speaker as a most effective campaigner. And so it has been for each group of student reports following each of his appearances in the classroom. Last year my one Communist student said, "We look to the political leader for guidance in the world today and he gives us a smile and funny stories." Other students have remarked, "It would not be unreasonable to suppose that part of his success is due at least to the fact that he was drawn along, as a faithful henchman, by the still more successful Progressive party." One student observed that, "My father always refused to vote for any La Follette candidate with the exception of Sol." This year a girl student wrote, "I am sorry that I voted a straight ticket. Next time I will split my ticket and vote for Sol." One paper that was unique stated, "It has been a tradition at our synagogue that once each year Mr. Levitan leads the congregation in prayer and he has done this every year since I can remember." However, in an overwhelming majority of papers the following

NICHOLAS FISHBOURNE

SOL LEVITAN

*"He loves people, but even more than that he loves
to talk to people."*

expressions appeared again and again, so often and with such gusto that I cannot easily think of another politician that would have brought them forth in the same full measure of unfeigned delight; "personal magnetism," "sincerity," "friendliness," "simple, honest man of the people," "honesty," "sense of intimacy," "convincing," "his many Jewish jokes break down any racial feeling," "his jokes are about himself, they are not the ones you have been hearing in the past 500 campaigns," "he makes the listener believe that he is the equal of the speaker," "he believes in the Golden Rule and the La Follettes." One student was reminded of the comedian Weber in the team of Weber and Fields; another student thought of him as a prophet stepping out of the pages of the Old Testament.

At first blush, Mr. Levitan's address in the classroom or on the hustings may seem to be only a haphazard lecture that is tossed off without careful preparation or pertinent regard to the particular audience. Or again, it may seem to be a rather naïve performance that may hit or miss the fancy of the group. However, both of these ideas are precisely opposite from the truth of the matter. First the speeches are carefully, even laboriously, prepared; no effort is saved; no time or consultation with appropriate experts (newspapermen or professors, or others) are spared in Sol's aim to get just the right speech. When it is finally given it embodies a highly developed and selective appeal aimed at those stereotypes and blind spots in the listener's mind that are most certain to arouse a feeling of sympathetic superiority and good will, which will later be transformed into a vote at the polls. The faulty English, the foreign accent, the mispronounced words are aids in helping him win and hold attention and sympathy. (Some years ago he asked a professor of speech to teach him how to speak English correctly. He was told not to change anything or he would ruin his speech. Today he knows this to be true. He refers with joy in his heart to his lack of formal training at the very start of each address. "I went to the wrong school, I went to the school of hard knocks.")

His public speaking formula seems to be, first, Sol himself in his most expansive, cheerful, and engaging manner. Next he begins his speech with a joke—probably about himself and his race; then he presents something in a more serious tone on La Follette and the Progressive party, or on the superiorities and excellencies of the group before him. (In a broad sense all of his speeches are the same, and yet each one is different. The nature of this difference is determined by the difference in the various groups that he addresses. For example, when he first addressed my students he said, "One time, just before Christmas, some of your young men from the university were feeling pretty jolly in front of a movie house. The police thought they were disturbing the peace and took them around the corner to the police station. I followed the patrol wagon and signed bail bonds to let them go. Then I went to your Dean and said, 'Dean, what are you going to do to the boys?' He didn't know. I said, 'You want the university budget approved?'" [The preceding legislature had not approved the appropriation for the University. The preceding appropriation could be approved by an emergency board of three men. One of these was the state treasurer.] "He got the idea." The students in the classroom got the idea too.

In explaining the "emergency board" to the students, he characteristically used a homely illustration that he also uses in talking to the voters. "I am a member of the emergency board, and I oppose a good many things the board wants. The Governor, and the Secretary of State are members of it too. I want to tell you what it is. I used to send my children to school and they always needed money for books, and I says 'My, my they must have enough books to make a new library.' Well, their mother used to go through my pockets at night and take a nickel or a dime out of it and give the money to the children. That is what I call an emergency board."

A few weeks later he talked to the students at Tripp Dormitory. One fact that he stressed repeatedly in talking to the students at Tripp, and did not mention elsewhere, was the pertinent point that it was through him that the money was raised for the construction of the dormitories.

In his last talk to the students he told them about the scrupulous honesty required of the Wisconsin state treasurer, and then with a mischievous Puck-like smile on his beaming face, he pointed his finger at the professor who was standing against a side wall and loudly charged, "It is no job for a Philadelphia politician." The student response in hand-clapping was immediate. (Mr. Levitan

knew that the object of his remark had written a book on Philadelphia politicians; he likewise knew that the students were thoroughly aware of this fact. Thus, a campaign speech that had
already been given about 194 times seemed at that moment to be
an address prepared specifically for the students present.)

The third element in his speech is again a joke. But the joke is
uniquely arresting; and it is more than something "humoristic."
It may be folklore; something that has been for an unknown time
associated with the sorrows and struggles of the human race. This
idea is illustrated by the following:

McAdoo and Admiral Grayson, Wilson's doctor, came to Wisconsin to help launch a Liberty Bond Campaign. Mr. Levitan sat
next to Dr. Grayson at a banquet. The Admiral was from Virginia
and Sol had once peddled in his home town. The Admiral thought
that he remembered Sol and said, "When you come to Washington, be sure and visit the White House." Later Mr. Levitan took
all the ballots to Camp Wadsworth, S. C., for the Wisconsin
soldiers. Coming back, he stopped off at Washington to see Admiral Grayson. "He was friendly to me—says 'Sol, I want you to
meet Tumulty. Tumulty, I want you to meet a man from Wisconsin—that loyal state!' I said, 'Yes, we're loyal. My son is in the
navy, my daughter is working for government insurance allotment,
and sings at Camp Meade to soldiers, and I at home have bought
Liberty Bonds. All I have left at home is my mother-in-law, and
my country can have her too. A man who is willing to spare the
peace-maker of the family is a hundred per cent American.' "

Or possibly the joke is used to present a significant fact, or is
based on a current public question prominent in the minds of the
audience. During the latter part of the prohibition era Mr. Levitan
described the recognition that he had received in this manner. "I
was made an honorary member of one of your social science fra-
ternities—you called it Pi Gamma Mu? I was made honorary
president of the State Treasurers Association for life. I was also
made a chief of the tribe of Winnebago Indians. I said I would
rather be a member of the tribe of Israel. I get ten gallons of sac-
ramental wine."

In any case the joke is stamped with the original flavor of Sol.
Finally, Mr. Levitan says that the one thing that he has contributed

to the ancient art of campaigning is this: "Never talk anything against nobody."

In his 1936 campaign for re-election he answered the critics who said that he was too old to hold the office with the following observation. "Wisdom comes from experience. Handling the people's money is not a job for a politician. There's too much temptation. It might be good to let an elderly man handle your money. He's looking for the Golden Gate, not the Golden Calf."

v

Mr. Levitan's genius for publicity, his energy in pursuing it, and his amazing wit in achieving it are subjects that require special mention. Publicity not only helps him in his trade of politics, but is a form of recognition. And the desire for recognition is the dominant motif in his life. He loves people, but even more than that, he loves to talk to people. The warm embrace of the crowd to him is like the baying of the hounds to the fox hunter, or a sharp increase in the price of milk to the dairyman. Different times when I talked to him in long evenings when he was out of office, he would be sure to say, "Professor, get me some speaking engagements—Chautauquas and like that. I only want my expenses and you can have the rest." I pleaded total inability and lack of connections to do this sort of thing, but I suggested that he obtain the desired introductions from a prominent Progressive who often gives public addresses and must have the necessary connections, but Sol said, "Oh no, he thinks only of himself."

And then on the midnight and after of November 3, 1936, right at the very moment of victory, when he was surrounded in his home by his closest friends (and the interloper—the Professor) he suddenly turned to me and said, "Now I am elected. Now you will find places for me to speak." There was no thought then of quitting now that the campaign was over, victory had been gained, and he must have been tired to death because of the laborious and forced marches over the state during the preceding three months. The one thing in his mind seemed to be—"Now maybe I can get opportunities to talk to more people than ever before. The treasury office is a detail on my march to better recognition. Not money

—that has limited uses and it may pass away, but glory. Not the people now, but Sol!" After he had won the nomination in the primary that year, he said, "It makes me feel as though Senator and Mrs. La Follette, Sr., were living again. They were the greatest people Wisconsin ever had. They were always kind and sympathetic to me."

As an indication of how well he succeeded in the past in satisfying his yen for talking, I quote his own statement, and this of course merely suggests his activity in this field but does not cover it:

"I was invited to every normal school in the state of Wisconsin, and I talked to the students, give them good advice. Then I talked to the P. T. A., that is very valuable. Then I used to go in the schools when they invited me, every Friday night. Then I talked in the high schools, when they invited me, and in the public schools. Also in the industrial schools. Then I talked in the colleges, Lawrence and Ripon. I was invited to talk to the Women's Club and the Lion's Club, and the Kiwanis Club."

The man that hitch-hiked to the Crimea and traveled from there to the state treasurer's office in Wisconsin never got where he is today by hiding his light under a bushel, and he knows that. None of the world's literature moves him as does the sight of his own name in print. At his spacious office in the Capitol he has proudly shown me massive drawers filled with newspaper clippings about him—the contents of two of these drawers would fill a trunk—and he points out that the greatest metropolitan dailies as well as the country weeklies celebrate him in their columns. One time he said that he was one of the best publicized Jews in America. At his home he eagerly shows these printed tributes to him. One is a scroll framed and hanging. It bears the names of less than a score of Jewish men prominent in both public and private life in America. He points to his name and proudly says, "See, Solomon Levitan, next to Felix Warburg and Julius Rosenwald."

When he is among a group of public officials whose picture is about to be taken he has a tendency, sometimes curbed, to get right in front of the group. This last Fourth of July, he "happened" to be at a park where a picnic was in progress. They had thirty minutes on a state-wide hook-up. Just before the festivities over the radio were to begin, Mr. Levitan asked if he might say a few words to his friends. The secretary thought it a fine idea. The secretary spoke first to the friends of the group all over the state, and on the meaning of the Fourth of July. He then introduced "our friend, Mr. Levitan, who will say a few words." Mr. Levitan started right out as though he were going to make a speech. He took notes from his pocket and spoke with animation about his own campaign for re-election to the state treasurer's office and the glory of living in a free land where independence from all outside control has been established. Before he had quite finished, the secretary had to announce that their time on the air was gone, and all he could do was to wish all their friends "good-by."

A short time ago he was in Fond du Lac right at the moment that the Chamber of Commerce was holding its annual convention. Mr. Levitan asked the Madison secretary if he might say a few words to the delegates. He was finally granted the permission, but only on the condition that he would not tell the delegates that he was a candidate for re-election to the state treasurer's office. The first words that Mr. Levitan spoke to the assembled Chamber of Commerce Secretaries were, "Gentlemen, your very kind Mr. ———— has made me promise that I will not tell you that I am a candidate for re-election to the state treasurer's office, and I won't." He then gave a non-political address.

One-time he said, "My publicity costs me a lot of money. I was surprised there are so many countries. There must be two hundred. I sent out a picture of me conducting a service at Yom Kippur to the Jewish organizations in all foreign countries. I sent the Wisconsin Treasury report to the finance minister in all countries."

Later, in 1932, after he had previously been elected five times in succession to the office of state treasurer, he neglected one detail in the attention-getting game of publicity, which might have caused, or at least contributed to, his defeat in that year. "I saved $1,000 in 1932 in not sending letters to people for signing my nomination papers. In the past I had always sent these letters. But I was already feeling the depression in 1932 and I tried to save some money. This was a big mistake. When you are in a fight, money should be the least part."

Here is another example showing Mr. Levitan's ability to get publicity. One time after he spoke to my class he immediately returned to the state Capitol. I had a class the next hour, but when I returned to my office I found a secretary's memorandum on my desk to the effect that I should call the state treasurer on the telephone. When I spoke to him over the telephone, he said, "See, I bring glory to you too. Look on the front page of the *Chicago Tribune*." And there it was—Hon. Solomon Levitan, State Treasurer of Wisconsin, delivers address on government to the students in Professor J. T. Salter's class at the University—save that the brief condensed paragraph that followed was no more descriptive of Sol's talk than night is like day; it was merely a statement that a secretary had prepared for the press. Later, I found by actual count that twenty-seven newspapers in Wisconsin mentioned the fact that the State Treasurer had spoken at the University.

Last March Mr. Levitan spoke to my class and following his talk I sent him a three-page letter containing excerpts from student papers on him. He turned the letter over to Betty Cass, our local Heywood Broun, and she published the letter in three columns, after editorially stating, ". . . judging from the impression he made on the class, he can be state treasurer five times more if he'll just wait until the present crop of university students are voters." Mr. Levitan bought twenty-five copies of the state journal containing his article. He sent one to Governor Lehman, one to Brisbane, one to the A.P. and the others to Jewish newspapers. In November, after the election of 1936, I again asked Mr. Levitan to speak to my students. He replied, "I have just been over to talk to Bob La Follette. Had a heart-to-heart talk with him. Now I'll let you know about the students. I got to see Nathenson [his campaign manager] first. Got to see him about the release. You know—the press." Nothing is left to chance. Hope is eternal in the politician's breast.

Informed people hold different opinions about the value to the public of Roosevelt as president or Sol Levitan as state treasurer of Wisconsin, but each man has demonstrated to the world his uncanny ability as a candidate. If a politician is one who is a vote-getter, these two men rank high in the galaxy of politicians who know the ropes. (Sol, however, does not like the name "politician"; he says that all politicians are fakirs.) In the spring of

1936, after five elections, followed by one defeat, to the treasurer's office, when he was practically in retirement as a pensioner holding a minor position under a New Deal agency, at an age (his age is a debatable question in a campaign year) when one is apt to be in his grave or in seclusion, and a member of the Jewish race with scarcely any capital, a friend came to him with secret news. This friend had heard the Progressive leaders discuss a slate for the coming primary. It was the leaders' opinion, said the friend, that if Sol were a candidate, "no one can beat him." Mr. Levitan said, "I am a candidate. I do not like to disagree with the Progressive leaders." Other people said that he did not have a Chinaman's chance, but they did not know. Sol began talking to the people, and told some friends of the press that he wanted to see his name in print each morning along with his grapefruit at breakfast.

As state treasurer Mr. Levitan compares favorably with the majority of other Wisconsin treasurers since the turn of the century. He knows money. He told me that he had accumulated $500,000 before the crash. In an off moment he expressed the opinion that he has the shrewdness of an animal that lives close to the ground. The characterization is apt. He is best in handling the state's moneys, and less effective in directing such specialized agencies as the Beverage and Gasoline Tax inspectorships that were for a time assigned to the treasurer's office. He is inclined to listen to the great ones in the Progressive party in matters that require unusual decisions. This brought him to grief in the Capitol City Bank case of 1931. However, the people have faith in Sol's integrity; and as for his ability, they point to his position as a banker and owner of two department stores before he was ever state treasurer. He tells them that he can count their money in the dark and never lose a nickel, and they believe it.

He is unique in his outgoing friendliness to an anonymous public. When he first took office, he placed a large sign over the treasurer's door, saying, "Uncle Sol welcomes you." The building superintendent said it made the capitol look like a Jewish fire sale, and removed the sign. A few days later Sol and the building superintendent and other officials were guests of the legislature. Mr. Levitan was called upon to speak. He began, "When I took office I wanted the people to come and see me, to feel at home. I put a big sign of welcome over my door. Somebody took it down. Who took it down? He [pointing to the superintendent who was seated before him, in the first row] took it down. I didn't vote for him or he didn't vote for me, but he took it down." The legislature sustained Mr. Levitan. He did not use the sign again, but his friendliness remains.

VI

Kindliness may, or may not, be next to godliness, but in either case it is part of the bone and sinew of Sol. And it is a big part, for he is a genuinely kindly man. He has that goodness of heart that one is pleased to discover in one's friends. He has an awareness of other people as people, a sympathetic interest in them and their needs. He has lived a life that has made him sensitive to the suffering of others. He says a smile goes a long way even today. His rise, from what seems to some of us at a point somewhere below zero and in spite of handicaps that would have buried a lesser man, is incontrovertible proof that a smile—a kindly spirit—is appreciated in the world today. He knows too that a smile is the same in all languages and among all classes. He is a concrete example of one who brightens the corner where he is. He brings cheer to the person that he meets.

To those who might say that Sol gives a smile for a sale—for a vote—I agree, but I must add that there is more to his warm fellowship than the idea of a commercial or political transaction. His spirit *is* the man, and if his natural feeling for his fellows were different, he would die of nervous exhaustion in so persistently maintaining an attitude foreign to his nature.

He believes in sweet reasonableness rather than in force as a way of gaining his objective.[3] The fact that this method pays dividends does not detract from its charm and effectiveness as a method. One time in the early pack-peddling days, Sol invested $75 in a horse and wagon. It seemed like a good bargain, until he tried to drive the horse. But, at the most inopportune times or in the midst of a long march, the horse would stop; he was balky. Now Sol might

---

[3] But Sol also knows the value of force. He says, "If the other fellow treats me as a gentleman, I treat him as a gentleman, but if he is a Jesse James, I get the first shot."

have cursed his luck, but instead he bought a bag of corn, and when the horse stopped, he would get a nibble of corn, a gentle pat on the nose. Soon the horse would be going at a better clip than he had gone at first.

In his 1936 campaign he said, "I have never discharged anyone, and I paid good salaries. . . . The best investment we can do is to pay people best salaries when they work for you. You see, you can't make a bird sing for you unless you feed him well. . . . In all my life I have never foreclosed a mortgage; I have never sued a person in my life, and I have never refused a person, man or woman, a sack of flour whether they have money or not. . . . My dear people, sometimes it pays to cast your bread on the waters. It comes back—sometimes. I have always been for the Labor Union. I put up a building. A contractor offered to do the job for $7,500, but he was not fair to labor. So the secretary for the Union came to me and I was mighty glad to have the nerve to lose $7,500 and make the laborers happy. They come back to me when I run for state treasurer."

One might end this fragment of a biography with the statement —the Life of Sol Levitan or the Golden Rule that Pays. But it has not been a bed of roses for the man who made good in the land of opportunity. Man's unkindness to man has troubled him more than he has ever publicly indicated. At times he has felt that he was "sorrow's bone." He approached a group at a county seat this year who were holding a picnic. He chatted with one of them. "And this fellow told me that Hitler was a great man." Mr. Levitan told Father Bloodgood when the two were in my office "Reverend, people are not as kind as you think they are. You will have to give double-barrelled sermons on kindness." But to "the people" Sol is always the merry old gentleman who says something funny and cheerful.

This blithe spirit saved him or his driver from arrest last June. He was driving through Beaver Dam, and his campaign manager who was driving the car accidentally drove through an arterial. A cop came up to them and ordered them to pull up to the side of the road. Nathenson, the campaign manager, said to Sol that he thought they were in for it. When the officer approached the car, Sol smiled, held out his hand, and before the officer could say anything, he exclaimed, "Hello, officer, do you want to circulate my nominating petitions?" The officer was surprised, but on taking a second look said, "Why, you are Sol Levitan, aren't you? Yes, I will get a petition filled out for you." And he did.

16

SICKLER OF SALEM COUNTY: A STUDY OF RURAL POLITICS

By Robert C. Brooks

TIME: 3:00 A. M., WEDNESDAY, NOVEMBER 4, 1936. PLACE: DEMO-cratic Headquarters, Salem, New Jersey. At his desk after a strenuous twenty-hour day, County Chairman Joseph Sickler—very tired, also very happy. Tables, chairs, and floor littered with poll books, telegrams, newspapers, hastily scribbled tabulations of election returns. Inevitable odor of stale tobacco smoke left by precinct leaders and other local politicos who have just gone home over-joyed at the tremendous sweep of the Democratic landslide. Out-side belated roisterers are still whooping it up for Roosevelt and Garner. Republican Headquarters has been dark and deserted for hours.

To Joseph Sickler, naturally enough, the returns from Salem County meant more than the figures from all the rest of the state or even from the country as a whole. So far as the electoral college was concerned, while not confident to the same extreme as his generalissimo, the Honorable James Aloysius Farley, still he had never felt the slightest doubt. However, his deep concern in the local result was not due solely to his official responsibility as county chairman. As a matter of fact, Salem County had been rockribbed in its Republicanism for so long a time that even if it had given a majority to Landon on the day before few would have found that fact worth comment. Nor, considering the tidal wave that had swept Roosevelt to victory, was there anything remarkable in the actual Democratic majority of nearly four thousand. Viewed in the cold perspective of election statistics, all such upsets, whether on a small or a large scale, seem impersonal. For all his Quaker mod-esty, however, it would have been impossible for Chairman Sickler to regard the Salem County result wholly in that way. To him the Democratic majority thus achieved after so much striving must have appeared as due, in some small part at least, to studies which he had begun in college more than twenty years before, to the nine years of hard bread-winning work which he had been obliged to put in after graduation until he was able to secure his first foot-hold in local politics, and finally to the expenditure of every ounce of energy he possessed during his three years as county chairman.

Undoubtedly also Salem County represented a highly specialized case to Joseph Sickler. It was not just any county to him; it was *his* county, the county in which he was born, to which he had always returned whenever circumstances permitted, and where he expected to live and work permanently—in short his *home* county. For his fellow Salemites, of whom he knows personally a large proportion, he has great admiration on the whole; however, he regards most of them as having gone astray in the matter of their proper party allegiance. Several years earlier Sickler had made up his mind to set them right, nor has he ever regarded it as "cursèd spite" that this apparently hopeless task was assigned to him as Democratic county chairman. If he had cared only for office and quick promotion he would have gone over—as so many ambitious youngsters of his own age had done—to the ever-victorious G. O. P. As a matter of fact, he received several flattering invitations, one accompanied by an offer to nominate him for the Assembly, from local Republican leaders who wished him to transfer his allegiance to their organization. Instead, he dug himself in as a member of the Democratic minority, studied the situation as thoroughly as he could both while at home and at a distance, and was prepared to fight it out on this line indefinitely. Certainly no one knew better than Joseph Sickler why Salem County had remained so firmly fixed in the Republican column. Once having learned this primary les-son, he had to overcome many difficulties before he was able to appeal effectively to its electorate, largely rural as it was in char-acter. Nor was it an easy job for him, essential as he knew it to be, to win over the Negro strongholds which had contributed so heavily to Republican success ever since the Civil War.

While not a special case, from an outside point of view, still Salem County possesses certain distinctive characteristics. Organized as early as 1675, it now has a population of 37,000—or as Sickler usually states it, of 20,000 voters. Some 4,000 of the latter are Negroes who have been long settled in this section of southwestern New Jersey. In a sense it may be classified as southern, for if the Mason and Dixon line were projected eastward it would cut through the northernmost part of Salem County. Hence the large colored element. On the other hand, the population of foreign origin makes up a very small percentage of the total. There are about 500 Italian-American voters, Democrats all, in the Pennsgrove district bordering on the Delaware River. Here the Du Pont industrial empire, operating from its smokestack-studded capital immediately opposite in Wilmington, Delaware, has carved out a sizeable enclave for the production of dyes and high explosives within the confines of Salem County. In Pittsgrove Township there are some 400 Russian-Jewish voters, all successfully engaged in farming, as a result of the wise benevolence of the Baron de Hirsch Fund. The first emigrants of this group were brought to the county in 1881; at present they are so thoroughly naturalized as scarcely to be considered foreigners. In any event, they have lost touch completely with Russia. Politically there is not a Communist among them; having been cultivated by local Democrats ever since their arrival they are now members of that party to a man. In addition, there are a few scattered German families, mostly farmers; also a small number of Lithuanian and Polish industrial workers. Of course the Swedes of Salem County long since ceased to be considered foreign; indeed, as first settlers, now making elaborate preparations for the celebration of their three-hundredth anniversary, the Dolbows, Rambos, Vannemans, Sinnicksons, and many other families of that ilk are not without a certain aristocratic pride.

The county boasts a county seat of the same name which reflects credit upon it in every way. Indeed Salem is as lovely an old town as the wayfarer may hope to find anywhere in New Jersey. Its central streets, broad and shaded by ancient elms, are flanked by stately mansions of red brick, all with shutters, columns, and porticoes immaculately white. Here colonial history still lives in dignity; here revolutionary history has settled down amid long unbroken peace. Only toward the outskirts of Salem town is one brought back to modernity by newer frame houses built in the atrocious style characteristic of adjacent shore resorts.

Apart from the giant Pennsgrove plant of the Du Ponts, a large glass factory, and two or three other smaller industrial enterprises in the county seat, Salem County is predominantly agricultural. Its farmers are famous for their bumper crops of potatoes and tomatoes. Also the population, with the exception of the colored and foreign elements noted above, is overwhelmingly of English origin. Very old English be it noted; the first settlers of this stock, founders of the principal families, far antedate the Revolution. Among them the Quaker element is very strong; there are meeting houses not only at the county seat but also at Hancock's Bridge and Woodstown. Bearing the above facts, economic and demographic, in mind it is not hard to understand why Salem County has been noted until quite recently for its rockribbed conservatism.

Indeed, with such a background, the possibility of a sudden and complete political turnover seemed hopeless down to the latter half of the ill-fated Hoover regime. Consequently it was with a distinct shock of surprise that Jerseymen generally learned of the election to the State Assembly in November, 1931, of Joseph Sheppard Sickler. Two years later Sickler became Democratic county chairman, working so effectively at that job during the last three elections that he has not lost a single contest. At present his party has placed in office ten out of the fourteen county commissioners and all but two of the other officeholders of the county. These two remaining Republicans, by the way, are the clerk and the surrogate of the County Court, recognized generally as old and faithful public servants, and the Democratic organization has made no fight against them.

Before entering upon the usual biographical data regarding Mr. Sickler—family, birth, education, and the like—the present writer is under obligation, not at all unwillingly, however, to state for him that he desires no special credit above others for what has been accomplished by the Democratic organization in Salem County. On the contrary, he looks upon it as essentially the group achievement of a number of younger men, faithfully aided by the old wheelhorses of the party. He feels himself most deeply indebted both for advice and valiant assistance at every turn to another young leader, Mr. Orvyl Schalick, a former classmate of his at the University of Pennsylvania, to whom, more than to any other single person, he ascribes the success of the party in the county. Mr. Schalick is now a member of the Democratic State Committee of New Jersey and as such continues to watch over and aid in local affairs with unabated interest. Few writers on politics have failed to note the importance ascribed by active partisans to the virtue of personal loyalty, the "the dear love of friends" as Professor G. E. G. Catlin finely phrases it. Certainly there is more of this sentiment among politicians than among members of the average church, club, business association, or college faculty. No one can talk even casually to Joseph Sickler without becoming aware of the fact that he possesses this virtue to a marked degree.

Joseph Sickler was born in Salem, December 1, 1897, his parents on both sides being of old English stock. The house in which his father still resides was built about 1843 on ground that had been in possession of the family since 1815, and has never been occupied by anyone but Sicklers. On the paternal side the family had been active in Democratic affairs since the days of his great grandfather, Adam Sickler. Throughout his long life—he lived to be ninety-three—this worthy ran for office, beginning in 1810, at least forty times, a record that probably would have been impossible were it not for the fact that the usual term for elective positions then was a year only. Adam ran for assessor, dog-catcher, councilman, highway director, justice of the peace—it did not seem to matter which or how often. Sometimes he lost; usually he won, for prior to the outbreak of the Civil War the Democratic party was in the ascendant throughout the county. During his whole career of intermittent officeholding the patriarch carried on the active work of his farm, being celebrated locally for the enormous size of the tomatoes he raised. His son, Zacheus, grandfather of Joseph, was also active politically although he did not run for office so often as Adam had done. Nor so successfully, for toward the end of the career of Zacheus the War between the States brought with it disastrous consequences to Jersey Democratic candidates. To the credit of the stalwart old gentleman it must be said that he was an ideal "ticket-filler," accepting hopeless nominations

JOSEPH SICKLER

"In ancestry, historical interest, religious affiliation,
most of all in close association with people of all walks
of life, he is Salem personified."

gladly and always putting up a stiff fight. Never did he make any concealment of his Confederate sympathies, accepting with complete equanimity the resultant heavy political losses and the outspoken condemnation of many relatives and friends. Joseph's father, William, was also a Democrat and deeply interested in politics, but with the exception of one unsuccessful candidacy for the Salem City Council never ran for office.

On the side of his mother, Ruth Evans Sheppard of Cumberland County, New Jersey, the subject of this sketch was connected also with the Bradway and Fithian families, renowned throughout the state for their ardent black Republicanism. To them the only good Democrat was a dead Democrat, nor did they hesitate to say so openly. Naturally there was much high and heated argument when the two clans got together, but in the end the Quaker counsels of the mother prevailed. Even today at family gatherings of the Sicklers and Sheppards it is tacitly understood that the subject of politics is not to be discussed.

Naturally in such an environment the boy Joseph absorbed political information—and misinformation—both in large quantities, from his earliest years. He is inclined to date his first conscious identification of himself with the Democratic party from the time he overheard his father—this must have been about 1902—declaiming upon the unspeakable injustice committed in 1876 when the Republicans stole the presidency from Samuel J. Tilden. A few years after the turn of the century Joseph began attending political meetings in Salem, listening to the speakers with rapt attention whether or not he understood what they said. In 1910 at the age of thirteen an event occurred which made a deep impression upon him, fixing in his mind the determination to enter politics if an occasion to do so ever offered itself. Among the speakers scheduled to appear at a local Democratic rally was one, Woodrow Wilson, then nothing more than the "Schoolmaster of Princeton." Joseph's father took the boy to Democratic headquarters and there introduced him to the visiting orator. In paternal fashion Wilson patted Joseph on the head and gave utterance to the hope that he would grow up to be a good Democrat. Altogether banal as the incident was, young Sickler formed the impression on the spot that he had met a very great man. Or *thinks* he formed the impression on the spot; as a matter of fact, the initial good impression was probably fortified by his idol's quick ascension to the governorship of the state and then to the presidency. However this may be, the incident had the ultimate effect of setting him to study Wilson's public activities intensively, with results that have been most helpful throughout his own later career.

Joseph received his preliminary educational training at the Salem Friends School and the Salem High School. Destined by the Quaker connections of his mother for Swarthmore College, he was obliged by the low state of the family's finances at the time to work his way through that institution. Even in the summers he took such jobs as he could find, no matter how hard, dirty, or even dangerous they might be. During one vacation, for example, he shoveled gun-cotton at the Du Pont plant in Pennsgrove. The experience gained at this somewhat hazardous occupation was to prove of value later when he canvassed for votes among the industrial workers of that section of Salem County. Financially handicapped as he was, Sickler made a generally creditable record in college, his marks in political science and in public speaking being excellent as a rule. From Swarthmore he received the degree of A.B. in 1920, subsequently spending two semesters in the law school of the University of Pennsylvania and the same amount of time doing postgraduate work in pedagogy at his alma mater. Still under the necessity of maintaining himself wholly by his own earnings and certainly being in no position to make a start at a political career, he was evidently at cross purposes during this period. So far as law was concerned, he loathed it as dull and tedious in the extreme; obviously he would never have undertaken to study it except for the hope that it might prove to be a stepping-stone to politics. Later he tried to read law while working for the Pullman Company, but again his heart was not in it and his hours on duty were long. Several times he took the state bar examinations, each time without success. Thereupon a rule was handed down by the Supreme Court of New Jersey providing that any one who had failed to pass such examinations three times should be debarred thereafter from taking them. The next year—although this is anticipating our story somewhat—Joseph Sickler was elected to the Assembly, thus becoming a lawmaker of the sovereign state which, ironically enough, had barred the way to his qualifying for the practice of that profession within its confines! In spite of his failure to break into the ranks of the lawyers, Sickler did manage to acquire a considerable assortment of knowledge on legal subjects which has been of material benefit to him in his political life.

Reviewing his educational career as a whole Sickler attaches greatest importance to the training received at Swarthmore. As a major in political science he found that subject entirely to his liking; moreover the injunction often repeated to students by the head of the department, namely that they should go into active politics, coincided fully with his own inclinations. Also from the professor who taught public speaking he received training and encouragement which have proved most valuable in all his subsequent campaigns.

Ever since his own undergraduate days Sickler has found himself growing more and more confirmed in the conviction that it is the duty of college men to go into politics whenever possible. Nothing delights him more than to return to his alma mater from time to time to advocate this conviction. He notes that in the whole vast organization of the Democratic party of New Jersey there are at present not more than half a dozen committeemen who graduated from college with the major in political science. And he believes most firmly that a large proportion of men so trained would add enormously to the intelligence, efficiency, and honesty of our party machinery. In his own experience he has found that a knowledge of political science is most useful in giving a background of pertinent facts and theories, plus the ability to think clearly on the problems that come up from day to day. At the same time he concedes that college men have some things to forget when they enter upon a practical political career. Especially in rural sections one must NOT be highbrow. "If you talk about Machiavelli or Hobbes or Montesquieu the people will think you are 'nuts'—and you are if you try to do so." Along this line he recounts, with a wry grimace, one incident of his first legislative campaign when he had been sent out to speak to the farmers of the district. With his insufficient knowledge of agriculture he did the best he could, only to learn that an irate bucolic constituent had called up the County Chairman on the telephone, saying: "Keep that damned college boy home; he don't know nothing about cows." Thereafter, perforce, Sickler became an assiduous student of the bovine species. Not without success, either, for at present he is one of the most highly regarded of political orators on the local rural circuit.

Sickler was a freshman in Swarthmore College when the United States entered the World War. For a time he continued his studies but in May, 1918, made an attempt to enlist in the Navy only to be rejected because of a highly astigmatic eye condition. After the passage of the second enrollment act which applied to all male citizens from eighteen to forty-five years of age, he appeared before the Draft Board in Salem and waived the exemption which as a Quaker he could legally have claimed. Meanwhile he had transferred to the University of Pennsylvania, where he managed to get himself accepted by the Students Army Training Corps exactly one month before the armistice.

Following his college career, Sickler spent nine years working for purely bread-and-butter reasons with the Pullman Company as conductor and clerk, being promoted finally to the position of Platform man in Philadelphia. Long as was this enforced term of service outside his chosen field, he managed to learn certain useful lessons from it that have stood him in good stead since he became county chairman. Thus he became adept at soothing the multifarious grouches developed by members of the great American traveling public, which apparently are not unlike the grouches common among the voters in any political district. Also he learned something about patronage by serving unofficially as an employment agent for the Pullman Company, incidentally finding summer jobs for large numbers of college friends. Indeed, as the writer can testify, it was impossible at that time to take a sleeper or chair car on any train leaving Philadelphia without being waited upon courteously by a Swarthmore undergraduate, temporarily refulgent in blue uniform and brass buttons.

At the end of this period of service with the Pullman Company, Sickler secured a position as teacher of history at the Boys' Latin School in Baltimore. Always, however, he had maintained his voting residence in Salem, intending to return there at the first opportunity. His chance came in 1930 when he was offered a position on the local party newspaper which rejoices in the artless appellation of *The Salem Sunbeam*. Let city slickers laugh if they will; *The Sunbeam* shines brightly, always with a strictly Democratic light, each week illumining the broad fields of Salem County with ten pages devoted to town and rural affairs and to pithy comment thereupon, interspersed, particularly during campaigns, with hot political editorials shrewdly adapted to meet local conditions. As such it is a force to be reckoned with politically, probably influencing its readers much more potently in proportion to circulation than many metropolitan journals. In accordance with the sacred American principle of check and balance, a rival Republican weekly, *The Standard and Jerseyman*, see to it that Democrats generally, and particularly those of Salem County, and most particularly Mr. Joseph Sickler, are properly "viewed with alarm."

On *The Sunbeam* Sickler's duties were to gather news notes, hustle for the all-important ads, write occasional editorials, set type at rush periods, and then to spend his spare time, if any, in concocting special feature articles. Certainly in breadth his journalistic apprenticeship far exceeded anything that the cub on a large city paper ever finds thrown his way. Already deeply interested in county history—it would be impossible to live in Salem without developing that trait—Sickler devoted himself to an intensive study of the old houses of the town and vicinity. With their glazed brick scroll work in intricate designs, and exhibiting the date and initials of their builders in bold characters, many of these ancient homesteads are as picturesque as they are famous in local annals. Out of these studies grew a series of illustrated feature articles which were later collected and published as a fifty-six-page booklet under the title: *The Old Houses of Salem*. Subsequently Sickler contributed to *The Sunbeam* an extended series on the history of Salem County, which is also to make its appearance as a volume in the near future. He also confesses to having written "a bum novel," as yet unpublished. Undertaken originally in a purely antiquarian spirit the studies published in *The Sunbeam* proved somewhat helpful politically in that they have made the name of the author a household word throughout a county, many of the inhabitants of which are deeply interested in the doings of their forebears. It is useful also in that whenever he makes a speech locally he is able to refer familiarly to past events and illustrious family names. Finally this special interest on Sickler's part secures him invitations to address historical societies and even Rotary Clubs, the members of which are seldom numbered among his political supporters.

Active entrance into politics as a candidate came fortuitously, perhaps as a jest, in April, 1931. Visiting the office of Mr. Schalick, then state committeeman, in his capacity as a reporter, Sickler was greeted one fine morning with the question: "Joe, where can I get a sucker to run for the Assembly?" "How about it if I run?" flippantly replied the newspaperman. "Done," said the Committeeman, entering the name of Joseph S. Sickler on a blank nomination form. "Hold on, what are you doing there?" interjected the candidate-in-spite-of-himself; "I was only kidding you." "It's too late now," was the calm reply; "you're it, and thank you."

Thus told it is a good enough story. Undoubtedly it does throw some light upon the processes by which candidates were selected for apparently hopeless contests in South Jersey—and elsewhere— at that time. One need not insist too much upon the jocular element involved; Sickler himself wrote later that some slight portion of the inspired must have perched upon his shoulder as he coyly consented to run. After all, he had been considering such a step for years. Moreover Sickler well knew that he also serves who merely stands and waits as a "ticket-filler." Apparently he did not bother himself with securing the needed one hundred signatures to his nominating petition. Willing party workers are always at hand to look after such petty details, which, nevertheless, are insisted upon by direct primary laws. As a matter of fact, he did not undertake to make a canvass until shortly before the final election. For in spite of the excellent work accomplished by Committeeman Schalick in building up an organization within Salem County, the likelihood of Sickler's success, short of a minor miracle, did not enter the fondest dreams of local Democratic party workers.

Well, something very like a minor miracle did happen. Only a little over a month before election day, at that! On October 10, Sickler's opponent, then the Republican assemblyman, voted "wet" on a resolution urging Congress to permit the sale of beer. Now Salem County—rural, American, church-going Salem County—is "dry," overwhelmingly "D-R-Y." Here, of course, was the political opportunity of a lifetime. With Schalick at his elbow Sickler proceeded to exemplify the adage about making hay while the sun shines. Forthwith he sent out to every voter in the county a brief pungent letter accusing the sitting Assemblyman of taking orders from Boss David Baird when he voted "wet." "I am pledging myself," continued Candidate Sickler, "that if elected, I will vote for the retention of the Hobart Act, the upholding of the XVIIIth Amendment and all existing dry legislation. . . . I also pledge myself to make every effort within my power to stop the waste of public money and to relieve the burdens of the taxpayer. This is the people's fight and I earnestly ask your support in behalf of the above-stated platform planks."

In making this appeal Sickler did not attempt to conceal the fact that he was anything but a "dry" in sentiment. Or in his personal conduct for that matter; he does take a drink on rare occasions when he happens to feel the need for one. The case was simply this: knowing the county to be opposed to the return of liquor he proposed to represent it as such, regardless of his own opinion on the subject. He left himself free to advocate liberal policies at a later date; as a matter of fact, he has done so. But until the expiration of his mandate he pledged himself absolutely to act in the "dry" interest. The decision to do so was made quite voluntarily; strange as it may seem, there was no interposition on the part of the Anti-Saloon League or of any other pressure group of that character.

Unquestionably the letter sent out by Sickler to all voters was the main agent in overcoming the strong Republican sentiment then prevalent in Salem County. However, he followed it up with a vigorous round of speeches and by a prolonged tour of "door-bell-ringing"—the local vernacular for a house-to-house canvass. No doubt the old-time Republican "drys" found themselves in a ticklish position. They hated the thought of voting for a Democrat, any Democrat, like poison. Moreover they harbored sundry dark misgivings about this precise Democrat's personal views and personal habits. On the other hand—and this helped materially—he was a Quaker and "a Quaker's word is as good as his bond," a popular aphorism which Joseph Sickler has lived up to scrupu-

lously all the days of his life. Finally there could be no doubt in
the minds of candid "drys" that they had been scandalously betrayed at Trenton by the vote of the Republican assemblyman on
the beer bill, especially since he had pledged himself to their cause
when a candidate for that office. In the end enough "drys" overcame their anti-Democratic phobias to elect Joseph Sickler to the
New Jersey State Assembly by a safe margin of 640 votes in a total
of nearly 13,000. Thus it was that Salem County sent a Democratic
Representative to Trenton for the first time in eighteen years.

At the State Capitol Sickler kept his word faithfully. With
monotonous regularity he voted "yes" on every "dry" bill and
"no" on every "wet" bill. As news of each of these exemplary
deeds was blazoned forth to the local world in the columns of *The
Salem Sunbeam*, good church members throughout the county
sighed with unctuous satisfaction, reflecting that after all there
was at least one politician who was honest. Believe it or not, while
all this was going on Mayor Frank Hague of Jersey City, Democratic boss of the state, maintained an absolutely correct attitude.
Probably he was too delighted at having a Democratic member
from Salem County to care to interfere; in any event he is understood to have enjoined a strictly hands-off policy so far as Sickler's
"dry" votes were concerned. If so, he was obeyed scrupulously;
the young member from Salem County was never "sweated" in
caucus with regard to his attitude on measures of this character.
Toward the end of the term, however, an issue came up which
caused him much searching of conscience. It took the form of a
proposal to submit the Hobart Act, i.e., the dry-enforcement law
of the state, to a referendum vote of the people of New Jersey. As
a convinced democrat—this time with a small "d"—Sickler could
not withhold his approval; moreover he knew that the proposal
was overwhelmingly popular. In the end, however, he reached the
conclusion that since the "drys" regarded it with hostility, since
moreover he had pledged himself specifically to act in their favor
on this measure, he was obligated to vote against it. With the
result that when the vote was announced in the Assembly it stood
57 to 1, Sickler of Salem County being the only member recorded
in opposition. By way of postscript it may be added that when the

Hobart Act was submitted to the people on November 8, 1932, it was snowed under by 1,012,526 to 223,865.

While his votes on wet-dry measures attracted the largest share of attention outside, Sickler's real interest as an assemblyman centered in run-of-the-mine measures of greater workaday importance. He was a member of two committees—the Steering Committee, and the Agricultural Committee; and chairman of two others—the House Joint Committee on the Bordentown Industrial School (colored), and the Fish and Game Committee. It was to the last named, a committee of considerable importance in a state so beloved by the followers of Nimrod and of Izaak Walton as is New Jersey, that he gave most of his time. He fought consistently for the poor trappers and fishermen of South Jersey as against the wealthy owners of exclusive private preserves, many of which run into thousands of acres. Although successful in securing the passage by the Assembly of his own bill, which provided for a substantial reduction in gunning and license fees, it was killed by the Republican Senate. Sickler took an active part also in the discussion of several bills, including one dealing with railroad consolidation which was of considerable importance. This particular part of his legislative experience he found easy and pleasant, as indeed it should have been considering his training in public speaking at Swarthmore and later. In connection with a bill affecting the shoe manufacturers he was offered his first—and only—bribe. The lobbyist concerned, now by the way a fugitive from justice for ballot-box stuffing, suggested that if the young member "voted right" on the measure he would "find something in his overcoat." Feeling somewhat nauseated Sickler promptly and forcibly requested the gentleman to get out and not to talk to him further about any subject, including the weather.

With this creditable record of legislative service behind him it is somewhat painful to record that Sickler was defeated when he came up for re-election in 1932. He made a strenuous fight, however, losing by only 222 votes out of a total of nearly sixteen thousand, and had the satisfaction of polling one thousand more votes in defeat than he had received in his victorious contest of the year before. Certainly no other Democrat could have overcome the heavy handicap of a presidential year in a county which had lined up in the G. O. P. column so long as Salem. Incidentally it was the last time the Republicans were to have the undivided support of their large block of Negro voters. For immediately after being freed from legislative duties Sickler went to work as a missionary among them, seeking their conversion to the true faith of Democracy.

Politics is at best a precarious calling. It would be even more so, perhaps to a degree making it prohibitive to all except men of independent means, were it not for the practice, common to both parties, of taking care of defeated candidates so far as possible. In June, 1933, Sickler was appointed postmaster of Salem, being one of the first one hundred and fifty such appointees by the new administration in Washington. Naturally there has been criticism because he retains possession of the county chairmanship, although of course the latter, as a purely party office, pays no salary. Technically he ranks as a second-class, presidential, non-assembled postmaster, which leaves him some leeway to continue party activities. As a matter of fact, the Salem Post Office has been filled by political appointees ever since it was established in 1794.

Shortly after taking over his new duties Sickler, who is a glutton for work, was asked to accept a non-salaried position in the local administration of the NRA. To this and to similar positions with the WPA, the CWA, and the ERA to which he was subsequently appointed, he has devoted almost all his leisure time. Party advantage counts for little with him in these relationships; he has simply undertaken four heavy additional tasks because he considers them not only necessary under present circumstances but also profoundly helpful to the poorer citizens of Salem County. He would not be a proper politician did he not take particular pride in the fact that through them he has been able to secure jobs for some four hundred persons. Still there is a good deal of humanitarian feeling as well in the way he regards this achievement. In filling jobs he acted wholly without regard to the party affiliations of applicants; indeed some for whom he found places had opposed him vigorously during his two candidacies for the Assembly, including a few who had been personally ugly about it.

Sickler is five feet, eight inches in height, and weighs 155 pounds. Not in any sense an athlete, still he leads a fairly active life. He is quick on his feet, and easy of manner, and he has learned in the hard school of experience to restrain a certain tendency toward emotionalism which was characteristic of his younger years. There is a slight cast in one eye which gives him a rather quizzical look. The alleged deleterious effects of practical politics have not sufficed as yet to deprive him of the appearance of an old-time Quaker; indeed, with a little more attention to his garb he could sit upon the "Facing Benches" in any Meeting House and look the part perfectly. His mother was given to saying: "Joseph, thee is a good-looking boy—when thee is dressed up." Questioned regarding his apparent carelessness about the clothes he wears, he refers this trait to a certain native slothfulness, also to a desire not to appear to be too well dressed. It would seem that there are limits in matters sartorial which a rural leader does well not to overstep.

Although what is known as a "good mixer" Sickler belongs to few organizations apart from the political and administrative committees which demand so large a share of his attention. In college he joined a fraternity and was elected to membership in an honorary public speaking society. He is a member of the American Legion but not active in its affairs. The only enthusiasm—mild at that—which he displayed when questioned along this line was for the Railway Fans of America. Membership in this organization costs only a dollar a year, its main purpose being to arrange cheap excursions to out-of-the-way historic spots. Sickler's lack of interest in such matters as secret societies differentiates him from the ruck of rural politicians who are "joiners" if they are nothing else. As he himself remarked: "Many sheriffs and county chairmen are members of every lodge in their bailiwicks. Long regarded as a shrewd way to political success, I believe that nowadays this sort of thing is grossly overdone. Really it belongs in the limbo of old and forgotten things."

Apart from speeches and direct personal appeals Sickler placed chief reliance in his two campaigns for elective office upon letters sent out to constituents. He had no financial resources of his own, and his expenses, the only large item being a printing bill of $500 in 1931, were met out of the funds of the local Democratic organization. In both cases the totals were well within the limit of

five cents per vote fixed by the New Jersey Corrupt Practices Act
of 1911. Sickler also used handbills to a slight extent while a candidate; he regards them as of some stray advertising value but much
less effective than letters carefully drafted with the psychology of
the voter as a target. He attaches great importance to direct personal appeal which must be neither too effusive nor too cool. In
his opinion "an unemotional politician is as interesting to his public as a last year's newspaper. . . . You must convince the electorate
that there is some heart in you. If you are too cold and unemotional you lose color and if you lose color you are on your way out.
Here is one of the open secrets of political appeal: a sincere pat on
the back, a smile, a wave of the hand or friendly recognition on
the street will do more for you than a thousand speeches or thousands in money." Further he maintains that a candidate must be
assertive although that also is a trait that may be carried too far.
"My habit has been to tell the truth, in a kindly way if possible,
if not, to tell it anyhow. There is another 'don't' as old as any copy-
book maxim. Never lie. That also is a rapid down-grade for the
politician. In fact it is the quickest I know. Once a subordinate lies
his usefulness is forever destroyed, and this is a thousand times
truer in politics than in business."

No matter what his earlier shortcomings may have been, Sickler
has developed into a highly effective campaign orator. He possesses
a pleasant tenor voice, more than strong enough for any Salem
County auditorium and for open air speaking. During the presidential campaign of 1936 he enjoyed a telling advantage over
many of the political orators in the field because he knew the principal alphabetical agencies of the Federal government not only
from reading books and newspapers about them but also, and to a
far greater extent, from actual experience in their administration.
Admittedly he resorts to "demagogy," that is, to picturesque or
sensational appeal, when it seems likely to be useful with the particular audience concerned. Thus in the Roosevelt-Landon campaign he often began with the remark: "Sunflowers bloom in July
but they are dead in November." As already noted he made a
particular appeal at this time to the 4,000 Negro voters of Salem
County, an appeal which was not without its effect in detaching
the overwhelming majority of them from their long-continued

affiliation with the Republican party. At many meetings devoted to political proselyting among colored citizens Sickler was the only white man in the hall. Often the fervor he aroused found expression not only in clapping and stamping but also in soulful "Amens" and "Halleluiahs" from his auditors. His usual form of appeal followed the line, first, of glorifying the race for their ancient gratitude to Abraham Lincoln, the Great Emancipator, then carrying this sentiment over to Franklin D. Roosevelt as their Great Preserver from the myriad evils entailed upon them by the Hoover Depression. At a certain schoolhouse where Sickler addressed a colored audience there hung upon the wall three pictures, one of Abraham Lincoln, one of Booker T. Washington, and the third, which occupied the central position between the other two, of a white benefactor, a certain well-known Jersey Democratic politician and business man who need not be named in this connection. Using the three as texts the County Chairman from Salem praised each of them in turn; then lifting his discourse from the local Democratic Chieftain to the Great White Father in Washington, he crashed into the following peroration: "Take your Landons and your Lemkes, take your Hearsts and take your Knoxes, take your Reeds and your Breckenridges, take your Elys and—yes—take your Al Smiths—pile them all, end on end, pile them all a million miles high in the sky, and even then—AND EVEN THEN—you couldn't get the whole damn bunch high enough to look with level gaze into the eyes of Franklin Delano Roosevelt!"

Hooey? Yes, of course. Particularly distressing hooey to issue from sober Quaker lips, to say nothing of the "damn" included therewith. But certainly no more malicious than the outbursts of the they-hate-Roosevelt anvil chorus coming from the other side of the political fence. Still, as hooey, effective; oh, yes, very effective. For Salem County went Democratic on November 3, 1936, by 3,943, including the votes of nearly all the Negroes that had been cast solidly for Abraham Lincoln ever since the Civil War.

It has often been remarked of local politicians that they reflect their environment closely. To a considerable degree Joseph Sickler is typical in this regard. In ancestry, historical interest, religious affiliation, most of all in close association with people of all walks of life, he is Salem personified. In other respects, however, he is clearly a most unusual sort of county chairman. While performing —and that evidently with rare skill—the ordinary duties of this purely party office, namely building up the organization and getting out the vote, he devotes himself to active campaigning and particularly to public speaking with a gusto and to a degree that has few imitators among his colleagues. In addition to his fondness for oratory he even cherishes ambitions as a writer; Brand Whitlock has long been one of his heroes. Finally, it is seldom indeed that one will discover among the more than six thousand county chairmen in the United States cases of men who prepared themselves intensively for party activities by the study of political science in college.

Too busy as a party leader to devote much time to social life Sickler nevertheless enjoys it keenly at off-periods between campaigns. He even found time—one wonders how—on May 28 of this year to marry Miss Grace Mildred Plummer of Quinton, New Jersey.

As we have noted, Sickler was forced by bread-winning necessities to postpone for several years his active entry into politics. In this respect he resembles those Labor party leaders in England who, as Professor Laski has shown, seldom reach Parliament or ministerial posts until they are ten or more years older than their well-heeled Tory competitors. Nevertheless it is probable that Sickler is still much below the average age of county chairmen throughout the country. Perhaps it was not altogether a personal misfortune that the delay occurred. Certainly he had something to learn from his various earlier occupations; even more certainly he extracted everything of a political character that was worth learning from each of them. And once started in his chosen field progress has been rapid. If energy, ambition, and versatility count for anything he may go far. Meanwhile he is engaged in the performance of the job in hand, giving everything he has to making it a success. Although he is temporarily concentrated upon local details, it is evident that he has a grasp of wider affairs that can be brought to bear if opportunity beckons. Jerseymen are noted for their state patriotism, and in this respect also Sickler is thoroughly typical of his environment. What he learned in the Assembly, brief as was his term therein, may be needed at a later stage of his career. Perhaps the most significant of his recent activities is his part-time service with the federal agencies represented in Salem County. They amount to a highly practical postgraduate course for which he prepared himself originally while a student of national questions at Swarthmore College. If a call should come from Washington he could qualify easily as an "expert," indeed as that *rara avis* among experts, namely one who has gumption and who knows something about party politics as well.

17

ANNA BRANCATO:
STATE REPRESENTATIVE

By Frances L. Reinhold

ANNA BRANCATO AND FRANKLIN D. ROOSEVELT WERE ELECTED TO public posts by popular acclaim in 1932. Both passed the goal line by a comfortable margin of twenty-five hundred votes in the First Congressional District of Philadelphia—she to the great office of state representative, he to the mere office of president of the United States. She was the first woman Democrat ever to hold such a position in the Keystone State, and he, after all, was not the first Democrat to fill the role of chief executive.

Elected to the Pennsylvania legislature in her twenties, Miss Brancato has now served three terms in the lower house. Anna made the laws at home long before she made them in Harrisburg. "She was a vixen when she went to school; and though she be but little, she is fierce." When five feet two inches of Anna Brancato is fierce, that is a definition of fierceness. Yet she can be gentle as well as stern, and the combination is delightful.

"The first thing you'll want to write down about me is that everybody likes me. I'm the best vote-getter that the Party has among women." Then as a corrective afterthought, "You'll find that I am modest when you get to know me." And with the merriest of twinkles, "You may take my picture from any angle you wish, but when you come to that inevitable question about my age, you'll have to plot your own figure."

A sleek thirty-four, cut to the windward, could not be far amiss either as to age or figure. 'Twould be an author's boon could Anna be described as a beautiful woman. But no. She is merely interesting. Still one must admit that here is a decidedly captivating personality. To that her male colleagues will testify at once. Indeed there is one who vouches for her unsurpassed loveliness, as a handsome engagement ring bears witness. This romance is too genuine to be treated lightly; yet the betrothal of a lady legislator to a deputy-attorney-general cannot long go unmentioned when either's name is spoken.

Anna's feminine assets seem to be accentuated by the smallness of her stature, but on long and close inspection she betrays a certain callousness, even hardness, which is partially cause, partially effect, of her political experiences. An oval face, provocative in its mobility, provides a disconcerting contrast for bright blue eyes that are naïve because of a genuine—or perhaps an assumed—width. Woe to the transgressor who thinks he can presume upon this naïveté. More woe to him who thinks he cannot. Her light skin is greatly enhanced by dark brown hair, braided in the classic Greek style now so popular among sophisticated women. Unlike most members of her sex, she is better looking without a hat. In any case, one always finds her smartly dressed. She is a novelty in politics—the kind of novelty that begets a welcome. Indeed, her contribution to the legislative processes is a smile as well as a vote.

First-born of the traditional "seven stalwarts," Anna is still the pride and joy of a devoted Italian family. Whatever triumphs she has had, have been shared first of all with them. The two small produce stores by which the Brancatos earn their livelihood are well known in South Philadelphia, where Anna was born and reared. Asked whether she was at all domestic, she replied, "Wouldn't you be too if you had had to be satisfied with a grammar school education so that you could help raise six small children?" Later she took a business-school course, but her childhood ability to speak Italian, English, and Hebrew has no doubt served her in better political stead than a formal education.

One of the most prepossessing of Miss Brancato's characteristics is her perpetual desire to improve herself. No doubt this stems directly from a feeling of inferiority created by the void in her higher educational training. A natural orator, she would nevertheless take up the study of elocution to reassure her on her native techniques. Knowing as much as or more than most college professors about applied political science, she feels the need of taking courses in this subject at the University of Pennsylvania because she shares the respect of the uninitiated for academic institutions.

She would like nothing better than to have time to study law. Who knows if the world has lost another Portia and gained but one more legislator? As a compensatory drive, this lack of formal education has probably been the major spur to her political ambitions.

Miss Brancato has a fundamental proclivity for philosophizing, which is a source of great power. She enjoys discussing attitudes toward life, disappointments, and hopes. Thus, at once she sweeps aside all superficial conversation and treats her casual callers as old friends who speak her language. This is a tremendously compelling factor in her personality. Yet the same quality which makes her sensitive to the significance of life also makes her sensitive to its anachronisms. That is probably why she has such a splendid appreciation of humor, as well as a certain talent for expressing it. To be sure, she is far more emotional than otherwise, but it is an emotion ordinarily tempered with safe judgment.

Anna's voice is not heavy but it carries at low pitch before a large audience. Because she can be heard and because she can entertain, she is always a popular attraction at a public gathering. Moreover, her radio voice is excellent and she uses it to good political advantage. Every Saturday night Representative Brancato addresses her constituency in Italian over Station WDAS and tells them of her day-by-day activities in the legislature. They are proud of their prodigy and they listen to her with avidity. One query might be raised—namely, why do these Italians tolerate this Latin girl as their legislative spokesman when their whole philosophy places woman in the home? If there is an answer it can probably be found in the partial Americanization of the Italian district.

Before becoming active in politics, Miss Brancato was a professional photographer's assistant. Here she learned to be tactful, encouraging, and sympathetic. She had to flatter her subjects—had to bring out the best that was in them. So she attained a camera presence that makes her the joy of newspaper photographers today. Nevertheless, her pictures reveal but a fraction of the vitality and good fellowship which are her most obvious characteristics. On the other hand, they do betray her flair for the dramatic.

Anna's political debut was not spectacular considering the nature of debuts, politics, and ladies in general. It was a mere happenstance that a friend took her to the local Democratic Club's social hour one Saturday evening. In those days a Democrat was virtually illegal in South Philadelphia, and a Democratic Club was something of a secret society. Moreover, in that Vare stronghold a good looking woman who was also a Democrat was an unknown phenomenon since the Republicans held a monopoly on feminine pulchritude no less than on everything else. Small wonder that Anna became the center of attraction in her new circle. She enjoyed the dancing. She enjoyed her popularity and she caught the enthusiasm peculiar to minority groups. To be sure, there was that matter of personal revenge for a minor Republican injustice which heightened the zest of being an honored guest in enemy territory. One comes to realize that Anna is the kind of person who forgives great injuries but cherishes slights.

Having become a member in good standing of the local Democratic Ward Club, Miss Brancato advanced to membership on the Twenty-sixth Ward Executive Committee. There is no avoiding the issue. Anna found her place in a new organization where she could never have cut a niche in the old. Moreover, she would never have achieved prominence had it not been for the Democratic landslide which swept so many accidental politicians into office. She has made the most of her opportunities, but the fact remains that luck played a large part in her success. She became a member of the Independent Democratic City Committee, and then a member of the Young Democrats of Pennsylvania, in which organization she served a term as vice-president. But this was at a time when there were more places in these associations than there were members. Most of all, however, as a Democratic watcher at her precinct poll, she thoroughly enjoyed the miracles wrought by the power to challenge Republican voters. This was the effective spur—the taste of blood as it were—that sent her into open campaign for office. She was acceptable to her party on two counts—first because she was an Italian girl in a district where the Italian women's vote was important, and secondly because the leaders thought she would take orders. On both scores their judgment was eminently correct.

Anna's first experience with newspaper publicity was disillusioning. The female reporter who interviewed her after election asked her at once about her love affairs. Anna's father, like most doting

fathers, told all—which meant all about the one adoring gentleman who was most interested in her election. As a result the story
read like a dime novel. She was reputed to be torn between two
rival suitors, each of whom worked loyally for her success in order
to determine their respective places in her affections. While this
made a romantic story for the fourth estate, it made complications
for Anna. Naturally, she found it difficult to convince her favored
friend that his fictitious rival did not exist. Moreover, her father
had offered this same female reporter an apple as she was leaving
the store. Poor Père Brancato was confronted with an irate wife
as well as a stormy daughter when the newspaper said that he had
attempted to give away the entire store in his elation over his
daughter's victory. Since that time Anna has been skeptical about
the newspaper profession though she deals with it adequately
enough when she chooses. Nevertheless, she has proved to be
hypersensitive about the press and has incurred no little resentment because of her diffident, unreliable, suspicious attitude toward reporters. She would be a better politician if she met them
halfway and treated them like human beings. They admit that she
is a good fellow. They like her. But they think they are as important to her as she is to them. They are right, of course. It is a
glaring defect in her political makeup that she does not appreciate
this fact.

Equipped with all the requisites for a successful political career
save experience, Miss Brancato determined to maintain a discreet
silence until she learned her way about the State Capitol. This
watchful caution is one of her soundest instincts and she has the
intelligence to rely upon it frequently.

The Old Guard, not missing an opportunity to initiate such a
promising subject, immediately asked what she was doing in
Harrisburg—so young, so attractive, and so far from home. The
Republican Chief assigned her to a seat in the midst of the Republican representatives. "I guess they hoped it would keep me
quiet. I didn't like my surroundings at first even though I had
lived in Republican South Philadelphia all my life. But I was glad
that I was there. It turned out to be an excellent place. The Republicans forgot about me after a while and I had a box seat in
their business quarters." But when sightseers began to visit her as

they visited the Zoo, the Executive Mansion, and other points of interest—just to see the "Lady Legislator"—she rebelled. Being a lady legislator was one thing. Being an exhibit was another. But being a good politician she resigned herself to the latter and became actively engaged in the former.

Elected originally on a platform advocating modification of the Sunday blue laws and the repeal of prohibition—both planks later to be adopted—Anna has since devoted her legislative career to the improvement of social conditions for the poor of her district. There is no question that she seeks the interests of her bailiwick, her class, her race above every other consideration. Broad general issues mean little to her unless they can be interpreted profitably for Italian South Philadelphia. She is particularly interested in the protection of women and children. One of the first measures which she introduced into the House of Representatives was designed to prevent widows from losing their rights under the intestate laws. In Pennsylvania a man may deed his property to another in trust, receiving income from it and controlling it during his lifetime, but effectively removing it from the jurisdiction of his wife after his death. The lawyers were opposed to Miss Brancato's efforts to make this illegal, and so her bill was defeated in the Senate. This was a disappointment which she has rarely been called upon to experience since her apprenticeship—not because she wields omnipotent influence, but because she learned not to sponsor unpopular measures.

While still a newcomer to the Capitol, she introduced an "anti-eviction" bill which would have allowed the Courts to prevent the dispossession of unemployed persons. When the bill came out of committee, she was surprised to find that it no longer bore her name but carried instead the name of a prominent Republican. Upon inquiry, she was told that her opponents had no intention of allowing her to sponsor a bill that was bound to be so popular. She was doing it for her constituency, but she wanted them to give her credit for it. And she was not inclined to favor it under other auspices.

There is no more ardent advocate of minimum wage laws, short-hour weeks, child labor protection, and anti-sweat-shop laws than Representative Brancato. A list of her affirmative votes on social welfare bills reads like a social workers' Bible. She worked zealously in behalf of the Pennsylvania Old Age Pension Law. And when the Social Security Act was passed in Washington, she introduced a measure to bring the Pennsylvania Mothers' Assistance Bill into conformity with it. Fortunately for her, large groups outside her constituency profit by the measures which she supports for her own people; so a kind of social welfare myth has developed about her throughout the state's poorer classes. Moreover, she profits by the accident of the growing governmental popularity of her class.

A Catholic by birth and by conviction, Miss Brancato's political attitudes understandably are colored by the traditions of her religion. She it was who propelled the Hasty-Marriage Act through devious legislative channels to its final resting place upon the statute books. The law provides that three days must elapse between application for a license and performance of the wedding ceremony. An amusing corollary developed when the Court interpreted this act to mean a five-day waiting period rather than three, which was not what its sponsor intended.

Her personal popularity with the men was enhanced by the introduction of a bill outlawing breach of promise suits in Pennsylvania. Needless to say, she had little difficulty in steering such a measure through the legislature, though she was subjected to unmerciful teasing and broad badinage at the expense of her prospective husband.

The Assembly temporarily elevated Representative Brancato to the post of acting speaker of the House at the opening session of the 1935 legislature. This was the first time that a woman had ever held that position in the history of the state. The gavel with which she was presented and the resolutions which were passed in her honor are framed and displayed in her business office in Philadelphia. She is proud of the responsibility and of the recognition which they signify.

Representative Brancato's office possesses other framed testimonials as well. Being human she naturally is touched by manifestations of appreciation. Without the least evidence of vanity, and full of simple dignity, she will exhibit her trophies to all who will see. She is an honorary police commissioner of the city of

WIDE WORLD PHOTOS

ANNA BRANCATO

" 'I'm the best vote-getter that the Party has among
women.' . . . 'You'll find that I am modest when you
get to know me.' "

Philadelphia, as well as of a number of small towns in the state, because of her successful efforts to improve the working conditions of policemen. For the first time in forty years, the state legislature passed a bill in the interest of the municipal police service. When the Mayor of Philadelphia asked whether she wished to wear the police uniform to which she was now entitled, she most emphatically declined. Anna is as pleased with her badges as college girls are with their fraternity pins. To her credit it may be said that she lacks the conqueror's arrogance which they often possess. Philadelphia's firemen, too, are in her debt for the passage of a bill granting them shorter hours—a welcome innovation long overdue.

The measure of which Miss Brancato is most proud is the enactment of her Pawnbroker's License Act. Ever since she became a public figure, she has been distressed by the complaints of her poor constituents who were constantly harried by rapacious pawnbrokers. When the *Philadelphia Inquirer* ran a series of articles exposing the exorbitant rates charged by pawnbrokers for loans—frequently between 66 per cent and 72 per cent in Philadelphia and 120 per cent in other parts of the state—she stepped forward and offered to sponsor a bill in the legislature that would curb the evils of this particular profession. One sometimes suspects that she reads the newspapers with a single idea in mind—namely, to run down some item that would bear popular legislation. Of course, there were pressure groups and private interests to be battled, but the bill finally became a law, though because of lengthy court proceedings its effectiveness is still to be proved. A copy of the measure which she cherishes bears the inscription by the Governor, "With kindest regards to Anna Brancato, the sponsor of this most constructive bill. George H. Earle." These autographed bills are excellent vote-getters when shown to the right people at the right time.

Besides being the first Democratic woman representative in Harrisburg, and the first woman acting speaker of the House, she is also the first woman ever to hold a committee chairmanship. Anna is now Chairman of the important Committee on Cities, of which there are thirty-six members. She can be a veritable dictator in that post if she thinks her cause a good one. She has been known to bring a bill out of Committee despite the opposition of thirty-two of her members—and then to have it passed by both Houses and signed by the Governor. In addition to her chairmanship, she also serves on the Appropriation Committee, the Education Committee, the Judiciary General Committee, the Law and Order Committee, the Public Utilities Committee, and the State Boards Committee.

An interesting sidelight on the perversity of women, on legislative procedure, and on democratic government in general is to be found in a single instance when Anna was given party orders and refused to take them. There was a bill before the committee to abolish capital punishment in Pennsylvania. Miss Brancato favored the measure anyway, but the party leader ordered her to vote affirmatively without prior consultation. Resenting the dictatorial attitude, she voted negatively in Committee, much to the amazement of the leader. When the bill came before the House for roll call, she wrote the latter a note and sent it by page boy, to the effect that her constituents demanded that she vote in the affirmative on his measure so she would have to change her original ballot. In order to teach her not to disobey orders, the leader had her vote recorded in the negative "for the benefit of her constituents." In other words, he had her recorded on the unpopular side of a good vote-getting measure. No doubt "if women were humbler, men would be honester." But this was an isolated instance, the importance of which should not be exaggerated. For the most part, she takes her party's orders.

Most recently Representative Brancato has served as secretary of the State Legislative Committee which investigated Philadelphia's government. This committee held hearings for the investigation of county officials twice a week for six months, and ultimately recommended far-reaching changes, some of which have since been made effective by state law.

During the legislative session, Miss Brancato's time is divided between the state Capitol and her constituency. She spends the first three days of the week in Harrisburg, the next three days at her Philadelphia office, where she conducts a brokerage business, and her Sundays at home with her family and personal friends. Like all politicians her time is not her own and there is never enough of it to satisfy the demands made upon her. Yet she knows that a political public is ruthless and impatient when not served, so she obtains jobs for her constituents, pays bills for her poor, visits her sick, and graces the halls of her social friends who want her for display.

There are times when Anna longs for the financial remuneration that she thinks her talents would bring her as a full-time insurance broker, but desire for the power and prestige that come with a public career has subordinated the urge for material blessings. She does not suspect it in the least, but she is goaded by a lust for power. Her sincere conviction that her social conscience is her *élan vital* is a rationalization of motives—unconscious to be sure, but wishful thinking none the less. The truth of the matter is that she possesses the knack of foreseeing the popular side of a political question. Of course she does have unusually keen social sensibilities because of her heredity and environment. But regardless of motive, the results of her work have justified her endeavors from a social point of view. However, one cannot watch the light in her eyes when she reads her praises in the press, or note the blush of pleasure when she gains another personal triumph, without understanding how much these things mean to a girl who has won her spurs by her own efforts despite meagre opportunities.

While political power has sufficed to date, there is no doubt that financial considerations are becoming more and more important to her. She is continually complaining about the cost of politics and the low salaries given to state legislators. It is whispered and denied that she is being reimbursed by lobbies—notably by the beauticians' associations—for promoting favorable legislation for pressure interests.

An unusual personality in her own right, Miss Brancato has many characteristics that are generic to the "American Politician." As has already been indicated, her outstanding attribute in that connection is her ability to win votes. The accident of sex has little to do with such a fundamental requisite except, perhaps, to enhance or diminish a marginal electoral quota. In her case, it seems to have increased the potential ballots for the office she holds.

Despite her personal charm and political aptitude, Miss Brancato owes much of her success to the fact that she is a regular in politics. She is a party servant first and a woman after that. With all her talents she would not survive the competitive struggle as an independent. To this extent, she is a tool in the hands of party leaders. Still there is no doubt about it—she does control the votes of the Italian section of Philadelphia—almost to a man. There are four Socialists who remain unaccounted for, but the rest of her constituency seems to be loyal. So the party cannot afford to lose her any more than she can afford to lose the party. They humor her because she is a woman, and they enjoy doing it because she is such a delightful one. In her way she wields her sceptre—provided it does not interfere with the interests of her party.

There are times too when one suspects that Anna is being used by the party to obtain some particular favor that threatens to be difficult. If this is true, one feels that she is not unconscious of her role. She knows the intricacies of politics too well by now to be deceived. However, she plays the game safely and shrewdly by clearly distinguishing between the ethics of politics and the ethics of other social institutions.

Miss Brancato believes that as long as the Democratic party is dominant in Pennsylvania and as long as it does not become factionalized, there will be a place for her because "The Party needs women, and I am the best vote-getter that they have." It is the Party that finances her elections. She herself regularly files an affidavit that she has spent less than fifty dollars on her own campaign. She is ambitious for higher office but is not hopeful of attaining it in the immediate future. She seems to be too valuable to the party in the position she holds. Essentially she is the right person in the right place, and that after all is what Plato dreamed of in his theoretic Republic.

Because of her salesmanship, her vote-getting ability, her regularity, her lobbying activities, her amenability, her publicity value, and her political aptitude for her job, Anna Brancato shares the characteristics of her prototype throughout the United States. Because of her personal charm, her sex, her championship of the lower classes, she has developed attributes that set her apart. Commanding the respect and affection of all who know her, she seems to have been pardoned for her success as well as to have been praised for it, thus triumphing over the old observation, "It is less difficult for a woman to obtain celebrity by her genius than to be forgiven for it."

18

ROBERT HEUCK AND THE "CITIZENS" MOVEMENT IN HAMILTON COUNTY, OHIO

By Murray Seasongood

THE COMPARATIVELY BRIEF CAREER OF ROBERT HEUCK IN HAM-ilton County, Ohio, politics affords an interesting proof that it is not necessarily the form of government that is the conclusive factor in either good or bad government. A superior form helps in the attainment of good government, but it is possible to have bad government under a good form and a good government under a bad form. In this case the county government set-up is as archaic and unscientific as can be—with the various county offices independent of one another and under no central authority. Nevertheless, the Heuck administrations of the county offices of recorder and auditor to which he was elected, were carried on in co-operation with other "citizens" (reform) officials with a high degree of efficiency and economy; and the merit system, which, written into the constitution of Ohio as far back as 1912, has been practically nonexistent throughout the state and in the eighty-eight counties thereof, was put into effect by Heuck before any official machinery was erected for that purpose, because he had the sincere wish to fill positions in his office on the basis of merit.

His career in public office further shows what a determined "citizens" movement can accomplish in a locality, and how sinister forces of privilege and machine politics can put back into private life a splendid public servant, despite his admirable achievements, and smother any movements for reform.

Heuck was born in Cincinnati forty-five years ago, of a father born in Germany and a mother born in Lancaster, Ohio. The father owned and operated certain theatres in Cincinnati. Heuck's Opera House was the home of melodrama, then in its prime, and People's Theatre, of burlesque, before it descended to the low form of amusement the word now connotes. Weber and Fields and other famous entertainers had their early appearances at People's Theatre. The Lyric Theatre, where Shubert first-class attractions were presented, was also one of Mr. Heuck's theatres.

Heuck has lived for thirty-five years in the suburban part of Cincinnati, that known as Clifton, and has lived all that time in the same house. His family had no political traditions except to vote Republican, and he himself had never taken part in politics before becoming a candidate in 1926. Heuck is a stocky, athletic, pipe-smoking person, whose weight varies between 170 and 190 and his height is five feet seven and a half. There is nothing peculiar about his appearance, which is agreeable, or his manner of dress, which is not "expressed in fancy." His personality is delightful, he is full of fun, and his imitations of a German senator (in Rogers Brothers manner) or of irate constituents complaining about valuations, are as well received as were any of the famous imitations of the professionals in his father's theatres. At the same time, under an appearance of lightheartedness he is extremely sensitive, and the calumnies to which he was subjected caused him very real unhappiness. He is the father of five children, and his family is indeed a happy and hospitable one. Their eggnog reception on New Year's Day each year is an event to which fortunate participants look forward. He has a fine resonant voice which he uses very agreeably in speaking and singing. He wriggled a good deal in answering certain questions for this sketch, because he dislikes speaking of himself, and replied to an inquiry regarding his voice, "When in cups, tenor." [1] Heuck is an extremely modest person. As an instance, he did not mention and I learned only by accident that in the World War he was a lieutenant of field artillery. The economic position of his family and himself can be best described as comfortable and reasonably well-to-do. He was engaged in business as a manufacturer of vitreous enamel.

Heuck received his education in the public schools, the Cincinnati Technical School, and the University of Cincinnati, at which he received his A.B. in 1913. At the University he was a leading undergraduate, a successful captain of the football team, organizer

[1] In politics, as elsewhere, humor is dangerous. One must "speak by the card," or equivocation will undo you. Heuck is not a total abstainer, but he is never in his cups.

and president of the C Club, editor of the *Annual Year Book* (considered a great honor), president of the Senior Class and later of the B.A. Alumni Association. Perhaps what he studied did not directly help him in his later life in politics, but a wide acquaintance, public speaking, and the heading of various organizations undoubtedly were of value to him.

After graduation he was a team captain in a Community Chest Drive, president of the Gyro (luncheon) Club, a member of the University, Cincinnati, and Golf Clubs and of the Cincinnatus Association.

This last organization was originated by another remarkable personality, Victor Heintz, who is deserving of a separate monograph and whose achievements I shall touch upon as a prologue to the story of Heuck's political experiences. Heintz was Republican congressman from the Cincinnati district, one of the two congressmen (the other being the present Mayor La Guardia of New York) who did not limit their patriotism to oratory in the congressional halls during the Great War, but resigned their seats for active service at the front. Heintz became a captain, was wounded in battle, and decorated for bravery. When the war was over, he thought to translate into peace-time activities some of the fine idealism, high purpose, and unselfishness engendered by the great conflict and he organized the Cincinnatus Association as a means towards accomplishing this purpose. Its objects were to discuss and take action on matters of general interest, with particular reference to public and local affairs. It was composed of fifty young men of promise, many of them members of prominent Cincinnati families, and from its inception it became a powerful influence in the achievement of good government by Cincinnati and Hamilton County. Numerous public and unofficial positions of importance in the good government movement have been filled from its ranks.

In 1926, the first year of the reform government in Cincinnati, a number of us reached the conclusion that the advance in city government which had been secured in Cincinnati was unsafe, because the same machine, styling itself Republican, which had debased Cincinnati municipal government for forty years, also had control of the county government and sniped viciously at the City Hall from the Courthouse. It was found that persons separated from the city pay roll for reasons of inefficiency or disloyalty promptly found places in county positions from which to renew their attacks, and almost all the county personnel was composed of ward and precinct executives of the machine. Hence, we organized what was called the "Citizens Party," composed largely of the same persons who had brought about good government in the city. It is one of the difficulties, however, of an unbossed organization that differences of opinion are allowed to develop freely, and some of the Charter group refused to cross city lines and join in the Citizens movement. Cincinnati and Hamilton County at that time were predominantly Republican, and almost all of the members of the Cincinnatus Association were of that political stripe in national affairs. The effort of the Citizens group was to elect its candidates at the Republican primaries. Very shortly before the deadline for filing nominations for these primaries, Victor Heintz and others called on Heuck and urged him to stand for the office of recorder. Early in the movement he had refused to be a candidate for sheriff, but was prevailed upon to allow his name to be submitted for the office of county recorder. Before that time Heuck had had no interest in or acquaintance with politics. The *élan* which had recently brought about the change in the city charter and the election of charter councilmen, carried over into the county primaries, so that many of the Citizens candidates for county offices received the Republican nomination at the primaries and were subsequently elected. Heuck was one of those who saw clearly the importance of having the county offices manned by friends of the city administration. He became chairman of the Men's Organization of the City Charter Committee and later served as vice-chairman of the Campaign Committee of the Russell Wilson Charter Committee. Wilson was elected overwhelmingly on first-choice votes in the city proportional representation election for councilmen, became mayor in 1930, and has continued as such, in successive elections.

Heuck had a large personal following, based on his wide acquaintance, the excellence of his record, his engaging personality, and his excellent speaking ability. Such support as he mustered was not based at all on patronage, since he had no interest in that. Neither did he receive any recognition from or have any contact with the national administration. It is one of the defects of party system in this country that the contacts of the national administration are only with the political machines entitled by law to call themselves Republican or Democrat. The independent is an outcast and receives, not recognition, but opposition, through the appointment to federal offices or positions of those recommended by the bosses, who are almost invariably bitterly opposed to a reform administration in which merit is prized above party affiliations.

Heuck gets along with people and has initiative, energy, and problem-solving ability, courage, vision, and imagination, besides having a genuine sympathetic interest in other people. Aside from these characteristics and those previously mentioned he has none which are thought to spell political success. He has no unusual memory for names of people, has not much self-confidence, and is not interested in being tactful. He is content to do what he thinks is right and make a good job of any position he fills.

Heuck was recorder from 1927 until 1931. All the employees in the office had opposed his election at the primaries and were not under the merit system. He realized, however, that some had acquired proficiency in their positions and that their opposition to him had been required by the dictates of the political machine. He made few dismissals and gave the employees a chance to show their ability, seeking no promises from them except that they would resign political positions, such as ward or precinct executiveships. This was a settled Citizens policy, following the precedent which had been established (perhaps to extremes) in the City Hall.[2]

The office of county recorder is not one of the most important, but will serve as an example to show how much is needlessly exacted from tax payers for the maintenance of offices administered by a machine politician and how much efficiency can be increased and savings effected when operated by a competent citizen free

[2] Theoretically, this is a fine and generous attitude. It has many dangers, particularly if the beneficiaries are not in the classified service under a Civil Service Commission, which prevents active participation in political affairs. It was found that a number who resigned their political positions resorted to the ruse of having a wife or other relative assume such positions. The almost feudal loyalty to the boss and the political affiliations of a lifetime are not easily cast aside, and a number of such beneficiaries did not hesitate, when opportunity offered, to turn savagely on their benefactors. On the other hand, it must be admitted, some who were able were delighted to show what they could do when freed of political encumbrances and displayed complete loyalty to the official appointing them and to the good-government movement.

of organization control. The cost of this office to the Hamilton County taxpayers in the last year of organization incumbency was, in round figures, $91,000 and by 1931 it had been reduced to $55,000, a saving of $36,000.

When Heuck came into office, he found that deeds and other instruments were recorded in bound volumes by officeholders who had no skill as typists. It was almost amusing to see large-bodied, one-fingered operators, sitting, by necessity, a considerable distance away from their machines, pounding keys. Heuck noticed that one of these men had made a particularly large number of glaring mistakes in copying deeds and when telling him he could not be retained longer asked him where he had gained his experience in typing. The reply was that he had had none and his last previous occupation had been that of blacksmith.

Heuck immediately obtained skilled typists at reasonable salaries and earnestly set about trying to use the photostat process. He was met with a legal opinion that, under existing law, such process could not be used for recording. For two years, he was blocked, by the machinations of the local Republican political boss, abetted by certain political title-examining lawyers with specious objections, from obtaining permissive legislation; but, by persistence, he finally obtained the necessary legislation and set about immediately, amidst a great outcry against the reliability of the system, to put it into effect. In the meantime, he had introduced loose-leaf recording books, and by this, and by increased efficiency of employees in the typing department, he saved $22,000 a year as compared with the last full year of his predecessor. Naturally there was increased efficiency in his typing department, since he selected his typists through the means of a civil service examination. As the State Civil Service Commission was unable to hold an examination for the positions, he used the good offices of the Civil Service Commission of the City of Cincinnati.

When the photostat process was put in use, the savings were increased, the possibility of errors or forgeries of instruments was avoided, and the recorded instrument was returned to the owner in a day, by mail if desired, instead of in a week or ten days and only through a personal visit to the recorder's office, as under the old system. That the office became self-supporting, for the first

ROBERT HEUCK

*"His career in public office shows what a determined
'citizens' movement can accomplish in a locality, . . ."*

time, under Heuck, is the more remarkable because he reduced the fees for recording to the legal limit, whereas previously they had been above that limit, and he also instituted the policy of giving receipts for docket and recorder's fees.[3]

Before Heuck's advent, Hamilton County had been at a disadvantage, in the cost of the Recorder's office, as compared with Cuyahoga, the county in which Cleveland is located. But in the last year of Heuck's incumbency, Hamilton County had an advantage in this one office over Cuyahoga, in fees earned over salaries, of $34,000.

In 1930, Heuck was elected county auditor, the office often regarded as the most important in the county service. The auditor is the chief assessing officer in the county and must pass on all valuations of property. He is a member of the Budget Commission, the Sinking Fund Trustees, and the Board of Revision. He is the auditor and bookkeeper of the county. He must account for all special assessments, transfers of property, and delinquent as well as current property taxes. He is the collector of the inheritance tax and was also the collector of the personal property tax. He sells licenses such as automobile, barber, dog, peddler, show, retail and wholesale beverage, cosmetics, and malt. The county sealer is also under his direction, and even this list does not cover all of his duties.

The same efficiency and economy, on a larger scale, were shown in this office, the savings in 1934 over the last year of his predecessor, 1930, being over $60,000. The auditor's office is not self-supporting, for the auditor performs many duties for which his office is not credited with fees. In 1933, the fees earned were $62,000 less than the total expenses of the office compared with the loss in 1930, the last year of his machine predecessor, of $131,000 of excess expense over fees earned.

On taking office, Mr. Heuck perceived that another bookkeeping and auditing system was necessary. This new system was installed, and despite the tremendous increase in the volume of work (in 1933 the increase being more than a hundred per cent over

---

[3] For other statistics showing the savings of Citizens county offices in comparison with the same offices operated by organization officers, see Murray Seasongood, *Local Government in the United States* (Cambridge, Mass., 1934), pp. 51-54.

that of 1932, and three hundred per cent over that of 1930) the cost of the bookkeeping department was less, the work more up-to-date, and information more readily available. The billing and tabulating department was installed and has been recognized throughout the nation as an outstanding installation. Heuck regards this as his biggest achievement. The tax billing and accounting system was installed in 1931 during the appraisal and includes the use of tabulating machines, punch cards, and an addressograph. It is used for the billing, distribution, and settlement work as well as for the bookkeeping department. It is the same system used in utility billing, but its use by Heuck in Hamilton County was the first one in a public office. People came to see this installation from widely different sources and some large corporations also sent representatives to see it and later installed it.[4]

This method could be used because the Citizens auditor and the treasurer combined forces and used one another's employees. The auditor made the bills for the treasurer and the treasurer paid the auditor's employees while so doing. In every other county, the treasurer and the auditor remain completely independent, have no co-operation in the use of one another's employees, and do not co-operate by reason of patronage, jealousy, or objection to labor-saving devices.[5]

The real estate department is recognized by the examiners of the Tax Commission of Ohio as the most complete and efficient unit in the state.

Heuck's special assessment department handled over six hundred special assessment projects, which included over 145,000 items billed annually and semiannually. Special assessments are levied by the county, cities, and villages and are certified to the auditor for collection and auditing. The codifying of assessment projects and the individualizing of the items within each project were a tremendous task not theretofore attempted, and the results obtained are permanent in their benefits to the county and the

---

[4] The company furnishing part of the machinery got out for general distribution a special explanatory printed pamphlet entitled "Billing, Collecting and Accounting for Taxes, County of Hamilton, Ohio, by the International Electric Tabulating and Accounting Machine Method."

[5] See Murray Seasongood, "How Political Gangs Work," *Harvard Graduate Magazine*, pamphlet reprinted by the National Municipal League, 1932.

municipalities in the billing, collection, and distribution of all assessments.

The transfer department had its efficiency increased so that by the use of the permanent tax list which Mr. Heuck installed, transfers could be made immediately instead of waiting several hours. Through the co-operation of Mr. Beckman, the successor Citizens recorder, a lift was installed between the auditor's and recorder's offices, and the services given greatly improved.

Owing to the efficiency of the certified delinquent department as well as by means of the mechanical installation of the auditor's office, co-operation was given Harry A. Freiberg, the Citizens treasurer (Harvard A.B.), in furnishing delinquent tax bills for the first time in Ohio.

The appraisal department, under Mr. Heuck, is credited with the outstanding equalization appraisal in recent years, and the system employed was studied by many communities throughout the country. During the appraisal $2,000,000 worth of buildings which had escaped taxation were placed on the duplicate. The general routine work of this department was much praised for the promptness and accuracy with which it was handled.

A mapping system, in which each parcel receives an identification number, was instituted, and the physical condition and accuracy of the maps were greatly improved.

The inheritance tax department became the outstanding department in the State of Ohio. In 1933 this department collected a total of $981,000, the largest amount recorded by any of the eighty-eight counties of the state. Cuyahoga County collected only $645,000.

In 1930, the cost of the personal property department was $47,000; in 1933 its cost had been reduced to $26,000. In 1930 the cost of collecting one dollar of personal taxes was about 1⅛¢, while in 1933 it cost only slightly over ½¢ per dollar. This department ranked first in the State of Ohio.

At Mr. Heuck's request, the prosecuting attorney brought suit successfully against the distribution on an unjust basis of the 1932 intangible tax, which saved the County of Hamilton over $1,-500,000.

Although the licensing department showed a deficit before 1932, it has been paying for itself since. This is due to the savings in operation through the introduction of new and more efficient systems.

The county sealer, whose duty it is to check scales, gasoline pumps, dry and liquid measures, etc., added the services of checking heavy duty platform scales such as coal and hay scales. This was the first time in the history of Ohio that such a service had been given the community by this department.

Because of the business methods incorporated and the efficient arrangement of the auditor's office, over fourteen hundred square feet of floor area were released by the auditor to the clerk's office, and a similar amount of floor area was turned over to the Tax Commission of Ohio. Heuck let out sixteen in his office almost immediately, because the office was over-manned.

The auditor and the other Citizens officers set about diligently to install the merit system in their respective offices. They were delayed by an unfriendly opinion from the Republican organization attorney general from Cincinnati, but finally did bring it about so that the State Civil Service Commission had in Hamilton County its one examiner and representatives in eighty-eight counties of the state. The Commission paid half of the salary of this examiner from its meager funds, and the county commissioners paid an equal amount by employing him as budget commissioner. But neither political machine, Democrat or Republican, liked the merit system in the county and they vented their dislike on the examiner who had been obliged to fail in examinations some Republican and Democratic machine stalwarts.

Heuck's appraisal, as of April, 1931, was made under trying conditions, because of uncertain values in the depression and because valuations were somewhat lower when the appraisal was completed, than in April, 1931. In the midst of the appraisal, and shortly before the municipal election of November, 1931, the Republican organization attorney general of the state from Cincinnati, undoubtedly acting in concert with the local machine, released a long opinion very quickly (which must have been written up in advance), that anyone could see the appraisal as it progressed, at any time, and that the auditor had no private records. In previous years, organization auditors would postpone the appraisal, or not make anything public regarding it until after election, so as not to incur anyone's ill will through dissatisfaction with the valuation of his property. The result of the attorney general's opinion was to interfere seriously with Heuck's progress in the appraisal and to let loose a tirade of objections to influence the municipal election.

The downtown property owners fought the appraisal savagely and unfairly and put Heuck in the position of opposing blanket reductions made by the Tax Commission of Ohio. Heuck fought further reduction in land values because he believed his appraisal to be just and because such reduction aided business and investment property at the expense of the home-owner. Downtown land is often more valuable than the building placed on it. As to homeowners, however, reduction on the home building is usually more important than on the land. As proof of the justice of the appraisal, over ninety per cent of the appeals to the State Tax Commission from the Board of Review, were denied. The ordinary political auditor curries favor with individuals, whether influential or not, and especially with large contributors to the party campaign fund, by "making concessions" on valuations. A political county treasurer in Ohio was heard to say to his colleague the Auditor, "It's a cinch for you to be elected, because you can give favors to so many people. All I can do is to collect from them." But Heuck was not that kind of auditor: he was standing up for a just appraisal and the reduction in tax rate and continuance of proper governmental functions by preserving the real taxable value of the lands and buildings from which necessary tax revenues were derived. Heuck again used the City of Cincinnati Civil Service Commission to obtain efficient appraisers on the basis of competitive examinations. Several hundred were examined and ninety selected from the Civil Service list. This was something unheard of as, with previous auditors, such appraisers were appointed for political or personal patronage reasons.

One of the obstacles with which Heuck had to contend was a biased and unrepresentative press. Cincinnati has but one morning paper, housed in its own large building in the downtown section of the city, and the editor of that paper was allied with the utilities and downtown property owners group. It is true that, eventually, the editor endorsed Heuck for re-election, but the endorsement was just another of the many instances where the editorial and news columns of a newspaper do not coincide. This paper had a policy of permitting its Courthouse and City Hall reporters to accept favors to piece out their salaries. The perquisites of the Courthouse reporter from the Republican machine, in the shape of appointments such as a county building commissioner, appraiser in estates, etc., amounted to several thousand dollars a year. During all the time that Heuck was at the Courthouse, his splendid achievements received no recognition in the news columns of this paper and only garbled and hostile accounts of what he did and tried to do. The same was true of the afternoon Republican (Taft) newspaper, the editor of which was hostile to the whole Citizens movement and was also dissatisfied with Heuck's appraisal of his downtown property holdings; and an influential part owner of this paper was also actively allied with the downtown property owners and the Republican organization machine. The Courthouse reporters of this paper and also of the Scripps paper, which favored the Citizens group, were not over friendly, so Heuck, particularly, and all the Citizens incumbents, were misrepresented and did not have their accomplishments fairly presented to the voters.

It had been found by the Citizens group, in 1928, after the first primaries in 1926, that it was practically impossible to succeed in the party primary. And here is another defect of the American party system. In Ohio, and doubtless other states, the election machinery is in the hands of the two political gangs. When an independent seeks to win at a party primary, the two groups combine to defeat the intruder. The grossest frauds are permitted and abetted. Moreover, except under most unusual conditions, it is impossible to arouse enough enthusiasm in midsummer to induce the independent voter to cast his ballot at the primary; but the regulars will be out to vote at the primary because they are instructed to do so, and their livelihood depends upon the showing in their ward or precinct. Hence, after defeat in 1928 at the Republican primary, the Citizens group learned a lesson and decided that a coalition with the independent Democrats in the county, as successfully achieved by the City Charter Committee in the city elections, was the proper procedure. And in 1930, the Citizens party elected all of its candidates for the seven county offices voted on.

In the 1932 county elections this alliance was again successful, electing six of their nine candidates in a presidential year and with a form of ballot that discriminated grossly against them.[6]

Before the election of November, 1932, the following pledge was signed:

"We, the nine Citizens county candidates, pledge ourselves, if elected, to co-operate in immediately completing the classification of all offices, positions and employments in the Civil Service of the county.

"We pledge ourselves, if elected, to co-operate with the legally constituted officials in the installation of the Merit System and the carrying out with vigor the Ohio laws on that subject."

Unfortunately, the Citizens clerk of courts, an old-time Democratic politician, did not live up to this pledge and, while his administration of the office was superior to that of his Republican machine predecessor, it was conducted in defiance of the Civil Service Commission. Abetted by Democratic machine lawyers, he framed an inquiry to the Republican organization prosecutor so that he was told that he need not even put typists under the merit system. As a result of this and dissatisfaction with another Democratic Citizens official, the Citizens refused in 1934 to renominate them on their ticket, and an unfortunate split occurred by which the Democrats put up these officials and other county officers at the primary and on the regular Democratic party column ballot, and the Citizens nominated Heuck and others by petition on an independent ticket. Heuck and his associates who had agreed to run knew that their chances of election were practically nil, but they adhered to the motto of Seneca's pilot, "Oh, Neptune, you may save me if you will, you may sink me if you will, but I shall hold my rudder true." They felt that almost certain defeat was better than putting no Citizens candidate in the field and thereby disappointing and dissipating the Citizens organization.

Here, again, party administration of the election machinery prevented the people from continuing the services of those who had served them so well. Not alone were the Citizens county candidates denied a circle and emblem on the ballot such as is permitted

---

[6] For a sample ballot and more of the history of this election, see Seasongood, *Local Government in the United States*, pp. 45-51.

for a straight ticket voted for the Republican and Democratic candidates from governor down to coroner, twenty-nine offices, but the local Democratic boss, one of the Hamilton County Board of Elections, connived with the Democratic secretary of state in charge of elections to change the order of the county offices on the official party column ballot prescribed by statute (4785-109 Ohio General Code). This statute required that the candidate for county commissioner should come first, and the Board of Elections had prescribed that the Citizens should take out their nominating petitions in that order. Following this, the Citizens had their sample ballots and cards printed and distributed in that order. The Citizens candidate for county commissioner was very widely and favorably known and had twice been elected county treasurer on the Citizens ticket. It was difficult to educate the voters as to just where to find the Citizens ticket on the ballot as well as to induce them to make a cross mark for each candidate. So it was very convenient to tell them to look for the column headed by the name of Edgar Friedlander, the Citizens candidate for county commissioner. The Democratic secretary of state changed the order of offices on the official party column ballot for no other reason than that the little known name of William Holmes, candidate for clerk of courts on the Citizens ticket should be at the top. Moreover, the local Board of Elections did not submit proof of the ballot showing this change of order to the chairman of the local Executive Committee of the Citizens, as required by 4785-115. Hence, this skulduggery was not discovered until the ballots for all the counties had been printed in that order, and when suit was brought, the Ohio Supreme Court, in an ill-considered and hasty decision, refused the Citizens the right to compel reprinting of the ballots for Hamilton County alone, on the ground that the application came too late after the ballots had been printed and distributed and some mailed to absent voters.

Aside from this chicanery, the election proved the futility of a three-cornered fight where two of the parties have advantage of a party emblem and circle. Heuck and three of his Citizens colleagues up for re-election had rendered, as county officers, distinguished services for the taxpayers on a merit basis and without a suspicion of partisanship. All were defeated by Republican straight ballot voting, although the sum of the votes for Democrats and Citizens, for each candidate, exceeded the votes for the successful Republican. It was impossible to educate enough voters to come over to the Citizens column and to risk, as they thought, spoiling their ballot for state and national officers and representatives to the General Assembly. Even the Democrats obtained more votes for inconspicuous persons nominated for county offices, through the straight ballot voting under the Rooster and in the circle, than the distinguished and deserving Citizens candidates. During campaign Heuck was subjected to a tirade of vilification and abuse, but nevertheless he ran the best of the Citizens candidates. The Citizens, with a record of saving to the taxpayers in their seven years in county offices of over $800,000, were defeated by a thimble-rigging form of ballot and a crooked administration of the election machinery by two political gangs.

The one crumb of comfort for the Good Government Movement in the election of 1934 was that by favor of the County Home Rule Amendment to the State Constitution passed at the November election in 1933 the issue, "Shall a county charter commission be chosen?" was submitted at this election, was resolved favorably, and a majority of those elected at the same time to frame such a charter for submission to the electorate, were Good Government hoplites. The platform of this group called for the submission of a county charter for Hamilton County which would co-ordinate county governmental functions and reduce expenses, so that the county might operate under an economical and efficient home rule plan of government that would help townships, villages, and cities to transfer any of their functions to the county government should they choose to do so; for a simple, direct and responsible control of administration and budget; for county elections by a majority vote on a separate non-partisan short ballot; for the extension of county responsibility for health, hospitals and welfare; and, most important, for a merit system under the jurisdiction of a local home rule commission providing for security in public employment, with a just and adequate retirement plan free from any state control.

An excellent charter to carry out these objects was submitted in the 1935 election. Both political machines misrepresented and opposed it. The afternoon Republican paper was filled with expressions of misgiving as to the effect that such a charter would have on the salvation of the Republican party. Even some of the Charter party governing body were lukewarm in favor or actually opposed to this charter and it was defeated.

In 1936 the Democrats were so confident of the ability of their county candidates to ride in on the coattails, i.e., party column ballot, headed by Franklin D. Roosevelt, that they would have refused any attempt at coalition with independent Republicans. When the Republican machine got hold of the county commissioners, they speedily did away with the representative of the Civil Service Commission as budget commissioner, and the Democrats who were elected to county offices on a straight Democratic ticket aided in the sabotage of the merit system. So Hamilton County has again become the eighty-eighth county of the state where the merit system is nonexistent.

Hamilton County is to have a reappraisement this year, as required by law, but the downtown property owners have already triumphantly announced it is to be an "equitable" one. All, save some slight residuum of benefit, obtained by the heroic efforts of Heuck and other Citizens independents, seems lost until a more enlightened age makes it possible for Citizens again to conduct their own government in the interest of citizens.

19

HONEST TOM McINTYRE:
AN OLD-STYLE POLITICIAN

By J. T. Salter

THERE HE STOOD, TALKING TO FOUR OR FIVE MEN IN THE COR-
ridor of City Hall just outside the door of the sergeant at
arms' office—Honest Tom McIntyre, the Abe Lincoln of the organization, the "millionaire contractor" who got right down into
the ditch with his men and then on Thursdays came right up out
of the ditch to go to council. When he was first elected, legend has
it, two men had to hold him while a third introduced him to his
first white shirt. Now as he stood there in the great hall he seemed
too big for his clothes. His rugged form would not be entirely
confined. He is the athletic type, his head is large, and he has curly,
grizzled hair, so thick that it must be wetted to be held in place.
His skin has a deep, ruddy color that might have come from the
wind and the sea or from the drinking of much rum. He is the
most profane man I have ever met, but for some magic reason the
profanity is not revolting on his lips. It goes with his seaman's
color and heightens the illusion I always have when I see him that
here is the captain of a ship, home from a far port. Civilization has
not put him in a groove, nor broken him. His face is luminous and
infinitely expressive—it is the chiseled Irish sort. His eyes are
drooping, and remind one of the eyes of England's poet laureate,
John Masefield—except that Honest Tom's eyes are always twin-
kling.

There he stood, telling some friends a story—in that short section of the corridor, the observed of all observers. Councilman
Phinney Green of the Eleventh Ward was going by, and I asked
him to introduce me to McIntyre. I will not say that Honest Tom
was in liquor, for I could not prove that he was, but he was highly
exhilarated. When he heard that I wanted to write about him he

smiled, put his hand on my shoulder and said, "Young man, I wouldn't want all of my record printed!" and laughed. A few minutes later he said: "I am Honest Tom, and if ever I am dishonest, I have never been caught. I can drink rum better than any man in the Hall, and that goes whether it is good rum or bad—I can drink it." Just at this moment another councilman came out of the office. In jest Honest Tom pointed his finger at him and said, for all to hear: "There is a crooked councilman that changed his vote. If I voted one way, I would stay that way. I would not care what they said." And with that he walked down the corridor a few steps and turned into the council chamber.

The session was about to begin. When McIntyre entered he spoke to nearly everyone standing along the wall, and everyone spoke to him. He had not gone twenty feet before he stopped and talked to two men. He was with them for several minutes; then he pulled away, and with a few more salutations sank into the cushions of his seat in time for roll call. He partly rose, answered, "Present," and said, "No bills, Mr. President." (His voice is low, and his answer never varies. Once I heard an old-timer refer to the Councilman as Silent Tom. I was surprised. In the corridor or in his office he is the ribald talker—only he is so good-humored and he looks so clean and lusty that he never seems ribald—but he never addresses the chair in council. He told me that he gave up the practice when Butler was director of public safety. At that time he made an impassioned plea for the police that was not supported by his colleagues. "I have not spoken in council since. What's the use?" However, when it comes to voting, he votes right, and the organization never worries.)

Shortly after the roll call he grew restless; he quit his seat and desk and walked back to the rear of the chamber. He turned to the right, and there, at the end of the room, sitting on an ample, leather-covered lounge, were seven old-time politicians and myself. Tom ambled towards us and one of the men called out, "Hey, Tom, come over and have a seat!" The councilman was pivoting about on one foot, with something of a smile on his face. To our invitation he laughed and replied that he wouldn't associate with a damned bunch of crooks. One of the group said, "How are you, Tom?" Quick as a flash he said, "Damned near drunk!" The old-timer next to me said that Tom was awfully strong, and that he could remember the day when he was so drunk it took ten men to keep him out of the council chamber. A minute later, Honest Tom came up to me and said, "Young man, I will talk to you some time, and give you the real stuff."

Since that time I have seen Councilman McIntyre many times, usually on Thursday afternoons in City Hall, just outside the council chamber. His attitude is always the same. He is a man of high spirits, and a most pleasant fellow to meet. He can never walk from the elevator in the southeast corner of City Hall to the councilmanic chambers without speaking to a dozen people, and sometimes he greets as many as fifty. (One of his lieutenants told me this story: "One time Councilman McIntyre almost came face to face with Bill Vare as he was walking down a corridor in City Hall. A crippled bum happened along at the same time. Honest Tom just waved his hand to Vare, saying, 'Hello, Bill,' and stopped and shook hands with the old bum.") Sometimes he will stop and chat, and when he does a small group will immediately gather around him. It never matters what he is talking about—he is always interesting to hear. His great heartiness and charm enliven everyone and fill his spot in City Hall with color and light. He is always greater than his words. His spirit stirs the heart. He is not all things to all men, but one thing to all men.

One Thursday, just before City Council convened at 2:00 P.M., I found him talking to Magistrate L—— in the corridor on the fourth floor. I went over to them, and when Tom saw me he smiled and put his arm over my shoulder and drew me closer to them. He was in prime condition and most jovial—in happy contrast to the swarms of worried looking people who were jamming the corridors on the fourth and fifth floors of City Hall to protest against a threatened increase in the tax rate. "Here is a man," said Honest Tom to the Magistrate, "that is going to write the story of my life. I'll give him more damn stuff than he can put in two books, Judge!" The Judge emphatically agreed that he could do it. I then asked McIntyre if he would speak a good word to Uncle Dannie Turley for me. "Hell, yes!" he answered. "Come on!" And arm in arm we started down the corridor for the councilmanic chamber. But when we got to the sergeant at arms' office we stopped, and the councilman, forgetting all about Uncle Dannie when he did not see him there, gently pushed me into the swivel chair, started out of the doorway, gave an incoming politician a hearty whack on the middle of the back, and disappeared into the council chamber across the hall.

But not many days after that, I walked into a spacious office on the fourth floor of Philadelphia's "hall of a thousand sorrows" and found the city's most exuberant councilman sitting at his desk there. He gave me a hearty greeting and pointed to a colleague on the lounge across the room. "There," he said, "there is the man you ought to talk to. Doesn't he look like a politician? If he had on a striped suit he would be the perfect picture of a gang politician." I looked at Councilman Turley. He had a bull neck, a big, baggy middle that covered his lap as he sat, a small head and small eyes that were always partly closed. He merely blinked as McIntyre spoke, and looked straight ahead. And during our whole interview, there he sat, not like a wooden Indian, but rather like three sacks of grain.

"I was born in Philadelphia," Honest Tom began. "My father and mother were from Ireland, my father from the County Derry, my mother from County Down. They were never in politics. My father always said I was a dirty bum for going into politics. I was eighteen years old when I started. Just about that time I got into the contracting business. When I started out in politics, we used to be in a cellar. We would have a half barrel of beer, some limburger cheese and crackers and, damn it, we had an awfully good time! There were stables behind our house. Every night there were so many fellows sleeping in the stables that I counted on their votes. My first job was judge of elections. This was the only job I wanted, for if we could control the judge, we could control the election. From twenty-one years of age on I was elected as judge of election either in this ward or in the Seventy-ninth Ward.[1] For fifteen years I was judge of election in the ninth division of the Sixty-second Ward. It was known as the 'Bloody ninth' and it was a s-o-b! You should see the *Bulletin* for 1895. They have an article about me and how I voted forty people from my stable. They called me a small contractor then, and said I voted forty men from

[1] When I use ward numbers above 50, I do so to hide the identity of the wards.

my stables. The bastards were all there, too. They wouldn't vote unless I marked their ballots and I always marked them, for I wouldn't trust any one of them. The night that article appeared my mother said, 'You're sorry now, ain't you?' I had just brought home a load of gravel. I told her, 'Mother, there is a million people that know me today that never heard of me before.' " And then he again declared, "The forty-five men were there too, by God, they were there.

"Calkins, the ward leader of the Fifty-sixth Ward, refused to seat me on the ward committee, although I was elected every year from the time I was twenty-one years of age until I was elected to the city committee and the select council in 1907. In those early days I would be elected to the ward committee, and Calkins would fire me out.

"Later I went over to the Seventy-ninth Ward and got elected as judge of elections over there. I wanted to help the boys out and show them just how politics were done. However, they talked about putting me in prison for voting away from home; so I resigned as judge. When I was elected to council from the Fifty-sixth Ward, the boys of the Seventy-ninth said, 'You're a fine s-o-b to be elected to council!' But I won, and I won for my friends! I never took a drink of rum until I got elected to council. I've been elected to council ever since and have served under seven mayors. In the old days I was always elected to select council.

"Now Turley never had any trouble in his ward, but I always had the whole damned bunch against me. I was with Jim Mc-Nichol, and the Martin people were fighting against me. Pretty near all the ward committeemen were place-holders, and they would vote me out. They threw me out because their boss, Calkins, told them to. He was afraid I would get too strong and get his hide. He was first a magistrate, then a real estate assessor, and finally a mercantile appraiser, but I beat him at last. Dave Martin and Billy Knight were against me because I refused to put one of their friends in common council. I said, 'He is a Democrat.' 'What difference if he is, he will do as you say!' But I wouldn't take him.

"The Washington party [an anti-organization group] was strong then. Some of the leaders in my section asked me if I wanted them to endorse me. I said, 'Yes.' Later I asked them what it would cost. They said they would let me decide after the primary. One night eight of these leaders sneaked over to my house the back way. They explained that they did not want to be seen in my presence. I said, 'All right.' I got out a quart of whisky and gave each of them a good drink. I won the nomination by a large vote. None of these fellows ever came back to get their pay. When I saw them I said, 'Why don't you fellows come and see me?' 'Tom,' they said, 'you got such a big majority that we thought you would forget all about your promise.' I said, 'No, I never go back on my word.' I asked them what their help was worth. They said, 'Fifty dollars apiece.' So I took out a roll of bills and put one hundred dollars before each of them. I then got out a bottle of rum and gave each of them a drink. They took not only one drink, but two, and after that no one could ever lick me.

"The organization gave Fox money to get elected to the City Committee. Fox actually had four more committeemen than I had. The night of the election one of my committeemen was going in the room, and he was asked who he was going to vote for. He knew then that I could not be elected. But Rainer, my committeeman, said, 'Old McIntyre is good enough for me.' That was in 1906. Fox beat me for the last time in that election. The next year I was elected, and I have been ever since."

I asked McIntyre how he inspired such high loyalty in his men. I had talked to seven of them, including the leader of the women's organization in the Fifty-sixth Ward, and they are all, lock, stock and barrel, for Honest Tom just as Rainer had been twenty-five years ago.

"I can answer that question in a minute. I never met a soul that was on the ward committee that I didn't use my best efforts to make him a friend; no matter if he had voted against me before, I still tried to get him to go along with me. It all depends on how you use the people as to how far or how well you will go. Ask the colored men in my ward. They will tell you that I am the only 'white man' that they know. Some people want to be too stingy, and will not give anything away, or they want all the credit for themselves. I know enough to believe that I wouldn't be worth a damn if it wasn't for the fellows that go with me. I made a study of that at the start. I realized then that there was room enough for a good leader if he gave credit to those that helped him. Play fair with your neighbors and they will never fail you. Some time ago, in 1920, Parker, my opponent, wanted ten of my committeemen to vote for him for the city committee, but they refused; so Mayor Moore fired all ten. However, I paid each of them $100 a month until I got another job for them. When Parker asked them to vote for him they all said, 'Go to hell!' It cost me between ten and fourteen thousand dollars to take care of these ten men who had been fired for loyalty to me. One day I spoke to Ed Vare about it. Vare said that he would write me a check. I said, 'Damn it, Ed, I am paying these men, and I don't want a check, but I do want them to get a job!' Vare got them a job. You see, I was paying only $100 a month, and when they got a job they were getting at least $1800 a year. One time I asked Judge B—— if he had a place for niggers. I said 'Haven't you got any damned place for a nigger?' B—— said to a friend, 'Have you got a damned place for a nigger?' (B—— is a shrewd judge and shrewder ward leader.) We got a place for him as a janitor.

"Both in my contracting work and in politics I stay close to my men. I work with them now. I throw the stuff in mixers. I work with them and keep them going. The sooner we finish a job the more money we make."

I asked if he had belonged to any boys' club. The councilman misunderstood my question and said, "Hell, yes—I joined all of them!" And then he started talking about the Masons and he added, "But the club that I think most of is the Fifty-sixth Ward Republican Club. I am president of it. For twenty years I went there seven nights a week, but don't go there so often now, for I am often at Atlantic City. Our club is on —— Avenue between X and Y streets. Come on over sometime and see us. We have everything there, cards, billiards, pool and a bowling alley." I inquired, "When will I find you there?" He said that he did not know. "I might not be there for a month, and I might be there tonight." (When he is there the boys gather around him and the room is packed with good listeners and animated talk. When the leader isn't there, neither are the followers. The club house is deserted save for fifteen or twenty men who talk and play games and wonder if the Old Man will show up.) "Ask the people in the section where I live. They are all for me." (I talked to about thirty of them, almost at random, and each one of them seemed to feel that Honest Tom was his personal friend.) "I was born in the Nineteenth Ward. My father was in the milk business—he always kept about sixty head of cows. Till I growed up to be damn near a man I herded them around the vacant lots. But when the country got built in around us we moved with the cows to the Fifty-sixth Ward section. The cows would get the sidewalks dirty and the board of health got after us, and so we had to move. For the last sixty years I have lived in the Fifty-sixth Ward, and when my sister died, she left me the property, though I now live in Atlantic City."

As McIntyre talked his face was flushed and his eyes sparkled, and he seemed to relish the idea of talking about his life in politics. His three party workers and Councilman Turley sat there without saying a word. There was nothing extraordinary here to them but the professor, and ten minutes was plenty for looking him over. Honest Tom talked with gusto, and much of the time he looked at his companions as he talked. I was merely a prompter. When I asked if his father had been in politics, he said, "Hell, no! My father said that I was a fool for going in. He voted for me the first time but never after that, because I learned to drink in city council. At one of my later elections he asked a friend how I was making out. The friend said, 'What do you care? You won't vote for him.' My father said, 'I know, but then you see, he is my son, and I would like to see him come through.'

"I know many of the people in my ward and they know me. I know the boundary lines of each division in my ward. I know pretty nearly the name and address of all my committeemen, but there have been so many changes lately that I would not know all at the present time. I have experienced committeemen that help me on party details. They never miss, and if I'm not here one of my men is.

"In the old days I was always there. Once after I began drinking liquor I got home at three o'clock—I had a hell of a load on, so I laid down on the hay and went to sleep. In the morning my father said, 'Tom is a queer one. Instead of sleeping in a nice bed here with us, he will go out in the barn, and sleep with the bums.'

"At times people would come to the house and ask for me.

My father would say that I was away, and ask them if he could do something. They would always say, 'No, I guess not.' You know my father used to believe that all I ever done was to get these bums out of the station house. I enjoyed that life a lot. It was an expensive piece of business, though—this being in politics, for me. Once I spent so much money paying rent for my ward committeemen that I overdrew my account $800. My bank carried me. I never took any help from the city committee. I had to pay all my own bills. My old man thought he was going to make a minister out of me [Tom is Presbyterian] but I didn't like that kind of business because there were so many damned women around."

I suggested that politics was a strenuous game. He disagreed. He said, "Oh, no, not if you play it right. I go to Atlantic City at six o'clock, look the papers over, have supper, and go to bed at nine. I go to sleep at once. In the morning I read the *Record* because I know if there is any scandal about the politicians the *Record* will publish it. At night time I get the *Bulletin*. In the morning at Atlantic City I get six or seven papers and give them to my friends." At this point, Dick Moore, his friendly lieutenant, spoke up and said, "Tell him about the lunches, Tom." Tom smiled and said, "Oh, yes, I take my friends to lunch."

I asked him if he read books. He said that he did, but, "I can't think of the name of the book." He added, "Oh, damn it, I bet my sister had five hundred. I just pick them up and read the one I come to. I like to read about shipwrecks and that sort of thing."

I told Honest Tom that I thought that I could understand why he was a leader, but, "Take Grimm, for instance; what has he got that makes for leadership?" The councilman paused and answered, "I wish I knew. A fellow like Grimm is a disappointment to a real leader. He was made overnight by Vare. Such an outrage!" One of McIntyre's standers-by expressed the opinion, "He is a counterfeit!" Honest Tom answered, "Yes, but his job is not a counterfeit!" The councilman's reply demonstrated his ability to strike at the jugular vein in an argument. Almost invariably the organization leader places the toga on an old-time committeeman, but in the case of Grimm he was placed in a ward specifically for the purpose of being made a leader. Vare wanted a man he could trust implicitly.

Several times Honest Tom exclaimed, "I could write that book myself!" When I thanked him, he gave me a hearty handshake and said, "That's all right, young man—you come back some other time and we will talk about politics some more." I offered him a cigar, which he refused. "If that were a pint of liquor, I would drink half of it with you."

One morning when I saw Honest Tom in Dick Moore's office I thought of Albert Jay Nock's feeling about the characters in Dickens.—"But how interesting! Why, one would walk miles unending to meet one of them and, having met him, would haunt him and delightedly follow him up and down the earth!" He gave me a lusty greeting; he was in top form. He asked me and Zeke Moran, the detail man of another ward leader, to come down to his office. There he passed around a box of Antony and Cleopatra cigars. We each took one. Just then two men came in, one a rather humble and ordinary looking man of about fifty, who went up to Tom and, with a most appreciative expression, started to thank him. His ward leader interrupted. "Did it cost you a hundred?" The man answered, "No, he gave me three years' probation!" Honest Tom gave the man a friendly pat on the back, and the grateful caller went out. He doubtless had a new feeling of independence; he was beholden to no man, but forevermore he would feel that Honest Tom was his friend. A more human acknowledgment of a service rendered could not well be imagined. But the benefactor thought no more about it. To him it was merely a matter of course. "I told the judge to give him probation—that he had no money—that he would not handle, drink or sell any wet goods again," he said as he dismissed the incident from his mind.

Zeke Moran, tall, slender, stooped, with black hair and a hatchet face, was painfully worried. (He had been told by his ward leader to support Mackey in the primary, and Vare's agent had told him that he would be fired from his job, his nice berth at City Hall, if he did. Vare was against Mackey, and for his opponent, Long.) Moran said, "I went to see that big gazabo at Atlantic City. He was as vindictive as hell! He said that he was for Long for the legislature and would not break his word. I said, 'That is the same way with us. We won't break our word.' 'Hell,' said Vare. 'Don't try to pass the buck that way.' We couldn't come to any agreement, and I will lose my job. I lost my job twice for Vare already. Once I was taken to Ed Vare. My friend said, 'You know Zeke Moran.' He grunted, 'Yes, I know him.' I said, 'You don't know me, Senator. But every s-o-b from Mulberry Street to the county line knows that I am for Vare.' He said, 'What's the matter with you—you won't lose your job.' 'Like hell I won't! Here is my notice.' I showed Ed Vare the notice of dismissal. 'I have lost it already.' He said, 'I'll put you back,' and he did. But in tomorrow's fight Mackey can't carry his own ward."

Honest Tom remarked, "The trouble with you damned bastards is that you wobble too much! Can't tell where you stand." Zeke came right back with, "You are a damned liar. We always stand one way."

A state senator came in, and sat on a big leather-covered lounge. Honest Tom began talking about the grand jury investigation in 1928. "When Mackey went in, the booze sellers asked me who I wanted as collector for my ward. They said, 'We have been paying twenty-five dollars a week for protection.' I said, 'Hell, don't pay any protection. Instead of charging a poor man fifty cents for a drink, sell it to him for twenty-five cents.' But they didn't. The cops or someone got the protection money. When the grand jury investigation came along I told the boys to stay open and sell near-beer, but the word went out to close, and every damned one of them closed. Everyone was in hot water except me. I danced around as if there was a jig tune being played. The trouble with M—— was, he took too much money. X [ward leader] went to jail. Hell, he should have gone to hell for the money he took! You got to play fair with the people.

"Last week the Yorks wanted to know if it would cost much to take me away from Dorgan in this fight. I said it wouldn't cost anything. You fellows [the Yorks] worked against my going to council. Dorgan helped me. Besides, I'll never go back on my word. My people know that if I say 'Yes,' I mean 'Yes,' and all hell can't change me!"

In personal conversation or in talking to a small group, Honest Tom is as alive as a character in Rabelais, but on a platform, before two hundred or five hundred people, part of his magic is lost in thin air. The distance is too great. One night in the summer of 1932, I was one of a hundred and fifty on the lawn in front of the U.V.W. Ward Club. Several ward leaders made rather effective speeches. When Honest Tom stood in the spotlight he smiled, and everyone cheered. He told the people that he couldn't say much there. "But I got a nice farm on the other side of the county line. After this primary I want all of my friends to come out there and have a drink of rum." The applause was immediate. Later in the campaign he spoke before six hundred in a neighboring ward. The night was sweltering hot, as Philadelphia nights in September are likely to be. Again McIntyre made the briefest of speeches. "I think we got awful nerve. We got an awful gall to keep you people here in this hot building. Anyone here for any time at all knows who I am and where I stand. I guess my two minutes are up." Again there was great applause, not because of the words that had been said, but because this man was the man they knew and loved.

Honest Tom went to the Republican convention in 1932 just as he had gone to earlier national conventions of his party since 1904, but this time he did something that he had never done before. He made a brief speech to the members of the Pennsylvania delegation concerning the need for immediate repeal of the Eighteenth Amendment. He rather laboriously unwound himself from his chair, and then said with some deliberation:

"I come from the workingman's section of the great northeast of Philadelphia. They have sent me to conventions for years. They sent me this time to get some change in the prohibition laws. Back home, the workingman wants a glass of beer or some stronger stimulant. I would hate to return home and think that I stood out here as a figurehead, and not vote to help the poor working man." [2]

Back in his chair again, the speaker knew what he had always known—that the votes in the Pennsylvania delegation are never changed by speeches. That night I saw him standing on the curb in front of the Congress Hotel. He was wearing a white badge about the size of a silver dollar. In red ink was printed, "My Vote Goes Wet," but the badge was upside down. I started to adjust it to an upright position. "Here, stop that!" he shouted. "I want

[2] *The Evening Bulletin*, June 6, 1932.

that badge so that I can see what it says myself. I don't care whether you can read it or not."

Honest Tom's innate spirit is as blithe today in 1938 as it was when his party was the only party in Philadelphia. But the *élan vital* has gone from his people, or they have become more restive under Republican leadership in general and the Councilman Mc-Intyre brand in particular. The depression, the great destroyer of jobs, traditions, wealth, and personalities, had squarely settled on the voters and their families in the Fifty-sixth Ward, and they knew it. They, like the man with the shoe that hurt his foot, knew something had to be done. They did not know any solution for their ills or the ills of the economic system under which they lived, but thousands who had never voted Democratic before did so in the years from 1932 to 1938. Honest Tom lost his ward in these years because his people were suffering, and he could not make it up to them. Some were impelled positively toward Roosevelt and his work-relief program, and others were merely bent on voting against the party in power. I do not believe that Councilman McIntyre could have changed had he wanted to. He, like City Hall, is built according to a certain rigid plan. He may expire, but he cannot change. His people, however, could not very well keep from changing.

In the fall of 1934 I called at the Philadelphia home of Councilman McIntyre. (He has two houses—one in the city and one in Atlantic City.) His house, surrounded by a high board wall-like fence, stood on the corner. The house was of brick and both high and narrow, and as somber as a fortress. There were no lights visible. I had been told to go around to the side gate, and it was on this gate that I pounded. Dixon, both political and personal helper, appeared and unfastened the tall gate; the door leading into the kitchen was opened, and I walked in.

There was Honest Tom in his shirt sleeves, sitting at a small table eating a supper that he had just prepared. He gave me a jovial welcome, asked me if I had eaten, and then noticed that the room was very smoky; Dixon opened one window and Honest Tom opened another. He had just fried two slices of eggplant and was eating them, with two extra large baking-powder biscuits and coffee. He told me that he often cooked his own food and washed the dishes. The appearance of the room suggested that he was camping out for a few days or a week, but he assured me that he lived there when he was not in Atlantic City in the hottest part of the summer. I commented on the unusually high ceiling. He replied, "This house was built sixty-six years ago; my old daddy paid three times as much, because he wanted everything double good." I noticed that he was cold sober, and mentioned reports that had come my way about his being on the water wagon now. "You bet I am; I haven't taken a drink since last August. One day I was down at Vare's home telling him that I was a candidate for register of wills. The Big Fellow refused to endorse me. Jim Davis was there. He said, 'You will have to have about [indicating three fingers] before you speak in this campaign.' I said, 'No—I will never drink again.' " (But "never" proved too long a time!)

We contentedly sat in the stark kitchen—the Councilman eating, I smoking a pipe and occasionally asking a question, Dixon a-straddle a turned kitchen chair, with his hands and chin resting on its back and his eyes following Tom.

Tom spoke of the restlessness of the voters of today, voters who had always voted Republican before. He blamed it all on the lack of employment in his industrial-manufacturing district. Today voters say, "I had my breakfast in my belly in those times, and I had my dinner in my hand. I am going to my work and dragging my feet and legs behind me. And now I am getting $450 without work. I want a change in politics." The situation looked hopeless because Mr. McIntyre did not see how he could keep up with the Democrats when they had a treasury behind them.

His mind went back to better days. "Once Dave Harris called on me in 1914 and said, 'Can I see you a minute?' 'You can see me an hour,' I told him. He explained that Connolly wanted to bet him $200 in 1919 that I would never go back to the council. He asked what my chances were in going back. $1,000 then was nothing. I said, 'Here is $1,000—bet this for me.' 'No,' Harris said, 'I will bet my own $1,000. I just wanted to get your opinion.' "

Mr. McIntyre then remarked that he was a candidate for the state Senate. The new leaders of the organization wanted his vote there, and he had agreed to make the race if they would get him the contracting work from the General Electric and Reading Railroad. "You know Ike Hetzell [former councilman and leader of the Eighteenth Ward] had this work, and when he died he left $1,700,000."

At the end of an hour I started to go. He said, "You are not going already?" I told him that I had heard that he went to bed early. "Hell, though, I don't go to bed at eight o'clock."

(I should go back at this point to say that when I talked to Honest Tom in 1933 he was a candidate for one of the important county offices, that of register of wills. He campaigned without the help of the central organization's workers or its gold, and was defeated. He now spoke of his 1933 campaign, and his resentment against the Big Fellow, which arose out of it. His resentment was not caused by his defeat, however, but it sprang phoenix-like from the failure of the Boss to pay back to Honest Tom the money that he had spent in his unsuccessful campaign.) "I polled 48,900 votes, and spent $15,000 in cash. We campaigned against Vare and his hand-picked candidates. We do not want Vare to govern the northeast." And later, "Of course, I was beaten. The sinews of war are the almighty dollar. Schwarz had that behind him and he had the organization, but this time it didn't do him any good." (The year 1933 was a Democratic year.)

The Councilman spoke of Vare—the Big Boss—who had just died, and who had been deposed two months before his death. "Bill Vare could have saved himself if he had put up a million dollars." I interrupted to quote one of Vare's lieutenants who had said that the Big Fellow could have kept his leadership if he had put $100,000 into the campaign, that Vare had given nothing in the 1933 primary, and had contributed only $10,000 this June. Honest Tom smiled and said, "Louchheim didn't put up $10,000." (Louchheim is the contractor who put up the money in the revolt against the Boss.)

He then commented on the most delicate task that confronts an organization leader—the preparation of a slate of offices and candidates. "Vare was wrong in switching old officeholders for the important jobs of coroner and register of wills. You can never measure a snake until he is dead. That is the way it is with Campbell.

Campbell made $120,000 a year for twelve years. Now he says he is broke. Got to have a job. Babies up in his ward going hungry. Let them go hungry. Ed [Vare] was too easy, and gave his money away. Bill took the bit in his teeth. He wouldn't let anyone know about the damn thing but himself. He even had Wilson [city controller then, now mayor] change $600,000 in city bonds to small denominations in order to avoid the tax. *But Vare made his biggest mistake when he let me go away mad.* I spent $15,000 in the primary [1933] and he never said a word about making it up. Vare was too damn tight. He fought Earle, Penrose's candidate for mayor, in 1911. When Earle was nominated, Penrose called for Bill Vare and said, 'How much did you spend?' Vare thought that he had spent about $250,000. 'All right,' said the Senator, 'I will give you my check!' Bill Vare never did this to me."

In the fall of 1935 I stopped in Honest Tom's office several times without seeing him. One afternoon just five days before the primary, I went in again. He was not there but about thirty of his lieutenants and colleagues were there, including Councilman Punker, leader of the Fifty-ninth Ward. I was chatting with some of these men when Councilman McIntyre himself walked through the doorway. Everyone looked up with a pleased expression and there was a broad smile on Honest Tom's face. He walked straight up to me, clapped both hands on my shoulders, and pleasantly ejaculated: "My old Southern friend! Say, I never would forgive you if you would come to town without seeing me. How are you?" Then he said, "Let's go out into the corridor. We can't talk here."

Outside the office, leaning against the far corridor wall, we talked. We had no sooner taken our position than people passing called out cheery greetings to the Councilman. One particularly fine and trim-looking man of about sixty darted over to the Councilman, and with a friendly twinkle in his eye held out his hand, and said, "Tom, I am surprised, but I am for you." (A remark which had to do with an election episode with which the papers were filled that day.) We talked of the Vares. "Bill had the most brains; Ed was too easy. Bill didn't ask for advice. He would fix a slate and then talk turkey. Ed would sit down with me and a dozen others, and we could all be heard in fixing a ticket. Ugly part of it was McNichol and some of the men tried to get rid of

Ed, but they couldn't do it. But we did cut the ground under Bill's feet."

The Councilman was running as candidate for sheriff in the following election. A little, abject-looking old man came up to within six feet of the leader, took off his hat, and stood waiting. (Honest Tom had helped this man in the past, but he was now living in the Twenty-second Ward. The leader of this ward, Dave Watson, was the Hadley candidate for sheriff.) The decrepit old man apologetically inquired, "They want me to be for Watson for sheriff." The Councilman cheerily sang back, "I'm for Watson too. You be for him. That's right. It would be too bad to hang your friends." The man breathed a sigh of relief, thanked Honest Tom more than enough, and backed away with his hat still in his hand.

"I have eighty-five hundred votes in that ward in my pocket, but I wouldn't ask them to support me. I said I would go along to help out, but I wouldn't ask any of my friends to lose anything by supporting me."

I asked why he made the run at all if he were not intending to win the nomination. His reply was instantaneous, "If it weren't for me they wouldn't have a s-o-b of any consequence on their ticket."

A clerk in one of the courts, an old-time friend of Honest Tom's, stood there against the far side of the wide corridor with us. He nodded in approval of the Councilman's estimate, and then drifted downstream with the traffic going past us. I remarked to Honest Tom that he was a rare character, and that men coming up in politics now seemed different. "Probably the die from which you were made has been broken."

Smilingly he inquired if I knew what a hooker shop was. I thought I did. He went on: "One night we were in a hooker shop; it was when I was first in Council, more than twenty-five years ago. I had plenty of money and bought the girls all that they could eat and drink; lobster, crab, chicken, beer, and rum—anything they asked for. One night one of the girls said, 'My Gawd, men and women, I want to tell you something about my man. When they made the pattern of Tom McIntyre they broke the mold. There isn't another man like him anywhere. And I know men!' That is the compliment I got from a lady in a hooker shop."

A prominent City Hall employee under civil service came up to tell his friend that he should not support a candidate for mayor who didn't have a chance. "Why do you do it?" The Councilman replied, "Organization, boy, organization; without organization we ain't worth a damn. I'll waste my *vote* this trip, but we have wasted votes before."

The City Hall reporter from the *Evening Bulletin* stopped and asked the Councilman if the Hadley group was going to win. Honest Tom replied, "Listen, my friend, ask me no questions and I'll tell you no lies." But the reporter insisted. The ward leader said, "Sure, we're going to win. That's why we are in politics—to win. We got Judge Brown and Louchheim—the best brains and the best money—with us." [3]

The newspaper man started talking about next November, when Mr. McIntyre interrupted. "You are talking too far ahead for me. I can never see beyond the next election. And just now it is a little hard to see that far."

Next, a little old Jew wearing a grotesquely large black felt hat that would have covered his face had it not been for two nearly horizontal ears serving as props, edged up and said, "I am not going to vote for Jake Dogole or Costello." McIntyre replied in hearty tones, for all to hear: "All right, I don't give a damn who you vote for. Get on a soap box and tell the world, I don't care." The Jew looked frightened at first, then his face brightened, he waved his monster hat and went away saying, "Hoooray."

Again and again I have been struck with Honest Tom's ability to measure men with a lightning glance, or merely, it seemed, by the sound of their voices. All kinds of people have spoken to him during the hours that we have talked, and I have necessarily observed him under all sorts of conditions. If a person of some merit came up—either of high or low degree—Honest Tom had time

---

[3] But Hadley did not win the nomination for mayor, largely because the politicians thought that S. Davis Wilson was a better vote-getter, and if the Republicans were to win in November they needed the best vote-getter available. Wilson won because he had more organized support and a bigger bundle than Hadley. And Honest Tom lost the Republican nomination for sheriff. He is probably content, for what sense would his politics make, if the man with the best organization and the most cash did not win?

for him. But if a liar and an utterly undependable individual came along, the Councilman was plainly not interested. One time the fat and oily Lolatow walked over to us, oozing conceit and wallowing in his hopes of the future. A lot of talk was pent up in him. I knew him to be a liar, and evidently the Councilman did too, for he patiently waited until the sleek one had finished before he said a word. And then he spoke of other matters as though the sleek one had never been born or heard from.

For some minutes on this last day, I had noticed two of the lesser ward leaders and two other individuals leaning against the opposite corridor wall not thirty feet away. They were waiting to see Mr. McIntyre. I finally said, "I think I had better go now and call some other time. There are a number of men over there waiting to see you, and this is a crucial time in the campaign." He put his hand on my shoulder and said, "You stay right where you are. They will be here when you are gone." And then, rather pensively, "I may not have much time left, and I ought to have some pleasure before I go." Then, looking straight into my eyes, "You know I talk to you because I believe that you are fair and honest; if I didn't, I wouldn't give you a damn bit of information. My wife tells me that you will have a better answer than mine for everything that I say." I remarked that my only purpose was to describe him exactly as I found him. He was satisfied. "That's all I ask for. For years I have talked to my people in the Fifty-sixth Ward, and they are for me. I guess if I can stand on my own feet in my ward, I can do it in your book."

A messenger came up and said, "Councilman, Judge Stern wants you to come down to his office."

As we said good-by I noticed again how good he was to look at. His complexion was still ruddy, and even though his teeth were not good one rarely noticed that; they merely indicated that he was human and seventy-six.

As he started down the corridor for Judge Stern's office, I thought how long ago it was since he had begun his strenuous life in dead earnest—before he was eighteen! For more than fifty years he had been on the winning side in politics; now it must seem hard to face a series of defeats. One hundred victories in the past cannot add up to a sum as impressive as one defeat in the present. Not only was his candidate for mayor defeated in the primary but the winning Republican candidate in November failed to carry the Fifty-sixth. Today in City Hall the Republicans say that this ward has turned sour; Honest Tom says that his people have no jobs; he thought he saw the handwriting on the wall and was not a candidate for re-election to council. Had he been, he would have won his eighth term, for Philadelphia went Republican in 1935. The Great Depression has liquidated personalities as well as fortunes. (Herbert Hoover is another Republican who has been returned to private life by this inexorable force.) However, Honest Tom's skin is thick; his heart is stout. He may be beaten today, but he will not give up. Only death can remove men of his breed from politics.

I started gathering material for the foregoing sketch several years ago, right at the beginning of Democratic victories in the City of the Union League Club and stalwart Republicanism. Since that time many of the details of politics have changed, but the pattern remains the same. Honest Tom drinks less, devotes more time to buying and selling tax delinquent properties, still manages his ward (although he has another person represent it on the Republican Central Campaign Committee), and instead of being in Council, is one of the three members of the Civil Service Commission. The other two members are politicians too. And if you ask, "Isn't it odd to have a ward leader as the one who administers the merit system? Aren't the very spirit and content of his training, background, and interests hostile to the cardinal principles of the merit system?" And if, instead of glibly saying "Yes," I remind you that usually two out of the three members of the United States Civil Service Commission are politicians—regulars in an art or trade that stems back in history before "Absalom stole the hearts of the men of Israel," you will see that Honest Tom is not unique, nor is he an individual, but rather he is a symbol of a civilization. His tragedy and ours is that we naturally are loyal to people and organizations that we know and can see and love or fear. Abstract principles or artificial persons like municipal corporations weigh little with us. The City of Philadelphia may be invisible, it may not be articulate, it may not even be a still small voice in our deliberations. If I were to go to Honest Tom today and say, "Suppose I want to get on the public pay roll but I cannot pass the examination, what could you do?", he would give me his most engaging smile and say, "Young man, you wouldn't want me to tell you just what I could do, would you?" And then, after a pause, "But I could do something, and I would—for I always help my friends."

POSTSCRIPT

A final justification for a sketch of Honest Tom is that he is the sort of politician that any one of us who may decide to take a hand in the governing of his own community may be forced to deal with. One may have to co-operate with him or fight him. In either case, it is important to know him. A physician would not be worthy of his medical degree if he refused to study a pathological condition that did not please his esthetic sense. A voter, no matter how distinguished in his own right, cannot strengthen the democracy in which he lives by merely deploring the Honest Toms, without trying to comprehend them and their roots and the needs they satisfy. Honest Tom has been, and still continues to be, a ward leader in a powerful party organization; for more than twenty-five years he was a councilman in a great city and now he is a civil service commissioner. Of those that think he is not the sort of person to determine the policies of the government of Philadelphia—and I know that there are many such—I ask what the one who protests is doing about it. He may make some indignant remark in the bosom of his family, but is he doing anything to stir, agitate, or guide opinion for getting a better qualified person into the government of Philadelphia? Some other writer has well remarked that votes, like babies, require both time and labor to produce. Neither are dropped down chimneys by storks. Honest Tom and his friends give this time and labor to produce votes 365 days each year. They take infinite pains to capture the voters' attention. Citizens who contribute nothing in educating or in guiding the voters' attention are even less useful to democracy than Honest Tom.

A few weeks ago, while talking to Carl Sandburg about politics, in a cabin on the edge of Lake Michigan, I asked if he had ever thought of becoming a candidate for Congress. He gave me the most honest answer that I have ever received to this question. He said, "I am a writing man and I do not know the political game. But if I had no more books to write nor any more songs to sing, and I wanted a life of routine misery, I would become a candidate." He paused, and then added, "But if things go on as they have been going on around here, I am going to begin to ask some questions. I am going to ask Lynn Edinger and Kenneth Holden [two of his neighbors] why we do not get some better men to represent us in our government."

THE CONTRIBUTORS

DUNCAN AIKMAN was born in Terre Haute, Indiana, forty-nine years ago, was graduated from Yale in 1911, and has served newspapers from London to Los Angeles, covered Washington for three years for the *New York Times Sunday Magazine*, and is now a special writer for the *New York Post*. He is the author of two books, *Calamity Jane and the Lady Wildcats*, and *The Home Town Mind*. He is a contributor to *Harper's*, the old *American Mercury*, and other magazines. He has a rare and intimate knowledge of politics and politicians.

HOLMES ALEXANDER was born in 1906 in Parkersburg, West Virginia, and lives in Maryland, where he farms, teaches school, foxhunts, and writes. He served a term in the State Legislature, has published three books, and has had articles and stories published in current magazines. His latest book was a biography of Aaron Burr, called *The Proud Pretender*, which received the Baltimore Civic Award last year.

ROBERT C. BROOKS is professor of Political Science at Swarthmore College. His principal interest is in political parties and their leaders. He is the author of *Political Parties and Electoral Problems*, now in its third edition, and has begun the preparation of a fourth edition which is to incorporate the results of the national campaign of 1940. Several years ago Professor Brooks inaugurated a course at Swarthmore dealing with the motives of political leaders as revealed by biographies and state papers. Subsequently work of this character has been offered widely in the colleges and universities of the United States.

PAUL M. CUNCANNON was born in Chester County, Pennsylvania, and is a descendant of the early Quakers who settled that region.

He was educated at Swarthmore College and Princeton University. He is the author of *The Political Ideas of Theodore Roosevelt.* He was private secretary to Joseph Swain at the International Congress of Education at San Francisco in 1915. In 1922–23 he was special aide in administration to Andrew F. West at Princeton. He has lived much of his life in Washington. He teaches political science in the University of Michigan at Ann Arbor.

LINDSAY HOBEN has been on the editorial staff of the *Milwaukee Journal* for thirteen years. He has contributed to *Current History, Collier's,* and foreign magazines. He has visited thirty-six countries for news and features, often off beaten paths—Inner Mongolia, Soviet Central Asia, Finnish Lapland, Canadian Arctic. He was born in 1902, is married, has two children, belongs to no church, no clubs, never any political party, but has voted Republican, Democrat, Progressive, Socialist—all in same election. He was educated at the University High School, Chicago and at Carleton College (Phi Beta Kappa and Sigma Delta Psi). He has worked briefly as factory and farm laborer, salesman, chemist, and in general business before journalism. He cuts wood and gardens.

CLAUDIUS O. JOHNSON is professor of Political Science and the head of the Department of History and Political Science at the State College of Washington. In 1934–35 he served as a member of the Governor's Advisory Constitutional Revision Commission, and in 1937 he was appointed a member of the Board of Sponsors for the Merit System of the Department of Social Security. He is the author of *Carter H. Harrison, Political Leader; Government in the United States;* and *Borah of Idaho.* He was a member of the Executive Council of the American Political Science Association, 1936–38.

PAUL J. KERN was born in Ann Arbor, Michigan. He received his A.B. at the University of Michigan and his LL.B. at Columbia University Law School. He was law secretary to Congressman La Guardia during the Seventy-Second Congress, and was for a time assistant to Professor Thomas I. Parkinson of the Columbia University Law School. He was law secretary (assistant corporation counsel) to Mayor La Guardia, 1934–1936. Since 1936 he has been Civil Service commissioner, and since January 4, 1938, he has been president of the New York City Civil Service Commission.

Don D. Lescohier. Professor of Economics, University of Wisconsin; sometime lecturer in Economics at the Universities of California, Minnesota, and Pittsburgh; professor of Social Sciences, Hamline University; chief statistician, Minnesota Department of Labor and Industries; special agent, Wisconsin Bureau of Labor; collaborator, United States Department of Agriculture; author of various books, articles, and government reports.

John C. O'Brien was born in Hartford, Connecticut, forty-three years ago. He attended Clark University in Worcester, Massachusetts, receiving A.B. and A.M. degrees. After two years of teaching in secondary schools, he entered the newspaper profession, working successively on newspapers in the West and in New York City. He was legislative correspondent of the *New York Herald-Tribune* for three years and since 1936 has been a member of the Washington staff of the same newspaper.

Frances L. Reinhold has been an instructor in Political Science at Swarthmore College since 1932. She received her Ph.D. degree at the University of Pennsylvania. She is the author of *Provisional Appointment in City Civil Service* (University of Pennsylvania Press, 1937), and is a contributor to the *National Municipal Review* and to the forthcoming *Dictionary of American History*.

J. T. Salter has been associate professor of Political Science at the University of Wisconsin since 1930. He is particularly interested in human nature in politics and in administration. Each term a variety of politicians and administrators are invited to come and address his students at the university. In 1930 and again in 1931 he received Social Science Research Council fellowships in order to make first-hand investigation of political leaders, methods, and voters in Philadelphia. His book, *Boss Rule: Portraits in City Politics,* and articles in scientific and literary journals represent part of his findings, as does also one of his chapters in the present volume. Before going to Wisconsin he taught politics at the University of Pennsylvania and was assistant editor of the *Annals* of the American Academy of Political and Social Science. He also taught at the University of Oklahoma and while there was secretary of the Oklahoma Municipal League and editor of the *Oklahoma Municipal Review*. He was graduated from Oberlin College in 1921, took his Ph.D. degree at the University of Pennsylvania, is married, and has five children.

WALLACE S. SAYRE has been interested in the politics of Wisconsin and in the La Follette political careers for several years. As a graduate student he wrote his doctoral dissertation on the political methods of Robert M. La Follette, Sr. He is now writing a full-length biography of the elder Senator, and has written several articles on contemporary Wisconsin politics in the *New Republic* and elsewhere. As a member of the faculty of New York University he has taught courses in public administration and party politics. He has been active in New York City civic affairs and is now a member of the New York City Civil Service Commission.

MURRAY SEASONGOOD is a native of Cincinnati. He took his A.B., A.M., and LL.B. at Harvard and was admitted to the Ohio Bar in 1903. He has been part-time professor of Law at the University of Cincinnati since 1925; mayor of Cincinnati for two terms, 1926–1930; chairman of City Planning Commission; president of the Hamilton County Good Government League; holds a number of important trusteeships and has served on numerous civic, state, and national commissions and committees. Author of *Local Government in the United States* and other books and articles.

JASPER BERRY SHANNON, born and educated in the Bluegrass region of Kentucky, was graduated with distinction from Transylvania College in 1925. He took advanced degrees at the University of Wisconsin in 1928 and 1934. In 1935 he was created first Henry Clay Professor of History and Political Science at Transylvania. He was research associate in Public Administration, Tennessee Valley Authority, 1936 and 1937. At present he is associate professor of Political Science, University of Kentucky. He has written:

Henry Clay as a Political Leader; Farm Tenancy in the Big Bend of the Tennessee River; and *Regional Population Trends in Kentucky.*

PHILIP TAFT received his B.A. and Ph.D. degrees from the University of Wisconsin. He is co-author of *History of Labor in the United States, 1896–1932,* with Selig Perlman, and he has contributed to the *American Economic Review,* and to the *Journal of Political Economy.* At present he is assistant professor of Economics at Brown University.

T. HENRY WALNUT is a lawyer practicing in Philadelphia. He began his political career as a reformer shortly preceding the election of Mayor Blankenburg. He was elected as a reformer to the legislature in 1910 and re-elected on the Progressive Party ticket headed by Theodore Roosevelt in 1912. He was an active participant in the legislative proceedings in both sessions. He continued active in independent political movements and was appointed as a special assistant United States attorney for the Eastern District of Pennsylvania shortly after the war opened. He remained in that position until March, 1922, and supported Gifford Pinchot in the campaign of 1922. Subsequently he was appointed chairman of the State Workmen's Compensation Board, a position which he held until 1927. He has been active since that time in political movements and is listed as an independent Republican.

HAROLD ZINK was born in Roswell, New Mexico, on May 15, 1901. He received his A.B. degree at the University of Denver in 1921; his A.M. and Ph.D. degrees at Harvard in 1924 and 1926 respectively. He has done post-doctoral study in the Far East, 1933; in Europe, 1934; in South America, 1935; in Central America, 1937. He has been assistant in Government, Harvard University, 1924–25; professor of Political Science, DePauw University, 1925– ; visiting associate professor of Political Science, Amherst College, 1928–29. He is the author of *City Bosses in the United States* (1930), and of articles in the *Dictionary of American Biography, Dictionary of American History,* and other publications.

INDEX